Caul

Using Hypnosis in Family Therapy

Michele Ritterman

Using Hypnosis in Family Therapy

Jossey-Bass Publishers

San Francisco • Washington • London • 1983

USING HYPNOSIS IN FAMILY THERAPY
by Michele Ritterman

Copyright © 1983 by: Jossey-Bass Inc., Publishers
433 California Street
San Francisco, California 94104

&

Jossey-Bass Limited
28 Banner Street
London EC1Y 8QE

Library of Congress Cataloging in Publication Data

Ritterman, Michele.
Using hypnosis in family therapy.

(The Jossey-Bass social and behavioral science series)
Bibliography: p. 339
Includes index.
1. Family psychotherapy.   2. Hypnotism—Therapeutic
use.   I. Title.   II. Series.
RC488.5.R57   1983   616.89'156   83-48162
ISBN 0-87589-581-6 (alk. paper)

Manufactured in the United States of America

The paper in this book meets the guidelines for
permanence and durability of the Committee on
Production Guidelines for Book Longevity of the
Council on Library Resources.

JACKET DESIGN BY WILLI BAUM

FIRST EDITION

Code 8328

The Jossey-Bass
Social and Behavioral Science Series

ꙮ ꙮ ꙮ *Foreword*

At first thought, the idea of joining such disparate fields as hypnosis and family therapy may seem like trying to meld gin rummy and bridge. Hypnosis has been a method of using the unconscious to promote change within the individual; most family approaches traditionally bypass the idea of an unconscious and deal with social fields and patterns of interaction. However, the coming of age of Ericksonian hypnosis creates new possibilities for joining hypnotic and family approaches. Milton H. Erickson, M.D., this century's premier medical hypnotherapist, created new methods of using hypnosis in psychotherapy. He championed naturalistic approaches, thereby revealing methods for successfully using hypnotic techniques without the necessity of applying a formal hypnotic induction. Ericksonian hypnotherapy, with both its formal and naturalistic varieties, has a place in family therapy. These effective techniques can promote change in hierarchies and systems as well as within symptomatic individuals. Milton Erickson did, in fact, use his techniques with families, but he neither clarified the possibilities nor systemized an approach. This job was left to his students—notable among them, Michele Ritterman.

Ritterman does not merely take Ericksonian techniques and apply them in families. Hypnotic models do not only have utility in promoting change. Modern hypnotic methods can advance theory as well as practice because modern theories of hypnosis emphasize the microdynamics of influence communication and thereby provide a tool for precisely examining the way in which individuals interact and induce pathology.

The idea of examining hypnotic induction procedures and comparing them with the induction of pathology is not new. Jay Haley introduced the idea in *Strategies of Psychotherapy* (1963), and R. D. Laing discussed the induction process within families in *The Politics of the Family* (1972). However, until the present volume, this idea was not developed. For example, R. D. Laing briefly pointed out the similarities between hypnotic induction and the mystification and induction of roles by patients in symptomatic families. Laing provided an example of the induction/attribution process by citing the following dialogue between a mother and a fourteen-year-old girl (1972, p. 122).

M: You are evil.

D: No, I'm not.

M: Yes, you are.

D: Uncle Jack doesn't think so.

M: He doesn't love you as I do. Only a mother really knows the truth about her daughter and only one who loves you as I do will ever tell you the truth about yourself no matter what it is. If you don't believe me, just look at yourself in the mirror carefully and you will see that I am telling you the truth.

Subsequently, Laing shocks us by suggesting that we change the attribution by substituting the word "pretty" for the word "evil." Leaving us reeling from the eerie qualities of the impact of this "small" change, Laing challenges us to "reflect upon the structure of the induction, not only the content thereof" (p. 123).

Thinking about Laing's admonition can leave more questions than answers: What are the actual mechanisms by which the induction is accomplished? To create an effective induction, is it not important to change extraverbal components in conjunction with manipulating the verbal components of the communication? Realizing that induction is unavoidable, how can we use that fact to therapeutic advantage? Can we create effective therapeutic counterinductions to combat negative suggestions and mystifications? Laing provides no specific answers. He merely points out that "the clinical hypnotist knows what he is doing; the family hypnotist almost never" (p. 80). Awareness and objectivity seem to be powerful tools.

In the present volume, Michele Ritterman takes up Laing's challenge and attempts to objectively answer the previously mentioned questions. She is particularly well-suited for the task, because she is an accomplished family therapist with training in the strategic and structural schools from Haley, Salvador Minuchin, and Braulio Montalvo. Additionally, she is an accomplished hypnotherapist with personal training from Erickson.

Actually, I first met Michele Ritterman during one of her visits with Milton Erickson. I know that Erickson valued his relationship with her; she was not only a student but also a special friend who was included in the extended Erickson family.

In *Using Hypnosis in Family Therapy,* Ritterman demonstrates both her admirable professional and personal qualities. The book is comprehensive, innovative, and humanistic. In regard to its technical contributions, new diagnostic formulations and therapeutic innovations are presented.

Ritterman discusses a twofold framework for understanding symptomatic systems; both macrodynamics and microdynamics are considered. A macrodynamic diagnostic framework for systems is presented first. In evaluating the family, one should consider the intrapsychic, familial, and social dimensions. Binding conflicts among these levels lead to dissociated symptoms through a sort of pathological "hypnosis." Symptoms are metaphors for the active conflict among levels and subsequently become a rigid organizing force in the life of the family. Ritterman does not just pay lip service to her hypothesis about levels. Rather, she provides clear categories and examples of the dynamics of problems within levels and of binds across categories, and she discusses how they lead to rigidity and dysfunction in systems and hierarchies.

A microdynamic diagnostic framework is also presented. For example, Erickson contributed two important techniques to the field of hypnosis: the confusion technique and the interspersal technique. Ritterman takes these techniques and explains how families specifically use the same techniques to induce symptoms in the immediate setting. Her work on microdynamics is important. For therapists, it opens up new vistas into the complex interventions that occur in families. We need to know more about the microdynamics of interaction that induce pathology, and Ritterman's work is an important pioneering step.

Ritterman also presents innovative therapeutic techniques for promoting counterinduction. As far as therapy is concerned, the goal is functional flexibility in the interaction among individual, familial, and social levels. Families need to learn how to interact to induce effectiveness and subsequently eliminate the need for a symptom as an organizing force. Case studies are used to introduce such skillful techniques as using cue words, convergent trances, complementary couples inductions, shared family reveries, and so on.

Ritterman also addresses the proper, humane attitude of interaction that is needed between patient and therapist. Technique is not enough. Ritterman uses a pleasant and provocative style to confront the reader with new perspectives. I find her insights on viewing the symptom as a "gift" in the context of exchange rituals particularly illuminating and useful. Additionally she invites us to view resistance as interactional instructions rather than as an impediment. These new humanistic perspectives are important in promoting flexibility, and they underline an emphasis on the positive that was central to Erickson's approach to his patients and that should be an integral part of any psychotherapy.

I hope that readers will approach the book with the same interest that I did, incorporating Ritterman's ideas into their practice to provide new sustenance for themselves and their patients. It is an honor for me to introduce this important volume.

Phoenix, Arizona   Jeffrey K. Zeig, Ph.D.
September 1983   Director,
                                         Milton H. Erickson Foundation

᎒᎒᎒ ᎒᎒᎒ ᎒᎒᎒ *Preface*

This book is about a therapy that selectively uses hypnotic techniques in the context of the family. As such, it is intended for therapists and counselors seeking to widen the range of strategies they can effectively employ with individuals and their families. Although one need not be a hypnotist to understand and make use of the various ideas presented, readers will find principles of hypnosis interwoven throughout. Indeed, the book's purpose is to integrate hypnotic techniques with family therapy and thus develop a new approach appropriate for a diverse clientele with a variety of problems.

I call this new approach *hypnotic family therapy*. It differs from the more familiar forms of family therapy and from hypnotherapy, even as it draws on both. Family therapies, especially the strategic, exemplified by the work of Jay Haley and Cloé Madanes, and the structural, exemplifed by the work of Salvador Minuchin and Braulio Montalvo, are designed to produce a shift in power and responsibility in relationships among symptom bearer and family members. These approaches intentionally disattend to the inner workings of the individual. They bring to the clinical foreground that diversity of observable individual changes that derive from *situational rearrangements*. In contrast, hypnotherapy, exemplified by the work of Milton Erickson, is designed to catalyze *reorganizations within the phenomenal reality* of the individual symptom bearer. Internal transformations then reverberate outward into new psychophysiological, behavioral, and interactional changes. The changed individual changes his context.

Each approach recognizes that a symptom has an inner and outer reality. Each focuses on one side of that two-sided reality. Clinically, the family maps suggest that the therapist step outward at the first sign of resistance; but just as clearly, the hypnotic map suggests that she* turn inward. Many therapists, arriving at this historical juncture, have found themselves confused. The terrain from individual interior landscape to family collective property, and back, seems difficult to travel.

Hypnotic family therapy incorporates significant features of both the interior concerns, approached through hypnotic techniques, and the exterior factors, approached through family therapy methods. This approach regards symptoms as *partly* family and societal abuses of special individual capacities. Consider that hypnotists are not the only ones who use hypnotic techniques; a number of persons with whom a "subject" is intensely engaged, such as family members, can make constructive or destructive hypnotic-like "suggestions" to a person. A family's power to transmit unseen messages to members can be especially problematic if the family structure is in need of realignment. If a family arrangement is confused—as when a person holds two positions in a family that nullify one another in terms of what he believes he ought to do—the family may inadvertently abuse the person's capacity to either focus inward on problems of the self or act outward to change his circumstances.

The dual approach of hypnotic family therapy is a response to a common thread in many presenting problems—conflict between a person's inner reality (or self-directional system) and his outer realities of family and social contexts. In fact, a person with a problem is often one who is asked to play seemingly incompatible roles across all three levels of his functioning. Most poignant is the tug-of-war between the individual's belief about how he should behave and the exterior requisites concerning his behavior. Insofar as the symptom seems principally a signal of dis-ease between inner and outer realities, negotiating a new balance between them is often a desirable therapeutic goal. In hypnotic family therapy, the therapist searches for the essential connections between symptom-related external contexts and individual mental-sets. Throughout, the therapy is shaped and staged to catalyze the production of new bonds and new

*The pronouns *she* and *her* will be used when referring to the therapist; *he* and *him* will be used in other instances.

boundaries both within the individual's self-suggestional system and between the individual and his larger external world.

The therapist using this approach employs a number of specially developed techniques to create an atmosphere in which she is permitted to observe the kinds of intimate family- and self-communicational processes that may culminate in symptom expressions. The therapist then initiates a therapeutic counterinductive process. Because the symptom is appreciated as a kind of economical summarization of a central conflict in the symptom bearer's life, the therapist is respectful in all aspects of the handling of the symptom. She is not trying to eliminate all features of the symptom. Indeed, it is important that she "receive" the symptom as if it were a gift from the symptom bearer—recognizing fully that in the act of "offering" the problem the person is revealing vital clues about himself and his context. The therapist thus seeks to salvage those parts of a symptom that are benevolent and use them to activate new behavior. The goal of a therapeutic counterinduction is not to produce a set of counterdirectives (suggestions that defuse the effects of family and individual directive) but to help a person alter his life situation to his advantage. The therapist works to restore dignity, as well as freedom from incapacitating symptoms, so that the individual can better choose from his own potential repertoire of behaviors. If symptoms are counterfeit attempts to be free, therapy hopes to secure for the individual a crack at the real thing.

Hypnotic family therapy draws on special individual resources as part of a broader plan to facilitate change in family patterns of communication and organization. Capacities associated with "trance" states in one or more family members can then be employed to initiate individual and family change. The task is to build a dialectical therapy so that interpersonal changes will not meet with overriding rigidities in an individual's mind-set and individual changes will not meet with relentless family or social constraints.

Toward the development of such a dialectical therapy, this book provides interventions designed to activate interrelational sequences that, it is hoped, will *culminate* in the "spontaneous" expression of new behaviors and ideas in the symptom bearer, *while* using special states and other individual-based capacities of the symptom bearer and others to serve as *starting points* for interrelational change. The book introduces a number of new techniques, including various modes of trance induction with one or more family members in a family therapy interview.

Even though I call my approach hypnotic family therapy, I do not always use trance and I do not always work with entire families. Each family and individual is unique, and therapy works best when it adapts to special needs. With each case, the therapist decides whether to use hypnosis and, if so, with which family members. She then determines the level of trance appropriate to the goals at hand, with care to protect the individual from opening up unnecessarily in front of his family. It is my hope that this book clearly sets forth principles of using hypnotic techniques in family therapy without insisting on a rigid, made-for-every-case strategy.

Truly, human problems seem complex enough to warrant a therapy that works on multiple levels. By intervening both from the inside (readying individuals for new action) and from the outside (enabling family and social groups to construct helpful suggestions), we have a better chance to effectively challenge the reign of a symptom. Along the way, we hope to restore to a person the dignity that has been lost in his efforts to make sense of disjointed contexts.

The book is organized into eight chapters, moving from the conceptual to the specific and concluding with a brief wrap-up and comparison with related therapies. Some readers may choose to start with the case material, especially that presented in Chapters Five and Six. The principles underlying the approach could then be read with a clear picture in mind of how the therapy progresses. (The contents headed "Case Studies," p. xxi, identify the major cases presented, although examples are given throughout.) Other readers may want to read the early chapters quickly and return to them later for a closer look.

Chapter One lays the conceptual groundwork for using hypnosis in family therapy. It first describes a three-level model of symptoms that includes the individual's mental-set, his family context, and his social situation. It then provides a dynamic way of thinking about the relationships among these levels. Special emphasis is placed on the connections between interactional processes (outer levels) and special-state phenomena (inner levels).

Chapter Two outlines the therapy, in particular the three stages often included in an hypnotic family therapy interview—the preinductive stage, therapeutic counterinductive stage, and postinductive stage.

Chapter Three deals with the stance of the therapist and considers structure and power transactions in the therapeutic context. It proposes a therapeutic model of "cooperative exchange," whereby the therapist in effect receives the client's symptom as a gift. The therapeutic arts of receiving the gift and therapeutically repaying for it in kind are exemplified with case material.

Chapter Four examines the capacities of families to induce trance-like states in family members and, using a case transcript, reveals how certain family interactions can also induce symptoms.

Chapter Five presents a detailed transcript of an interview with a young hemophiliac who has stress-related bleeds to demonstrate the development of a dialectical intervention. Techniques used to work hypnotically with the boy and his mother to strengthen needed boundaries have general applicability for other psychosomatic problems and other chronic illnesses with psychosomatic concomitants.

Chapter Six provides a thorough explanation of what the therapist did and why she did it in a transcribed study of an interview with a suicidal young woman and her family. Included are descriptions of the steps used in creating an hypnotic atmosphere and in "reading" a family induction. The chapter also demonstrates the creation of a therapeutic counterinduction with a whole family and shows ways to elicit and work therapeutically with objections raised by the family after the therapeutic induction.

Chapter Seven summarizes six case studies on a session-by-session basis. Each case is used to introduce a therapeutic technique or to demonstrate some of the ways to size up the best points of therapeutic entry.

Chapter Eight highlights the essential elements of the present approach and compares it with related hypnotic and family therapies.

A glossary of terms—either unfamiliar ones or ones used in an uncommon manner in this approach—can be found at the end of the book.

Acknowledgments

A pleasurable ordeal like writing a book gives one an opportunity to thank the people who in some way sustained the writer through the process. I express my gratitude to Jay Haley, who taught me to use and keep my wits while charting difficult therapeutic sequences; to Salvador Minuchin, who instructed me in the arts of proximity and distance in therapy, supervision, and teaching; and to Harry Aponte, Ronald

Liebman, and Lydia Linan, who helped me get challenging work opportunities. Braulio Montalvo and the late Milton Erickson, in believing in
me, illuminated my way. I am grateful to Braulio also for his careful
reading of drafts of this book, which helped me unravel some mysteries in
my own ideas.

To my friends, David Heard, who cared and gave me a forum
through which to clarify my ideas; Barbara Waterman and Bertholde
Carter, who critiqued chapters of this book; to Ed Bassis, who was a
therapist for a case discussed; and to Anne Ritterman, who helped me
secure a writing room of my own, thank you. Also, I am appreciative to
those who see me in therapy, for offering me opportunities to "change my
mind" and expand my skills of give and take. Above all, I am grateful to
Jeffrey Ritterman, without whose challenging suggestions, endurance of
my exhilarations and doubts, and real well of love there might have been
no book; and to my children, Miranda and Judah, who found clever ways
of getting me to "hurry up" and finish the book, so I would not lag too far
behind them.

To paraphrase from "Initiation" by Rilke, one of my first teachers
about "the unconscious": Now, tenderly, I let this book go.

Oakland, California   Michele Ritterman
September 1983

ᗛᗘ ᗛᗘ ᗛᗘ Contents

Foreword   ix

Preface   xiii

Case Studies   xxi

The Author   xxiii

1. Basic Principles: Symptoms, Families, and Hypnosis   1

2. Stages of an Interview   42

3. Exchanges of Power in the Therapeutic Relationship   66

4. Role of Family Interactions in Inducing Symptoms   85

5. Case Study of a Hemophiliac   143

6. Case Study of a Suicidal Woman   189

7. Adapting Intervention Strategies to Particular Problems   281

8. Hypnotic Family Therapy: Summary and Comparative   320
    Assessment of Related Approaches

    Glossary   333

    References   339

    Index   343

 *Case Studies*

Getting Mind Control: Hemophilia   143

The Young Woman with the Bad Body: Suicide   189

A Study of Family Hydraulics: Enuresis and Alcoholism   282

A Matter of Growing Pains: Psychosomatics   288

Over My Dead Body: Suicide or Self-Ectomy   294

The Turtle with the Cracked Shell: Intractable Back Pain   299

Too Close for Comfort: Claustrophobia   302

Divorcing the Dead: Alcoholism   306

In loving memory of Milton Hyland Erickson,
this book is dedicated to

Jeffrey, Miranda, and Judah Ritterman
Morris and Esther Klevens
Braulio and Margarita Montalvo
and Elizabeth Erickson

☙ ☙ ☙ *The Author*

Michele Ritterman is a therapist in private practice. She received her B.A. degree in English and psychology from the University of Wisconsin at Madison (1969) and her Ph.D. degree in clinical psychology from Temple University (1979).

Ritterman interned at the Philadelphia Child Guidance Clinic from 1972 to 1974, during which time she studied family therapy with Jay Haley, Salvador Minuchin, and Braulio Montalvo. She served on staff there from 1974–1979, conducting clinical research on hyperactivity and hemophilia, developing hospital liaison services, and providing supervision and training. Also during this period, through 1980, she studied hypnotherapy with the late Milton H. Erickson.

Ritterman has lectured and given workshops and seminars in the United States and Canada and has published several papers and produced a video teaching tape on conceptual and clinical issues in therapy. Since 1980, she has conducted therapy and supervision from her home-based office in California, where she lives with her husband and their two children.

Using Hypnosis in Family Therapy

Chapter One ⚜ ⚜ ⚜

Basic
Principles

Symptoms, Families, and Hypnosis

⚜ This chapter lays the conceptual groundwork for ideas and techniques of using hypnosis in family therapy. The first part describes the symptom as identifying three hierarchically organized structural referents: (1) structure of the symptom bearer's mind-set, (2) family structure, and (3) social structure. Facets of interrelationships among these three levels of the symptom are discussed. Most importantly, this part associates the symptom—as a destructive special state—with problematic positioning of a symptom bearer *across the three contexts he inhabits.*

The second part focuses on the dialectics of special-state phenomena—including both trance and symptom states—and interactional processes. A structural model of trance induction and suggestion-reception provides a broad frame of reference for any specific interaction between inner (individual) and outer (relational) processes.

1

Three Levels of the Symptom

A fairly well-dressed Spanish-speaking woman is brought by her friend to an outpatient clinic. She has not been able to stop crying for four months. She is alone, she is pregnant, and she feels that she is incapable of having a child in her present state. However, since the thought of abortion makes her feel like a murderer, she believes she should die. This first level of her situation—the individual mind-set she is trapped in—causes irreconcilable conflict between what she feels like doing and what she believes she should do. According to her present way of thinking, she can kill the baby or kill herself—or cry continuously. Her symptom "all I can do is cry" is her way of avoiding the other choices.

Consider the second level of her situation—her family context. How does her symptom reflect this aspect of her life? We learn that the woman had recently married a young doctor in Central America. They had decided to have a child together, but suddenly, without warning, he was missing, and she fled to the United States, leaving parents and friends behind. Clearly, her symptom of crying denotes her terrible loss of power, control, and meaning in terms of family life and family development. She had married a man of prominence but is now apparently a widow, and pregnant. The ideas of giving up the child or giving up her own life take on new meaning when viewed in light of this drastic shift in her family constellation and organization.

The woman's symptom also reflects a third level or aspect of her life—her social context. The woman had been a devout Catholic in El Salvador, where abortion is considered unthinkable, the greatest sin. The government had long killed peasants and clergy, and now it was killing doctors suspected of serving people with "antigovernment" tendencies. The woman's husband had disappeared in an area in which the disappeared rarely are found. She was warned to leave by someone who knew the government's plans. Truly, in her social situation, she is bereft of all sense of personal power and meaning in life. Catholicism was her source of philosophy about the world, yet she is aching to not bring a child into the world. This third facet of her symptom intersects with her options of despair and loss of family supports, producing a convergence of negative positions in all her hierarchies of meaning and doing. All she can do is cry.

If the woman had a different mental attitude, family developmental situation, or social context, she might not manifest symptoms, although she might be grievous. As things stand, her symptom is best regarded as the point where all three contexts that she temporarily inhabits converge in suggesting hopelessness.

In the therapy discussed in this book, we look for a single common thread that unifies, summarizes, and epitomizes the predominant problem in an individual's life that he presents to us as a symptom. Cases are considered in terms of the possibility that the symptom is a three-level metaphor (see Haley, 1976), with referents to an individual's interior belief system, his family context, and his social context, insofar as each level is observable or salient.

Ideally, as clinicians or social science researchers, we would have some marvelous instrument, the equivalent of a camera with a zoom lens, that would enable us to observe (1) individual phenomena as they accumulate, organize, and transform into social phenomena and (2) social possibilities as they recode into the individual idiosyncrasies we typically study. Lacking such a tool, we develop or discover ideas that help us see both the social and individual structures people inhabit. We need concepts of transition, change, and interaction; concepts encompassing man and woman as both private and public entities; concepts built on the recognition that private sufferings, or symptoms, may have a public or social precipitant, just as social and family phenomena may be disturbed by an individual's problems in day-to-day living.

We know that all human beings dream, hope, wish, pretend; that they relate within the contexts of friends and family; that they are somehow dependent on the broader socioeconomic system. As therapists, however, confronted with these people as patients, we may fail to see aspects of them that may be relevant for treatment. In other words, we may have a philosophically induced "negative hallucination" for some of their behavior. The tendency today is to perceive a symptom bearer in terms of either internal conflict or family relational problems.

Here we draw on a conceptual model called "holistic structuralism" (see Overton, 1974; Ritterman, 1977) to clarify certain assumptions. This paradigm of biological, developing systems provides a way of synthesizing understandings about related inner and outer features of problems in living. Figure 1 shows the model.

Fundamentally, this comprehensive model of symptoms suggests that the basic unit under consideration is the structured or organized whole, of which the symptom is a functioning part. We consider the

Figure 1. Holistic Structural Model of Symptoms.

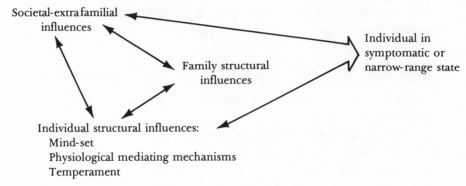

Source: Revised from Minuchin, Rosman, and Baker, 1978, p. 24.

symptom as a potential totalization of the symptom bearer's situation, the structure of "symptom bearer in social context." The symptom bearer's mind-set, his family context, and his social situation represent three levels of his life and three sources of suggestion about how to behave. The symptom itself can thus be regarded as a code for conflicts within the boundaries of each, or all, of these levels, or it can represent problematic connections among the three levels.

The three levels of the symptom bearer's situation are independent of each other, in that a change in one level does not automatically lead to a change in another level. Rather, the levels represent three different orders of reality that impinge in complex ways on one another.

However, the broader contexts of society and family have a more pervasive influence on individual mind-sets than any one individual or family typically has on society. Nevertheless, the relationships across structures are mysterious. For example, regarding relations between the levels of social structure and individual mind-set:

1.   The individual exists within a social situation characterized by certain epidemiological features, so he is personally impinged on or subject to the likelihood that any one citizen at any one place or time will manifest a symptom—drug addiction, sexual abuse, suicide, de-

linquency, depression, or hypertension. Within his context, he is subject to certain social odds. Although we cannot always identify broader social contributions to any one individual's complaint, we know that social structures do penetrate the "membranes" around family and individual, recoding into belief and relational systems, transforming, at times, into a haunting inner reality. In this sense, a symptom reflects troubled social relations.

2. At a moment of historical readiness, an individual's dream, when enacted, can alter the course of an era, as was the case with Einstein, Darwin, Freud, or even Hitler. Interestingly, people considered great often suffered through a period of symptomatology. In that life-stage, they were often personally "arrested" by those very conflicts that beleaguered their entire social order. By transcending their own personal embodiment of central racial, religious, or caste conflicts, they rose to greatness, offering others the option of transcending social problems. Martin Luther (Erikson, 1958), Malcolm X (Haley, 1966), and Mahatma Gandhi were individuals who affected broad social-set conflicts (see Ritterman, 1970).

Similarly, regarding the relationship between family structure and an individual's context of mind, the present approach suggests that there is not a one-to-one correlation between changes in family systems and alterations in individual functioning, or, conversely, between changes in individual mind-set and persistent, systematic family structural change. The nature of the relationship between symptom bearer and family system must be determined in each situation. Again, however, the broader structure—the family context—is regarded as having the potential to override changes in an individual's mind-set (See Ritterman, 1980).

The concept in structuralism that the broader structure classifies or shapes substructures is not only useful for thinking about relationships among the three levels of a symptom structure. The idea of different, hierarchical levels of power and influence is also a cornerstone in conceptualizing each context *individually:*

1. *The individual's mind-set.* We consider hierarchies of meaning and doing, with a special interest in ideas that exert an overriding influence over the symptom bearer's other ideas about his options. Once one idea becomes a kind of rule setter, the sequences of ideas that

follow logically contribute to the systems-perpetuating features of the individual's self-instruction.

2. *The individual's family context.* We consider what unit within a family has more power than another for sustaining symptom-related interactions. It is not enough to merely study sequences of interaction (see Ritterman, 1977). For example, if A fights with B about what B should or should not eat, there is a different approach if A is mother and B child than if A is child and B mother, or if A is wife and B wife abuser, or if A is grandmother and B forty-year-old married daughter. We consider interactions in terms of hierarchical configurations (see Haley, 1976; Madanes, 1981) and power and responsibility relations in terms of generational units and economic and gender subsystems. Regarding the impact of family systems on an unsettled individual family member, we look for nullifying or mutually exclusive hierarchical positions that contribute to an individual's confusion about how to behave responsibly at any one moment within or outside the family context.

3. *The individual's social situation.* We consider the cultural, racial, religious, gender, class, and generational hierarchies that are interiorized by families and individuals.

Within each context, we regard the person with a problem as having a dual role. On the one hand, the symptom bearer is, like all individuals, potentially an organizer of the three structures he inhabits. In his capacity to use and create structures, he can absorb, organize, and synthesize information; arrange it into priorities; prepare to find and use it; and, ultimately, transform it, changing his own belief system, his family system, even his society. He thus exercises his margin of personal freedom. On the other hand, the symptom bearer is subject to each context he inhabits, including the context of his own mind. In his capacity to be structured by existing contexts, he partly behaves automatically within the established (if unspoken) rules and roles of these contexts. Although capable of creating contexts, the symptom bearer at the point of entry into therapy often behaves as if he were merely their subject, a prisoner of one side of this human dialectic. It is in terms of this human feature that Frantz Fanon (1969, p. 53) wrote: "Madness is one of the means man has of losing his freedom."

The human's capacity to be structured by prevailing self, family, and social contexts seems also to enable him to be "hypnotized" by these systems. In fact, hypnosis is possible because an individual can attach to and detach from aspects of his immediate exterior situation. A context may affect a person's attentional movements, influencing what inner and outer realities become foreground, and what background. Certain contextual cues may then trigger thoughts or actions that appear to occur automatically. The structure of a context, whether that context is a system of socioeconomic relations, individual psychophysiological response patterning, or intimate interaction, is revealed as it functions in the world. Repetition—through sequences of thought and action—is the drone of structure. For example, in the context of a family with a member who suffers a chronic problem, repetition of many symptom-related sequences of thought and interaction occur automatically, given the guidelines of problematic rules and orderings of that relational system. Likewise, repetition in a family not suffering symptomatology suggests a certain lulling and automatic flow of behaviors resulting from mutually satisfactory relational rules. Such a family has little need to attend to context and can remain in an "automatic pilot" state. This arrangement enables the parents, for example, to "naturally" carry out their daily activities, including earning a living, caring for their children, cooking, socializing, and so on. Similarly, repetition is the drone of an individual's mental-set. Once established, his context of mind induces him to behave spontaneously; for example, he arrives at work without recalling locking the door of the house, walking down the front steps, stepping off the curb, unlocking the car door, putting the key in the ignition, or straightening the floor mat. Many aspects of unconscious programming, once memorized, may remain unshaken for a lifetime. An individual may have developed a way of walking that—except for slight modifications during the teen years, a broken leg, pregnancy, or a dramatic weight change—is built in and pretty much "tells" her how to walk. Although often elusive, once established, the structure of each context a person is subject to, including his own mind, makes him behave in certain automatic ways. Although entrancement by and suggestibility to structures is a human condition, the symptom bearer often does not balance these pressures with a sense of creating his own context. Thus, in terms of his symptom, he experiences himself as uncontrollably carrying out certain undesirable behaviors.

To grasp the symptom as a living conflict, we have to go beyond this static representation of the three levels of a symptom. One way we do this is by considering the symptom bearer as he integrates messages from multiple contexts. It is often useful to view the individual symptom bearer as a member of various hierarchical organizations that exist within and across the interrelated structures he is a part of (see Montalvo, 1973). We saw that within any one hierarchy, within any one context, there are certain messages about how one is to behave relative to others. We pay special attention to relationships among messages an individual receives about how he is to behave as he functions, given a certain belief system, within a certain work-related hierarchy, for example, and, given a certain position, within a central family hierarchy. We consider the possibility that a symptom is part of the process of the individual's functioning across the sectors of his life, which is the essence of the idea that the whole system structure may be transmitting messages about how to behave that are nullifying one another or that are converging in such a way that the individual consistently experiences a loss of power.

In a sense, the term "hierarchy" is our zoom lens, helping us observe the mysterious translation of social factors into individual structures and individual mental-sets into family and social structures. We use the terms "hierarchies" and "hierarchical imbalance" to help us grasp the ways the three contexts of a person's life may converge into a symptom. Establishing a balance of positions across the three functional contexts is a goal in the treatment of cases described.

Symptom Bearer's Context of Mind*

At the moment that, for example, a hemophiliac with stress-related bleeds, a chronically depressed man, a pregnant woman who cannot stop crying, or a boy who cannot think from one thought to the next arrives for therapy, the rules that organize his or her activity have culminated in an inability to recognize or act on options that might extricate the person from a symptomatic situation. Whatever the contributing factors, the symptom bearer has narrowed his potential range of behavior; his experience focuses on a particular trouble. We consider that this constriction of experience may be partly caused by the symptomatic individual having, or, more precisely, being subject to, a rigid mind-set. The person is partly a prisoner of his own self-directional system.

---

*The term "context of mind" is used to emphasize the structured nature of a person's mental-set; it denotes one of three levels of a symptom structure. It also is used to refer to the automatic pilot aspects of self-suggestion.

Generally, a mind-set is defined as that system of an individual's behavior that determines rules for:

1. Accumulating and excluding information and experience.
2. Arranging behavior, putting it into priorities, and sequencing it— including thoughts, feelings, sensations, and even aspects of physiological life.

If a symptom bearer has a rigid mind-set, his behavior system may be organized in a way that precludes the possibility of his using the very information he needs to dislodge himself from a problematic situation. However obvious his mind-set is to others, the symptomatic individual will not think of breaking his own self-imposed rule or redefining or reexamining a rule imposed by other contexts, such as a religious rule, a socially prescribed ethic, an assumption about gender roles, or standards for what members of one's own class or race do or do not do. The experience the individual needs to reorganize his behavior at a higher, more complex level is often taboo to his mental-set.

Every seasoned clinician has known a person who cannot recall a single positive memory at the start of therapy or whose every positive association is reduced to a prelude to inevitable disaster. In such cases, a rigid structural rule governs all the person's experience: "Nothing good happens to me. I am fated to be miserable." A person with a problem may follow a rule by which he is unable to recognize pleasurable physiological sensations and responses, experiencing only painful responses. A person may follow a relational rule he is not consciously aware of but that can be observed through ordinary or trance-evoked accounts of his patterns of thought. His prevailing life cycle principle, which handicaps his movements to his next life-stage, might be "To be loyal to my parents, I must not have children." Part of the clinical challenge in such cases is to help persons modify their own frames of mind.

As a heuristic device, useful for planning a point of therapeutic entry, we "map" such mind-sets, looking to both the hierarchical organization of ideas and that idea that prevails over all others for maintaining a symptom's rule. (Note that mapping was originally developed by Minuchin, 1974, to conceptualize *family* structure.) Figure 2 is a map of a rigid mind-set, based on observations of a man whose presenting complaint is tinnitus of thirteen years duration that has now become intolera-

Figure 2. Rigid Mind-Set.

Idea 1
I must not ask for help.

Subidea A   Subidea B

If wife and son talk too low   If I cannot hear my students,
to hear, that is the way   there is nothing to be done.
things are.   I am a sick man.

ble. He says that at dinner, when his wife and son talk too quietly to be heard over his perceived sounds of cars crashing and monks chanting, he turns down his hearing aid rather than asking them to speak up. When he teaches at the university, he misses what students say, and he often must, to his great shame, continue without having heard the questions. From this and many other pieces of data, an idea emerges that, having become elevated to the level of a private law, seems to contribute to sustaining this man's symptom of profound isolation. The central rule, idea 1, is: "I must not ask for help."

Once a person's way of thinking becomes rigidly organized, he tends to behave automatically within the confines of that structure, as if he is simply subject to his context of mind and social situation. Many thoughts and experiences, especially in a situation of chronicity, can be partly traced back to a source idea. Because many of these structuring rules exist outside the symptomatic individual's range of ordinary perception, they can be called "unconscious" principles. These principles may be recalled more readily in trance and be responsive to the kind of direct-unconscious communication that occurs in trance.

Part of the way a person develops and arranges his behaviors into a hierarchy is related to his human ability to osmose, or interiorize, structures and rules of the world around him. The man with tinnitus, for example, was an Asian who experienced himself as an outsider in a largely white professional community. From this experience, he interiorized a wish to not be bothersome. Also, his idea of dignity by self-reliance was based on certain Asian cultural values, pertinent to an oldest male child, and specific early family mythology that highly valued self-reliance in fear- and pain-evoking situations. This interiorizing became a problem, constricting his margin of asymptomatic freedom.

Another case concerns the rigid mental-set of a symptomatic young woman who interiorizes* the rules and roles of her family life. This twenty-three-year-old does not know why she has been so depressed for the last two years, why she made two nearly successful suicide attempts, and why she fears she will soon attempt another. Ellen's prevailing belief is that she should die—she is unworthy. This idea affects all her behavior— whether she is deciding to return to college, to make friends, to ask her parents for financial support. Her rigid mind-set, which regulates her behaviors and ideas, reflects her interiorization of certain roles she plays within her family. Figure 3 depicts the two main hierarchies of family life she has interiorized. Within these interior hierarchies, Ellen is the unlovable child; the allied-against child; at worst, the family destroyer. Her negatively convergent hierarchical positions, once taken into her interior reality, send her a lifetime of bad messages about herself, messages that women are not to be trusted and that men, although nicer than women, are uncaring.

Figure 3. Interiorized Hierarchies of Family Life.

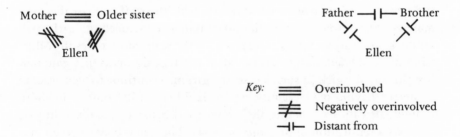

Often interiorized hierarchies like Ellen's derive from a salient and observable aspect of family functioning. Only a week before Ellen's graduation from college (the family's first child to graduate), her older sister wrote, "I have no choice but to write to you, you are the only one in the family who understands craziness." Her mother wrote her not "Good luck in school" but "Why won't you love me? I don't blame you if you hate me!" When her new dorm friends gave her a surprise birthday get-

*"Interiorize" is used instead of "internalize." Interiorize connotes at least the possibility of an active process. Also, whereas internalize refers predominantly to emotions, interiorize pertains to relational structures or representations of those structures.

together, Ellen's father said, with mild surprise, "Oh, you are going out with *friends?*", and her brother said, incredulous, *"You* got all those birthday gifts?" In the case studies, we will look at these variables as they affect family induction of mind-sets. For now, the important aspect to consider is that in Ellen's instance she did interiorize the family hierarchies she was part of, and they then contributed to her finding herself repeatedly contemplating ways to help everyone out by eliminating her crazy, bad, unlovable, disloyal self (see Chapter Seven, Case Study 3, "Over My Dead Body").

Once aspects of family context have been built into an individual's mental-set, these contextual influences take on a life of their own. Interiorized family contexts such as Ellen's thus have their own systems-perpetuating features. Ellen, in her first situations away from home, exteriorized her position in family hierarchies, by transposing it onto her relations with new acquaintances, building a battle with a girlfriend around old battles with mom, and finding a very noncommittal boyfriend, not unlike her dad. Another example of mind-sets exteriorizing themselves is an anorectic girl entering a hospital. Within a day, she may have an entire hospital ward, including housekeeping personnel, replicating her parents' management conflicts. Half the staff follows the strict managerial approach, while the other half is convinced the girl needs kindness and forgiveness. Each faction of the staff undermines the other. Like mom and dad, staff teams can also switch positions as they gain new insight into the girl. In such a case, the girl may continue to behave as an anorectic, having inadvertently exteriorized her family context. In short, individuals can, by enacting their own rigid behaviors, activate in *new* contexts a replication of *previous* contexts. These new contexts then may become part of the problem. Hence, it is useful to complement family contextual interventions with individual interventions designed to depotentiate a rigid interior relational system.

Individuals also may evolve rigid mind-sets by drawing on *interiorized social structures.* Issues of class, sex, gender, race, and age are often so fundamentally embedded into each individual's way of thinking about himself and others that they become features of his mental structure and organize his behavior below the threshold of his perception. Perhaps partly because society is stratified into economic and status levels, individuals often interiorize prevailing ideas of the self in relation to others and develop feelings of superiority or inferiority. It does not follow, however, that a member of a minority group, for example, will necessarily interiorize a sense of inferiority to members of a majority group. He may interiorize a reaction against the system of ideas that suggest his inferiority. The issue of concern is that the individual tends to respond somehow to prevailing social categories, and in turn these responses may contribute to a symptom. Let us look at a case in which a socially induced response shaped an individual's mind-set and led her to experience cross-contextual hierarchical conflict.

Patsy, a black woman from a lower socioeconomic class, considered herself as at least equal with a white coworker, based on objective assessments and time-proven skill superiority. The discrepancy between how she and the other woman were materially remunerated for their work became critical when her boss tried to prevent her from competing with the white worker for an available raise. At this point, the discrepancy between her interiorized representation of herself and the external world's representation of herself caused her conflict. Patsy became distressed over the incongruence (see Madanes, 1981) of her position in two hierarchies, one interiorized and the other social, as summarized in Figure 4.

At that point, Patsy's idea about how to behave at work was nullified by the way she was treated there. This conflict between her self-view and social reality caused insufferable lower back pain and led to uncontrollable crying spells. Her prevailing rigid belief, drawn from both hierarchies, became "I'm too good for this treatment but there's no real way

Figure 4. Incongruent Cross-Contextual Hierarchies.

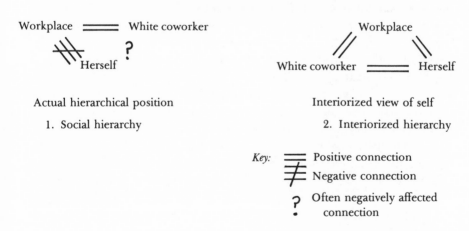

out of it." (See Chapter Seven, Case Study 4, "The Turtle with the Cracked Shell.") This rigid belief system, based on a hybrid of seemingly irreconcilable self- and social suggestion, then took on a life of its own, affecting all aspects of Patsy's life and self-esteem.

Individual mind-sets thus may represent both (1) interiorizations of aspects of rigidly repeated sequences of mythology and interaction that exist within the broader structures the symptom bearer is part of and (2) reconciliations of those directives with idiosyncratic self-directional beliefs. On the one hand, an individual may be immobilized by unhelpful edicts coming from negatively convergent hierarchical positions within a family. The person thus interiorizes (as did Ellen) these messages. On the other hand, an individual faced with a conflict between who she is and how she is to behave in relation to others—based on her self-evaluation— and the way the outside world evaluates her (as was the case with Patsy) may manifest a rigid mind-set. Interiorized conflicting messages, then, may derive from the family, social, and internal contexts the symptom bearer is part of. Once these messages are interiorized and consolidated into a rule, or rigid system of behavior, the symptom bearer's firm mind-set is no longer simply a culmination of family and social contexts; it also takes on a life of its own. These hybrid contextual beliefs often go under-ground, below a person's ordinary threshold of perception, regulating his behavior without his full intention. In this sense, an individual is subject to his own context of mind.

The individual mind-set is a treasured point of therapeutic entry. We hypothesize that a rigid mind-set presented at the start of therapy is not the only frame of mind an individual is capable of. To mobilize an individual's resources, this therapy attempts to activate and elevate secondary beliefs that may be developed to overthrow the rule of the symptom. The symptom can then become secondary, succumbing to a broadened context of mind. Through therapy, ideally the symptom bearer will come to play a more active role in the creation of his own belief system. Ellen, for example, after undergoing several family and individ-ual hypnosis sessions, described new abilities she had "spontaneously" evolved to disengage herself from externally triggered ideas that handi-capped her self-concept and to secure her private beliefs from intrusive outer realities. Coded in metaphors of family problems, a letter of Ellen's described her experience with a young man she liked: "On the morning we left for our trip, I felt so miserably angry—I was identifying Tom with

my father, and I couldn't take any word from him without reacting. I had
so much hatred and anger I felt like dying. I sat there crying, silently, not
really knowing what to do. Then I thought to go in my mind to the beach,
breathe in the goodness, and breathe out my father and the anger, have
him eaten up by a whale, throw in my mother for good measure, then
boot the whale into outer space. Even though it sounds silly, it had this
amazing cathartic effect. After that I had a great day!" Instead of letting
persistent interiorized family–life-style conflict limit her experience of
pleasure, Ellen decided to separate herself from those beliefs by mentally
sending them where they belonged, to *outer* rather than *inner* space.

Family Context

We broadly define family context as an hierarchically organized
and developing open system that, shaped by the broader social order,
operates according to certain family functional rules and roles and influences the mind-sets of individual members. Family structure encompasses
not only productive, reproductive, and other functional units but the
family's prevailing mythologies and beliefs. These include rules about
who is regarded as "us" and who as "them"; what family matters can be
presented to the public and what ones are to be kept private; to what
extent family members are to bow to social pressures that go against needs
of individual members; and to what extent individual members are invio-
late, even in the face of social reprobation or, as in wartime, the threat of
death. Regarding generational mythology, a family may carry out certain
long-held beliefs, for example, that children should grow up to sacrifice
themselves for their parents, an idea that may raise relational problems
when a child leaves home (see Chapter Seven, Case Study 2, "A Matter of
Growing Pains"). Another belief may be that men who lack education,
like father, are poor providers, and women who want an education, like
mother, are nothing but feminists, which can contribute to a young
woman's uncertainties about her future (see Chapter Six, "The Young
Woman with the Bad Body").

The contributions of family reproductive and developmental functions to symptomatology have been clearly described (see Haley, 1973;
Minuchin, 1974). Briefly, the family goes through stages of the family life
cycle, the nature of which varies across classes, cultures, and nations. The
family is identified by developmentally based functional substructures

delineated by age, order of birth, and other generational boundaries. Where roles are unclear, uncertainties about responsibilities and functions develop, and often unresolved conflicts emerge and become rigid through the mind or body of one family member. Developmental troubles are most likely to occur during periods of transition. At such times, fundamental interactional rules are tested as the family structure is called on to reorganize into a higher level of complexity. For example, the birth of a child transforms spouses into parents, but the spouses are not yet familiar with each other in their roles of "mother of child" or "father of child." They do not know how to behave toward or what functions to serve with this new parent person. The relationship "spouses-child" emerges, in which the child's role as it affects the parents' marriage and daily living must be defined. The child may also involve grandparents and in-laws with the parents in a new way. As a result, the old family models and mind-sets about who is in charge of what and how each person should behave in relation to the other may conflict with the many new developmental roles and functions.

Besides considering the reproductive and generational issues more commonly associated with symptoms, our approach adds an emphasis to the productive aspects of family life. In addition to life-stage developmental challenges, today gender role and economic conflicts permeate family life and affect the distribution of power and responsibility within it. I call these socially charged organizers of family functioning "hidden costs." Thus, conflicts in economic and gender subsystems activate or exacerbate family developmental conflicts. Therefore, in our approach, family developmental conflicts in and of themselves are often not considered the primary or sole cause of symptoms (see Case Study 2 in Chapter Seven).

The Gender Subsystem. Every family has a gender subsystem governed by rules designating those sequences of interaction that affect (1) the family distribution of gender-related notions of temperament, interest, worth, status, and even influence; (2) the distribution of material entities, such as money and food; and (3) the parameters of physical movement, including gait, amount of weight one can lift, range of gesture, facial expression, sexual experience, and educational opportunities. The gender subsystem may influence the way any content issue within the family can be treated because it affects the organizational rules whereby family members meet the requirements of their gender. Once certain rules of the gender subsystem have been established, then there can be no breach of the boundaries. Thus a mother or daughter who trespasses into male-associated territory will be confronted with whatever signs—from physical or sexual abuse to depression—the family system posts to state its rules. Likewise, a male child, such as a hemophiliac, whose father regards him as unmanly because of illness restrictions, or a father who steps out of his gender-identified position by failing to provide economically for his family, will be confronted with the subsystem's rules about gender boundaries.

Family hierarchies based on gender eventually may clash with individual members' desired functions or mind-sets. In one family, the mother recognized that she was a lesbian about the same time the father recognized that he was gay. Although never comfortable in the patriarchal role, the father had played it for years, being the breadwinner and having little to do with his two sons. Suddenly, his wife became symptomatic. Distressed, she decided to move away from her husband, and to break with the then-prevalent ideas of weakness associated with mothering, she left the children with him. In a sense, the couple temporarily reversed the sex-role stereotype, with the newly assertive wife leaving her newly nurturant husband. Considerations about who was in charge of what—which once had been, albeit unhappily, defined by socially normative rules of gender roles—now caused uncertainty, especially for the woman, who was most dramatically going against social norms. At that time, it was as if the man had to play the role of husband and the woman the role of wife. Eventually, however, the family found a most novel solution: They lived as friends in the same building, each with a new partner, and shared childrearing and finances equally. It took several years, however, for the ex-spouses to clarify the functional hierarchies and to attain a fair balance of power and responsibility.

The emphasis in our approach is on attaining functional and balanced hierarchies, but gaining clarity about gender roles will not necessarily further that goal. The patriarchal family, in which definite gender roles determine hierarchies in much of family functioning and males are to be clearly and consistently in a dominant position, produces more than its share of father-daughter incest (Herman, 1981), wives on Valium, and wife abuse (Barnett and others, 1980). Clear gender roles, in which, for example, females are constantly at the bottom of functional hierarchies (that is, congruent negative positions), may cause as many symptoms as entrapment in nullifying roles within family hierarchies (see Chapter Six).

The Economic Subsystem. This hierarchically organized substructure of the family establishes relational rules for (1) earning money for the family; (2) designating sequences of interaction that affect the actual distribution and use of the money (including clothes, nutrition, gifts) and the symbolic distributions of wealth (including power, status, affection, emotional gifts); (3) other service functions, such as childcare, dishes, garbage, yardwork. In the face of broader social conflicts pertaining to money, status, power, and recognition, family members must determine how they are going to deal with inequalities of earning power and actual earnings and how they are going to measure these economic variables against other family responsibilities, such as nurturance, domestic tasks, and so on. Even families who exert the greatest effort to believe that they do not have such relational rules tend to post boundaries they will not cross regarding how little or how much the other spouse can bring in economically. They also have conditions about what nonfinancial contributions in exchange from spouse or child are acceptable. Many marital problems and related breaches of generational boundaries involving children and grandparents are rooted in these hidden rules of family accounting and accountability (see Case Study 2 in Chapter Seven).

A family is partly a financial arrangement. If we discuss change in emotionally charged family hierarchies but neglect the economic implications, we may fail to account for the family's central conflict. Pain patients who are paid for their disability have been found most intractable to treatment because their problem gives them an uplifting balance in the social hierarchy via financial reward. Similarly, a symptom in a family system designed to compensate for an inability to provide certain expected economic responsibilities may be intractable to treatment if not considered within the broader context of the economic hierarchy. In Chapter Seven, Case Study 4, the woman Patsy exhibits a symptom partly born of her hierarchical position within her family's economic subsystem.

Perhaps most important to our therapy are considerations of how—through structuring of family life, in particular, through the hierarchically organized substructures an individual is part of—indirect pieces of information are transmitted, often unnoticed, about individual capacities, needs, sensations, even desires. Somehow, family structure is one of the means by which pieces of information, carried in sequences of interaction and in many codes, can be repeated and repeated so often, or communicated inconsistently but with such a special intensity, that a family member may consider them as "the way things are." When the messages transmitted help the person develop in a healthy manner, we consider such various family inductive phenomena as equivalent to "good hypnosis." When the family, through its structural and sequential cues and codes, "tells" an individual member that he is less than he is, or sends mutually exclusive messages about who he is, this may contribute to a form of "bad hypnosis." Chapter Four, "Role of Family Interactions in Inducing Symptoms," will discuss ways for therapists to read relationships between family structure and the induction of rigid, individual mind-sets. Family inductive capacities discussed there include:

1. The public versus private dichotomy.
2. Content versus structure confusion technique.
3. Intense rapport in family life and multiple-person inductions.
4. Conflicting messages, hierarchies in conflict, and automatic behavior.
5. Confusion, focusing inward, and the use of spontaneously occurring states of inner reverie and suggestibility.
6. Directives about who the person is, including the use of evocative cue words.
7. Parts-of-self, "bad twins," and other boundary-blurring techniques.
8. Family interspersal techniques.

We will also see how a dysfunctional family mythology can continue to have a life of its own even after a symptom bearer is no longer producing a symptom. In certain cases, like Ellen's, the individual symptom bearer may, by leaving the family, transcend his position within his family context, and the family system may persist in certain patterns of perceiving and responding to the individual, as if he were still the troubled child, anxious wife, or uncertain husband they once knew. As a result, some individuals, at least for certain periods, cannot go home again (see Chapter Seven, Case Study 3). Erickson said that such families had "earned the right to be disowned." Our approach includes the clinical study of family trancelike injunctions and actual symptom-inductive moments to explore the family as a point of therapeutic entry and possibly to develop related family therapeutic counterinductions.

In establishing new family sequences and new family induction techniques, the therapist, when possible, considers the needs of *all* family members to facilitate a developmentally sound balance of hierarchical functions. (The technique of "bartering" with the family is presented in Chapter Three, "Exchanges of Power in the Therapeutic Relationship.") Also, whenever possible, it is desirable to help a family with a symptomatic member use and expand those structures through which therapeutic counterinductions can occur naturally, routinely, privately, and repeatedly in the course of daily living. In short, our approach seeks to make the symptom bearer and his intimates the person's best hypnotists.

To increase the likelihood of changes in both an individual mindset and a related family structural arrangement, the therapist works concurrently on both levels of the symptom bearer's situation. The ultimate goals are for individual changes to not meet with overriding problematic family, work, or school patterns and for useful changes in the person's outer reality to be interiorized.

Social Context

Haley (1976, pp. 101–102) wrote about hierarchies: "Everywhere there are hierarchical arrangements that are unjust. One economic class suppresses another, women are kept in the subordinate position in both family and work groups merely because they are female. People are placed in subordinate positions because of race or religion, children are oppressed by their parents in the sense of being restricted and exploited in extreme ways. Obviously, there are many wrongs that need righting and involving hierarchical issues and any therapist must think through his ethical position." We view hierarchical conflicts within the broader social order and persistent injustices against specific groups as potential contributors to the likelihood that a certain number of families and individuals in that society will manifest symptomatology. This does not mean that there is a one-to-one correlation between social oppression and the manifestation of symptoms. Those on the bottom, the poor, are subject to worse living conditions, life expectancy, and other factors affecting physical and emotional well-being, but the rich and middle class are also symptomatic. Nevertheless, social stratification into haves and have-nots, exploiter and exploited, powerful and powerless shapes the substructures of society and affects individual members' experience of themselves. When social positions consistently handicap individuals or when social hierarchical positions nullify positions in family hierarchies or within interiorized ideas of self, individuals may manifest symptoms.* A clinician does not need an elaborate theory of society to engage in therapy. But by considering a person in his social situation, we can appreciate more fully the hierarchical conflicts he is part of and his dilemma about how to behave.

In this book, the term "social structure" encompasses prevailing ideas of status and economic arrangements that affect public thinking and action and, to the extent that social categories have been interiorized by families and individuals, the private arena. There are several ways society arranges itself into a hierarchy. One way is by *wealth,* with haves on top and have-nots on the bottom. *Gender* is another means by which economics and status are distributed, with males continuing, for example, to attain higher wages than women for equal work, and "women's work" (childcare, housekeeping) continuing to bring in no wages, retirement benefits, and so on. *Race* is a third way by which society is stratified, with a majority of whites on top, a majority of minorities on the bottom. The working class may be black and white, but the poorest sector of the working class continues to be black. *Age* is a social category. Often children and old people are less-valued social commodities than are people in their prime years of social productivity. *Religion* may play a role, with certain politically affiliated groups, such as the Fundamentalists, gaining in economic power, or certain groups' status being affected by whether they are involved in popular or unpopular political causes in other countries (such as Catholics involved in political causes in Central America; Protestants in Ireland; or Jews and Moslems in the Middle East). In these cases, as society accepts or rejects people based on religious-political commitment, membership in a certain religion, even by association alone, may affect families' and individuals' situations.

A woman who later became a union leader exemplifies how a social phenomenon penetrates family life. She reported that during the Depression in the United States, when many men could not get jobs, some factories took advantage of the situation by working hard the few men they had. Her husband, along with the other husbands in town employed by the area's biggest factory, were so stressed by work speedups and threats

---

*Because economic stratification suggests the inevitability of economic insecurity for some, real material threats can be transformed into symbolic fears about shifts in relative social altitude or status. These symbolic fears may in themselves cue certain psychophysiological responses.

about getting fired that "it had to come out somewhere." Men who had never been drinkers but who did not want to come home and take out their frustrations on their wives went to bars and drank until they were pacified. Meanwhile, the women grieved over their husbands being away and spending so much of the money they had worked so hard to earn on alcohol. The grieving women went to church for consolation. "That's all we had in Flint, Michigan: churches and bars." This woman's family, and many other families in a similar social situation, interiorized social problems, somehow. Families can "break down" and produce a distressed member in various ways. Numerous families who have to meet so many of the emotional and all the financial needs of members, despite a job shortage, often show the scars from carrying an overwhelming load.

A social problem can impinge directly on an individual through blame. A society may blame victims of a social order as the cause of society's problems, just as a family may blame a symptom bearer for its problems. This linear model of blame prevents people from facing problematic exterior realities and conceptualizing a holistic model of shared social responsibility. A symptom bearer may interiorize socially suggested notions of inferiority derived from race, sex, or age stereotypes. He may also blame himself and his peers rather than considering that he is affected by broader and more difficult to detect social contexts of which he is only a part. For example, an eighty-four-year-old woman who was a great educator, an incurable optimist, author of many books, is now isolated. Her parents, husband, and all her friends are dead; young people are treating her like a relic. She has a progressive illness that will soon leave her blind. She has no meaningful work, although her mind is intact. She has become deeply and suicidally depressed. Therapy may be able to help her reinstate the images of her influential self that she can draw on to construct a new social niche in these later years. But she is only one of many manifestations of statistical likelihood in a society that devalues its "less-productive," "old" members. The social label of inferiority may overpower her and will overpower others like her despite its obvious poor fit. Consider the black woman whose great-grandparents were slaves and whose parents were lucky to find work in someone else's fields, where they too labored like slaves from "can't see in the morning to can't see at night." Her story is one of relentless struggle and suffering from childhood through marriage, defending herself from poverty and lack of self-esteem. Individuals inhabiting a system that discriminates against women in general, but especially poor women, and most especially black women, are subject to a certain likelihood of developing such a chronic inferiority (see Chapter Seven, Case Study 6, "Divorcing the Dead"). Fanon (1967, p. 12) described the individual's interiorization of a sense of social injustice: "The disinherited in all parts of the world perceive life not as a flowering or a development of an essential productiveness, but as a permanent struggle against an omnipresent death. This ever-menacing death is experienced as endemic famine, unemployment, a high death rate, an inferiority complex and the absence of any hope for the future."

We can say that a social victim maintains the contexts he is part of. However, given a structure of inequality, we cannot say that he upholds it equally. Perhaps his induction into the social mind-set that "this is the way things are" or a perverted Christian ideology that he was put here "to suffer on this earth" is complete. He may not perceive options or openings into other ways of feeling or interrelating because he is "unaware" that he exists in a changeable context. Or sometimes a trapped individual who is aware of the context may be afraid of paying the personal costs of throwing off the shackles of a restrictive social code. And sometimes a person simply does not know what to do or who to join up with to stop feeling unworthy.

Regarding symptoms, in each case we recognize that individual and family have some margin of freedom from the materially fortified suggestive power of social context. However, in extreme cases, as with refugees from war-torn Guatemala and El Salvador, a poor family or physicians resisting government suggestions within their own margin of freedom may face exile or death. Sometimes an individual in our own society is free to be unemployed and free to go hungry because of a lack of jobs for all. Nevertheless, so long as a person can choose one set of realistic self-instructions over another set, he has a chance to at least remain asymptomatic.

Although this book does not discuss this issue in depth, specific ways social structures may activate certain individual beliefs and psychophysiological states are as intriguing to unearth as tools of family induction. Cannon's classic work on voodoo death (1957) is most interesting for considering how social structures can lead to specific mind-sets, including dramatic sequences of psychophysiological response. He described how all the members within a social context may so empower a witch doctor that at the proper gesture (or "cue") from him, an individual identified as evil will die suddenly (probably from sudden cardiac arrest!). Although the witch doctor made the gesture, he did so within a supportive social context, so his gesture was the economical summarization of many prior interactional sequences of which the individual was an active part. In our society, terms such as "nigger," "bitch," and "dyke" operate as structurally and materially empowered cue words or shibboleths that symbolically transfer power across a group (such as Klansmen or misogynists), or they indicate real exclusion from certain places, activities, opportunities, and even basic human rights. They can signal the legitimacy of violence. A single look from a person, in a context of racism or sexism, may "summarize" these social structures and thereby spontaneously activate certain feelings, sensations, or ideas in a primed recipient of the look. Social categories work on the society's members all the time. For example, hypertension, which afflicts an excessive number of blacks, is a symptom of a condition in which the individual's natural defenses are so chronically aroused as to be deadly. Several studies have hypothesized that the body's turning against itself is associated with experiences of helplessness within a racist context (see Harburg and others, 1973; Naditch, 1974).

We consider that work-related hierarchies (described as *contributing* to the symptoms of Patsy, the woman with back pain) may give individuals *sufficient exterior context* for symptoms. For example, a young psychotherapist who is a family and child expert is assigned to run an outpatient unit in a family-oriented therapy program. He was hired by the former head of the program, who now is the top administrator. The administrator had been the expert in family and child; he still likes to attend case conferences, and he does not want to relinquish his authority. Actually, the young doctor knows more about the field than the administrator. The young doctor becomes anxious and has trouble speaking at case conferences, especially when he is supposed to lead the discussion. On the one hand, as the director of outpatient, he is on top of the hierarchy; on the other hand, he is clearly junior, as seen in Figure 5. In one hierarchy, he is to behave as an authority or he will fail to do the job he was hired for. In the other hierarchy, the young doctor is to behave more submissively, as a person new to a system and as yet unproved within it. In this work-related situation (until he transcends these opposed structural demands), he may be confused and long to escape seemingly nullifying realities. Add to this situation the fact that his coworkers have the status of tenure, having been there longer than he, yet must work under him. Add to that some coworkers requesting that their own families become his patients, and one can see how the work aspect of social context alone can cause even highly successful individuals to develop stammers, hives, tics, impotence, and other strange forms of protest.

Figure 5. Incongruent Work Hierarchies.

As director of outpatient and in terms of clinical knowledge

Young doctor

——————————————————————————————————————

Coworkers   Administrator

Administrator

——————————————————————————————————————

Coworkers   Young doctor as
                                                             newest staff member

To summarize what we call the symptom structure, there are three major levels, one interior—the individual mind-set—and two exterior—family and social context. We also identify several subcategories (see Table 1).

In dialectical therapy, we consider the symptom a metaphorical referent to the relevant problematic hierarchical subcategories within, or across, these classifications. We consider that an individual manifesting symptoms may be caught in nullifying hierarchical positions and is therefore receiving conflicting suggestions about how to think, feel, and otherwise behave in at least two central areas of his life; or the individual is consistently on the bottom of hierarchies and denied an asymptomatic domain of functional significance. A common goal of treatment is to facilitate symptom relief by helping the person attain a functional hierarchical balance across the contexts he inhabits.

The Dialectics of Interaction and Special States

Thus far, we have focused on each of three proposed levels of a symptom structure. As mentioned, however, the symptom is in reality a

Table 1. Three Levels of Symptom Structure.

Interior Context	Exterior Context	
Individual Mind-set	Family Structure	Social Structure
1. Hierarchy of ideas 2. Interiorized hierarchy of family life 3. Interiorized hierarchy of social nexus	1. Hierarchy based on generational functions 2. Hierarchy of gender functions 3. Hierarchy of economic functions 4. Interiorization of social classification of family 5. Rigid mind-set about an individual's position in family	1. Hierarchical ideas of status and economically derived substructures 2. Class-, race-, gender-, age-, job-, church-, school-based hierarchical positions

Note: The reader may recognize a similarity to the existentialist's "eigenwelt," "umwelt," and "mitwelt" (Binswanger, 1958, pp. 328–329). In the present approach this existential model is informed by recent understandings of power and hierarchy in the shaping and interconnecting of these domains.

living conflict and often a manifestation of cross-contextual suggestion *in action*. To establish a more precise understanding of how, for example, a family may contribute to the activation of a symptom, we will address several other issues.

We have established the role of *power* in symptomatology through the concept of hierarchy. Certain people and ideas prevail over other people and ideas, both within and across the three contexts examined. When all is well, power walks arm-in-arm with responsibility. Sometimes, however, power joins with her lesser sisters, such as neglect or intrusion, such that, for example, one context, person, or idea penetrates the intrapsychic refuge an individual might otherwise seek for renewal. At this juncture the issue of *boundaries* is a central feature of power and symptoms. Boundaries represent the psychophysiological regulators of gates and timing of entry both into and across the three symptom-sustaining contexts of *mind, family,* and *society.*

Historically, boundary making has been the sacrosanct domain of privilege. The king surrounded his castle with an uncrossable moat and was guarded by knights with swords. He had strict and well-protected points of entry. The poor have often had no place to even consider delineating as "mine." And historically, men with physical strength, have drawn boundaries beyond which women cannot trespass, while the bodies of women, who are often legally regarded as male property, have been violated by even husbands and fathers. The sick, the imprisoned, and the mentally ill share a long history of lack of even self-rights. Consider Foucault's (1976, p. 12) statement: "The situation of internment and guardianship imposed on the madman from the end of the eighteenth century, his total dependence on medical decision, contributed no doubt to the creation, at the end of the nineteenth century, of the personality of the hysteric. Dispossessed of his or her rights by guardian and family, thrown back into what was practically a state of juridical and moral minority, deprived of freedom by the all-powerful doctor, *the patient became the nexus of all social suggestions; and at the point of convergence of these practices, suggestibility was proposed as the major syndrome of hysteria*" (italics added). The relationship between individual boundary regulation and rights to self-instruction and broader systems of external suggestion has been explored in politics, philosophy, and religion, but it is a relatively new factor in creating clinical models and therapeutic interventions.

We mentioned how powers from broader social contexts somehow penetrate the boundaries of all family systems. A family then may be more or less resilient in preserving domestic boundaries. For the greater or lesser good of family members, depending on the issues at hand (ranging from government-legislated acts of terror against family members for some reason to state protection of a child from parental sexual abuse), the family membrane is permeable, allowing the social categories of gender, economics, and authority to be interiorized from the broader socioeconomic system. To consider interiorization of social suggestion in families, the Kindervolk (young folk) prearmy organized by Hitler in Nazi Germany often gave a child member power over his entire family by virtue of his connection to the Nazi order. A son could breach generational boundaries, defy his father in the father's home, and even turn him in to the Gestapo if the father failed to exercise the "proper responses" to people labeled inferior. We suggested from such phenomena that families are inextricably connected to the world around them, and if the skies and seas are polluted, they too are likely to be somehow poisoned.

We indicated that families, whether they submit to unseen or direct social cues, also have their own special suggestive powers over individual family members and their own unique abilities to penetrate individual boundaries. Implicit in the field of family therapy is recognition of the powers of families over their members, powers that can be used intentionally, spontaneously, even accidentally, for good or for evil. In fact, the symptom is often a moment in a power struggle between individual member and family system, in which physical, economic, sexual, generational, or affective forces may help keep the symptom bearer in check. In families, sequences of interaction, rules of relating, dreams, real threats of loss of love, finances, sexual opportunity, or respectability converge. The resulting contradictions between a member's inner and outer realities can become difficult to transcend. The role the family context plays in relation to the individual symptom bearer's suggestive responsivity is the part of the multifaceted and dynamic symptom structure we examine most in this book. By what means can a family (or a social context) attain so formidable a hold on the mind-set of an individual member and gain the right to penetrate his psychophysiological boundaries in a manner at least partly harmful to him? How much can an individual afford to allow a particular family or social setting to permeate his psychophysiological system? To what extent can an individual permit his mind-set, including those aspects of his functioning considered autonomic, to be influenced by his family? How can a symptom bearer enjoy his societal rights as a free citizen within a context of a powerful family expectational system or a violent family? To what extent can he learn to modulate points and means of entry across his own private boundaries and maintain only useful family- and self-instruction? In what nonsymptomatic way can he create a self-suggestive response to reconcile seemingly nullifying contextual cues? How can broader social structures—including the family—be prevailed on to relinquish intrusive or otherwise irresponsible control, even that which is unintentionally and/or benevolently imposed?

When thinking of these profound issues, it is useful to make an analogy with the story of the three little pigs. The houses of straw and wood are symptomatic boundaries; huffed and puffed on, they leave the symptom bearer squealing. But with a good house of stone, windows on the world, and a secure door, the happy inhabitants can have their pie and allow the hungry wolf his domain.

As we consider links between family suggestive capacities and the symptomatic member's interior self-instructional capacities, we can draw on certain understandings of the relationship between hypnotist and subject. Decades of hypnotic research have demonstrated that a subject's response to any suggestion is in part a function of his ability to be hypnotized, as assessed by standard measures; that receptive capacities and trance skills vary across subjects, regardless of the inductive procedure employed; and that some subjects respond to nonstandard and indirect procedures (see Orne, 1959, 1977; Erickson, 1980). We thus recognize that ultimately across and within family members there is a margin of differential responsiveness to suggestions from self, family, and others. As we study in depth the power of family directives, we appreciate that the symptom is not simply an eruption of family and social conflicts and suggestions; it is also partly a creation, an effort at self-instruction, a product of a roving self struggling to reconcile self-messages with messages from others. The symptom is a logical hybrid of inner and outer realities.

Also, it is useful to remember that the subject of family suggestions need not be in an inferior position in the family hierarchy. And the subject is not *under* the hypnotist's spell. Indeed, the subject intentionally or unintentionally lets the hypnotist or the family influence; but the suggestive power is not solely in the magnetic hands of family mesmerizers. As we look at indirect and unintended family suggestions, it is not always easy or necessary to unravel who is the subject and who is the operator. In any hypnosis, but particularly that of the family or society, the subject himself must believe in and uphold certain structures for the messages to be suggestive. In fact, his own hierarchical position of power in one family subsystem may be the motivator that ultimately renders him responsive to other counterdemands in another subsystem. (The author uses subsystem and substructure interchangeably; see Ritterman, 1977, for philosophical rationale.)

In Chapter Four we will observe a family induction of components of David's symptomatic behavior. David is a young man who cannot think from one idea to the next. In his family, he occupies two hierarchically incongruent and seemingly nullifying positions. In one subunit, he has power that is excessive for his position in the family; in the other subunit, he is inappropriately infantilized. His "automatic" symptomatic responses, observably intensified in the course of family interaction, are partly reactions to suggestions or cues that derive their power over him in part from his position of power over his father.

Responsiveness to suggestion and a loss of power (or a compromised range of personal freedom), then, are related but not equal phenomena. In fact, as we have discussed thus far, the power of suggestive messages is often derived from a lack of balance throughout the hierarchically organized contexts of individuals' lives. The resulting incompatibility of messages intensifies the inductive potential of specific statements, enabling them to enter unnoticed into an individual's mind and tell him at once to "Go ahead and try it, you are the greatest" and "What's an idiot like you doing trying to accomplish something of this caliber?"

Thus far we have hinted at some elusive relationship between trance states and symptom states, between hypnotists and family members. To clarify what we mean by hypnosis, symptoms, and family inductions, we first briefly discuss conventional hypnotherapy.

Introduction to Hypnosis

A person hypnotized enters a special state and then uses that state. The hypnotist has to recognize and/or activate the state and then use the state therapeutically. Thus, the hypnotist *works with* the individual.

Depending partly on his level of trance, the hypnotized individual detaches more or less of his attention from his immediate exterior context. As he does so, he is increasingly able to attach his attention to interior psychological and psychophysiological realities and thus to his own individual potentials.

The hypnotist seeks to activate the symptom bearer to search through his psychophysiological memory system. During his period of internal scanning, the person inhabits subjective time and experiences internal events as if they were happening externally. The hypnotist uses this special state to help the person imagine and ultimately *reify* the imagined. The subject focuses on those memories that can help him go beyond the habitual frames of reference or mind-set by which his thinking and experiencing have been routinely organized. Trance thus becomes a chance to rehearse new actions to be used in a person's external reality.

Basically, the hypnotic state may be readily aroused by such diverse conditions as music, a boring lecture, a car accident, or a loving reverie. Any event, internal or external, that directs the subject's attention inward, away from his immediate exterior realities, can activate trance. For the hypnotist, Erickson wrote (1980, vol. 3, pp. 15–16):

One needs the respect, confidence, and trust of a subject, and then one suggests fatigue, a desire for sleep and
rest, an increasing feeling of sleep, and finally a deep sound
restful sleep. These suggestions are given repetitiously, with
gradual progression from one to the next, always with careful reassurance of the subjects as they make response to
them. . . . One simply, persuasively, and patiently suggests
sleep of a restful character until the subject does sleep, and
then the subject is instructed to remain asleep until all reasonable purposes are accomplished. There should be no forcing or rushing of subjects, and every effort should be made
to enable the subjects to appreciate any physical feeling they
have suggestive of sleep. This simple technique can be
learned by anyone, and anybody who has been hypnotized
can employ it to hypnotize others, given cooperation and
the patience to make use of it. As for awakening the subject,
one can suggest an arousal directly, or give the subject suggestions to the effect that he is slowly and progressively
awakening, repeating these suggestions until the subject is
fully awake.

However, recent research suggests that healthy people go through
certain ultradian cycles, in which every ninety minutes certain parasympathetic and right-hemispheric functions sharing many features of the
"common everyday trance" are activated spontaneously (Rossi, 1982).
People may regularly and naturally go into and out of these special states,
which are characterized by response attentiveness. The hypnotist may
thus wish to spontaneously activate this state by using the *internal* time
clock: "Trance readiness, or the common everyday trance, may be understood as highly individual and variable but behaviorally recognizable
portions of the ultradian cycle. . . . Hypnotherapy may be conceptualized
as a facilitation of these naturally occurring ultradian cycles, during
which parasympathetic and right-hemispheric processes can be maxi-
mized to facilitate healing" (Rossi, 1982, p. 30). By following this
ultradian cycle theory, the hypnotist can either facilitate the activation
of the state in the patient or recognize the manifestations of the state as it
occurs naturally within a session and amplify its duration, intensity, and
utility.

Directives. To formally activate the hypnotic state, the therapist can use one of three basic types of directives. The first directive is *the simple induction.* This trance induction technique can be a direct statement, such as "Sleep now," or a simple *indirect* statement, such as "You don't want to go into trance too quickly, do you?" More commonly, the hypnotist uses a *sequential directive,* either at the point of the individual's readiness to enter a trance—the person seems relaxed, receptive, already in the process of entertaining a brief inner reverie—or at whatever moment the clinician establishes the intense rapport often required to activate the state of trance. Erickson and Rossi (1979, p. 4) developed a five-stage paradigm of sequential trance induction and suggestion:

1. Get and keep the patient's attention by focusing his attention on what is going on inside of him (feelings, memories, and so on).
2. Defuse habitual mind-sets or ways of thinking by distracting the person or introducing doubts about the way he usually sees things.
3. Initiate an unconscious search by using indirect forms of suggestion, words, or events with certain implications.
4. Activate unconscious processes, particularly by mobilizing personal associations and sequences of personal lines of thought.
5. Recognize the hypnotic response, which is the result of these chains of behavioral evocations; physiological and psychological phenomena then occur, which the subject experiences as happening autonomously.

Progressive sequential directives can become more complex when several interrelated sequences are presented simultaneously to a subject. An excellent example of this event is Erickson's interspersal technique (1966), in which at least two lines of communication are taking place, one concealing the other. To the florist suffering cancer pain, the conscious communication sequences are about tomato plants and the unconscious communication is about comfort.

The third and less frequently discussed type of hypnotic event is derived from the power of contextual cues and *structural* directives. The hypnotist may use a hypnotic atmosphere—such as a setting in which a wife is hypnotized and all conversation is metaphorical, to increase the likelihood of the husband going into trance. So long as the hypnotist herself does not believe in them, she may play into mesmeric myths to intensify the husband's expectations of entering into and using a trance state effectively. Hypnotic and other therapeutic contexts have their own special suggestive capacities because they *are* outside a person's ordinary frame of reference and they represent a social force. Also, it is sometimes easier and safer for a symptom bearer to surrender to a stranger than to a family member who knows too well his touchinesses. The hypnotic context derives its special effectiveness from its temporary nature and social power and from trance being built in as part of its reality. In Chapter Four we will examine structural inductions in depth when we look at family suggestion. For now, contextual cues, which are more than the sum of simple and sequential directives, heighten the likelihood of trance manifesting itself. These include all relevant structure-function cues in which temporal antecedence is not the principle variable in activating trance responses. Rather, the very organization of the hypnotic context, the functions it is expected to carry out, and the suggestive weight a person outside the family carries all bear their own inductive capacities.

Trance Ratification. After a trance has been induced, the hypnotist has to ratify her effectiveness. How can she do so? To aid in this process, Erickson and Rossi (1979, p. 11) cited a number of indicators of spontaneously occurring or hypnotically induced trance, including:

> Body reorientation after trance
> Catalepsy
> Body immobility
> Changed voice quality
> Expectancy
> Eye changes and closure
> Facial features smoothed
> Feelings of dissociation
> Amnesia
> Anesthesia
> Body illusions
> Time distortion
> Feeling good after trance (no matter how one felt before)
> Loss of or alteration in reflexes, including blinking, respiration, swallowing, startle reflex
> Psychosomatic responses
> Pupillary changes

Response attentiveness
Time lag in motor and conceptual behavior (for example, taking
    twenty-five minutes to lift hand to cheek)

However, the issue is controversial. For decades, researchers of
hypnotism have pondered how to describe, explain, and ratify the trance
state. What are the stable psychophysiological concomitants of the state, if
any; what is the relationship between entering into the trance state and
following directives? What are the differences among the trancelike states
of long-distance runners; detached-from-external-reality yogis; and Zen
masters, who develop a heightened awareness, which maintains attentiveness to external stimuli? Relaxation and the relaxation response
Benson (1976) described are cardinal features of some entranced, but
other subjects exhibit increased tension. Some researchers prefer to
exclude or deemphasize those same nonvoluntary features Erickson
and other researchers, including Weitzenhoffer (1978), identified as classical. To date, hypnosis has been described as a special state with *stable*
psychophysiological concomitants; a special state with *variable* psychophysiological concomitants; that state an individual is in *whenever* he
follows a suggestion; or a state that has no *consistent* relationship to the
likelihood of a suggestion being received and followed.

Studies have shown that subjects permit the hypnotist's voice to
wander through the corridors of their experiential and psychophysiological life and then interiorize the events in a manner that may affect a wide
range of phenomena. For example, hypnosis has been used effectively in
telling a subject's body to cut off the blood supply of unwanted warts
(Johnson and Barber, 1978). Many studies have demonstrated hypnotists'
capacity to "tell" people in this special state to increase the blood supply
to one body area, making it warmer, and decrease the flow of blood
to another, rendering it cooler (Taub, 1977; Dugan and Sheridan, 1976;
Maslach, Marshall, and Zimbardo, 1972). Similarly, hypnosis has been
found significantly more effective than biofeedback in peripheral vasodilation and vasoconstriction training (Barabasz and McGeorge, 1978). It has
decreased capillary bleeding during oral surgery with hemophiliacs
(Lucas, 1959) and decreased the need for factor transfusions for hemophiliacs (LeBaw, 1970, 1975). Many researchers agree that the special state
of trance is one way to enter those human systems typically thought of
as "automatic." Additionally, hypnotists appreciate the importance of

getting out quickly, so that the body can return to its own time-honored protective mechanisms.

It seems from such studies (also see Crasilneck and Hall, 1959) that hypnotic suggestion often does use the special psychophysiological variables classically used to ratify the trance state. However, more than twenty years ago, Barber proved that a wide range of suggestive phenomena previously associated with trance—color blindness; modified transmission of photic impulses to the retina in hypnotic blindness; hypnotic deafness; altered gastric functions, blood-glucose-content levels, respiration rates, pulse, temperature, and cutaneous functioning, including the formation of herpes blisters—could also be activated by direct forms of suggestion, that is, without any of the externally choreographed chain of events associated with formal trance induction. His review of that literature led him to emphasize that: "Further investigations into the nature of hypnosis 'might help bypass the concepts of hypnotic induction' and 'trance state' and focus on biographical and situational factors that may account for certain individuals' responding to symbolic stimulation from another person with so-called 'hypnotic behavior,' whether primarily motor responses (for example, limb rigidity, eye catalepsy) or primarily physiological responses (for example, tachycardia, wart involution)" (Barber, 1961, p. 419).

We propose that each human being has a capacity for suggestion-readiness, an idiosyncratic ability to *turn on* (or off) to a certain type or format of suggestion that can then affect aspects of his psychophysiological functioning. Any student of hypnosis has observed certain subjects' special capacities of memory, time distortion, accessibility of emotional experience, dissociation, or heightened ability to ignore painful stimuli. The capacity to focus on Y and to hear but not be distracted by X, to see but not respond to seeing Z, and other skills of selective inattention to exterior cues is heightened in hypnotic subjects. We believe that although direct suggestions to a motivated or cooperative individual can have a powerful effect, in other cases the likelihood of the readiness-to-respond state being activated and specific heightened subjective capacities being used can be increased by taking advantage of the phenomena described— if not explained—as characteristic of trance. If an individual is overly suggestible to certain indirect family cues, or unable to turn off to those cues, the therapist may want to use the trance state to immunize him against such "invisible" directives. We regard the trance state—using classical automatic responses and classical ratification variables—as providing the "entranced," his family, and the therapist with a special opportunity to affect, for better or worse, his context of mind. Just as body builders exercise certain muscle groups to shape their physiques, symptom bearers can spontaneously integrate trance "exercises" into a program of shaping up their relations with self and others.

Symptoms and Family Induction

Trained hypnotists are not the only ones who may gain entry into otherwise automatic human processes. The human body's own ebb and flow rhythms affect its openness to suggestion, permitting other diverse and even negative influences to make their way. Eyer and Sterling's (1975) work on hypertension noted that whereas hunter-gatherer societies produced few hypertensives, up to half the people in modern societies have high enough blood pressures to cause death. Community disruption and increased work pressure have been correlated with the ups and downs of individuals' blood pressures, suggesting that social systems can penetrate individuals neurohormonal and cardiovascular systems.

Family stresses have been shown to somehow violate the natural rhythms of human psychophysiology, leading to increased bleeds in hemophiliacs and rises in free fatty acids in the bloodstream of superlabile diabetics (Minuchin, Rosman, and Baker, 1978). External systems thus can stress and penetrate individuals, creating a neurohormonal, cardiovascular, or other psychophysiological event. After this event has been activated enough for the body to become familiar with it, the body "learns" this self-destructive routine, reconciling its messages with these new constrictive regulations. The body, in trying to live in synch with these external systems, becomes out of synch. A wart appears; then a colony of warts; more bleeds than genetics can account for occur in a hemophiliac; the muscles in the neck tense spontaneously, radiating down the back; intercourse sends a referred pain through the sympathetic nervous system to the cut nerve fibers in a foot, causing a familiar burning pain; a husband, wife, or child becomes immobile with depression and subjective time stops.

Sometimes a destructive version of the trance state is cued in, a symptomatic state that occupies periods intended for rest and renewal. The trance state, the state of receptivity, is filled with the intrusions of others. Experiences are introduced into the human system that the system is not yet equipped to readily absorb, process, or remove. The individual experiences himself as occupied by his symptom and its "bad-trance" state.

As we look at a symptom bearer's preoccupation with family conflict, we consider automatically occurring phenomena as indicators, if not of trance, of the reception of suggestions by the unconscious or by those aspects of human functions generally choreographed spontaneously by the autonomic nervous system (ANS) and other automatic systems. We also consider that certain aspects of the symptomatic state and its component behaviors, including special subjective experiences, can be regarded as one form of a trance state and may in fact represent an abuse or perversion of aspects of that state. In other words, we consider the symptomatic state as partly a destructive utilization of trance capacities, in which the symptom bearer is carrying out some reconciliation of seemingly irreconcilable suggestions from another person or social context, a family context, and/or his or her own context of mind. We recognize that symptoms also have functional uses and may derive partly from active coping and defensive attempts. Symptoms thus are mysteriously multipurposed.

We do not attempt to prove that symptom bearers are in a certain level of trance at a certain moment when seemingly automatic symptom components are activated in a certain family interview. However, we do clarify what variables we use to differentiate a family induction from ordinary family functioning. We focus on instances when specific family rituals, which correspond with recognized hypnotic induction rituals, can be observed within specific therapy sessions. Certainly we do not use the eye-roll or arm levitation techniques as standards of family inductions. Instead, we pay special attention to the culmination of observable family sequences in the seemingly spontaneous manifestations of *components* of symptomatic behavior, particularly those components that are associated with the classical ratifiers of the trance state.

We look for (1) simple, sequential, and unique family-structural inductive capacities in association with (2) the activation or intensification of automatically occurring trance concomitants or symptom components in the symptom bearer. We recognize that just as the hypnotist's subject determines the efficacy of her procedures, so the symptom bearer, even in the expression of seemingly automatic and psychophysiological responses, contributes to the shaping of his own mediating self-instructional capacities. Although we appreciate that the family has a special generalized power of emotional and suggestive continuity, clinically we are most interested in actually observing clear-cut *inductive* events. In using hypnosis in family therapy, we pattern our therapeutic counterinduction on such processes, using family suggestive routes to carry new messages about behavior and to activate new internal processes in several family members, which can lead to family transforming behaviors.

Certainly there are cases when, even if family life is contributing to activation of a symptom, the therapist may not be able to observe an induction or may not realize the direction or pull of seemingly discontinuous fragments of suggestion scattered across family members, diverse interactional sequences, and over time. That family voice accompanying the symptom bearer may be part of an impressive cacophony of many different voices of family, self, and society to which the clinician is tone-deaf. In fact, we recognize that part of the power of family suggestion and moments of intense family inductive efficacy may lie in its elusiveness, its slipperiness, and its inconsistent appearance. A *variable inductive reinforcement schedule* may be most irresistible. When an inductive event occurs, an undertow of family emotional life may suddenly open up, momentarily pulling the symptom bearer with it. Then just as suddenly it may close, leaving the symptom bearer wondering "Am I making all this up? What's wrong with me?" As one young "schizophrenic" man expressed it, "When my mother looks me in the eyes and talks in that voice, she hypnotizes me. I lose thirty seconds in your time. But to me, I lose eternity. A hole opens up. Then, I can't remember where I was or what I was doing." This opening and "vanishing" (Montalvo, 1976) of a symptom-inductive moment is discussed in Chapter Four.

We invite the clinician to search for, activate, or increase the likelihood of the family opening up to the therapist its own inductive secrets. Because of our interest in participating clinically in this family inductive process, we emphasize the importance of creating an hypnotic atmosphere, which increases the likelihood of both (1) observing actual inductive moments and (2) being invited in at multiple points to counter destructive aspects of such moments.

Table 2 lists potential activators of trance states and conceptualizes multiple points at which responsive readiness and bad-trance-like states of symptoms may occur. Once again, note that the family induction is only one facet of the induction dialectic. In Chapter Six and the last case study in Chapter Seven, we focus on self-instruction in symptoms.

Table 2. Potential Activators of Trance States.

I.   Interior
     A. *Spontaneous*—as in common, everyday trance, perhaps occurring with
        ultradian rhythms, as in the manifestations of symptom components
     B. *Planned use of self-hypnosis* to immunize self against harmful external
        suggestions or otherwise instruct and inform the self; maximal use of
        the margin of intrapsychic freedom

II. Exterior
     A. *Family induction* procedures
     B. *Social induction procedures or other exterior events*
        1. Listening to a boring, lulling, repetitive lecturer or piece of music
        2. Traumatic event
        3. Racial, gender, age, and other broad social suggestions
        4. Actions of the hypnotist or other purposeful trance activator
III. Hybrids of interior and exterior suggestion

Because we are interested primarily in *change* in therapy, we need a
model for the induction of symptomatic behavior that indicates movement across the three contexts the symptom bearer inhabits. Figure 6
transforms this linear outline table into a dynamic model. It is an open-
systems model of trance induction, useful for conceptualizing the family
and hypnotist inductions discussed throughout this book.

Again, society may entrance a family, and a family may entrance an
individual member. A member may entrance himself or a responsive family or society (as examples, Hitler and Gandhi). Chains of sequences
across suggestive contexts activate and utilize individual trance and automatic phenomena. We use this model as a general picture of potentially
multiple points of inductive entry into a symptom structure.

For a family induction to transgress the clinician's threshold of just
noticeable difference (JND) of family context (see Chapter Four), the
clinician first must be informed of family systems' inductive capacities. To
help recognize these capacities, in Chapter Four we will look at family
interactions in terms of Erickson and Rossi's (1979) five-stage formal induction sequence, outlined earlier in this chapter.

If an individual hypnotist, usually a stranger to the patient, can
compel that person, often a family member, to focus his attention inward;
can confuse that family member; can cue him to private memories and
associations; can activate changes in respiration, physical sensation,
blood flow, temperature change, and other psychophysiological processes
associated with trance states, certainly family members may be able to do

Figure 6. Holistic Model of Trance Induction and Suggestion-Reception.

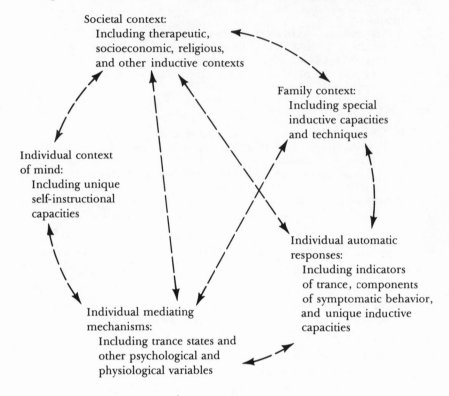

Key: ———— represents a single line or convergence of multiple suggestions that are explicit or implicit from the context(s) identified.

Source: Revised from Minuchin, Rosman, and Baker, 1978, p. 21.

the same. The family influence can be very frequent and inconsistent and can carry threats of economic and emotional withdrawal. If indirect suggestion is associated with enhancing a suggestion's irresistability, the family has a number of unique characteristics that intensify its ability to carry unconscious or even unintended messages unseen, below the JND of contextual perception.

Summary

A symptom can be regarded as representing a problem across the three contexts a person may inhabit. Each context has suggestive power over the others, with the broader contexts of family and society tending to wield more power than self because of real, in-built economic and survival dependencies. However, the lesser structures do appear to have some margin of freedom. An individual's symptoms often appear related to efforts to reconcile messages from his three contexts. The reconciliation of incompatible inner and outer realities may produce a rather bizarre symptom hybrid.

We describe the symptom as partly a kind of abuse of the trance state, in which the individual carries out certain automatic responses to strange and often bizarre cross-contextual suggestions. We also recognize it as a coping effort, a defense against undesirable suggestions, to increase one's margin of personal freedom. It is both reflexive and intentional, embodying the dialectics of conscious versus unconscious processes within the individual and interior versus exterior demands. The goals of therapy are to (1) enlarge the individual's exercise of his margin of freedom from restrictive cross-contextual injunctions, by enhancing his self-discipline or his powers of self-instruction, and (2) at the same time to help his family reorganize in a manner that expands its repertoire of developmentally useful directives by affecting its symptom-related processes and structures. We thus develop dialectical interventions into related points of therapeutic entry, whereby the therapist searches through family, social, and self-inductions, gathering the connections to be used for creating a therapeutic counterinduction.

Chapter Two ⧉ ⧉ ⧉

Stages
of an Interview

⧉ Chapter Two outlines the three-stage family therapy that is clinically demonstrated in the rest of the book. The reader may want to return to this chapter after completing the book, to flesh out this approach to healing.

The preinductive stage is the creation of an hypnotic atmosphere and the maximization of chances of glimpsing a family-based induction of certain symptom components. The more intense therapeutic counterinductive stage focuses on only essential factors relevant to the symptom and includes the use of multiperson hypnotic techniques. The postinductive stage offers the therapist an opportunity to invite and address objections to her counterinduction.

Therapy is a science that encompasses the relative assessment of the symptom bearer's problem, which is revealed by the therapist's immersion in the individual's mind-set, family, and even work life. A symptom exists in a certain therapeutic context for a specific client and a particular therapist; the science of therapy includes all the idiosyncracies of the therapist, therapeutic context, and symptom. The goal is to stay close to the essentials of the case.

Because therapy is based on the creation of a new social contract between people and involves both physical and purely subjective concepts of space, time, and motion, it requires immediate and automatic response from the therapist. The therapist, like a ballerina, is only as excellent as her ability to move, at the required moment, with precision, perseverance, and grace. Thus the spontaneity of an artist is an essential skill in the science of therapy. A theory must help the therapist move with disciplined agility: our approach does so by increasing the clinician's familiarity with contextual suggestions so that therapeutic counterinductions will be more automatic or "intuitive."

The structuring and sequencing of this therapy is based on five assumptions:

1. Therapy is most often effective if it derives from intense engagement and persistence within a context of cooperative exchange.
2. A goal of therapy, especially during the initial interview, is to assess self-, family, and societal symptom-induction techniques, such as sequences of thoughts and action that seem to contribute to activation of the symptom.
3. To influence central dysfunctional sequences of both private and public behavior, the therapist can conceptualize her task as one of activating therapeutic counterinductions, using a spectrum of techniques—from trance events to related family interactional events—to do so.
4. Therapeutic interventions are often made through several points of entry at once, in that the therapist plans a strategy that will affect dialectically or isomorphically related systems-perpetuating features of the symptom bearer's mind-set and family or societal contexts.
5. Because symptoms often represent hierarchical conflicts across the inner and outer contexts of a person's life, the impact of therapy on these hierarchies often leads to seemingly automatic relief from the domination of the symptom and other beneficial changes.

Before identifying the specific steps of the therapy, which are examined in depth throughout this book, let us discuss briefly the nature of the therapeutic context itself and the use of the unique features of that context.

Structuring the Therapeutic Context: A Model of Persistence and Cooperative Exchange

As Bateson elucidated (1972), the way relational statements are contextualized carries their meaning and the sequences of their messages. For example, monkeys may act the same way when starting a fight or initiating play. But the overriding communication that "this is in play" takes the bite out of a nip. The contextual message colors the meaning of events that occur within that context. The therapeutic context automatically carries its own messages about the nature of relationships within its boundaries. If it carries the message "This context deals with mental illness," therapeutic transactions will be injected with medical metaphors. In a different vein, Madanes suggested that introducing pretending into a nurturant model of therapy helps activate less painful, less autocratic approaches to human dilemmas (1981). We regard therapy not as a social control vehicle but as an agent of individual and family service. It is a unique type of human service because it requires personal involvement from the parties concerned, including rapport and cooperation. Although change is fundamental to therapy, and change often implies struggle, we emphasize techniques for maintaining a context of cooperation throughout that process. Perseverance and consistency frame many strategies.

This therapy is derived partly from vestiges of a broader social structure that has, across civilizations and cultures, provided rules and roles of noncombative or cooperative transaction: the model of gift exchange (Mauss, 1967; Levi-Strauss, 1969). The rituals of gift exchange (described in depth in Chapter Three), are governed by a society's rules about joining kin to nonkin, about what constitutes a fair and equitable exchange for all parties concerned. If properly conducted, it effects the hierarchical elevation of all parties concerned and provides steps one can follow to influence shifts in hierarchical relationships during the exchange process itself. If this model is followed, from start to finish the therapeutic context becomes a malleable and prototypical situation for attaining certain goals.

The three most general categories of the therapeutic process are (1) therapist-client interactions around the client "giving" the therapist the living conflict of the symptom as a kind of offering; (2) interactions around the therapist "receiving" the symptom; (3) interactions around the heart of the therapeutic process, with the therapist "repaying" the client(s). This model is useful for:

1. Helping to activate the therapist's attitudes of positive expectation and eagerness to be of service and minimizing unintended, undesirable combative attitudes, even if the therapy prescribes an arduous treatment plan. A respectful rapport is thereby quickly established.

2. Activating throughout therapy a spirit of client cooperation and a sense of enhanced control over one's mind and relationships and minimizing unnecessarily therapeutically induced dependencies.
3. Facilitating intense engagement and building in from the start a logical sequencing of therapeutic events, from involvement to disengagement, by establishing multiple functional hierarchical relationships within the therapy itself.

The sequential steps and the temporary, dynamic hierarchical arrangements they prescribe determine the nature of the therapeutic context. They frame the substeps of therapeutic strategy, which are designed to tailor to fit a unique set of symptom circumstances. Because this therapy tampers as little as necessary for as briefly or as infrequently as necessary with a person or family, the primary therapeutic attitude is enhanced by this approach. The therapist becomes curious about a client's response patterns, and ideally the client is hopeful of positive therapist-client exchange. The process starts simply with the therapist's admiring reception of the many functional uses of the client's "gift."

The Three Stages of the Therapeutic Interview

There are three basic stages in a therapy session, designed to produce interventions into dialectical or isomorphic intrapsychic and interactional contributors to a symptom structure. The interventions are multinodal, to ensure that unconscious mental processes will not be overridden by interpersonal influences and interpersonal structural changes will not meet persistent individual rigidities. Hypnotic family therapy seeks to eliminate the existential basis for a rigid, symptomatically coded communication. Within the context of giving and receiving the symptom, the preinductive stage involves identifying individual, and where relevant and possible, family and social contributions to the induction of certain components of the system. Within the context of repaying, the therapist sets in motion a first needed structural event that will evolve into a therapeutic counterinduction. In the post-inductive stage, the therapist raises and addresses objections or resistances to the therapeutic counterinduction.

Stage 1: Reading Contextual Inductions

The two main skills required for Stage 1 of a therapy interview are the ability to establish an intense rapport with those present at a session and yet observe what suggestive effects people are having on one another. The clinician is especially interested in witnessing activations of symptom components in the session. To accomplish these goals, the therapist (1) creates an hypnotic atmosphere and (2) learns by experiential observation the structure of inductions and suggestive sequences.

Creating an Hypnotic Atmosphere. While the therapist gets acquainted with her client(s) and the problem, she must perform four tasks designed to facilitate trust, curiosity, a sense of security, and an intense multilevel connectedness:

1. Become engaged as intimately and as intensely as possible with all present at the interview, as individuals and as a family system.
2. Avoid, as much as experience permits, immersion in the individual's or family system's destructive symptom-perpetuating features; convey appreciation for benevolent aspects of the symptom.
3. Create a sense of "abrogating the usual rules that structure reality in order to reshape reality" (Montalvo, 1976, p. 333).
4. Establish individually with each family member meaningful cue words.

An intense engagement with family members is established so that the therapist can be introduced as rapidly as possible into the more private and less socially formal aspects of the symptom. Because families and individuals have public and private selves, therapists initiating treatment while still "outsiders" are often considered objectionable by clients (see Chapter Four, the subsection "The Public versus Private Dichotomy"). The rapport includes both joining the family, well-described elsewhere (Minuchin, 1974), and connecting with each individual member (as in individual hypnosis). Although the clinical atmosphere, except in cases of crisis, may seem casual at this point, the therapist is beginning to "seed" for more indirect and multimeaning communications with family members and to build toward the possible observation of a family symptom-activating event.

In Chapter Six, we examine in detail the steps for creating an hypnotic atmosphere in the therapy of a young suicidal woman. One technique common to our approach is establishing individual cue words with each family member. If we appreciate that coming to therapy is often in itself an ordeal for many people, we can assume that what people convey directly or indirectly to the therapist, even in a first casual exchange, includes some hints at what concerns them personally about the symptom. Responding to "unconscious" communications is most important for hypnotic rapport. In Chapter Six, the therapist responds in kind to father's *tone* of despair while he describes his optimism about his daughter. She establishes cue words with father about carrying emotional burdens. With mother, she talks in code about two issues mother has offered her while chitchatting about who she is and what she does. These coded interactions are cues to mother that the therapist is talking to her (regardless of who the therapist is looking at) when she speaks of "getting support from men" or of "separating from one's reproductive years." Each family member will recognize these cues as they come up in the treatment of the symptom. These cues are also one part of the seeding process for trance phenomena.

Although the therapist seeks intimacy, she does not open up or enter into areas of family life unrelated to the symptom. She accepts benevolent features of the symptom. Also, as discussed in Chapter Three, it is important that the client is not invited to offer too much, especially during a first visit. In many instances, an excessive outpouring may cause the client to lose face or render the therapist ineffectual. Similarly, the therapist, to the best of her clinical foresight, does not simply enter into the family system. She is careful to avoid accommodating herself to systems-perpetuating features of the symptom bearer's self-instructions or family context. For example, in Chapter Six, the therapist does not let the index patient have the upper hand by threatening suicide; the therapist— in opposition to the family pattern—challenges that lethal coping device on every front.

By behaving intimately with people, the therapist becomes kinlike. Yet she maintains her separateness by not practicing such harmful features of rapport as, for example, allying against a certain family member or nodding in agreement that a child is sick with mental illness. In maintaining this dialectic of engagement and disengagement, she clears the way for a sharp focus on a particular area of distress. As this focus intensifies, the creation of the hypnotic atmosphere is used to ensure a minimum of rigid response from family members to the therapist. As in all respectful hypnotic therapy, the therapist tries to respond *in kind* to messages transmitted by family members. In Chapter Six, father's tone, an indirect message, is responded to indirectly. The therapist, to the best of her ability, helps family members within the framework of their wishes. Nevertheless, when *essential*, the therapist is prepared to totally reject the symptom as untreatable as offered.

Finally, the clients' uncertainty about the therapist's role in their lives is best transformed into excitement, enthusiasm, curiosity, and, when appropriate, anticipation of a major life-transforming event. In this phase of therapy, all social categories can be converted into subjectively pliable and synthetic artifacts, as learnings to be transcended by new learnings and experiences. Montalvo described most lucidly (1976, p. 333) aspects of this therapeutic magic in terms of time:

> From therapists and patients who render time elastic, and from hypnotists who have experimented with time distortion throughout the ages, we learn that time is a social category. The consciousness of time can be handled in therapy as an alterable dimension because the basis of therapy is a social contract. Therapy is an inter-personal agreement to abrogate the usual rules that structure reality, in order to reshape reality. By agreeing to use either open-ended or closed notions, time can be stretched or circumscribed, according to need. Agreement around these notions varies with stages of the process and therapeutic orientation. But generally, during beginning sessions, the agreement is to use time as an open-ended context. Most comments during that period indicate that no systematic ordering of time is necessary. The redundant phrases are, "Start any place," "We are in no rush." "Take your time." And requests for binding time are often answered with, "We'll see," "It depends," "I don't know when." In this way, a framework of temporal imprecision is established. As most reliance on conventional chronological units is eroded, a new framework for timing and ordering events is applied. In this new framework, time is hinged increasingly on social events that allow both therapist and family to punctuate reality differently. "We'll finish when Janice feels better." "When she stops hollering, you'll know we are almost through." By

having impersonal standards of minutes, hours, days, months treated as secondary to the measuring of events through interpersonal sequences, a different time consciousness appears. This change comes about in the same way that man probably organized the first views of his own life cycle and those of his family. By attaching his attention first to the standard flow of the seasons he could then apply the standard of the seasons to draw stages in his own growth and that of his family. This capacity to attach, detach, and re-attach from different time frameworks seems to be basic to the construction and validation of social reality.

The therapist conveys to the entire family "Be alone with me" and "Where we are doesn't matter, the past is a vast well to draw on as needed; all that matters now is what we construct for the future." The arts of attaching, detaching, and reattaching to and from aspects of symptom-related contexts are described in the case studies in the following chapters.

Ultimately, during this stage, the family invites the therapist to become involved as intimately and as privately as possible with them. The therapist introduces herself to the family and mind contexts, without inhibiting the freedom of interpersonal and intrapsychic movement essential for her to be of service to the family. She does so within an hypnotic atmosphere that defines her position of leadership in the therapeutic context as she uses family attitudes, myths, and styles to establish special cues and communications with each individual and to redefine the rules of space, time, motion, and, eventually, relatedness. In this way, private and multilevel communications can occur, and an atmosphere is set in which a potentially life-changing event is safely expected.

Learning by Experience the Structure of Inductions. The goals of this second phase of stage 1 are:

1. Assessing family structural conflicts, including considerations of hierarchical contradictions among family developmental, gender, or economic subsystems and of family mythology, including role assignment and other forms of typecasting. If possible and desirable, the therapist tries to set up the circumstances to observe a family symptom-inductive event to get the sharpest focus on family contribution to symptoms.

2. Assessing the rigidity of the individual mind-set, that is, symptom-related rules about what is public and what is private, about "the way life is," and so on.

3. Assessing rules imposed by social context and their possible contributions to hierarchical conflicts.

4. Mentally mapping sequences of interaction that culminate in *or* are activated by specific aspects of symptomatic individual behavior.

5. Collecting case idiosyncracies and details and outstanding family habits or quirks and incorporating them into the generalities of a therapeutic counterinduction, to facilitate rapport and enhance one's therapeutic bargaining position. Toward this end, the therapist assesses *privately* possible developmental disadvantages of the symptom for the symptom bearer and the family. These disadvantages can be used as motivators later in the interview.

In this phase, as in any structural family therapy, the therapist invites family members to talk with one another about the symptom that brought them to therapy. The therapist thus seeks a new level of interactionally coded information about the symptom. The therapist permits any form of interaction to occur—*except* that which would be anathema to therapy. For example, in some therapies, talk of the past might be forbidden. In this therapy, the clinician often wants to see what modalities the family currently is using inadvertently that may be activating a component of a symptom bearer's problem. The therapist seeks data on how family structure in action and the symptom bearer's handicapping descriptions of self contribute to the activation of observable features of the symptom. For example, in Chapter Four we will learn to note the point at which routine family interaction stops and a symptom-inductive moment begins. We will note who starts an induction sequence, what inadvertent trance-induction techniques are employed, what unintended self-handicapping responses the symptom bearer seemingly automatically makes. In a family induction, we examine certain suggestive sequences, including symptom-related psychophysiological changes in a young man with psychosomatic problems. His rate of respiration changes markedly; he begins gasping, proceeds to gulping, and ends up with trouble breathing or thinking straight. In the case of the suicidal young woman (Chapter Six), a family interaction is sustained that is pregnant with indirect suggestion to the young woman. In their best efforts to succor their child in distress, two demoralized parents inadvertantly seed their comforts with messages of loneliness, failure, and despair. In an intense moment of family rapport, the young woman responds with guilt and fear, which she reconciles into her own belief system as proof of her basic "badness" and "sickness."

During this phase, the therapist listens to different messages from various family members that the symptom bearer may feel obliged to somehow reconcile into a single metamessage about how to behave at any one moment. The therapist attempts to identify specific rules, roles, and cues of family suggestive life that may be unintentionally plugging into a symptom bearer's behavioral patterns—producing, for example, trouble in breathing, a rush of blood to the cheek, a reluctance to move the hand, a perception that the room is turning around, a feeling of shame.

As interactional sequences and, ideally, an inductive moment occur in the family's identification of its problem to the therapist, by both description and transaction during the session, the therapist may wish to explore in greater depth more unconscious symptom-related aspects of an individual's mind-set or family and social structure. Because the therapist has established an hypnotic atmosphere, she can shift quite naturally and at any moment from observing family members interacting to using formal or informal trance-deepening techniques with one or more family members to obtain another more private level of communication about the symptom.

In "The Young Woman with the Bad Body," the therapist uses a trance induction of the young woman, after her family induction, partly to explore the secret rules of her mind-set. In this way, she can begin to challenge the woman's own contribution to her family's symptom-sustaining interventions. Throughout this book we discuss when it is best to cloister individual trance experiences from family events. We consider several variables the clinician is called on to weigh in each case. Chapter Three's example of the man reading the poem "I Sing the Body Electric" and Chapter Seven's case studies—1, "A Study of Family Hydraulics," and 2, "A Matter of Growing Pains"—all deal with when and when not to use the private deep-trance event within the less-private domain of the family.

Also, the therapist considers possible messages the symptom bearer's role in a certain social situation carries that may be contributing to a certain mental-set or family dilemma. In Case Study 4, "The Turtle with

the Cracked Shell," in Chapter Seven, we will see how racial discrimination problems on the job converge with gender discriminations on the
home front to suggest back pain to a young woman.

In this observation and multicontextual data-collection phase of
treatment, the therapist assumes both the existence of unseen aspects of an
individual's context of mind and unseen interrelational connections and
subsystems. She gently challenges ideas and rules to "test the limits of
tolerance" for the expression of these hidden capacities within prevailing
structures. What memories are taboo? How are past events colored? What
ideas are considered ignorant, naive? What do affection, separation, pun-
ishment mean within prevailing symptom-sustaining contexts? Chapter
Six examines in depth how to recognize specific family induction techniques by identifying uses of cue words, nicknames, and other contextual
abbreviations. Ultimately, one probes to rub up against the structural
rules—often unspoken and out of family members' ordinary frame of
reference—that support the symptom. One also ponders what alternative
rules there are to render the symptom an odd quirk of a partially forgotten
past.

Given the hypnotic atmosphere, the therapist can shift, when
ready, to a *different level of communication* from dreaming and remembering, for example, to planning and thinking and enacting. All the while,
the therapist can remain focused on a single and solvable therapeutic
problem.

Stage 2: Creating a Therapeutic Counterinduction

Stage 2 consists of two parts: (1) assessing what doors are open to
the therapist and how to enter into the inductive system and (2) developing a therapeutic counterinduction.

Determining Points of Entry; Possible Intervention Strategies.
This is the private phase of therapy, in which the therapist maps the
structural conflict that seems central to the presenting complaint and
considers possible intervention strategies. This phase is best conceptualized as repaying the family for their willingness to share this more un-
pleasant side of their lives. The therapist pulls together the essential
information gained about mind-sets, how family induces certain ideas of
self in a symptom bearer, and how the symptom bearer activates dysfunc-

tional patterns of interaction. Theoretically, a therapist has a number of potential points of entry into the symptom structure:

1. Within the individual mind-set
   a. Unconscious structure (including interiorized family and societal hierarchies)
   b. Conscious structure
   c. Relationship between (as demonstrated in amnesia or insight, for example)
2. Outside the individual: family and social contexts
   a. Family interaction (including developmental, gender, and economic hierarchies)
   b. Societal (as in work or school)
   c. Family-society interface
3. Both inner and outer points simultaneously = dialectical

To begin, a therapist may wish to mentally or graphically represent the whole structure the symptom bearer inhabits as she perceives it at that moment. Using triangles for hierarchies is helpful. The therapist considers whether a symptom bearer received consistently "bad" suggestions about himself because he is caught in negatively convergent positions across hierarchies or confusing mutually exclusive messages because he inhabits nullifying positions across hierarchies. (Chapter Five demonstrates in detail this phase of therapeutic strategizing.) For example, Patsy, who has lower back pain, will not tell her husband about her symptom because he gets angry when she is weak. He thinks she is weak whenever she cries, but she is crying because she is being harassed overtly on her job. Lately, she believes she is worth more than all this but is afraid she will cry uncontrollably at home and work. Indeed, when she does tell her husband about her situation, he tells her she is weak and that he wants no part of her troubles. A map of her problem via an holistic model results in a hypothetical reflection of her whole problem situation (Figure 7).

The conflict that seems to explain "why now" or why Patsy has sought help at the present time is caused by a change of mind, to thinking that "I don't deserve to be treated badly." This new idea has made the messages from her old family and work positions problematic. In fact, the behaviors suggested by work and husband ("bear your burden, girl") and

Figure 7. Holistic Hierarchical Model of a Three-Level Problem Situation.

1. Societal

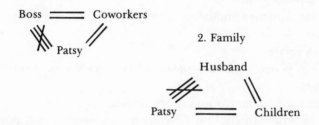

2. Family

3. Mind-set

Key: ═══ Adequate   Patsy ═══ Husband ═══ Coworkers

≢ Very negative

Symptomatic lower bank pain,
uncontrollable crying

the behaviors suggested by her mind-set ("I shouldn't have to carry so much weight") are now contradictory. The symptom is seen as a dialectical structural metaphor for this conflict in the organization of Patsy's life: "My boss and husband are on my back; I want to stand tall, but it's hopeless."

At this point, in examining hierarchical problems in general, the therapist wonders and decides:

1. What hierarchical problems are essential supportive structures for the symptom?
2. Is the resolution of one hierarchical problem the negation of another within the present ordering of the symptom bearer's life?
3. If so, the broader system may need to change form—as in the case of divorce or getting a new job.
4. If not, the broader system may not need to change, but modifications within existing hierarchies can be facilitated, which will alter the mind-set about position or otherwise alter communications channels *within* the same basic structure.

For example, Patsy may ultimately work for the same boss but not care what the boss thinks of her. She may remain in a function-by-gender family system but may negotiate sufficiently clear domains of authority and usefulness in specific functions of family life to feel self-confident. There may be something she can do for her husband to help ease his rigid mind-set. In this case, the broader work-and-spouse systems do not need total renovation; the basic contract holds. However, modifications within hierarchies can be made to alter Patsy's relative hierarchical position and therefore ideas and self-instructions about how to behave. In Chapters Three and Seven, two marital therapies will be discussed. In the one in Chapter Three, a shift in the symptom bearer's interiorized self-view is a precurser to divorce; in the other case, the shift is met by a complementary readjustment of the spouse's self-views. Thus the basic marital agreement simply stretches to contain two transformed selves. This case demonstrates that a shift in positioning in one functional unit of family life is not automatically the negation of the broader family system.

At this point, the therapist seeks to identify the simplest, most readily accessible, and most direct points of entry into the multilevel problem situation. Considerations when selecting a means of entry include who is willing to come to a session, what relational modalities are most akin to family and individual functioning, and what techniques can incur the fewest family and individual objections. Hypnosis is used only if needed to affect a family context or individual mind-set. Only workable families are worked with! The therapist looks for the door that is open. It is only a slight exaggeration to say that the ideal intervention is invisible.

In Chapter Three, we see that there are cases—such as Sandra's and Ralph's—in which multinodal interventions are not essential. Sandra has an intractable callus; individual indirect hypnotic induction alone will affect her mind-set and awaken aspects of self that help her break even a family contextual induction. Ralph has a school phobia; a simple family structural intervention breaks the inductive power of the family context, and the boy's mind-set automatically shifts. Most of the cases we examine, however, required dialectical intervention designed to affect the relationship between a rigid mind-set and a rigid social structure. Human dilemmas are often complex enough that when we are able to enter into a problem situation from both sides of a central conflict, we have a better chance of success.

Once the specific point(s) of intervention, such as mind-set, work system, or marital relationship, have been chosen, the therapist considers general categories of interventions, including, for example:

1. Focusing on the individual symptom bearer's mind-set by using hypnotic techniques while metaphorically discussing a family structural aspect of the symptom. When attentive family members are present for this event, the therapist's communication with the symptom bearer is used to offer them indirect suggestions.
2. Focusing on family interactional sequences while seeding these interactions with insertions of events that will alter family-induction sequences and the structures sustaining them. These insertions include distorting and simplifying messages, redirecting suggestions to other family members, selectively introducing trance events, immunizing individuals against harmful contextual cues.
3. Alternating between setting up family interactions and introjecting, through any form of direct or indirect suggestion, including trance, different individual responses, including feelings about or physiological reactions to family "attempts" to organize an individual's behavior.

Hypnotic techniques in family sessions, although not always needed, can accomplish a number of special goals. (1) They can demonstrate to the observing family member(s) other aspects of an individual they thought did not exist and so inspire hope (as in "The Young Woman with the Bad Body"). (2) They can activate needed nonhabitual sequences of thought in an individual at the precise moment he would be induced otherwise by persistently destructive family induction. This technique thereby depotentiates destructive family inductive power (as in Chapter Five). (3) They can immediately immunize family members to each other's harmful suggestions (as in Case Study 2, "A Matter of Growing Pains," in Chapter Seven). (4) They can be used as an opportunity for all family members to be involved in a family imagining (a structurally needed event is imagined to have occurred). Afterward, following indirect suggestions, the family can begin to work to make the imagined event happen. (5) Most importantly, they can be used to make boundaries, to set aside, through suggestive and interactional techniques, *new domains of privacy* from the intrusion of family by using related but separate-track trances (as in Chapter Five).

In Chapters Four to Seven we will consider these techniques in depth, as well as counterindications of the use of trance for the symptom bearer in a family session. These counterindications include going against a global therapeutic pattern of maintaining the symptom bearer in a position of deviance or risking his baring private aspects of himself in a hostile relational domain. The hypnosis must be used to improve boundaries between self and others, not to weaken or eliminate them. Chapter Five includes a clear case of using two parallel but separate-track trances to enhance relational boundaries between a mother and son.

Once a *general modality of intervention* has been selected, the therapist considers how to incorporate the case's specifics—such as cultural values, family metaphors and cue words, and even quirks—into a more refined way of tailoring this intervention to a specific family or person. The therapist has several techniques to choose from, including (1) shared trance relaxation, (2) shared memories, and (3) direct and indirect suggestions to family members (see expanded list of techniques at end of chapter). For example, shared trance relaxation can be used to affect a family mind-set about a frightening transfusion technique. Shared memories of a time when a suicidal child was happy and a source of pride can activate hope for father's support when a child returns home for a visit. And a choreography of hypnotic and waking directives to family members can break dysfunctional induction sequences centered around alcoholism.

At this point the therapist considers the details and fine points of a person's life and how to challenge the person, drawing on his private longings for a developmentally fuller future, his discontent with the circumstances of the symptomatic present, and, of course, the unique attributes of the therapeutic context. With increasing experience, this step of Stage 2 often, but not always, becomes abbreviated. If it is sufficiently condensed, it is considered "intuitive."

Techniques of Counterinduction. Often counterinduction techniques incorporate the modalities of family induction (described in Chapter Four). If family cue words seem to activate certain immature aspects of the symptom bearer's mind-set, the therapist may help the family render those words taboo and insert other cue words. These words can be paired, via hypnotic techniques, with associations the symptom bearer has for new systems-transforming behaviors. If denied aspects of family relating are central to the problem, hypnotic techniques can be used in many ways to depotentiate the undetected contributory dysfunctional sequences. For example, whenever mother criticizes son, when she is actually angry with her peripheral husband, we can use hypnotic principles to suggest that son will tend to feel mildly puzzled or become absorbed spontaneously in a developmentally useful problem, rather than intensely enraged, breathless, or otherwise symptomatic. The therapist makes maximal use of moments in which an interaction might ordinarily activate an automatic response in a symptom bearer. It is at such points that she will employ special states to help the person activate less frequently used feelings, actions, and ideas. These new feelings, actions, and ideas can then spontaneously induce a reorganization of broader family structures.

The therapist can now develop a specific counterinduction, or a first step in this direction, and does so in a manner acceptable to or, even better, unnoticed by those present at the interview. A therapeutic counterinduction designates the therapeutic approach used to depotentiate the symptom as a regulator of individual or group behavior. Although often the result of a counterinduction is elimination of symptomatic behavior, that is *not* our measure of success. In fact, inclusion of an economically abbreviated form of the symptomatic behavior (as in "A Matter of Growing Pains") as a cue for needed new behaviors is one of our fundamental techniques. (Symptom cuing is discussed later in this chapter.) Our main purpose is to eliminate the symptom as a primary organizing principle in the contexts the person inhabits. However, there is a place for a moment of previously symptomatic anxiety in a new self- and family-instructional process. In this approach, benevolent features of symptoms are salvaged. The therapeutic counterinduction is usually dialectical; that is, it is designed to impinge simultaneously on related inner and outer reflections of the symptomatic state. The approach entails the creation of carefully designed hypnotic suggestive techniques. Suggestions are made to one or more family members in whatever depth of trance is required for that person(s) and given the characteristics of the family (intrusive, disengaged). Hypnotic approaches are designed to produce multi-person shifts in rigid symptom-related belief systems; they encompass suggestions of classes of outwardly directed and often relational transactions that, *when carried out in family concert,* can transform contextual or outer features of the symptom. The counterinduction is often developed using the

Erickson-Rossi guidelines for induction (see Chapter One) and draws on the unique family induction techniques observed in the previous stage of the interview. For example, in Chapter Six, a mother uses a "bad twins" technique with her daughter by conveying her own sense of self-evil and then intensely pairing her ailing daughter with her by saying "We are a lot alike, you and I. . . ." The therapist may wish to incorporate this "twins" technique into her own therapeutic counterinduction, to distort the mother's approach and thereby help mother modify her self-analogy into one that may activate different attitudes within her daughter.

The therapeutic counterinduction is a stage of higher energy than either of the two terminal stages of an interview. It must be so to help the family move from one stable state to another. In this intensive moment of largely indirect suggestive communication with family members, often at least one member is in a ratifiable trance state. In an hypnotic and emotionally charged but receptive atmosphere, the therapist invites each family member to connect specific complementary aspects of self with specific benevolent aspects of others. The therapist uses both metaphorical or coded language *and* the sustained, indirect, and inwardly focused communication associated with trance. The specific therapeutic goal often includes making it easier for a person to construct a fresh boundary between his interior and extracerebral, or outer-related, self and between himself and other family members.

Although symptoms are complex, the actual induction—like most hypnotic processes—remains specific and intensely focused on what is perceived as the single most important structural conflict between the symptom bearer's inner and outer realities. The closer the therapist is to "home," the more likely she is to have an effect. Also, the induction draws its power—not unlike family inductive moments—from disappearing quickly when the job is done, meddling as little as essential, and leaving the contents inaccessible to excessive and premature scrutiny. Sullivan, describing his own style of interviewing, addressed several of these issues (1970, p. 227): "You cannot do magic with reassuring language. The magic occurs in the interpersonal relations, and the real magic is done by the patient, not by the therapist. The therapist's skill and art lie in keeping things simple enough so that something can happen; in other words, he clears the field for favorable change, and then tries to avoid getting in the way of its development."

It is important to note that we are not suggesting that trance work is *always needed* (see Chapter Seven, Case Study 4, "The Turtle with the Cracked Shell"). In some cases, the therapist can just make a simple interactional suggestion or a direct suggestion. Likewise, an intervention that is designed to affect related inner and outer symptom realities need not always use the special trance state features to do so. Trance and dialectical interventions are prescribed for cases in which these approaches will provide the needed therapeutic challenge. Throughout, we will discuss ways of deciding about the nature of an intervention.

When the therapist decides to use trance, she considers what *level* of trance is needed to accomplish the work at hand. For example, in Chapter Six, following an indirect induction process, the therapist uses a shared family reverie when *all* family members are demonstrating the characteristics of a light trance. It is at this depth of trance that the therapist invites a collective memory of an event that can inspire the hope needed for the family to solve its present problems. In Chapter Five, the therapist uses a formal trance-induction technique to induce a moderate trance in a mother and her son. This level of trance is desirable for affecting the psychophysiological problems in the case. In Chapter Seven, a sustained deep trance is employed to deal with a woman's consciously unbearable problems (Case Study 6). In this case, the deepest level of trance was necessary to help the woman resolve guilt about a long-buried traumatic event. In other cases in Chapter Seven, it suffices at certain points in the therapy to interject sustained indirect communications with family members (Case Studies 1 and 2). The important issue is that the therapist must consider for each case whether the special features of the trance state are desirable and whether relations within the family threaten an abuse of the state. If trance is indicated, the therapist assesses what level of trance is desirable for any one family member.

Following are several techniques used throughout this book to develop dialectical counterinductions. It is assumed that the symptom bearer often has to reconcile cross-contextual positions about how to behave that seem to nullify each other. This hybrid message produces a bizarre symptomatic response. Therefore, a common therapeutic goal is to set in motion those processes that will make it easier to establish balanced self-serving hierarchies and more easily reconcilable cross-contextual suggestions as a new equilibrium in a symptom bearer's life is created. These techniques are predicated on working to challenge the present suggestive structures by facilitating a new balance across contexts.

The self-voice induction* technique can be used, for example, for one "blamed" member of a couple in the presence of a spouse who refuses treatment. The partner seeking trance, by initiating it himself, thus maintains self-control in the treatment process. The therapist can then help the client explore and utilize his special state-related capacities. Indirect communications relevant to the marital contributions to a symptom can then be more readily made to the spouse. (See, in Chapter Three, the man who reads the poem "I Sing the Body Electric.")

Shared positive hypnotic events take two forms. In a *shared reverie* or convergent trances, the family participates collectively in recalling an event that serves as a rehearsal for the attitudes or relational valences the therapist hopes to help them mobilize toward resolution of the symptom (see "The Young Woman with the Bad Body.") In *separate-track trances,* the entranced family members are simultaneously assigned separate but parallel trance experiences or technologies, such as "imagining watching different television screens." Although the content of the trances is important, the *format* is primary. In and of itself it may "suggest" to an enmeshed dyad, for example, the potential pleasantness of building some separateness into their love (see Chapter Five).

In *complementary separate-track hypnosis,* completely individuated trances are used with multiple family members to suggest actions that, if undertaken in concert, will disrupt an interactional symptomatic process (see Chapter Seven, Case Study 5, "Too Close for Comfort"). Certainly, trance for one partner and direct suggestion for another may also be used in many cases (see Case Studies 1, "A Study of Family Hydraulics" and 3, "Over My Dead Body").

Parts-of-self techniques can be used to evoke those aspects of a person's capacities that are latent or forbidden within a certain family while metaphorically evoking related parts of the family that merit activation. For example, in a young woman, the part of herself that is a "baby" has been making her decisions, just as the infantile unrealistic parts of her family have been making emotional responses. The therapist uses this model of parts of self to suggest to the woman and her family, while they are in a light trance and in the indirect modality they prefer, the acceptability and indeed necessity of psychosexually mature aspects of self coming to the fore. (For another example of this technique, see Chapter Seven, Case Study 6, "Divorcing the Dead.")

---

*Erickson (1964) used the sound of a client's own voice as a trance-deepening technique.

In *symptom cuing*, a commonly used technique, the therapist inserts an abbreviated component of the symptom structure into ongoing sequences of interior individual behavior (such as thought) and interaction as a cue to turn on a new sequence of suggested countersymptomatic behaviors. This way, the symptom is not abolished but removed from its position as destructive regulator of behavior. In fact, it is transformed into a signal for change. Several varieties of this technique are demonstrated throughout Chapter Seven (especially see Case Study 2, "A Matter of Growing Pains"). In *family contextual cuing*, it may be suggested to a symptomatic child, for example, that his parents' unresolved arguing, which has been part of the exterior contribution to his symptoms, will now cue him to focus inward and intensify his resolve to plan for college. In *self*-symptom cuing, a young man's anxiety habit may be abbreviated so that an economical form of anxiety on meeting a new male or female at college can be established as a cue to go into trance and evoke an hypnotically developed good body image and all the sensations and actions associated with it.

Other dialectically related techniques, which may or may not use trance states, include acting as if the intentional is unintentional and the unintentional intentional and other distortion-introducing approaches (see Chapter Five); readying a family before the present problem is solved for the problem that will occur after it has been solved, that is, probing for concealed hierarchical opposites (see Chapter Seven, Case Study 1, "A Study of Family Hydraulics"); and family bartering in and out of trance (see Chapters Three and Six).

Stage 3: Postinduction

After the therapist has presented her goal-directed and multipurpose suggestions, she invites what therapists call "resistances" and business people call "objections."* I think business people have a good idea. Thinking of family members' doubts and hesitancies as objections helps the therapist maintain a respectful attitude toward the person with reservations and reminds her that the person is not just "crazy" to pass up the great therapeutic deal just offered.

---

*I am indebted to Larry Barnette for making this distinction.

In the postinductive phase of a session, the therapist hopes objections will be raised so that they will less likely be enacted outside the session. A primary technique with this phase is called *trance insertion*. As family members raise doubts about capacities to carry out suggested counterinductive plans, the therapist draws on cue words and other elements of the hypnotic atmosphere to return with that person to an abbreviated moment of a relevant aspect of the trance event. For example, just after the two-track counterinduction in Chapter Five, mother begins to resume her level of anxiety—which seems to contribute inadvertantly to the orchestration of her son's stress-related bleeds. As the mother begins to get anxious, the therapist says, "So when you do this (relaxation technique) with him (your son) and then talk about that you turn on the TV screen. Turn on the TV screen and imagine . . . whatever you would like . . . for him." This way, at the inception of mother's anxious objections, the therapist reintroduces earlier trance-competence suggestions and mother briefly reenters trance, spontaneously using that state to calm herself.

Similarly, this period is used to create amnesias for aspects of the counterinductive suggestive process that need time to settle in without conscious or interpersonal intrusion. The therapist is careful to keep the deck of trance events well-shuffled during this period. She may wish to address objections and refer back to a trance event partially out of its context. However, especially before any new family action has taken place, she does not wish to open to public comment the entire interior event.

Summary

A therapist is invited to create an atmosphere of intense rapport, multilevel and private communications, a sense of abrogation of the usual social categories that structure routine life. In a spirit of cooperation, receptivity, and willingness to persist, the therapist intensifies an anticipation of the potential importance of the therapeutic events to follow and increases the likelihood of observing inadvertant ways the symptom bearer and family contribute to a symptom-suggestive situation. She then identifies ready points of entry into the symptom structure; assesses the need for the use of special states and the best level of trance for accomplishing her goals; and weighs possible techniques of activating therapeutic counterinductions to—as unobtrusively as possible—depotentiate related mind-set and family-contextual symptom catalysts. After the induction, the therapist activates objections to suggestions and uses those objections as opportunities to modify her suggestions to better fit the symptom or to selectively reintroduce trance events into the waking routines of family life. The following lists summarize important techniques and therapeutic steps in this approach.

Techniques Based on Hypnotic Principles for Use in Family Therapy

1. Self-voice induction.
2. Convergent trances.
3. Separate-track trances.
4. Parts-of-self and parts-of-family inductions.
5. Symptom cuing.
6. Preparing for opposites.
7. Distortion techniques.
8. Family bartering.
9. Trance-insertion techniques.

Outline of Therapy Steps

1. Within the giving and receiving contexts:
    a. While socializing and then identifying the problem, establish an hypnotic atmosphere that encompasses all present.
    b. Immerse in and withdraw from interactions with all present and their interactions with one another, to learn both the individual and family structure of instructions that culminate in the activation of symptom components.
2. Within the repaying context:
    a. Privately hypothesize a central structural conflict (across or within the hierarchies of three potential levels of structure); determine whether to use trance states, with whom, and at what level; identify multiple interrelated points of intervention.
    b. Set up a first-needed multilevel structural event that will evolve into a therapeutic counterinduction, using, as much as possible, prevailing family interactional patterns and individual mind-sets to do so.

c. Elicit objections to counterinductive material and suggest the material in a different or more acceptable manner or reintroduce select, isolated trance events.

This approach stays close to the symptom, working through coordinated tasks on those aspects of the symptom that reflect related problematic inner and outer realities. Through participatory observation of them, the therapist "reads" the inductions of the contexts the symptom bearer is part of and then, often using trance states to do so, introduces dialectical therapeutic counterinductions into those contexts.

Chapter Three ⧉ ⧉ ⧉

Exchanges
of Power
in the Therapeutic
Relationship

⧉ The issue of possession of a problem and transfer of it to a healer is not new. Many cultures follow a long historical tradition in which sins, crimes, and evil spirits are given over to a thing (totem), another person or animal (scapegoat), or a priest or healer (Frazer, 1922). This chapter offers a cooperative model of exchange of power over symptoms. The model is fundamentally designed to quickly connect the therapist and clients and to create the circumstances for a balance of functions within the course of therapy. A basic give-and-take is established that minimizes undesirable dependencies and feelings of helplessness. The first part describes the symptom as a gift and defines the steps of giving, receiving, and repaying the gift in therapy. The second part cites moments within therapies that capture some of the essential points of transition encountered when using this model.

Chapters One and Two emphasized the power of family and social structures to plug into individual response patterns and activate seemingly automatic responses. We considered the potentially pervasive impact of broad social structures as their material and ideological forces are somehow interiorized by smaller social units. To round out our broad overview of the relationships between context and mind-set, this chapter addresses the most general structuring of the therapeutic context. The therapeutic relationship more or less intentionally draws on broader social rules and roles to establish its guidelines. Particularly important in family-oriented therapies is clarifying the nature of the connection of kin (the family) to nonkin (the therapist and the therapeutic community) (Mauss, 1967; Levi-Strauss, 1969). The stance of the therapist derives partly from her grasp of this connection.

Since people's earliest history, two basic sociocultural structures have provided the sequence of rituals that both link kinship groups and join kin to nonkin. The first structure, and the oldest economic system, is total "prestation," a series of exchanges of gifts and favors between clans and individuals that binds them into a comprehensive relationship of reciprocity. All rituals of gift exchange derive from this earliest human economy. Gift exchange affects aspects of all interactions between individuals and groups and is a primary modality for clarifying dynamic hierarchies of power and responsibility. The second fundamental social structure is warfare, a series of opposing exchanges, including slaughter and sacrificing (giving) oneself for others. This institution also affects part of all human relationships.

These two social structures are mutually exclusive in that to trade and exchange gifts, people must first lay down arms. In therapy, notions of "strategy" and "crisis induction," in which family conflict is intensified to facilitate change, and "ordeal," in which a major life-transforming and difficult task is prescribed, all derive from a *recognition of the struggle inherent in most therapy*. These ideas are occasionally misconstrued, however, as implying a combative attitude or approach with patients. In fact, these approaches are effective only if they take place in a context of joining, rapport, and collaboration.

This chapter highlights the less-examined contributions of gift-giving rituals to therapy's most general level of shaping and sequencing. Comparing therapy to the prestation transactions helps clinicians avoid confusing strategy and needed intensifications of stress with an *unintentional* fighting approach. This therapy, because it depends on clients' *maximal receptivity,* clearly frames the struggle within a context of cooperation and persistence. This therapeutic format maximizes the likelihood of creating an hypnotic atmosphere, of facilitating exchanges of power, which are positive for both therapist and client(s) and of increasing a client's willingness to accept the therapist's offer: a therapeutic challenge repaid in kind, to match the symptom offering.

With this model, the symptom is regarded as a gift from client(s) to therapist. Interactions around the symptom are prescribed within the guidelines of certain rules of the gift, which include rules of giving, accepting, and repaying. Additionally, the structuring of the therapeutic prestation sequences enables multiple and dynamic hierarchical arrangements between giver and receiver to be established, which leaves the clinician in a position of power over the client(s)' problem as briefly as possible. Case examples are discussed here to demonstrate rituals of gift exchange at the start, middle, and end of therapy.

The Symptom as a Living Conflict

In the previous chapters we saw that a symptom is often a metaphor for conflicts within three socialized contexts: individual, family, and social. Existentionally, it can be viewed as a representative of the state of the union of inner and outer realities. As such, the symptom often has practical and material implications for the symptom bearer; for example, a symptom can break up or sustain a marriage, enhance or destroy a child's future, create or eliminate a job, allow a person to break the shackles of a historical era or suicidally turn the weapons of that era against himself. As Sartre put it: "The simple and inert juxtaposition of object (person) and epoch is replaced by a living conflict" (Laing and Cooper, 1971, p. 61). This living conflict takes a long time to develop, often serves multiple functions in a number of contexts, often is hard-earned—in efforts to reconcile multiple and seemingly conflicting messages—and is accompanied by a great deal of real suffering. When family members are willing to bring this real problem to an outsider, they do not come empty-handed; they bring the "pearl" produced by the irritation. According to Sartre (1960, p. 246): "The person cloaks a thing via action with a human signification, but in return, his action, by becoming objectified in the realm of matter, is at least in part made into a thing or reified."

In the case of psychophysiological symptoms, the totalization of a person's existential situation may have produced actual material damage. Even at other levels of the problem—such as affective, perceptual, and emotional—however, the symptom can be described as objectifying, in its own special code, basic contradictions or antagonisms in a person's life.

Family members may not always like the symptom; nevertheless, it often serves multiple functions. Consider a family who regards a daughter who went away to college but is now returning home as a sign of family failure. The family, logically, is reluctant to "admit defeat." When their daughter threatens suicide, she may be partly amplifying her message of duress to get permission to come home. The young woman needs to come home; therefore, using her best self-equipment, she produces, partly intentionally and partly unintentionally, a lethal coping device. The therapist, regarding the symptom as a gift, certainly rejects the time-bomb aspects of the offering: the suicide threats. However, she carefully salvages the benevolent aspects of the gift: the woman's wish to come home briefly to regroup, heal herself, feel at home in a confusing world. Similarly, the therapist rejects the parents' idealized standards for their daughter but appreciates their wishes for her to do well and to use their refuge to do so. The therapist secures a place in the background of a person's existential reality for positive facets of the symptom.

Resistance: Here Is a Moat and There Is an Alligator. With each symptom comes a set of personal and contextual instructions for proper handling. Sometimes these instructions are explicit, such as "I'll try anything you say, Doc, except challenge my mother." At other times, they are more implicit, such as "My problem of swinging my legs to put myself to sleep originated when I was a newborn [it is too old a habit to totally eliminate and meets a deep-seated need] and is only a problem for my wife [we are not to talk about it as something bothersome to *me*]. Sometimes they are hidden in interactions. A man who had had a habit of becoming withdrawn and depressed instead of actively voicing his wishes finally asked his wife to keep her dog out of his office, and she conceded—but only after a few days. He rejected her consensus by acting resentful to her or ignoring her, thereby enacting his "rule" of "If you don't do what I want when I want it, I won't accept it when you do it later." Such *rule enactment* also conveys certain instructions for symptom handling. What we usually call resistance is actually most often a well-developed set of injunctions that, if received graciously, is a good chart for a therapeutic course around the symptom, in all its contexts.

We can afford to be especially gracious recipients of resistance if we recognize it as both a concise set of interactional instructions and a guide to the individual's habits and mental rules. We have seen that the symptom bearer plays a role in his family and his society. He is often the recipient of contextual messages, including: "You must stay with us, your problem belongs with us." "You must be unwilling or unable within our relational context to respond to (certain, or any) suggestions of others about this problem." Often the symptom represents the patient responding within cross fire between a number of contexts. The therapist can prematurely "demand" that the patient "battle" these often-absent others to get them to "join" him, or she can, at least temporarily, join those others by appreciating the power of their injunctions as part of the symptom. The symptom comes complete with the negative injunctions of others that the new therapeutic system will have to encompass. It forewarns the therapist about who may be threatened or affected indirectly if the symptom bearer sheds his problem. The therapy attempts to activate, mobilize, and incorporate many of a client's and family's objections to a treatment into a viable and powerful therapeutic counterinduction. Looked at from this vantage point, resistance in therapy is actually most problematic when it comes from the clinician, who out of loyalty to an ideology of her collegial community rejects the client's initial exchange rules.

The Three Rules of the Gift

The model of regulated gift exchange is fundamental to cooperative social life and a therapy based on negotiations about power. It is important to identify the three basic substructures that regulate gift exchange: giving, accepting, and repaying. Each phase of gift exchange involves certain steps and has hierarchical and structural implications. The entire system of transactions is based on a cooperative social endeavor between mutually respectful parties.

Giving. Giving is performed by the symptom bearer as he presents himself and others in reference to the central living conflict. The client brings both the symptom and a more or less implicit set of instructions for handling. If the therapist handles the symptom improperly, the offering can humiliate the client or induce doubt about whether the therapist can measure up to the client's offering. If the therapist handles the symptom properly, it will be clear to the client that (1) he is recognized as the sole owner of his problem until he and the therapist have agreed on the rights of transfer of power over it; (2) the therapist subordinates aspects of self-interest to the common therapeutic interest, although not in a self-sacrificial manner; (3) he is in control of himself as a person and in hierarchical control over the therapy *until* he has handed over to the therapist some aspect of control. Not until the next step—receiving the gift—is the therapist elevated *by the patient* to a position of leadership in the therapeutic hierarchy. Proper giving—itself an interactional phenomenon—elevates both giver and receiver, activates states of reciprocal readiness for exchange, and creates a mind-set of positive expectation.

Receiving. Receiving is performed by the therapist. The steps of receiving facilitate the transfer of power over the problem from the client to the therapist. But before reaching out to take a gift, the receiver first admires it, considers its special features, and identifies its important and even unique uses. Upon first receiving the valuable gift, the therapist spontaneously draws it close, as if touching a part of the giver, to examine it carefully, in a different light and from all angles. This substep is important for linking the outsider, the therapist, to client and clan. *The two steps of appreciating and taking into one's hands some aspect of the problem may be critical to the course of therapy.* These are the first moments of establishing trust, respect, rules of obligation, power, responsiblity, and intense connnection. Indeed, therapist and client come together to share the many facets of the symptom.

If the transfer of power over the gift is transacted in a manner satisfactory to giver and receiver, an unspoken, automatic agreement is established, joining client and therapist and entitling the therapist to certain temporary rights over the negotiation of the problem, which, until that moment, was the indisputable possession of the giver and his family. At this stage within the therapeutic system, two simultaneous hierarchical relationships are established. As a person, the patient is in possession of his life, including his problems. In this context, the therapist *serves* the client. When the therapist fully appreciates and then receives the symptom, the client automatically elevates her to a temporary position of power over only essential aspects of the problem and its solution. This dual hierarchy paves the way for a therapy that temporarily gives the therapist power over the symptom, but within its framework it contains the structure for returning the client to a position of not needing a therapist when treatment is terminated.

Issues of separation in therapy, so often inadvertently induced by the therapy itself, can be minimized if not eliminated by recognizing from the start that the client temporarily transfers power to the therapist, but the therapist, through fair and equitable exchange, will as quickly as desirable facilitate a course that ends, as it began, with the life of the individual being his private domain. At the point of receiving, the therapist becomes head of the therapeutic system. Receiving has implications for the therapist's repaying—of giving back to client and family powers over the problem in a new and transforming way. Before moving to that third stage, it is important to note that not all symptoms or all the strings attached to symptoms are to be received. Receiving is the point at which a therapist presented with what is to the best of her understanding an unsolvable problem must refuse the gift or any of its potentially destructive aspects. This rejection of an unworthy gift is not always the end of a relationship or a proclamation of war. In certain circumstances, refusing a gift is not an admission of defeat but an assertion of "therapeutic invincibility." In extremely difficult cases, such as with one who has attempted suicide, this approach may be needed to establish authority; the therapist, anticipating herself being rendered impotent by the gift, can instead transform the gift or part of it into a booby prize and offer the family a different, commensurate, but workable problem (see Chapter Six).

Repaying. In repaying, the third phase of gift exchange, the therapist gives back something to the client and/or family and ultimately sets the conditions for a relationship between equals. In a sense, repaying is the task in psychotherapy; it often includes the creation of a therapeutic counterinductive event.

In repaying the therapist creates the circumstances in which the client(s) can affect the problem. In this phase, the therapist is bound to give back something; what is given back and when and how is determined largely by her clinical judgment. At this point, stress may be intensified as the usual structural thresholds are challenged, but the stress is framed in the broader context of cooperation. A difficult or unusually pleasurable therapeutic challenge may be offered in a therapeutic counterinductive event. At this stage the therapist may (1) hand back to a patient a new problem; (2) expand on positive uses of an otherwise negatively employed symptom habit (as Erickson did when approaching a young man who claimed to be Jesus Christ, saying to him: "I hear you are a carpenter"); (3) use an abbreviated form of the symptom to cue the client to a new action (see the symptom-cuing technique discussed in Chapter Two); (4) use the patients' objections in designing a counterinduction; or (5) facilitate bartering among family members for parts of the symptom that they must give up power over. Whatever approach is used at this time, the therapist's task is to set up a certain act "that changes the agent, the acted-upon, and their relationship" (Sartre, in Laing and Cooper, 1971, p. 13). Through this middle phase of therapy, the therapist builds up to the total return of power over the problem to the symptom bearer.

Like the other steps of gift exchange, repaying is interactional. When the equitable exchange has occurred, the patient often demonstrates recognition of completion of the ritual and the wish to leave the therapist by "giving the therapist something else." Thus the client's culmination of the repaying process often includes a verbal or material gift of termination. Hierarchically, this process ends with both client and therapist elevated in a sense of social competence, with client once more sole owner of self and life's routine problems and therapist as head of therapeutic systems for others. Therapist and client part as equals. (Haley, 1976, pp. 126–127, also described shifts in therapeutic hierarchies.) Now we look at these three rules of gift exchange in specific clinical cases.

Giving: When to Look a Gift Horse in the Mouth

There are three ways the therapist can err at this stage of the therapy. First, the therapist can let the client give *too much*. At a child guidance clinic, a woman came in for help for her seventeen-year-old son, who had low self-esteem and was beginning to miss days at school. Finding herself in the presence of an unusually supportive listener, the woman proceeded to pour out her heart, much to her own shock, despairing of everything in her life, especially the boy's father, and crying and hiding her face. Despite all the mother's openness, the young therapist sensed something was wrong and discussed the case with her supervisor, who predicted accurately that the woman would never come back. She had been *allowed* to shame herself and her son as well as the male image the son would need to look up to to enhance his own self-image—that of his father. Erickson grasped this point when he emphasized that the client should be encouraged to tell the therapist *as little as necessary* and go only as deeply into trance as *necessary*. Generally, if a patient is encouraged to focus on only one central problem, he can leave early sessions feeling proud about having given away only what was essential to the task at hand. Another example of "giving too much" will be discussed in Chapter Seven, Case Study 1, "A Study of Family Hydraulics." The therapist who allows the client to give too much may also be letting him lose face in the exchange situation.

Second, the therapist can err by accepting (what is for her) *an unsolvable problem*. This is tantamount to graciously accepting a dangerous gift, like a bomb, or cheating the client by implying that the therapist will have an exchange with him that the therapist will *not* have. In Chapter Six, "The Young Woman with the Bad Body," the suicidal young woman's infantile and mischievous tone associated with her "power" to threaten suicide is regarded as potentially lethal and therefore indirectly challenged, even in the first moments of therapy. On the other hand, the woman carries a stuffed animal. The therapist is able to safely incorporate this creature—with some transformation—into treatment. Generally, unacceptable problems center around issues of patients' abdicating responsibility in a manner that lessens the therapist's authority or leaves her subject to the symptom's rule. In the case of a family with an anorectic daughter, the daughter Coreen stole food from cancer patients, ran away from the hospital twice while naked when her parents failed to visit, and was thrown out of the hospital as soon as she had a minimum of body fat. The parents want nothing to do with the child in any sense of helping her function. The problem they offer the therapist is for her single-handedly—if not magically—to do something about Coreen maintaining her weight. This is an unacceptable, unsolvable as presented problem for the therapist because she would have no support from either the hospital or the family. The therapist is virtually being requested to adopt the child. The whole notion of "Here's a broken person, you fix it" as the gift is rarely acceptable. The therapist must clarify that the individual or the problem belongs to the family and that she will simply help them begin to exercise some benevolent and effective power over it. A gift of irresponsibility—like any other unwelcome gift—merits rejection.

Finally, the therapist may err by failing to recognize when *a gift has not yet been given over*. It may take a long time for client(s) to initially separate from even a piece of the hard-earned living conflict, and this separation may include the client(s) raising doubts, fears, and objections. In the case of a young man with hemophilia (Chapter Five), it was when mother said "Go with whatever you're comfortable with because I can pick up these steps . . ." that she indicated readiness for therapeutic intervention. Until that time, she and her son had been voicing reluctances, hesitancies, and prerequisites for the hypnotic treatment.

In some cases, the therapist may wish to help the client give up some power over the symptom. In France, it was the custom to whip a sheep to help detach it from the owner and move it to the buyer (Frazer, 1922). The case of an anorectic girl clinging in a lunch session to her power to reject eating the hotdog her parents have tried ineffectually to force down her throat is a dramatic example. The therapist (Minuchin) approaches the girl, picks up her hotdog, and throws it on the floor, saying, "So this is your victory." Especially for chronic problems, the therapist may wish to help the patient give over some control by transforming the gift, before the patient(s) very eyes, into a booby prize.

Receiving: The Miser Is Always Groaning over His Gifts

A pediatrician on an adolescent unit and learning about interviewing techniques had been all but physically assaulted by an angry mother and her fifteen-year-old daughter when he was trying to get them to "calm down and stop being so hard on each other" in order to get a sense of their problem. He could not understand what had happened as they both suddenly turned on him and began harassing him, much as they had harassed each other the moment before. Inadvertently, the pediatrician had used a family therapy strategy designed to join two people who are fighting by getting them both angry with the therapist. This pediatrician was "only trying to help" and "to get a logical history" and did not know what to do next, given the technique he had used by accident. I asked him what he thought about what mother and daughter were doing to each other. He thought it was wrong; they should not be acting like that.

In this case—common within adolescent clinics—the young doctor was rejecting the mother-daughter gift, which in their case was a wholehearted presentation in actions rather than a flat description of it. The physician failed to show either of them an appreciation for what they had brought in the door: a hard-earned, time-proved, well-deserved disrespect of each other.

The physician refused to see them alone or to join me in interviewing them because he was so frightened by the result of his help. However, the matter was quickly rectified. I went in to the mother and daughter and expressed proper gratitude for all that they had shared with the doctor. I then addressed the daughter first, saying I was certain that she was quite correct in stating that her mother was an impossible, self-centered, and utterly immature woman. Daughter quieted down immediately, becoming extremely receptive as I turned to her mother, who was attentive with amazement, and said, "And mother, I am certain that you are right that you have had to endure the upbringing for a seemingly intolerable length of time of a disrespectful, ungrateful, stubborn brat. Now, how can I help you?"

Those tigers continued in therapy as lambs. They did not need to waste any more time convincing the clinician how bad things really were. Their initial offering had been agreeably received.

The therapist who says to the parents who bring in their hyperactive child as the gift—even when it is clear that the child can act out at their injunctions—"The problem is your marriage" has spit on their gift. Therefore, the therapist, like the problem-solving therapist, must stay close to the symptom offered. In this model of gift exchange, asking for a different gift amounts to great rudeness and is just cause for discontinuing the exchange: "I don't like this gift, give me something else."

Receiving the gift is *not* equivalent to taking away the symptom; it is equivalent to having some hierarchical power over the symptom. Erickson emphasized how important it is to respect every line in a fingerprint because the fingerprint is unique. If dental x rays and x rays of the optic nerve also reveal original patterns, how much more so must aspects of our thinking, behaving, and even our problems be unique. Working with the problem of menstrual cramps, Erickson helped a patient gain control over the cramps when it was useful, leaving the potential for pain on a p.r.n. basis, to use for getting out of a date or taking a day of sick leave from work. This approach develops that tradition.

A frustrated physician referred a mother of a seventeen-year-old for hypnosis. The mother would call frantically for an appointment to get her daughter's long-term facial warts removed and then not bring the girl. Finally, accepting that the mother objected to being present, the therapist invited the girl to come alone, and she did. With the idea of removing the currently wildly proliferating facial warts, the therapist carried out a medium-trance induction for the girl, in which she imagined starving the warts of blood or burning them off. But after this session, the warts continued their advance, traveling toward the girl's mouth. The therapist modified her approach of generalized ill will to warts, this time appreciating the relational uses of the symptom. She wondered if there were not one wart the girl would like to spare. In trance the girl said: "Yes. Secret. Favorite. Between my toes." The girl had a delicious wart, a sensuous refuge well-guarded from mother's panics and intrusions. The therapist then suggested that the girl decide carefully which wart to keep and treasure and which ones to banish. Within a week the facial warts disappeared. The secret wart remained. The girl needed enhanced decision-making power and control over her problem, not to have the therapist get rid of it. Mother, still refusing family therapy, then came in for hypnosis for the insomnia that had been present throughout her entire married life. A guiding principle in receiving the symptom is to do so in such a way that permits the client to salvage its benevolent features. Symptom removal per se is not the essential goal.

Repaying: The Task in Therapy

Repaying can take a number of forms. The ultimate goal is to initiate a transfer of power such that this phase ends with completion of the exchange and the patient in charge of his problem. Following are several brief examples.

Resistance as Features of the Gift: The Therapist Is Not Afraid of the Gift. After twelve years of marital conflict, a childless marriage, and many previous rounds of behavioral and analytic therapies for his depression, a successful architect requested to see me. After all his treatments, both he and his wife had come to believe that his problem was biological. He requested individual hypnosis for his problem as a last resort for coping with his "genetic" handicap. Over the phone, I told him that he would get individual hypnosis only after I had had enough sessions with him and his wife to obtain the fullest possible understanding of his problem. He agreed.

After three sessions of marital therapy, it was clear to me that the man's relationship with his mother, who until he was eight had literally wiped him clean after every observed bowel movement, was replicated by his wife, who dominated the marriage. The wife dictated and critiqued his movements to the point where he had minimized them, becoming the epitome of physical immobility and emotional constipation, unable to participate any longer in sports; even emotionally he had gone limp. The man's wife seemed to hope he would get so angry that he would leave her, but he appeared too beaten down to get up the courage to leave. Even though he occasionally attacked his wife verbally in the most insulting way, both of them agreed that he was the problem, he had always been impossible, and he was the one in need of therapy. I believed the wife wanted out of the marriage, but she indicated that the husband wanted out, because divorce was against her philosophy and religion. I said I would conduct individual hypnosis with the husband with his wife present so that she could critique what I did and how he responded and that no trance work would be done with her. They were both happy with that idea.

During the session designated for the husband's hypnotherapy, he expressed doubts about his ability to enter trance, fearing a loss of self-control. He asked if before we started he could read a list of some things about himself that would help me understand him better, things about himself that needed changing. I agreed. He then proceeded to remove from his suit pocket a neatly folded four-page indictment of every feature of his personality, physiology, work life, recreational life, and ability to have an intimate relationship. The problem of helping him overcome his depression by discovering his central complaint was now further complicated by having this anxiety-provoking list precede an already difficult induction, given the patient's mind-set about loss of control.

For this man (and for several other clients also in primary guilt-modulated relationships), I used a "self-voice" trance-induction technique (see also Erickson, 1964). In a monotonous voice, I began defining trance to the architect and his wife, saying how he had often been in one before, and asking "Perhaps you would enjoy finding out just how much control you *do* have over yourself in trance . . . if so, all you need to do is to *allow yourself* to go into a trance while reading aloud *dispassionately* (as he did everything at that time) the list of things about yourself you'd like to see improved." The need for self-control, the dispassionate style, the presence of his wife as a nonpatient, and the list were all accepted and built into the induction.

The previously anxiety-provoking list became long, boring, and repetitious for the man, and after the nth reading, his eyes began to open and close as he spontaneously "checked on the dimensions" of his mental state. I demonstrated to him his ability to bring about temperature changes in his hands and to experience an arm catalepsy and levitation to confirm and deepen his self-voice trance. I asked periodically if he realized that he was in charge of himself, although in an extraordinary manner. He enjoyed recognizing this strange power over himself, which transcended his usual logic. While in a moderate to deep trance state, he spontaneously studied his wife and me dispassionately. We then worked on certain pleasant and painful memories of his choosing, maintaining throughout his ability to disassociate from the emotion. My hope was that he would demand his right to feel in the next trance.

In the second trance session, I accepted his overt wishes once more. Because his list included numerous psychosomatic complaints and he ostensibly was continuing to assert his wish for marital bliss, despite what seemed to be a most disinterested wife, I asked him to read Walt Whitman's poem, "I Sing the Body Electric," dispassionately to his wife.

Not only was this man, who had become frozen with an apathetic depression, reading to his wife, one of the all-time most passionate songs of love of the human body, he was saying every unmentionable word to her and surely inadvertently, *feeling* every forbidden feeling in her presence and at his own command. These factors heightened his desire to "escape" into trance, which he promptly entered, becoming glassy-eyed, and physically immobile and speaking in an unusual tone. Suddenly, for one of the few times in his life, he burst into tears, sobbing through the poem, as if something in him had broken open, stopping literally in midphrase, where I had made a dot in the book, reading and reading the part before as if he were translating, thick-tongued, from a foreign language.

The man's reading of a loving, passionate poem to his wife (the wife had said she longed to have her husband read her a love poem) allowed the initiation of a gradually unfolding process in which the husband and wife could discover in their own time that they had no real desire to hear or say loving things to one another. In this case, the self-voice induction was woven from threads the client brought into his therapy: his own set of instructions about his gift of depression, his list, his emotional dissociation, his longing to feel deeply yet remain in control of himself, his need to believe his depression was an internal affair, and his wife's objections to receiving therapy. Ultimately, the structuring of the therapy allowed the man a secure journey from conscious to unconscious self-experience and self-control and was powerful in helping the couple divorce successfully.

Expanding on the Gift. For three years a girl had been rubbing a spot on the tip of her left elbow. She developed a callus that she enjoyed all winter but that was an embarrassment to her in the summer. The nurse practitioner at an adolescent clinic mentioned my availability to the girl, who decided to bring her problem to me. I found out that Sandra was the "good" daughter among three girls, cared for by an extremely rigid, authoritarian, and puritanical mother. (At a later date I met this woman and confirmed the child's description.) In front of the girl's two younger and more socially developed sisters, I marveled at that callus, at how big it was (about one-half inch in diameter). I acknowledged that a lot of Sandra's time and energy had gone into traveling that terrain. The fingers of her right hand had expert knowledge of the size, shape, contours, and textures of that callus. It was also enduring: Medical science had been unable to remove it. The best of her mother's good advice to "stop rubbing that spot" had been unable to help Sandra. In fact, I had never known anyone who knew more about that one-half inch of her body. The girl was satisfied with my reception of her gift. She was awaiting my repaying the opportunity to be in the presence of a tip-of-the-elbow expert and was delighted with this someone who appreciated her—albeit small— adolescent assertion of autonomy.

Starting with her right elbow, I asked Sandra how familiar she was with that spot. Only a little—she checked. We proceeded on a journey from head to toe. In this context of her expecting me to *give something back*, I did not need to be explicit. Anyone who admired her symptom admired her rebellion. I was not inviting her to stop touching that spot. Quite the contrary—I was repaying her by encouraging her to expand her kinesthetic and sensuous exploration.

Several weeks later, the nurse practitioner reported that Sandra had taken up occasional masturbation and that the size of her callus had mysteriously decreased. Basically, I had said, "This is a great gift. Let's not minimize its utility."

Facilitating Bartering Among Kin. When working directly with a family, repaying often entails the therapist redistributing her power among family members. If we look at the symptom as a living conflict, when modifying the relating around the symptom, we risk "taking something away from everybody." The skillful therapist redistributes to family members her gift of power over the problem in such a way that each member gets something back, in exchange for separating from some of the familiarities and benefits of the symptom.

Mr. Mott, a greeting card salesman, somewhat shabbily dressed, and his overweight wife came to a child guidance clinic because the oldest of their two sons, Ralph, had been crying daily before school for five years, and lately his episodes had worsened. He was staying out of school, and his peers were calling him "sissy" and "momma's boy" and beating him up. Also asthmatic, he was described by mother as "too sensitive" to defend himself.

In therapy, it seemed that Mrs. Mott had been given unlimited license to talk in exchange for carrying most of the emotional weight within the family. Mr. Mott, for example, had not known about Ralph's crying until two weeks before the first therapy session. He had no idea what was wrong; neither did the sons. The therapist set up a situation in which each person would benefit from a new family organization. Mrs. Mott was urged to let Mr. Mott take charge of getting Ralph to school and arrange for him to take karate classes. Mr. Mott's more direct contact with his son, in a position of authority, gave him more power in the home in general. With his dad home and more and more assertively and responsibly involved, Ralph was freed of his excessive emotional domestic ties to mom. As Ralph was detriangulated from marital conflict, Mrs. Mott had more opportunities to go out with her husband, as a reward for their hard work with the children. The younger brother received the gift of a big brother he could look up to. Previously finding Ralph a tremendous embarrassment, the little brother was now delighted. Mr. Mott, once he was elevated at home, announced "spontaneously" that he was going to buy some good, well-fitting shoes and collect military disability, for which he had never had the courage to fight, so he could get treatment for painful long-term foot problems. Mrs. Mott spontaneously dieted and lost thirty pounds. Thus a shift in the distribution of responsibility and power over the gift occurred. In Chapter Six, we will see bartering demonstrated *indirectly* during a process of family hypnosis.

Termination. Termination is the end of the exchange process. It is at this moment that the therapist no longer has power over the patient's problem, unless invited in at a later date. Often, operating from this model, the patient leaves by giving something else to the therapist. Sometimes it is a new problem, which is really a common life-stage developmental problem; sometimes it is an insight (if the therapist likes insights);

and sometimes it is a note or some small thing. The client *exchanges* a symbolic piece of himself, to *take* his leave in thanks.

During my first year of internship, a four-year-old ghetto child I worked with taught me about gifts of separation. Nathan exhibited every insulting diagnosis contained in the *Diagnostic Manual*. Indeed, he behaved terribly, setting fires at home, flooding his bathtub, and failing to cooperate at kindergarten. But his social context, its utter emotional and financial insecurity, provided explanation for his behavior. He lived with his eighty-year-old grandmother, who was alive by miracle alone, given her many illnesses, including severe heart disease. She was his sole support system; she was totally unwilling at first to discipline him with any consistency, but occasionally and unexpectedly she beat him. After a year of my working with the diad of Nathan and his grandmother and with Nathan alone, and with school and community resources, Nathan began to control his impulses and reach out for the help he so desperately needed. The school recognized his superior intelligence and his strong moral sense of the injustices of his life.

The week before our last session, Nathan ran into my office and said, "Look at this, this plant is just reachin' out to that one. This big one here's just reachin' out to the other one." But I did not get the message. The last week, Nathan tried again, this time recognizing the difficulty of getting through to me. Full of quiet emotion, as if afraid of offending me perhaps, he brought me a small ceramic lamb with a cracked ear, a small treasure he had found among the glass and rubble on the streets. "This is for you," he said, with tears in his eyes. Finally, I got the message. He was giving me his leave. "I will treasure this, Nathan, and always keep it close with me," I said. And I have. In Chapter Seven, Case Study 4, "The Turtle with the Cracked Shell," we will see another example of this termination phenomenon.

Summary

It is often useful to think of a symptom as a totalization of a person's problem on three levels of his experience: mind-set, family structure, and social situation. Because the symptom is born partly from certain material conditions within a person's life and may have real survival implications for him, it is a living conflict. As such, the symptom may represent aspects of a person's past that radiate into present decision-making processes, *and* aspects of the present that awaken and mobilize specific lines of past association. For the patient, the symptom is a main source of motivation to change. In fact, *the symptom is all the therapist has been offered.* In this sense, the symptom is the therapist's "ticket" into the symptom bearer's private life and kinship group; it is her option for having power in the eyes of this group, but the actual transference of power over the symptom depends on her proper reception of it.

If we consider the change process a means of helping a person restore his dignity and expand his use of self, our most general model of the therapeutic process must be shaped by a conception of an elevating exchange. The two fundamental and sequentially orchestrated modalities for attaining elevation in transforming social processes are gift exchange and warfare. In our age, power attained through *adversarial positionings* prevails. We have little frame of reference for the stance of *reciprocal empowering* that trade and gift exchange have held through human history.

Therapists can afford to appreciate symptoms and their set of handling instructions called resistances, or objections throughout therapeutic transaction. If we look at therapy from a gift-exchange model, implicit in such a treatment is cooperation. The expectation of things getting better (internal) often derives automatically from contextual cues (external) built into the very scaffolding of cooperative therapeutic suggestion. Implicit in this approach is a division of labor, in which "You do some things, I do others." The client need not feel wholly dependent on or one down with the therapist to accept the therapist's repayment. Fighting—even within the prescription of a therapeutic crisis or ordeal or transforming life event—is minimized or framed within a context of cooperation. The therapeutic prescription is designed to match in kind the symptom offering; the therapist's task is to actually give the client "something he can take home with him" because she "owes" it to him. The therapist is aware of "giving back," redistributing power over, or exploiting benevolent features of the symptom rather than taking it over or owning or abolishing it. For powers transferred to her over the symptom state, the therapist exchanges specific and powerful therapeutic counterinductive events. Built into the model of exchange are multiple and dynamic rather than unitary and statically conceived hierarchies among therapist and client(s) that facilitate, from the start, the end of therapy.

Part of the symptom offering is often a set of family interactional instructions for handling or family relational aspects of the gift. These instructions are often given in the form of opportunities to observe the ways family members and the family context itself may carry messages to a symptom bearer about how to behave. The therapist's likelihood of being presented with such an intimate slice of family life may depend on how graciously she received other symptom offerings.

Therapeutic graciousness in relation to the client's gift is not always easy to achieve; the therapist can offend a patient or shame herself in several different ways. The pitfalls to avoid include:

1. Letting the patient give everything. The therapist accepts too much, and the patient loses face.
2. Spitting on the first gift the patient offers. "Your symptom is not good enough, your real problem is." In short, the therapist is greedy and looks for the ideal gift rather than the one the patient offers.
3. Telling the patient his problem is not such a big one. This is insulting the gift and results in long-term lucrative therapy in which the patient spends time proving how bad the problem really is.
4. Criticizing the way the gift is transferred. "You ask me to help, but then you put restrictions on me." This amounts to cowardice on the part of the therapist in the face of resistance.
5. Hoarding the gift. "This is mine now. I'll tell you how to handle it." A hoarded gift exerts power over the recipient. The family then arranges for the therapist to maintain the problem, rather than having her transfer power and responsibility back to the family.
6. Giving back only advice, not something that can help people reorganize their mind-set and kin-structure: "To accept without returning or repaying more is to face subordination, to become a client and subservient, to become a minister." (Mauss, 1967, p. 72).
7. Accepting an unacceptable offering. The therapist thereby comes under the destructive power of the symptom offering.
8. At termination, continuing to act as if the private life of the person is under the domain of the therapist.

Perhaps Mauss (1967, p. xiv) said it most succinctly: "Generous and bold men have the best time in life and never foster troubles. But the coward is apprehensive of everything and a miser is always groaning over his gifts."

Chapter Four 🙰 🙰 🙰

Role of Family Interactions in Inducing Symptoms

🙰 A key component of hypnotic family therapy is observation of the contribution of family suggestion to symptoms. Part of the impact of family suggestions derives from the family's power to give contextual (meta) cues, including the family's feeling tone (blaming, proud, despairing) and very general role distributions. These metacues are hard to perceive because they often are transmitted below the threshold of perception. In the measurement of an individual's psychophysiological capacities, there is a point at which an auditory or a visual cue transmitted at a certain frequency is below the person's threshold of perception. If the frequency is progressively altered, at a specific moment, the cue transgresses the person's threshold to a just noticeable difference (JND). This chapter will help the clinician enhance her skills in "reading" family inductions and decrease her JND for perceiving contextual cues.

The first part presents a compendium of family inductive capacities. These are normal capacities of kin systems that can have desirable or untoward effects; they are not diagnoses. It is important to differentiate these *capacities* from an actual moment of symptom *induction*. Because an actual family induction is a slippery event to catch, creating an hypnotic atmosphere is built into our therapy to increase the likelihood of glimpsing family hypnotic moments. An actual inductive moment often includes a number of a family's suggestive techniques, usually occurs in a period of intense rapport among family members, culminates in the seemingly automatic production of a symptom component within the symptom bearer, and disappears or is quickly transformed by ongoing family interaction. The later part of this chapter analyzes an actual induction, in which a family contributes to an activation of symptom components.

It is important to keep in mind that the symptom is often a confluence of *three* suggestive bodies: the individual's belief system, family context, and social situation. In this chapter, self- and social-suggestion are temporarily placed in the background while we sharpen our skills of observing family contributions to symptoms.

We use the Erickson and Rossi (1979) five-step paradigm of the induction process (discussed in Chapter One) as a basis for category headings in this beginning glossary of family inductive capacities; we precede this model with our own step, a step Erickson also regarded as essential, that of establishing an intense rapport. To understand this mode of organization, consider that the hypnotist may begin her induction with the statement "Be alone with me" both as her first step in establishing rapport and as a beginning toward her second step of focusing attention inward. We begin by looking at special family capacities to convey "Be alone with me" to a symptom bearer.

Establishing an Intense Rapport

The first step in a formal indirect hypnotic induction is to establish an intense rapport with the client. In fact, in great measure this intensity of rapport enables the individual to shut out all other external stimuli as extraneous or peripheral to the job at hand, to let the rest of the world blur and haze and disappear, and to attend to, with heightened concentration, the internal relevancies of his own associative context. All the while, the hypnotist's voice goes with him, becoming a part of his internal landscape and, ultimately, causing that experiential domain to be experienced as a real, external event charged with the meanings of a life experience. Erickson wrote that "Without full cooperation between the subject and the hypnotist, there can be no hypnotism. Unwillingness to be hypnotized, admitted or concealed, signifies the failure of the essential cooperation and consequently a trance does not and cannot occur" (1980, pp. 8–9).

Unlike the hypnotist, the family does not always need to do anything special to establish rapport in beginning its inductions. Most often, rapport, connectedness, and even some degree of trust are built into the interdependencies of a family system that shares not only past and present but constructs some shared future (even in divorce, when relationships go on, albeit in new forms). *Built-in economic and emotional interdependencies empower suggestive rapport.*

Besides connectedness, rapport in the sense of trance induction encompasses the *establishment of rules about who is in charge of what at what moment.* Whereas the hypnotist may have to earn the right to have some power over the symptom bearer's problems, the family often inherits a certain power over members. When the young "schizophrenic" man (Chapter One) said, "My mother has me hypnotized—when she talks in that voice, I lose an eternity," he described, among other things, the built-in power connection that is part of the hypnotic hierarchy of rapport.

To establish rapport, and to make the rest of the world less interesting for the hypnotic subject, the hypnotist may say "Be alone with me." Part of families' power to extend a similar invitation derives from the public versus private dichotomy of family life.

The Public Versus Private Dichotomy. This dichotomy is present in all organized systems. For the family, it affects its general functioning, both in the protection and self-sustenance of itself as a discreet entity in society and in areas of its power over its own members. Specifically, determining what is "private" affects rules about loyalty, secrecy, competition against others, and, perhaps most importantly for symptoms, the rights of individual members and external social institutions to depend or intrude on each other. This dichotomy is heightened within the family relative to other "societies" because the family is the most private human institution.

For example, the family may permit incest (private) but not the discussion of it outside the home (public). The child who is a victim of incest, by virtue of family connectedness and the family's rules, may be prevented from either reporting the problem—via a taboo against such connectedness with outsiders—or being "permitted" to see the private event as a problem. Such a family "suggests" that society is at fault and the incest is acceptable. Clinicians experienced with physical and sexual abuse cases have been awed by the family's power over the jaws, tongue, and vocal chords of a maligned child (see Herman, 1981). Loyalty, shame, fear, and heroism converge into the induction of a vow of silence, even a "forgetting," in the face of intense family connection.

Similarly, a family's *public-private dialectic* is a vehicle through which a dysfunctional family may use external institutions (the public) to threaten a symptom bearer and ultimately to cue him to enter into or remain in his special problematic state. Even an extended family may become "other" or "public." For example, an adolescent child and oldest male sibling of an Italian immigrant family was brought for treatment of problems in thinking, exposing his genitals to his sisters, and other "craziness." In fact, this young man was permitted by family legislation to go to his aunt's house and act strangely. However, if he attempted to go to his aunt's house or to any therapist or teacher and report that his mother still bathed him; his father beat his mother and chased her with a knife; while in drunken rages, father exposed himself to the boy's sisters and tied his little brother to a chair in the basement overnight, his parents would work in exceptional concert to get the young man locked up. And so he remained "unable" to think properly or to "communicate clearly" with others, cutting up scraps of paper in an inpatient unit, locked into a sovereign private rapport with his parents.

In cases like these, the rapport is so great that family influence renders the individual member unable or unwilling to respond to or otherwise accept the suggestion of anyone who is outside the boundary of "private." (See discussion of resistance in Chapter Three.) In the face of suggestions of others, the individual is to behave as if unseeing, unhearing, and unfeeling. Meanwhile, the family voice, replete with self-deprecating suggestions, may go with him in his private journeys. If it is not acted on, this form of inner voice may loudly and clearly speak to him throughout his life.

Not all aspects of family privacy are trance inducers. Go to the grocery store and, among a crowd of cart pushers, witness a frazzled and harried parent with a three-year-old who is jubilantly reaching out for colorful items. The parent, unable to find something needed for the evening meal, mutters "Oh f---." The three-year-old smiles inquisitively and calls out at the top of her voice, "Oh f---, daddy?" The father immediately says "*We* don't say that *here!*" He had intended his curse to remain within the privacy of his family unit, but the child made it a public event. This is *not* family hypnosis. Family hypnosis bypasses the individual's ordinary frame of reference and culminates in automatic responses. Such *hypnotic private suggestions* are legislated by rules the respondent cannot either perceive or intercede against, given his life situation and mind-set. The young Italian man, even in efforts to defend himself, cannot break out of his symptomatic state; he is a captive to the unspoken rules of family privacy. In a sense, he is robbed of his margin of freedom as he responds to the family will.

Family We-ness. Another family feature of rapport, and a potential creator of a readiness for focusing inward, is *family consensus, or we-ness,* which is a spin-off of the public versus private dichotomy. In this case, the family calls itself "we." This we takes on the power of majority consensus that may prevail over either pressures of socially suggested conformity or attempts at self-instruction of individual members. The group can produce positive and negative hallucinations or amnesia, via arbitrarily starting and stopping sequential analysis, blame, and agreement (for example, self-blame or self-pride). In this way, families may shape the machinery of the self and its feeling tone. The symptom bearer is often an active contributor to his own induction into we-ness.

Consider sixteen-year-old Wendy. She left home and found a job and apartment because her brother physically abused her at home and her parents would not stop him. She requested therapy because she felt inadequate to go to school. During a family meeting, it was evident that no matter what Wendy did, father, mother, brother, sister, and Wendy regarded Wendy as a failure. Wendy might ask father, "Why don't you stop Jim when he hits me, like yesterday, when you said I could take your car and he hit me to get the keys?" "Well, how was I to know what was really going on?" mumbles dad. But it is often Wendy herself who prevents the therapist from intervening in family patterns by stopping discussions of either her successes or her brother's true failings. (He is much older, lives with his parents, is unemployed and seems doggedly determined to cultivate rejection from the military.) In this context, the family we, the intense connectedness, basically depends on negative hallucinations for whatever Wendy does right and whatever her brother does wrong, so Wendy contributes to this we-ness. Such collusion is a feature of family privacy and provides an intense rapport that is difficult for any outsider to penetrate. It can therefore be a source of family inductive power. The family member who wants to leave this system or "break its spell" may be threatened with banishment or madness. Surely, he is "not himself;" therefore, he must be "other than himself," and that can *only* be very bad or very "mad." Wendy, like Ellen (see Chapter Seven, Case Study 3, "Over My Dead Body") was indeed temporarily an example of such banishment because she tried to break the spell.

For the family to initiate step 1 of a symptom-activating process— the establishing of an intense rapport—the family need only draw on a unique version of the public versus private dichotomy of all social systems, or use forms of we-ness, the most basic of which entails systemic consensus.

Focusing Attention Inward

The trance state is characterized by intense attention to specific phenomena and freedom from being distracted by extraneous variables. As the individual withdraws from those peripheral or external events that might distract his heightened attention to designated experiential learnings and lines of association, he focuses on or intensifies his usage of an inner reality. Erickson emphasized that the inner reality may then become so absorbing as to be experienced as if it were an outer reality, complete with the emotional and psychophysiological power of a real-life event.

What are the family's special capacities for focusing the symptom bearer's attention inward and carrying an equivalent of the hypnotist's suggestion that "Where we are does not matter?" What are some of the special means by which actual family dynamics—regardless of intentions—can encourage individuals to *not* attend to influential aspects of family or other *outer* contexts but to *selectively* attend to certain largely *inner* processes or features of self?

Denying Significant Aspects of Family Context. Foremost is the ability of families to not recognize the pulls of family life on individuals and, in effect, to deny that there is a family system. When all is well, disattention to context frees family members to attend to other matters. When a family context is in trouble, the external components that contribute to the symptom dialectic can become dangerously elusive. In a family in conflict, the ordinary family message that the family context is "just the way things are" tends to give members a distorted view of the symptom bearer as problematic. If a person is symptomatic, there must be something wrong with the person. In this way, the family focuses on what is often partly a *property* of its system, such as an individual member's symptom, as though it were *not* a feature of the system. Simultaneously, the family denies or does not attend to other contributory family difficulties.

This phenomenon of denial and consequent (if inadvertent) splitting off of a family member from the family system appears in scapegoat processes. A problem emerges in a family, sequences ossify, hierarchies or alliances crystallize, and suddenly the spotlight is on an individual member. Since helping professionals also often look under the skin for a problem, the problem person is confirmed, the system denied, and the focus goes inward. Sometimes individual denial can represent a whole family's denial of symptom-sustaining aspects of the context.

Contextual denial is nowhere clearer than in the anorectic family, in which there may be no confirmed organic basis for a young person's irresistible urge to starve herself to death. For example, consider fifteen-year-old Coreen. She denied that her body was thin and so starved herself to the point of having no body fat. Miraculously, she lived like this for a year, until a neighbor, who was a nurse, urged her mother to have her medically examined. Before the girl's therapy, she had a two-year history of severe anorexia and bulimia and two psychiatric hospitalizations. She had lost 35 percent of her body weight, was dehydrated, and had low potassium. She wanted no breasts, pubic hair, or thighs that touched. She wanted to die. Her anorexia, her denial of her body, was perceived as her problem.

However, in an in-hospital family interview, the therapist noted that the father talked about Coreen's tremendous beauty and sex appeal before her weight loss and observed numerous inappropriate gestures and comments about her legs—father was very possessive of Coreen's body. Coreen seemed to wish to both eliminate that which father sought to claim and to help out by reducing the threat that father's attraction to her posed for her mother. The therapist noted that mother glinted with anger when father said, "No doubt about it, Coreen was the best-looking gal in the family before she lost weight." Coreen's denial and shrinking of her body were products of a three-person problem, manifesting themselves in Coreen's effort to help amid broader uncertainties in the relationship between father and mother and in her troubled relationship with her own femaleness.

But this body denial and inner obsession with bodily phenomena occurred in a larger context and were more than the sum of individual denials. For example, when once forced by her parents to eat and locked with her father's handcuffs to her bed (father was a policeman), Coreen escaped from home naked. Clothed by a priest, she was beaten up and raped by a neighborhood boy in the basement of the parish church. This was Coreen's first sexual experience (unless there had been a prior father-daughter incest). At the next therapy session, mother brought the book *All Things Wise and Wonderful*, placing it like a rose on the table beside her seat, and proceeded to invite Coreen's seven siblings to behave as if Coreen had personally disgraced each one of them by "getting herself raped" and "getting it in print in the local newspaper." The circle composed of the mother and all the seven other children rippled with a wave of shame aroused by the ill wind of the cut and bruised Coreen. In fact, the mother was having an affair with a man at her office, a man of a higher class, wealthier, and better educated than her perhaps "unwise and unwonder-ful" husband. The advent of the affair corresponded with the onset of Coreen's denial of her body. *Mother denied her affair*—which father sus-pected and felt cuckolded by—even after reporting it to the therapist. While his wife had been seemingly eternally pregnant, supposedly be-cause "he liked pregnant women best," father had long used prostitutes on the beat. At his wife's disloyalty, he became more possessive of Coreen, and Coreen withdrew herself. Depending on one's vantage point, it was father or mother who had "shamed" the family and Coreen who played her role of the self-abbreviating martyr with aplomb.

Clearly, this family's upsets, which crystallized around gender con-flict and sexual disloyalties, were utterly denied. Even if once mentioned, they would be denied again later. Telling the truth was acute at best. In this case, there was a "transpersonal system of collusion" (Laing, 1972, p. 99), in which context was denied and Coreen was "the only problem."

In this family, all the members, including Coreen, colluded to deny any event or relationship that might point to other family members' contribution to a problem. *The problem was in Coreen's body; the focus was inward.* Whenever family imperfections began to show, they were quickly shifted to the background and Coreen was again brought to the foreground.

The following dialogue is cited not as a demonstration of a family induction but to convey how this system of family denial is a powerful milieu in which an inductive event can readily occur. These are brief excerpts from a session designed (from the therapist's vantage point) to shift Coreen's role as Satan in the sibling subsystem of angels:

Ther.: I'm sure your sister Patrice has told you about things she has done that have not been model-child things in her life.

Coreen: No one ever does anything wrong in this family. Only me.

Ther.: I don't believe that it's a perfect family!

Father: Not for a loooong time (gives Coreen an accusing look, the siblings follow his lead, as if to say, "Thanks to Coreen").

Ther.: (To one of the brothers) You open your vest and it says "Perfect Man"?

Brother: (Shrugs innocently; school has labeled him a behavior problem)

Coreen: No, but I meant, I know they do bad things, but not really bad, they don't do things that bad (Coreen is eager to self-efface).

Father: Well, what I think Coreen is referring to is . . . (father is eager to fill in the details of the especially bad things about Coreen).

Later father reports on how he had all the children, most of them younger, take turns watching Coreen to make sure she did not vomit after meals.

Ther.: My God! It sounds like the Gestapo.

Father: Well, none of *them* are that type of person. Oh, he might rat a little on Coreen, heh, heh, but, uh . . . they're all good kids.

Basically, the context of this family hiding from its own desperation inadvertently gives Coreen a potentially life-threatening message: "Don't see the problem outside of you. There is no context. There is only you. Look at you, inside of you, your badness, your special badness." Coreen, partly in an effort to absorb family shocks and partly because of profound obstinance, reconciling her own self-suggestion with parental suggestions, is in a state of chronic self-abnegation, practiced with her own "religious" fervor.

Let us now look at this capacity to deny family context from a *sequential* view. At the end of this chapter, we examine the actual induction by a family with the following chronic interactional pattern:

1. Father feebly tries to talk with son.
2. Hesitantly, son starts to respond.
3. Mother interrupts, introducing to son a tangential subject.
4. Mother and son argue.
5. Father is on the periphery until his next effort to . . . .

The parents deny marital conflict. The only problem in the family is that this son has trouble breathing and thinking straight. However, regardless of what is *said* about whom in this system, the family's *actions* carry the message that mother monitors the father-son interaction and treats son as more powerful and interesting than father. The pattern of interaction, invisible to the participants, carries messages that are hard for any of them to resist; the reflexes and automatic nature of family rituals have a life of their own. Because mother and father wish only to recognize and project the intimacy and respect between them, the very structure of the family gracefully provides an avenue for conveying that the symptomatic child is the sole problem. His father cannot talk sense into him; he is disrespectful to his mother. This denial of family structure and its plethora of sequentially coded messages below the contextual JND threshold of family members contribute to the creation of a milieu in which powerful family inductions can occur. Ultimately, we are suggesting *not* that such a family be required to *see* its own patterns. Instead, what is needed is that more of the family context than the projected intimacy and respect be worked with to prevent or supplant detrimental directives.

Sequence stopping is a technique that families can use in processes leading to inattention to symptom-based features of context. It tends to produce an amnesia for the one who actually activated the specific interactional sequence that culminated in a problematic event. Montalvo (1976) described this process in his "Observation of Two Naturally Occurring Amnesias." In a family like the anorectic Coreen's, even if big sister starts a fight with Coreen, the family members will reflexively, in analyzing the event, start the movie rolling several cuts later, at the moment of Coreen's response. That segment is deemed the start and therefore the cause of the problem.

There is a children's story about this phenomenon. A mother owl's baby falls to her death from the nest, and mother owl will not wake up the sun so the day can begin. The lion holds a tribunal. He first calls in the most recently associated culprit, the monkey, blaming him for disturbing the branch the owlet nested in. The monkey explains it was the crow's fault that he disturbed the branch because the crow's call of alarm conveyed to him he had to swing through the trees to help the rabbit, and then the branch broke under him. The crow, the rabbit, and many other animals are tried in succession, each identifying the benevolence of his intention and each blaming another. At each accusation, the lion is convinced of the newly named animal's guilt. Ultimately, the mosquito is blamed for buzzing in an iguana's ears and forcing him to put sticks in his ears and *causing* the entire sequence of events that followed. That is why people swat mosquitoes when they buzz in their ears—mosquitoes are what is wrong in life!

Because of the long ticker tape of family life, there are many sequences, *past and present*, to project onto life's screen, starting and stopping blame at moments that one readily remembers, if not always accurately.

Related to sequence stopping is using *effects of sequences as proofs*. In the case of David, "the young man who cannot think from one thought to the next," the effect of hidden family conflicts on him, which intensify his confusion, is used as *proof* of his being a bad investment risk for college. The reactive or reflexive symptom components become transformed into proof that the problem is the identified patient rather than evidence that the problem reflects in some measure the family system erupting through this responsive young man. (See Chapter One for a discussion of structural responsibility versus linear blame.)

Drawing on Shared History. An additional and unique feature of the family inductive context offers a second means of entry into the private domain of the individual's psychophysiological system and a source of suggestions to focus inward. Family members have a *shared history.* Therefore, whereas the hypnotist searches for the emotionally charged memory that will be drawn on to produce a specific effect, family members have a built-in ability to focus an individual member's attention on past experiences, anniversaries, associations, and memories that are connotatively important. Once the individual's attention is focused inward, a variety of spontaneously occurring phenomena may follow, depending on the nature and implications of the lines of associations for him.

Family members may select a memory or series of memories, colored by family psychomythology, pregnant with generations of implication. They may share in the revivification of an event, complete with specific psychophysiological concomitants, smells, sights, laughter, cold, tears. Just as when a family disciplines a child, the parents may become skillful in eliciting feelings of responsibility, shame, guilt, or regret, so the family in trouble may use shared history in a manner that inadvertantly activates guilt. The resources of shared family memories are vast, and family knowledge of responsive patterns makes it more difficult for the reacting family member to resist certain evocations.

Often, after the therapy, in which revivification of shared *positive* events is a common procedure, families spontaneously produce *subsequent* shared reveries based on more positive past experiences and apply those more positive learnings toward future goals.

In the induction of David Marad, the family fears dislocation of the family's connective joints as David is about to register for college. While intending to encourage David to stand up to his coming challenge in spite of his symptoms, mother makes a speech about a *shared history* that engages David in an argument with her. In this speech, broken up by other dialogue, mother inadvertantly activates the kind of *inner focus* that David then gets absorbed in, forgetting the pressing external tasks at hand. Mother's own uncertainties about herself as wife and mother permeate her suggestions to her son. David has expressed a doubt about carrying both a full college load and working. Mother's statements then begin:

Mother: Will you be able to handle responsibilities in college . . .? Academic excellence has always been David's thing. . . . Just in recent years, David has stopped doing homework and study and reading; that's what I'm concerned about. . . . In eleventh grade, this was also, it was already, you know, starting . . . I would like David to go to college, if he could demonstrate a willingness to take the time out to really do studies and this kind of work, and keep notes and records. We've been making sacrifices for five years while he went to Shoshanim, and somehow, we survived, because it was a positive thing. David was getting *something* out of the school; he has a skill, if he wishes to use it, so we feel that it was to his advantage. . . . We would continue [to support him] if David could, you know, could demonstrate that, you know, he's gonna buckle down and start, you know, doing something!

David was to have spent this session negotiating financial arrangements for the upcoming college registration, but his focus is now inward in a manner not useful to the realistic task at hand. Because of his individual capacity to respond with guilt and his unique position in his family, David and his mother fight, lost in a select slice of shared history:

David: Many times during those years when you got upset with me and thought I wasn't doing my work, you hung it over my head and made me feel guilty, and I'll never forget those times . . . as long as I live.

Structurally, mother and son argue while father observes from the periphery. Sequentially, the dialogue is mother-son-mother-son. Suggestively, the whole family works to turn the focus away from the threat of dislocation anticipated by David's move toward his individual future. Using shared common history, mother and son argue endlessly about son's past failings. The son is riveted inward, squirming to defend himself against guilt.

Family Usage of Spontaneously Occurring Reveries. We mentioned that modern hypnotists, increasingly respectful of the body's wisdom, try to enter as briefly as possible into the individual's psychophysiological system via words and movements. Some even await the individual's spontaneous readiness as he enters naturally into a common, everyday reverie and simply try to intensify this state. The family is in an excellent position to penetrate individuals' naturally occurring—possibly every ninety minutes—trancelike states. In its inductive process, the family may inadvertently take advantage of such times.

For example, in an enmeshed family system, if an asthmatic child is seated quietly, staring out the window, the overprotective mother might, with excessive goodness, put her arm around daughter's shoulder and ask "Are you feeling sad or lonely?" Although daughter may have been experiencing some of those feelings, actually she was studying an ant traveling the vast terrain of the windowpane. In the problematic family situation, the symptom bearer's private life can become occupied suggestively with unrecognized or projected needs and desires of other family members. The asthmatic child responsive to these needs may not breathe easily. She may quickly forget whatever enjoyable fantasies she had or observations she was making of the ant. Mother must be instructed that to care for this child is to look with her out the window, to study ants in the garden or at a hall of science, in short, to join the girl in a new and sometimes separate focus *outward*. Likewise, in Chapter Three, the moments of the husband's depression originally may have offered wife a chance to be protector and may have given him a retreat from family and work. However, this private state became not an opportunity to reflect on actions to change his marital and work circumstances but a mental space filled with familiar criticisms from mother and wife and with self-suggestions of inevitable likeness to his own depressed father: a psychic needlepoint of physical immobility, constipation, despair.

Also, whereas the hypnotist must work to return the individual to his state of mind prior to the spell of the symptom, and sometimes use early childhood memories to do so, the family pervades a young person's life experience, at a time when he is often in that special state of consciousness that allows uncurtailed exploration of physical and psychological potentials, from learning to move hands, to walking, to looking closely at something on a windowpane, to looking through the glass at something far away. Early periods are marked by responsive receptivity and inner reverie. The child easily hallucinates, enjoying the company of playmates who are invisible to others, and carries a playful and flexible boundary between inner and outer reality. Family life penetrates into the formation of his categories of being, and the child's fantasy life generates innovative outer realities. The child is no tabula rasa; nevertheless, the field of psychoanalysis is a testament to the powerful suggestive role of family life on a young person's early organization of experience.

Emotional and Suggestive Continuity. For better or worse, the family has a unique form of emotional and suggestive continuity. As we discussed in Chapter One, any system has the capacity to transmit certain messages in direct, sequential, or contextual forms, but a family system's ability to transmit a message over great gulfs of time, across multiple voices, on telephone wires, to pick up a line of association left off years before, is truly more miraculous than the power of any computer. The sound of a parent's voice, its tone, may so deeply reverberate within even a grown child that after sixty seconds on the phone, the person may sob with the abandoned sobs of children and dreamers or radiate an extraordinary sense of joy and pride.

In the Chapter Six case, "The Young Woman with the Bad Body," we will see how this emotional undertow of family life enables certain statements—for example, those of the father concerned that his daughter will kill herself—to have a symptom-inductive life of their own. The father's long-term sadness and his empathy, almost pity, for his daughter may *seem* temporally broken up by other family events. In fact, however, the daughter may experience them as the continuation of a single speech. Clock time contains the observing clinician, but the patient may respond to certain family pulls in emotional or subjective time. In this realm, the father's voice may be picked up at any time and still carry the weight of suggestive continuity. From this author's observations, this continuity often plays a role not only in activating but, more importantly, in *maintaining an inward focus.*

Let us look at father's speeches. (Temporal separation is indicated by ellipses.) Note that whenever he speaks, he carries a message tone of failure.

Father: Umm—I am a little bit leery. I think Gretchen has a hard time functioning on her own (voice lowers and speech becomes slower while looking at Gretchen). . . . Yah, you see, for a while there she was staying with that elderly lady and for a while she was alone up here. We didn't know what time the college started up here and she came up a week earlier. And, she was alone in the house and I don't think it is best for her. . . . I didn't want her to come back, but then she would be better off at home. (Several minutes later) I think that Gretchen has a hard time if she lives alone. I guess everybody gets lonely, but she has a harder time to function on her own, I guess. . . . Well . . . even to carry those thoughts [of suicide] in your mind is not right (shaken, biting lip). Well, I can understand that a person gets depressed once in a while. This is understandable . . . but why so depressed that you want to take your life . . . ? (Thirty minutes later) Well, it wouldn't be normal for her to, you know, be living at home, and I would like to see her go out and function on her own. And that was one of the reasons why when she came up here we thought, we were hoping, it would work out then, but she's not ready for it.

The therapist intervenes here in an effort to affect that frame of failure around a picture of daughter's coming home for fuel. This intervention breaks the ordinary power of father's suggestive continuity that, despite his intention to help, actually activates daughter to look inward with disappointment. It is as if a parent—himself temporarily stuck in a certain emotional state—offers the child a lens (the best he has) on the world. If the lens is one of sadness, and if the child reverberates to father's sadness, the child begins to cry his tears, even if she hears only a certain tone of voice. This child then "looks homeward and melts with grief," until the suggestive continuity is broken or emotionally charged in a different way.

Confusion Techniques of Families

The third step in a formal hypnotic induction procedure requires that the inducer, having established an intense rapport and secured the subject's sustained inward focus, depotentiates the habitual (or conscious) ways the person thinks through his problems. One may *distract* the person to disrupt his ordinary sequences of thinking, introduce *doubts* about the way he ordinarily sees things, or otherwise *disorient* or *confuse* him. At the moment of *uncertainty*, the *wish* for clarity is activated and the likelihood of responsiveness to a clear suggestion is increased.

A number of aspects of the family interactions that may confuse a symptomatic member or activate self-doubt derive from facets of family structure. Although there are other structural inductive capacities, we will focus on five confusion techniques: content versus structure, nullifying hierarchical messages, parts-of-self inductions, blurring of boundaries, and description directives.

Structure Versus Content. Dysfunctional families are in an excellent position to confuse a person (destructively depotentiating his conscious ways of thinking) via a discrepancy between what is said (the content of suggestions) and how it is framed (the interpersonal structural context in which the content occurs).

Chapter Two introduced the idea that human structures each convey a special level of communication to members of those structures, a message that cannot be reduced to either the sum of verbalizations or the sum of sequences of interaction that constitute the enactment of those rules. Once a family context has been formed, the family's organization carries with it often unspoken behaviorally enacted directives.

For example, consider a predominant modality in which a son or daughter receives an understanding of expected sex-role behavior. Sex-role delineations are derived from experiencing the family system in action. In the case of the young woman who thinks she has a bad body

(Chapter Six), father may *say* that he does not mind if his wife works, but he may *enact* hurt and anger with her at unexpected moments, perhaps by becoming increasingly unaffectionate when she does get a job. Mother may interiorize father's rejection as proof of her worthlessness or inferiority, carrying father's rejection as a message that she is failing herself and her daughter. The son may be *told* to respect his mother and father equally, but he may get the message that a woman's place really is in the home and the man ought to be a better provider to and caretaker of the woman. In short, there may be a discrepancy between what a family promotes as family ideology and what it does, between the *content* of family life, and the prevailing contextual *cues* and *rules* of relating.

Part of the power of any hypnotic procedure is its ability to convey to a person a sense of *who* he is rather than *what* he is to do (content). The content-structure confusion technique carries this force. There is constant shifting from the specific content being discussed to overriding enactment of dysfunctional interpersonal sequences that may culminate in a sense of self-identity, not necessarily positive, with the person having no idea where that idea of self came from! For example, a parent might state (content) that she equally loves and enjoys both her children, but she often enacts loving movements toward one child and attacking movements toward the other and confides to the first child about what the other child does wrong. Structurally, the rigid transgenerational alliance between mother and the more easily managed first child overrides the meaning of all specific suggestions of self-identity that the mother gives the second child. Whatever she *says* to the allied-against child, the enacted *message* is "You are second-rate." Like most indirect suggestions, this message is harder for a person to recognize and resist unconsciously than direct suggestions.

To conceptualize the effect of this technique, imagine watching a movie in which a father treats one son as inferior to his brother. Below the movie is a subtitle that says: The father demonstrated equal love for both children. Is the movie itself or the subtitle the truth? In real life, the *enactment* stings more than the words console, and the recipient often does not know what hit him!

Parental malevolence is not the issue. A parent may dislike a child and a child may dislike a parent, and no "bad hypnosis" need take place. It is the *confusion* between content and structural messages—sometimes in an effort to be nice or fair—that may *inadvertently* suggest to the recipient of the message an unshakeable sense of failure, inadequacy, or being second-best.

While innocently asking mommy "Why do we eat meat?" (content), a three-year-old may be getting on and off her chair (testing her structural relationship to mother by challenging a "We remain seated while eating dinner rule.") This is not hypnotic. However, if the parent consistently failed to set effective limits, such an event might ultimately trigger a behavior problem in the child or a request by mother for Valium. Chronicity and denial of or inattention to contributing structural problems are general prerequisites of a symptom-inductive content-structure confusion technique.

Nullifying Hierarchical Messages. Chapter One described aspects of how nullifying hierarchical positions produced messages confusing to a symptom bearer. As an additional example, consider the case of a couple in their twenties. They had been financially independent for a number of years but suddenly needed to borrow money from the husband's parents to buy their house. For all the members, because of consensual family psychomythology, this simple process activated a sense that the couple, although parents themselves, were now once again hierarchically back in the child position, vis-a-vis financial dependence.

Historically, the husband prepared dinner and the wife made breakfast and did the laundry. Shortly after giving her financial gift, mother-in-law decided it was time for her and her husband to visit, to help the couple get settled in their house. The timing of the visit was not good, but the young couple felt obliged to agree. Mother-in-law worked all day, assigning daughter-in-law tasks she really should do to enhance her new home. Father-in-law, who was deaf, retreated behind a wall of silence, not helping either his wife or daughter-in-law. Husband came home late each day from work. Near the end of each day, the grandchild became irritable, because, as grandmother explained it, "he was too hungry to wait for his father." Daughter-in-law would get a pain in her neck and have to go to bed. She realized that she was upset with her father-in-law for doing nothing, she felt obligated to help mother-in-law help her since she was working so hard, and she was becoming upset with her own husband for being late and leaving her with the whole situation. Nevertheless, she could not stand up to mother-in-law, who was financing her.

Hierarchically, as in Figure 8, daughter-in-law experienced herself as "supposed to" or "being suggested" to simultaneously play two roles that conflicted most intolerably at dinner hour, when the feeding of her child was at stake. Were the daughter's mind-set inaccessible to guilt, she might find an alternative to either or both of these arrangements. Indeed, she and her husband might have invited a visit at a later date and prevented the situation. When looking at the suggestion of family structures and special family confusion techniques, the important point is that *once the symptom bearer is operating within the reflexive structure of family life, he may become subject to conflicting messages about power and responsibility.* As these messages converge at a particular instant about a particular piece of behavior—such as "Feed *my* grandchild now" versus "In our house my husband feeds the children dinner"—the symptom bearer, caught in two nullifying prescriptions and unable to perceive a transcendent solution, may become confused and ultimately experience some symptomatic response. Like trance, this response may permit transient escape—if not relief—from a reality he inhabits.

It is worth noting that what a clinician observes in a family interview as a rapid shifting from subject to subject may actually, within the private code and structure of family life, represent *a shifting from one hierarchical position to another.* In the induction of David Marad (end of this chapter), we see this impact of changing "altitudinally related" subjects. In a moment of intense family drama around imminent shifts in power and dependency relations, mother alternately evokes content suggestive of David's conflicting roles in a stuck family structure. She brings up past school failings, suggesting his position of baby and failure, and then mentions her husband's illness, a cue for David the Rescuer to emerge. The son, looking dizzy and practically tearing his hair out, screams, "You're always changing the subject. I can't think anymore."

Figure 8. Nullifying Family Hierarchies.

Mother-in-law	Father-in-law		Daughter-in-law	Son
Daughter-in-law			Her own child Her in-laws as guests	
Economic- and gratitude-based hierarchy			Actual responsibility hierarchy	

Parts-of-Self Inductions. This procedure, related to nullifying hierarchical messages, uses various content issues to evoke different parts of self that have become compartmentalized within the family, such as the family savior versus the family baby positions. The parts-of-self procedure can have many effects. It may confuse the symptom bearer when two narrow and contradictory aspects of self—each of which are rigidly defined within separate hierarchies of family functioning—are evoked at once or in rapid succession. Parts of self may also be used to facilitate dissociation—as in the multiple personality who often has one or more "bad" selves, selves unacceptable to family life, hidden away from the world. These parts, which might ordinarily be angry or sad feelings in someone else, are broken off from the public personality as "not me" or "bad me" and at worst take on a vampirish life of their own.

Basically, in all parts-of-self inductions, the inducer is given power to delineate in the induced categories of intrapsychic functioning. The inducer says "This is who you are" or "These two categories represent who you are." In a family, there is the additional effect of hidden directive. "As rescuer, you are to stay home and help me; as baby and failure, you are a shackle and a financial burden on me, so leave!" The therapeutic use of parts-of-self counterinductions will be illustrated throughout the clinical chapters.

Blurring of Boundaries. The family can resort to a number of *boundary confusion techniques.* In "The Young Woman with the Bad Body" (Chapter Six), we will see a "twins" induction based on the family's capacity to merge individuals into units of likeness from which, even if undesirable, they cannot readily escape.

Family likenesses can draw on physical resemblances—even to family members long dead. For example, "Joan looks exactly like Aunt Milly" (who was a prostitute), or "Jim reminds me of Uncle Bill" (who never amounted to anything, was a drunk, but was good-looking). Likeness inductions may draw on certain temperamental features. Real, if thin, threads of commonality are in some way woven into the fabric of family alliance patterns and then radiate with tremendous suggestive color. When the mother of the young woman with the bad body begins, in a slow and religious tone full of insight and motherly compassion, "You know, we are a lot alike, you and I," the messages that follow may have a special significance to the child, a special hold over her, a special effect on her breathing (now timed to her mother's, her eyes now fixed to her mother's eyes) in a symbolic reverie in which the world goes away and only these "bad twins" are left.

Description Directives. Another phenomenon of family life that may contribute to the state of confusion that enhances certain forms of symptom suggestibility is the family description of the symptom bearer. This "technique" was first brought to my attention during a three-year research project I conducted on the treatment of hyperactive children within the context of their families (Ritterman, 1978). In the course of the initial service, the often bedraggled and fatigued parent(s) would naturally begin to describe the symptoms of the overactive child. In a percentage of these families, the child's behavior had attained a secondary advantage of helping the parent(s) get support from other adults in the face of a difficult charge. In a number of cases, if, during a parent's description of the child's inability to sit still, problems concentrating on the task at hand, and general uncooperativeness, the child sat like a model citizen, stationary and patient, the parent would begin to describe the child to the therapist in a way similar to this:

Parent: You see how he is. He's impossible. He can't sit still for a minute (child is stationary). He never stops talking (child is silent). He always wants to be on the move (child squirms). Look at him! (Child is stationary.) And he never stops swinging his legs (child begins to exercise his toes). . . .

Of course, there are many interpretations of this phenomenon. The child is "being bad" by "being good" in that he is again foiling parental efforts to bring him under their influence. Nevertheless ultimately the parent inadvertently orchestrates the child's activity level. In a chronic form of this pattern, the *description* of the child's symptomatic behavior gives the parents certain *secondary* "benefits"; the description comes to function as a directive. "Go ahead, show everyone how bad I have it, manifest your symptoms." Eventually the symptom bearer seems to respond, but not without experiencing some degree of confusion and doing some doubletakes in the meantime. It is similar to the hypnotist who says "You can't stand up; go ahead and try."

Let us look at this procedure more carefully in a sequence of such description directives that convey to a confused young man—who is mute for long periods each day—"You have the right to remain silent." Keep in mind Erickson's paradigm of a graduated series of suggestions, designed to culminate in the hypnotic alteration of any sensory-perceptual modality, including pain (see Erickson, 1980, p. 83). For example, to elicit hypnotic blindness, the hypnotist suggests steps, from inviting (1) the hope for the experience (the advantage of it for the person); (2) the expectation of it (it is likely to occur); (3) the realization it *is* coming; (4) the effort to resist (try but you cannot do it); (5) the realization that it has already occurred.

The following segments are from the third family session with a low-income black family living in an Oakland, California ghetto. The presenting complaint in the first session was that Arthur, according to his mother, older brother, and older sister, does not talk. Six months ago he had returned to his mother's after living with his father, father's various women friends, and his younger brother, who is favored in both family contexts. Arthur has refused to go to school, is staying home, almost catatonic, and occasionally erupts into rage when someone says the least little thing to him.

In the first session, the therapist noted that mother was not interested in taking charge of helping her son return to school. She was fatigued with the daily burdens of survival. The therapist used a typical family therapy technique of assigning the older brother charge of Arthur. As anticipated, in the second session two weeks later, mother reported that (1) things were better than ever and (2) she wanted a session alone with Arthur because he was not her son's child but her responsibility. And she demanded that responsibility.

Just before the session to help mother and son communicate, the older brother repeatedly taunted Arthur about his quietness in front of the brother's friend and Arthur went into a rage, raising a knife toward his brother's face, threatening violence. Because of the threat, a psychiatric consultation was called. The psychiatrist agreed to postpone the prescription of antidepressants and let the therapist try to activate calming family events.

Mother and son arrive two hours late for this session, which was planned to improve communication. Mother opens the session by mentioning her own physical illness. She has just said that she has postponed a needed operation for six months, associating this postponement with first getting Arthur back to school. In an effort to elevate Arthur to help him express himself, the therapist, to date unable to get a word out of

Arthur, now casually addresses him. Following are the steps involved in silencing Arthur; they focus on *progressive descriptions* of his mutism, which seem at first to function as a source of confusion to Arthur and, ultimately, as a directive.

Ther.: What do you think about what your mom is saying about putting off the operation?

Arthur: I don't think it's right.

Mother: (Interrupting) All of 'em been telling me.

Ther.: Why don't you let *him* tell you?

Mother: He did already. I just told you all of my kids have been getting on me about it.

Ther.: He's not all your kids. I only see one sitting here. You've got four.

Mother: Right, but he answered the question, too.

Ther.: He's not done, is he? He only gets to say two words? Isn't that what we were talking about on the phone, mama?

Arthur: (Looks gloomy)

Mother: I don't hear him saying nothing. Well maybe if I don't come, you won't have to worry about me overtalking. See, I been running after him all of his life; you can't tell me how he talks. You may be trying to change his way of talking, but he was finished whether you want to believe it or not. That's the end of it. When he says something, that's it. Now he's telling you the same thing. Like I said, maybe if I'm not here, he'll talk more, but I've been around him a long time. I know how he talks.

Mother has described her son in a way that might inadvertently motivate him to discontinue talking: If he talks, he is proving her wrong, making her description of his inability to speak seem to be partly her problem. Even this small step might serve as a needed *motivator* toward remaining silent, enhancing his expectation that he will remain silent.

In the following discussion, occurring after Arthur has expressed that he wants his mother to go to the hospital because he is "worried she's gonna die," mother goes off on a tangent about how it would not matter if she did die because "the kids" don't respect her anyway. The therapist has asked Arthur, who is fidgeting with his hands and huffing and puffing, for his verbal reaction. He makes a despairing sound and says, "It's got me mad." The therapist instructs him "Talk with your mom about this." Mother responds:

Mother: Not and tell me something like that. He ain't crazy.

Ther.: You mean if he tells you he's mad . . . .

Mother: No, no, you say tell me that I make him very mad. My children don't talk back to me.

Ther.: He's not allowed to say to you, "You make me mad."?

Mother: For what reason? I would prefer for him to say that makes me upset. I don't like that. Now for him to turn to me and say "Mama you make me very mad."? Uhuh, no.

Ther.: But he could say that makes him very upset. . . .

Mother: Yeah, but don't tell me that that makes you very mad, because I don't like that. . . . It's just like he does not say anything. . . . He doesn't say anything to anybody. He just clams up and he keeps everything inside of him. And then when he explodes, then it's to the danger point. See, he doesn't talk. Like I say, he talks when he wants to talk.

Mother's description of her son and her use of what is partly an *effect* of her own silencing techniques as *proof* of his peculiar mutism inadvertently help silence the boy.

When the therapist is able to reactivate Arthur to speak again, he begins talking freely and complains about mom's preferential treatment of his older brother, George:

Arthur: And I be on the phone when somebody call and I have to get off. Now when you be on the phone and somebody call, you don't tell them to call you back. You be on the phone and somebody call, but George comes along, he wants the phone . . . now you get off the phone.

Mother: Now, George never be home that much. (To therapist) That's the problem I have with him now. He stays up here all the time (Arthur), so why you sitting up here telling a story? When you go to the store for me, George's not even home. George not be here. Now you know yourself what time does George come home at night when you wake me up and tell me?

Arthur: When you asked me to go, you asked me to go Saturday, he's be there.

Mother: No, no, no. Nobody went out Saturday, it was freezing. We didn't go out Saturday.

Arthur: It must be every Saturday. I'm the only one that goes to the store.

Arthur is now called a liar. Indeed, he does manifest spontaneous memory lapses. In hypnotic inductions of deafness, the spontaneous development of sensory and motor disturbances is regarded as evidence of auditory changes since they imply a marked disturbance of general functioning. In this case, the *forgetfulness* is described as *lying* and suggests *indirectly* another kind of motivator toward Arthur keeping his mouth shut.

Mother: Every Saturday?

Arthur: Not every Saturday. Mostly every Saturday.

Mother: Okay, if you say so, we'll wait 'til next time when everybody's here and we'll see. (To therapist) I know that what he is saying is not true.

Arthur: What's the use of saying anything, if you all say I'm lying.

Mother: Well, you are. You knew you're lying. I didn't have to say it. If you're going to tell the truth that's one thing, but if you're going to lie, I'm definitely going to tell you when you're lying.

Interestingly, the symptom bearer often has a rationale for his problems, which suggests a greater degree of *voluntarism* than one might detect from an appreciation of the principles of family interaction and observations of his difficulties in self-expression. As Arthur moves from sentences to phrases and eventually to grunts, the therapist asks him, "Don't you ever get sick of everybody talking for you?" He explains:

Arthur: All the time, everything, every time we go somewhere everybody always, when somebody ask me something everybody else always say something for me, so I keep from talking . . . I just be quiet.

Minuchin (1974) described how a family can take a member's voice. It can, with a cooperative family member, also change it, forbid it, distort it, call it libelous, and otherwise invite its removal. These descriptions and actions, taken with the symptom bearer's efforts to break out of his symptom, often function as simple indirect directives. If sequenced, they may become progressive sequential directives. They are guaranteed to be confusing to the symptom bearer when, framed in a context of "speak up," the descriptions seem to direct the symptom bearer to demonstrate his profound silence. In Arthur's case, once the therapist intervened dialectically in this process, mother readily drew on more tender ways of relating with Arthur, and over three months' time, Arthur spoke back and functioned quite well at home and in a carefully selected public school.

Initiating an Unconscious Search

In families, evoking certain words or events with certain implications can initiate an unconscious search process for some members at special times. They may have an effect like that of the hypnotist who suggests that "Traveling along life's highway, you will come to a moment in which you. . . ." Here we describe the family usage of cue words and the associative pairing of past events with projected future plans.

Cue Words. The family is an organized system with functional rules. This system gives underlying emotional continuity to family life in terms of its metamessages. Within the limits of family structure, multi-level and seemingly incongruent messages piece together, across different speakers and over time, so that the repeated patterns become a familiar, if not always happy, route traveled. Just as a sequence of interactions—father talks to son, mother interrupts, mother and son fight—summarizes family structural rules, so a single word can summarize chains of family interaction and rules of relating. The cue word then becomes an economical signal, a form of shorthand, and the original inductive sequences need not be repeated. The cue word carries the hidden power of family structure.

In the earlier example of the couple borrowing money from parents, in family shorthand, a small movement from father-in-law indicating he is about to withdraw or a comment by mother-in-law about food can activate the daughter-in-law's pain in the neck. In a special case of "laying on of hands," a pain in the neck, which began with a father pulling on his son's neck, *placing* intense hostility and a feeling of failure into the young man's body, can become cued by others than family members. Sometimes a look from a male authority figure will do.

Interactional analysis alone may not suffice for the observing and participating clinician to grasp family inductive power. In fact, a single word may cue a family member into the automatic behaviors characteristic of the symptomatic state. A single word may carry behind it the hidden influence of the suggestive continuity of family structure. Part of the power of a family cue word derives from the public versus private dichotomy, in which suggestions or reminders by family may be so personal that no outsider, not even a clinician, will immediately recognize the implications of the word. In the actual family induction in the second part of this chapter, the words "garage sales," for example, spoken in conjunction with David's payment for college, might mean nothing to an observer but suggest at once the two irreconcilable positions David is holding in his family.

A child such as Arthur, with the right to remain silent, might have used the word "mad" in front of the therapist *knowing* that it would activate rage in mother, summarizing one hidden hierarchy of family life in which when son does talk, he "talks down" to mother. In such a case, the cue word can evoke certain parts of self in others and establish in shorthand: "I am talking to you within my capacity in *hierarchy 1* of family life, not *hierarchy 2.*

A family cue word can function as do the different forms of the word "you" in French, which designate automatically different levels of intimacy and different power relationships. This way, a cue word becomes a simple direct or indirect inductive technique, activating a certain part of self, a certain self in relation to others. Because it occurs within the unique family context, however, it draws its power from the nuances of family structure. Like any other evocation, once elicited, it activates the brain to continue to search unconsciously through the memory system, even after the person has consciously dismissed the family member's word. This unconscious search on an autonomous level is the essence of indirect suggestion, which enters "invisibly" and activates a search outside the respondent's ordinary frame of reference.

Regarding privately charged words and the evocation of parts of self unbeknown to the outsider, families may use a nickname that elicits certain sequences. A parent may have many different names for a child, each of which is used in conjunction with a certain state of feeling, a certain task at hand, often without the parent's conscious awareness of what name is used for what. In an immigrant Jewish family, the formal American name may be used in disciplining, the American nickname in routine usage, the Hebrew name (associated with the modern state of Israel) in times of intense pride, the old-country Yiddish name in times of deepest personal affection. In fact, in the Jewish culture, as in many cultures, there is a tradition recognizing the power of naming as a cue word. After a serious illness, a child may be renamed a name that will not ever again evoke the "self which became ill," only the new "healthy self." The child may be renamed "Godlike One" or "Blessed One" to serve this healing-cuing function.

In the case of the young woman who feels she has a bad body, the mood of loneliness and despair permeates all messages, even those intended to provide succor. The very word "loneliness" in this vignette of family life makes the index patient tense with fear, cuing her in to a lifetime of personal meanings attached to that word in her family. The meanings include failure, inadequacy, sacrilege, burdensome, bad, evil, sinful, sick, and so on. Affecting the impact of a cue word on family semantics may alter family mood and even the nature of relational connections between family members. The therapist thus must somehow affect the use of associated meaning of the word(s) that serve as summaries for and cues of central family conflicts.

Associative Pairing. A related but slightly different aspect of cuing is the activation of those processes in individuals that turn back their subjective time clocks into the past. In seeking to document, for example, "what kind of a person the child is," the family may give the therapist an example of an earlier event. This is fairly direct, and most often does not bypass anyone's ordinary frame of reference. The inductive power of such a reference lies in (1) its mention without explanation, so that it remains a private word; (2) its vivification of certain memories; and (3) its pairing of these memories and associations with anticipated future events. Families share a history that may be used in evoking certain past events; sometimes these evocations can be used as preceding evidence for predicting a certain future for a member. To explain this idea, consider several capacities of the unconscious mind. It is capable of what hypnotic terminology calls *revivification*—that is, an evocation of past events so vivid that to the subject it seems he is witnessing it now before his mind's eye—and *regression,* a subjective experience of memories, ideas, and understandings as external rather than internal events, a sense of actually returning to the past. In Chapter Seven, Case Study 6, "Divorcing the Dead," we will see the phenomenal capacity of the unconscious minds of certain individuals to return to the past with a sequential remembrance of a plethora of sensual-perceptual details.

If a family member wishes to bring a spouse or child or parent "back" to a past memory—for better or worse—he has cue words he can use, including nicknames for the person at that time, or for places or pets. Erickson and Rossi (1976) established a trance-state name for a person and found that later mention of the cue name alone could elicit trances. Because dysfunctional families tend to dwell on the past, they can easily and unnoticeably mobilize the symptom bearer's past failings as a kind of unconscious undertow that may draw him back into the family— especially when he is attempting to disengage. In the Marad family, reference to *Shoshanim,* a parochial high school David has been attending, serves this function, directing David's attention to what he has already cost his family and to what avail when he is trying to make plans for the expensive endeavor of going to college. He is thus cued in to guilt.

Out of context, this technique seems small. It might even seem unlikely to produce gasping and breathlessness in a young man with anxiety attacks. However, consider the fairy tale about Thorn Rose; the one bad witch, excluded from the birth banquet, intrudes on the event. With a simple action of pairing the princess's sleeplessness with her inevitable sixteenth birthday, the bad witch sets in force a terrible curse. Erickson recognized this power of pairing and often combined a suggestion with the future association of a person finding herself carrying it out at, for example, a next birthday or while eating an inevitable next meal. In a family in which, for example, the child is in the process of leaving home (David), or a husband is about to consider divorce (Chapter Three), the activation of aspects of that member's learnings and experiences may awaken doubtful thoughts of self and/or memories of times when others outside the family "betrayed" or failed to "come through" for them; amnesias for positive and "independent" periods of their lives may then disrupt sequences of thought, and, in a responsive subject, even trigger life-threatening psychophysiological responses. The activation of negative associations, memories, and physiological processes in conjunction with talk about plans for the future may have the power of a "curse." If, just as you move your right foot forward, I offhandedly refer to a time

when you tripped, and then quickly change subjects, you may find yourself more reluctant or cautious in moving that next step away. In the case
of David, references to past failings at Shoshanim have that untoward
effect. In the case of the young woman who thinks she has a bad body,
loneliness and past difficulties functioning on her own make her return
home to recuperate not a source of atavistic regression, not a movement
back that helps her prepare for separation, but a sign of failure for all and
a prognostic indication of likelihood of failing in the future.

Activating Unconscious Processes

Again, many of the inductive capacities described—including the
ability to draw on shared events and common reveries, to utilize cue words
charged with private associations and meanings, and the power to call
forth a certain part of self as if it were the ultimate representative of the
state of the union of the personality—can, in a symptom bearer, shepherd
unconscious processes beyond a certain psychophysiological threshold.
Two additional techniques are cited here because of their potential intensity. The first is the interspersal technique, and the second is the transmission of multiple, seemingly nullifying messages in a situation in which
the individual feels called on to transform them into some single higher-
order metamessage.

The Interspersal Technique. In Gretchen's case, (the young
woman who thinks she has a bad body), part of the therapeutic work
entails examining and evaluating in detail a family contribution to a
symptom induction. The study of the family induction helps the clinician
construct the scaffolding of therapeutic counterinduction and is a key
component of our approach. To study family hypnotic techniques in this
chapter, here we cull out select pieces of family inductive work from the
entire interview. The induction most resembles Erickson's interspersal
technique. As we mentioned earlier, the unique features of family structure provide a suggestive continuity in which, for example, an induction
initiated by one family member can, despite interruptions, be picked up at
a later moment when that family member speaks, as if nothing had occurred between speeches.

Additionally, another family member can pick up the induction
process. When several sentences converge, one may conceal the other, in
effect constructing an interspersal technique. In this technique, at least

two levels of conversation occur at once, weaving in and out of each other like two melodies. As in some scores, one or more of the melody lines is hidden, deriving its power from being in the background, less detected by the listener, unless that background suddenly becomes the primary theme.

In terms of hypnosis, to help a florist (Chapter One) deal with the pain of cancer, Erickson "sang" ostensibly only one "song," that of growing tomato plants. In this piece he "grew" the plant from seed through ground swell, stalk, leaf, bud, branch, to sun-ripened, rain-washed tomato plant. However, sprinkled throughout the tomato story was a fine rain of progressive hypnotic suggestions (a second sequential line of conversation in a different voice) about comfort, curiosity, things that work, listening without seeing or hearing, feeling more and more comfortable each day, desiring to have food in one's stomach, and taking one day at a time. It was the *embedded* message Erickson most hoped would get through to the subject's *unconscious* mind (Erickson, 1966).

In Gretchen's case, the messages from mother and father together have the effect of an interspersal technique. The family is talking about Gretchen coming home, why she has to come home. While *consciously* the family is discussing past events and problem times when Gretchen had trouble on her own, interspersed throughout is a message about loneliness, how unbearable life is, and even thoughts of taking one's life. Following is a synthesis of mother's and father's speeches across twenty minutes in a sesssion. The embedded lines of unintentionally interspersed *suggestion* to Gretchen in the mother-and-father speech are in italics.

Father: Umm—I am a little bit leery. I think Gretchen has a *hard time functioning* on her own (voice lowers and speech becomes slower while looking at Gretchen). . . .

Mother: She found it *lonely* here *where we live* . . .

Father: Yah. You see, for a while there she was staying with that elderly lady and for a while she was *alone* up here. We didn't know what time the college started up here and she came up a week earlier. And, *she was alone in the house* and I don't think it is best for her. . . . I didn't want her to come back, but then she would be better off at home. . . .

Mother: I *worry* about her, especially like—even when she is at home— when she cut her wrist, she *did it at home* and I am scared of what she would do if *she will do it*—maybe not, like, I think suicides are usually accidents. They try to prove something (nervous laugh). They do a good job, and I am *afraid*—like, I cannot imagine going and *finding her really hurt or dead,* like that bothers me. She says she won't do it anymore. . . .

Father: No—but I think that Gretchen has a *hard time* if she lives alone. I guess everybody gets *lonely,* but she has a *harder time* to function on her own, I guess. . . . I think the story with me—I *try to ignore* the fact that she wants to take her life because *I cannot understand it.* Personally, I am an optimist and *I cannot understand* why anybody would want to take their lives. You know what I mean?

Mother: I know *it's serious.* I can understand, in a way. When I was fourteen, *life* at home was *unbearable.* . . . (To Gretchen, leaning forward, gazing intensely into her eyes) And, I tried to—*I took* a whole bunch of *aspirins.* I took too many and so *all I did was get sick.* I just threw up. And, every time *I take an aspirin now,* my stomach goes yecch because I remember the taste of throwing up twenty-two aspirins. *And, life is so unbearable* and I can understand that feeling of *anything is better than living,* in me, but I *cannot understand* it in you because I am good (looks into Gretchen's eyes) to you and dad's good to you and we love you and we don't fight and I don't go out with men and I don't drink and dad doesn't beat me up. And that is why *life was unbearable* at home. Because my mother called me a whore and I was a virgin. Just because—I don't know why. And so, I don't understand it—like I don't understand—*I can understand life being unbearable* but I don't understand why it would be for you. Because, the circumstances aren't the same. And yet, if you believe that *life is unbearable,* why, why is *life unbearable,* and how can I help you to make it bearable? That's why I said to you, if you come home, one of the conditions is that we have to continue to see the therapist until you're better, because *I cannot handle it* on my own. Because *I don't know how.* You are a Christian and we are Christians. And you know that *the only reason to live is to go to heaven afterwards,* and if you *take your own life,* there is no—it makes it *hard for me to understand.* Because, that is *not right* as a Christian to feel that way. If I was a Christian then, I wouldn't have done it when I was a kid.

Father: Well . . . *even to carry those thoughts in your mind is not right* (shaken, biting lip).

Mother: And, I have to help you or else your being home would be *too hard on me* if *I can't help you* and you help me. And, I don't know why.

Why do you *feel* so *angry?* Do you *feel angry* because you *don't feel well* (crying)? Why *don't* you *feel well? Like—physically, emotionally? You know that we are a lot alike, you and I.* We have a lot of feelings the same and what makes me different from you—like, how did I cope and *you don't.*

Father: Well, I can understand that a person *gets depressed* once in a while. This is understandable. (To Gretchen) I do understand that you *do get depressed* sometimes, but why so *depressed* that you want to *take your life?* That's one thing I don't understand. So, *things don't always go the way we want them to go* and then we have a *hard time* dealing with problems here and there. It is no reason to *think about taking your life,* though. That is something I just *cannot understand* (bites lip, folds arms, holds back tears).

We will discuss this case in detail in Chapter Six. The point for this moment is that while mother and father are making every effort to dissuade their daughter from hurting them and herself, their tone and approach, their two voices converging, carry an interspersed message, which in the context of a family failing financially, feeling depressed and inadequate, carries an inadvertant suggestive power of feeling lonely, that life is unbearable, and so on. The sequences do culminate in the girl's feeling guilty, angry, and afraid rather than eager to carry on in the face of life's challenges.

Reconciling Multiple and Incongruous Messages. Gretchen's symptoms are partly an attempt to reconcile two *different* messages from each of her parents, one being father's feeling that if his daughter comes home for a rest he is a failure, the other being that if daughter comes home, it must cue mother into infantilizing her. The young woman, eager to come home, and herself having a mind-set of failure because she has not been a super student at college, reconciles these different messages into a single metamessage. In the seemingly bizarre logic of her symptomatic solution, she comes home suicidal and "disguised" as a three-year-old child with a stuffed animal.

Manifestation of Physiological and Psychological Phenomena

Of course, the proof of the induction is in the seemingly automatic activation of symptom components. This kind of family inductive process is difficult to learn to "catch." Certainly, in Minuchin's psychosomatic research (Minuchin, Rosman, and Baker, 1978), we can see that the activation of parental conflict culminates in an alteration in the blood contents of the superlabile diabetic child and that this alteration is followed by or induces a calming state, manifested by a decrease in the level of free fatty acids in the parents' bloodstream. In the case of a young man with hemophilia (Chapter Five), we will see that affecting the young man's symptom structure, including components of family inductive processes, leads to a decrease in the frequency of his need for transfusions and in the quantity of factor needed per transfusion. In Chapter Six, for Gretchen, we will see that as her parents focus inward when describing her loneliness, she becomes guilt-ridden and ashamed, two cardinal features of her depression and wish to kill herself. Earlier in this chapter, we saw how Arthur, who would not talk, first produces phrases, then words, monosyllabic responses, and ultimately grunts, and becomes inwardly absorbed and unresponsive to the therapist even as she practically turns herself on her head to look into his eyes for some nonverbal cue. Now we look at a family contribution to induction of components of David Marad's symptoms.

The author regards this interview as one of those lucky windows onto symptomatology because family inductions do not always follow the Erickson-Rossi induction paradigm so well. Often families do not need to. The following list summarizes the family inductive capacities and techniques described thus far. Note that any of these techniques may be transformed into therapeutic counterinductive tools. In fact, such a transformation is a basic part of the present approach.

1. *Establishing rapport: "Be alone with me."*
   a. Public versus private dichotomy
   b. Family we-ness techniques or consensus
2. *Focusing attention inward: "Look inside yourself."*
   a. Denial that there is a family system (there is only personality): sequence stopping; effects of sequences as proof of individual problem
   b. Denial of or inattention to symptom sustaining aspects of family context
   c. Shared common history
   d. Family usage of spontaneously occurring reveries
   e. Emotional and suggestive continuity

3. *Confusion techniques of families: "You're not certain, are you?"*
    a. Structure versus content
    b. Nullifying hierarchical messages
    c. Parts-of-self inductions
    d. Blurring of boundaries
    e. Description directives
4. *Initiating unconscious search—suggestive continuity: "Think along these lines."*
    a. Cue words
    b. Associative pairing of past events to future projections
    c. Shared history; also public versus private
5. *Mobilizing personal associations leading to activation of symptom components*
    a. Interspersal
    b. Integrating seemingly incongruent messages
    c. Parts of self; also cue words

A Family Induction of Symptom Components

Reading family inductions is a skill the therapist applies to create therapeutic counterinductions. Family inductions are part of what the client brings to the therapist, a feature of the hard-earned problem. By reading how family contributions activate symptom components, the therapist can plan how to *use* those suggestive channels to introduce new transforming suggestions. In observing an inductive moment, the therapist notes contributing hierarchical problems and identifies rigid or trespassed individual boundaries. She then uses her observations to initiate an idiosyncratic counterinductive process to help family members work in asymptomatic, nonintrusive concert with each other. Let us look at segments of a family therapy session within which an induction of the symptom bearer takes place. The case entails classic leaving-home conflicts. For this family, the challenges of separation are intensified by illness and economic problems, both chronic.

This is the case of David Marad, seventeen years old. He and his family came to therapy after David threw a piece of furniture at his mother several months ago. She had said that he could live part of the week with a cousin, and then she verbally and physically blocked his way when he tried to do so. Their battle ended and his symptomatic condition began formally with the throwing of the furniture.

David is the only son of a sixty-year-old traveling salesman who has recently begun to suffer from Parkinson's, a disease of progressive physical and psychological deterioration, and his wife, a fifty-year-old homemaker who has spent most of her married life raising David. David has always hoped to go to college.

At this important crossroad between considerable dependency on a specific family organization and movement toward a new, broad, and unfamiliar social context, David is suddenly "unable to think logically from one idea to the next," and fears "he is losing everything." Although repeated medical examinations have confirmed David's excellent physical condition, he believes that his intense stomach pain is an ulcer and that his gripping chest pains and trouble breathing indicate undetected heart disease.

We are looking at the fifth interview. The family has already made certain changes. Nevertheless, as described earlier in "Denying Significant Aspects of Family Context" (pp. 90–91), the basic family hierarchy of relating is manifested by the most rigidly repeated sequence of interactions: father son mother interrupting son mother son mother son mother and so on. This pattern (Figure 9) enacts one of the hierarchies of family functioning.

In this hierarchy, David is allied, if negatively, with mother, and he is acting as a surrogate husband, rescuer, and well-matched combatant while father sits helplessly or relieved on the sidelines. The therapist

Figure 9. Primary Hierarchy in Marad Family.

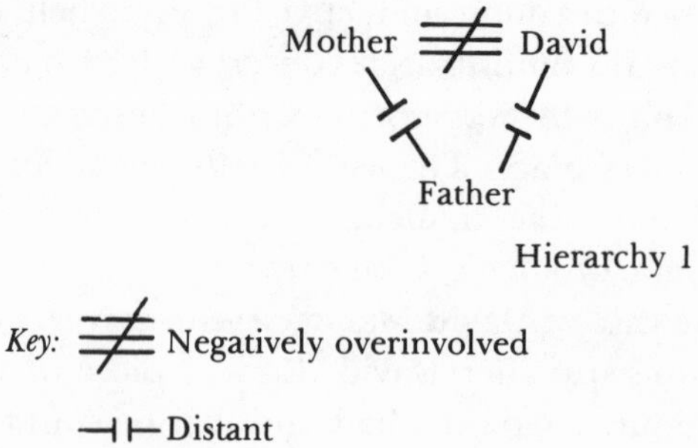

Mother ≢ David

Father

Hierarchy 1

Key: ≢ Negatively overinvolved

⊣⊢ Distant

recognizes that she must intervene in the sequences that enact this hierarchy because they send messages to David about a kind of overly important role he is needed to play on the homefront that will not help him go to college. An additional hierarchy of family life is available to be activated (Figure 10), although it too is currently abused and contributes to the family power to use various forms of the nullifying hierarchical confusion techniques. Hierarchy 2 represents an economic subsystem of the family. In this subset of family interaction, father is the sole breadwinner and does have the final say on family finances. In this domain, he and mother confer about "carrying" David, but in a manner that renders their "superhero" from hierarchy 1 a helpless, dependent baby.

The therapist knows that one of her goals is to have either father or mother make a financial proposal to David for mature discussion or to have David and father negotiate and then have father talk with mother. However, at this point, despite her knowledge of goals, the therapist too is organized by the family suggestive power. (Therapist dialogue is omitted to reduce the length of this section.) Basically, until the end of the segments we examine, she inadvertently maintained the structural-induction process.

The interview we are considering occurs at a moment of tremendous family separation anxiety. If David is to go to college, he has two days to make the registration deadline. In examining family inductive segments from this interview, we identify specific symptom inductive steps enacted by the family, in keeping with the Erickson-Rossi induction

Figure 10. Secondary Hierarchy in Marad Family.

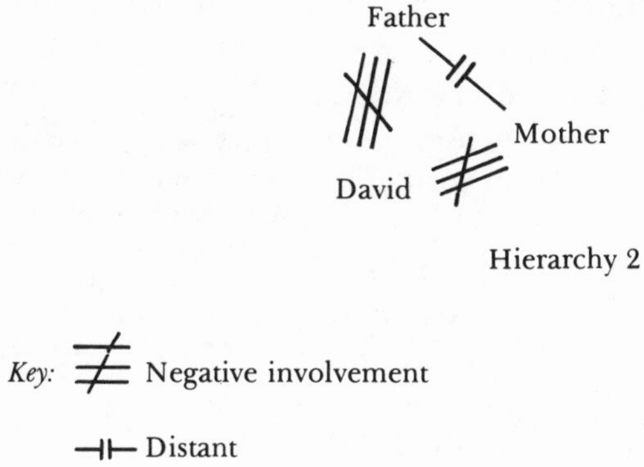

Hierarchy 2

Key: ≠ Negative involvement

⊣⊢ Distant

paradigm. The induction culminates in David saying, "I feel definitely crazy, like I've lost my mind." As in any inductive process, both inducers and induced are locked into a certain existential contract with one another and are affected by the experiential process. The induced response carries on as a stimulus of its own as well. For our limited purposes here, we focus on only the intensification of David's (not his parents') symptom components as our end point. Likewise, David's special symptom states can be seen as a starting point for both problematic family sequences and therapeutic sequences. We focus here on the exterior side of the symptom activation: the family contribution.*

Step 1: Establishing Rapport and Focusing Inward

The purpose of this session was to discuss family finances and clarify the parents' expectations for David regarding his contribution to college costs. However, the session opens with mother and father talking about illness. Remember that David's parents' illnesses may have special meaning for David because of his own mental-set *and* the hierarchies of the family life he inhabits.

In step 1, we assume that there is intense rapport between family members (although we see evidence of it as the interview progresses). Most importantly, we look for the general transmission of unconscious or indirect messages that constitute the hypnotic atmosphere and then for the focusing of David's attention inward. (Explanatory comments are to the right of the dialogue.)

Mother: (to therapist) I missed the last appointment because when the weather gets like I described to you the pain became more intense . . . uh, it lasted for about a day or so after I had spoken with you, and then it went away. Well actually, from the arthritis I have a chronic, a very dull pain all the time, but I've gotten so used to it, that I don't feel it any more. So now, it's just the usual, dull

Ostensibly mother explains to therapist why she missed the last session. Nevertheless, her "usual dull pain" lingers as a point of attention, especially when called "nothing" and yet contrasted with "good news" about Norman. Certain sad feelings might be initiated in a person like David who sizes up his own sense of well being by using his mother as a mirror.

*The symptom bearer can also be considered as a hypnotist of the family. This part of the model remains to be developed.

pain, which is nothing. But we had good news the other night, Norman goes to his doctor quarterly for a checkup for his Parkinson's, and the doctor is changing Norman's medication to one that is newer and more effective and more concentrated than Dopamine, because apparently, over the past couple of months . . . his condition has gotten a little worse.

The therapist, to shift respectfully from the real illness problems to the other school considerations, asks who in the family told David about dad's new drug. Her second interest is to find out whether David and dad are communicating more directly.

Father: Well, actually, mom got to the house first after the doctor's appointment, and I had to go upstairs to get washed, so while I was doing this, she was filling him in. So actually, I was . . . . But one good thing about it is that *David shouldn't feel guilt.* If I don't feel well, it's due, frequently due to my condition, it has nothing to do with David. (Therapist motions for father to tell this directly to David) You don't have to *have feelings of guilt,* which I know you do on occasion. There are dentists and surgeons also who have this condition, and they're able to go on . . . that's phenomenal. The medication controls the condition and they're able to go on.

Mother and David have talked, not father and David. From physical illness, suffering of mother and father, and all the feelings activated by raising the specter of these issues, father now focuses it all inward on David.

Unconsciously he suggests "guilt." His message has the unintended effect of saying "Don't think about the ocean." We must at least initially picture "ocean" to "try" to "forget it."

David: Gasps and sighs.

Part of David's problem is anxiety attacks and severe chest pains. Spontaneous alterations in his respiratory patterns suggest a possible initiation of part of this unconsciously activated process.

At the focusing of father inward into David's emotional life, David spontaneously gasps, gulps, and sighs. Whereas the trance subject might take a deep breath, David manifests components of his symptom of "difficulty breathing." It is as if he were responding to a directive, "Look inward and think of something guilt-inducing."

Mother now introjects a speech about father and work, which has a certain innuendo about financial pressures. Her speech structurally breaks up the father-son interaction and also breaks up father's inadvertent guilt induction. Looked at as an *interspersal technique,* mother's speech renders father's message *less detectable* and *more inductively effective.*

Mother: . . . observed the change—there's been a slowing down. His condition—do you mind, dear, if I talk about it, or would you rather . . . is that all right? has gotten a little worse. He's been up since like 5:00 this morning, so . . . . Anyway, so that it reached a point where Norm's body became conditioned.

If this is the good news, what is the bad news? The listener detects just below the thin-surface message of "We're hanging in there" a frigid anxiety.

Father: I've sort of slowed down—my speech, my . . . .

Mother: Which the doctor explained is natural, when the thing loses its effectiveness. Everything kind of slows down, the movement of the eyes, the walking, etc.

Again, mother's style of whisking away the seriousness of a problem she herself introduced. This is all "natural."

Father: And my eyes are constantly tearing. This is due to the condition. . . . Specifically, my mind, right arm, right leg, and my speech have been impaired by this condition, and this new medicine should be very good.

Had the listener considered it due to something else: Clearly, father's *tone* is inadvertently one of deep-seated fear, not hope.

Mother: Yeah, it's been on the market for like nine months, but the doctor didn't give it to Norm because

. . . he didn't want to use Norm as a guinea pig. . . . But he's found it's been terrific (tone of pseudojoviality). It's like a real miracle drug. If I may say something with regard to this, the doctor said, as we checked out about Norm's working hours, which are very long, and the driving that he does all day long, you know, how this is affecting his condition, and the doctor said that this is the best thing that Norm could be doing. . . . when a person is motivated, you can lead a very normal life. If a person is not motivated and has this condition, you know, you can get so comfortable with it that you can become, you know, like a vegetable, and the fact that Norman is a motivated person and likes to go to work. . . .

Father: I'm crazy about it! (Sarcastic)

Mother: Well . . . you know, no one has said, "well, Norman, you have to go to work." He wants to go.

This phrase of "terrific" in a not so terrific situation captures the saddening power of mother's self-consolations and efforts to "keep it all together."

From mother's and father's incongruent duet about work, father goes on to talk about stress. Because of *suggestive continuity*, his messages will tend to pick up where he left off in his last exchange with David, in which he had mentioned that David need not feel guilt.

Father: Every kind of stress will, to some extent, affect the condition, that's true of anybody's condition (looking at David) . . . when you're under stress, even if you have no disease. It will affect you in some way.

Is David affecting his father's status by stressing him?

Mother: The doctor said it's a *con-tributing* factor, but it does not create the condition or maintain it or anything, but it *contributes* to, you know, the tension, you know, with any muscle condition there's tension . . . .

One wonders is "it" the problems David is bringing on with his emotional problems and economic demands?

Father: Every condition and illness is affected by stress . . . .

David: (Anxiously to therapist and gasping for air) How long is this session? When can I see you alone?

Note in phase 1 of the induction of guilt and inability to think, father has shifted the discussion from his condition to a focus inside David and raised the issue of guilt. Mother has then interrupted the father-son dyadic interaction, changing the subject back to father's condition. Starting to get confused and focusing inward about guilt, David begins to feel uneasy. Finally, both parents end up implying that something about David is, in fact, stressing his father and worsening his condition. Unable to respond, David requests to leave the arena and be seen alone. The induction continues.

Step 2: Activating Doubt or Confusion

In the next segment, the family awakens self-doubt, initiating for David a process of inner search that begins to bypass his conscious ways of thinking. Besides the ongoing enactment of mother-son overinvolvement, mother's disregard for what father says, father's peripheral role, the constant shifting in subject matter to related subjects, note how mother—at a moment of David's turning inward, full of uncertainty about his abilities—asks him to *consider further along this doubting line of reasoning.* "If you can't work, can you go to college at all?"

The therapist has asked father to talk with son about the financial questions of registration.

Father: (To therapist, not David) Last session, we had a discussion about, uh, finances and things, like what David would like to do or wouldn't like to do . . . . In fact, I would really like to hear David talk about that. I don't know whether David accepts the proposals that I made. David is at a point of life where he's becoming an adult, and he has to have an opinion as to what he's going to do. Does he want to go to college, can he work while he's going to college? These things which would make going to college possible, and also reduce our sharing, reduce some of the stress and strain that has to do with me.

Tone is one of doubting self and David, of a future overcast with inevitable if mildly reducible stress and strain.

David: Dad (gulping), I just don't know if I can work going to college; in fact, I'm almost sure I can't if I feel the way I do now. It's enough just going to sleep and living, but I'm having a hard time doing anything, the way I feel now. I'm trying to get a job, but I just don't know if I'll be able . . . I'll see how I feel, I guess. If I feel like I do right now, there's no way I could work during . . . when I go to college. I just wouldn't go then.

David now reveals his interior reflection of outer uncertainties. He spontaneously expresses self-doubt, an emotional manifestation of his doubting his mental and physical intactness, perhaps intensified by his automatic and seemingly uncontrollable gasping and gulping. David is searching inward with an expanding sense of self-doubt about whether he can *both work and go to school*. Because of his own mental set, partly activated by his position in his family's hierarchy 2, he indicates he could not do both.

Mother: (To David, with hostile edge in her voice) Well, dear, will you be able to handle the responsibilities of college?

David: (looking down, head in hands, expressing great self-doubt) I don't know . . . I really don't know.

Son's focus is inward, his reasoning thrown off-balance with doubt. Now Mother suggests he *doubt further* along those same associative lines.

Step 3: Initiating an Unconscious Search

As David moves from doubting whether he can hold a job *and* go to school to doubting whether he can handle college at all, mother begins a revivification of past school failings, which seem to have the effect of indirect forms of suggestions. She is drawing on shared history.

Note that besides thinking about past failures, David is again enacting structurally his intense overinvolvement with his mother by fighting with her. This is a conflict that reverberates along their umbilical cord; it does not help them separate. Also, although David's anger is an active coping and self-defending attempt, not simply a carrying out of family directives, it does not work.

Mother: (To therapist) Academic excellence has always been his strength. It's just that in recent years, David has stopped doing homework and study and reading; that's what I'm concerned about. In eleventh grade, this was also, it was already, you know, starting, except . . . .

As David is now "suggested" to think dubiously about his capacities to handle future college work, this suggestion is paired with past failings, such as those in the eleventh grade. Note that it is hard for David to stop mother because she is ostensibly explaining to the therapist, not talking with David.

David: (To mother) Another thing I gotta say to that, you know . . .

Mother: (To therapist) Except at the age where, you know, by getting . . .

David and mother enact their structural overinvolvement and the hidden messages of proximity and connectedness it suggests.

David: (Interrupting mother, in a louder voice and more upset) Mom . . . mom! I don't want this to go on. I don't want you talking about my work.

Mother: (To David) I have a right to my . . .

David: (To mother, louder still) I don't feel I want to say, "Mom, I did work! I don't have to be a dog having to defend myself!"

The structure carries the message of the overly central position of the son.

Mother: (To David) You did the last quarter.

David: (To mother, much louder and more upset) I don't want to have to have—to have that thrown back to me by you. I don't have to say why I did, I did it, and I don't have to convince you of anything!

Although David is trying to resist this suggestive undertow, his anger, getting out of control, is a component of his symptom, which included throwing furniture at his mother.

Mother: (To therapist, sweetly, *not* to David) I would *like* David to go to college, if he could demonstrate a willingness to take the time out to really do studies and this kind of work, and keep notes and records. I mean, if he could demonstrate that, I think that's the best thing for him, because this *is* where David's excellence has always been. I mean, he's not mechanically handy . . . this is where it is, as far as, you know, his excellence is, and I'm in favor of, providing he is willing to demonstrate that he's going to do these things. Then, I think it would be great. This is where he belongs. We have always geared him in this direction. In fact, as a result of being so college-oriented and education-oriented, I have overlooked other areas of practical things in teaching David, which is not such a terrific thing to do. I'm not sure David is sure . . . .

As David gets increasingly agitated (while trying to defend himself from mother's agitating comments), mother's tone gets colder and pseudojovial, as if erasing her provocation, which temporally preceded David's upset. Ultimately this complementary process intensifies David's feelings of craziness. He is left with his rage and no external justification for it.

Backhanded compliment to herself and David.

David: It isn't that I'm not sure what to do, it's the way I feel now, I can't do anything. I have a hard enough time sitting in my room listening to music without feeling like hell. And going to sleep. I don't see how I can do anything else right now, the way I feel. It's not being

"Feeling now" is associatively paired with planning for "then." David now locks into doubts about whether he can do anything.

realistic. See, if I felt better, I'd . . . it
would still be very hard, but let's not
kid ourselves. It's unbelievably hard
now. The way I feel now. I'm gonna
have to start feeling better if I'm
gonna do that. *There's no way I can
go to college feeling the way I do at
this moment,* if I feel like I do now.
There's absolutely no way. I'm telling you . . . .

Again, David now spontaneously
pairs his present state with future
feelings. Now he definitely cannot
even go to college.

It is at this point of utter uncertainty and inner turmoil for David—
as he struggles to both accommodate and fight his family situation and
the thoughts in his head—that father introjects a message about their
financial reality. Under ordinary circumstances, father's message might
clarify things, but in the present undertow of indirect and unconsciously
transmitted messages, it further activates unsettling psychological phenomena in David.

Father: I would like David to go to
college, but it should have a realistic
outlook. I don't think we can make it
if we don't get some help from him.

David: And I'm saying that, look, *if I
felt better, I could do it,* it would be
hard to do it, but I'd have to do it. If I
don't feel better, I just don't . . .
there's no way . . . look, I'm gonna
have it . . . it's gonna be almost impossible for me to handle college, I'm
telling you honestly. And if I feel like
this (gasping), I couldn't even handle
college; and handle a job also, it's
impossible. I really don't feel like college, and I'm telling you, I just can't
do it. I'm not asking you to put up
extra money and put yourself under
more pressure, I'm just telling you: I

David doubts more.

"Forget that I stressed you, I quit."
David struggles in an attempt to
reconcile conflicting messages. He
manifests unconscious or automatic
psychological cooperation

just can't do it; the way I feel now. Let's see how I feel a month later (gulping) . . . from now. It's not normal "feeling bad." It's . . . you don't know what it feels like! It feels like I'm in a different reality now, that's what it feels like. You know, this feeling bad, that's a mild way to put it. It's like you've lost everything you've ever had.

with indirect family messages of doubt *while* he consciously struggles to escape their influence.

David is now manifesting and expressing the crazy feelings and thoughts that have impinged on him since he decided to go to college. He is full of doubt. He is periodically gasping and occasionally gulping. At this moment mother again shifts the interview's tone and content. Her impact is not unlike that of the hypnotist who changes the subject and tone, creating an amnesia for earlier suggestions and thereby intensifying their indirect power.

At this point mother also uses cue words, including "Shoshanim" and "garage sales," which implicitly cue David to personal associations of parental sacrifice for David's good and of David's failures and disloyalty. Ultimately, mother and David argue as if the past were happening now. Note how David and mother are lost in a shared revivification of dead-end memories.

Step 4: Initiating an Unconscious Search by Using Indirect Forms of Suggestion or Words or Events with Certain Implications

Mother: There is a realistic thing that we have to contend with. Two days from now, David will be registering. Which is great! I think it is terrific that we're going to have the money, now (pauses dramatically, dropping cigarette ashes in ashtray) in the bank . . . make out the check . . . and he'll have that, $325 on Friday. We've been making sacrifices for

Ignoring father's financial statement, mother structurally now ostensibly allies with son, acting as if they had not just fought and as if David had not just said he cannot go to college.

five years while he went to Shoshanim and somehow, we survived,
because it was a positive thing. David
was getting something out of the
school; he has a skill, if he wishes to
use it, so we feel that it was to his
advantage . . . . So we, uh, you know,
I went to *garage sales* and so forth,
but we didn't mind. We would continue if David could, you know,
could demonstrate that, you know,
he's gonna buckle down and start,
you know, doing something!

"Shoshanim" and "garage sales"
are cue words to David. They activate a sense of guilt about what his
education has cost his parents.

It is no mistake that the original
family conflict that rendered David
a symptom bearer erupted with
David throwing at his mother *a
piece of her own garage sale
furniture!*

David: Look, I just don't know if I
can! I mean you don't know how I
feel! You don't . . . .

Mother: David, that's good, I like to
hear what . . . you know. I enjoy the
garage sales! I have fun, I really do.

David: I bet you do.

Content-structure confusion technique. The content suggests that he
proceed toward college. The structure, enacted, pulls him developmentally backward into
problematic family affairs.

Father: (Half-heartedly to therapist)
This is a natural thing that goes on
all over the United States. There's no
reason he should feel guilty.

Again, the "don't think about
guilt" chorus interspersed
throughout.

Mother: It's a fun thing . . . .

David: I do feel guilty!

Guilt is activated.

Mother: Well, a lot of people go to
garage sales, honey, and they pick up
fine plastic, and it's cheap, and . . . .

Garage sales again.

David: (Yelling, as if in desperate
effort to make sense) Yeah, but that's
a bad comparison. Will you let me
talk, instead of goin' on and on and
on without saying anything? We're
not rich people, and the reason
you're going to a garage sale is

David *seems* to be defending himself. But *psychophysiologically, he
is not succeeding.* He is gasping for
air, screaming, grabbing his chest,
vividly recalling years when he
disappointed his mother and she
activated his mind-set of guilt and
so on.

because you don't have enough
money to go to a department store,
and that makes me feel guilty. And
many times during those years when
you got upset with me and thought I
wasn't doing my work, you hung it
over my head and made me feel
guilty, and I'll never forget those
times . . . as long as I live. . . . You
made me feel so bad. You made me
feel like s. . . .

Mother: Well, I felt that you should
cooperate. I mean, dad and I were
doing our share, and all we wanted
you . . . .

David: No, you made me feel guilty.

Mother: That's not asking too much!

David: You made me feel guilty.
When I got a B average in tenth
grade, you made me feel guilty.
When I flunked two tests, you made
me feel guilty.

Mother: I made you feel guilty?

David: You made me feel guilty. You
stormed into my room one night
when I flunked—when I flunked my
second test and the first test, and you
didn't let me hear the end of it.

Mother: What test?

David: Chemistry.

Mother: Oh, chemistry. But I got a
tutor for you and you passed chemistry, dear.

David: That wasn't my point. You
never seem to see my point . . . .

Again, structurally the messages
conveyed by an uninterrupted
mother   David   mother
David   mother   David
mother sequence simultaneously
activate mother and David's continuing symptom-sustaining
overinvolvement.

Revivification and emotional regression through shared events.

Note that the increasing *specificity*
renders the recollection more concrete, palpable, and real, much as
in Chapter Six, where a *counterinduction* with the *smell of daisies*
reifies associations of hope.

Mother: That was very constructive!

David: That wasn't my ... that isn't my point!

Mother: So you were not relating to chemistry.

David: That is not my point!

Mother: What *is* your point, David?

David: My point is, you made me feel guilty about math (gasping) ... about flunking.

Mother: You never told me about that. Why didn't you discuss it with me? I like to know your feelings.

David: If you had a brain, you could realize you made me feel guilty.

Mother: (To therapist) Well, David knows it's not his fault life is hard, because as I ... well, David, he knows that dad and I, and this is living proof, David, *as far back as you can remember,* before you went to Shoshanim, it does not take very much of anything to make us happy. Whatever we do, we're happy, and we don't have to spend a lot of money to do it. We did not spend a lot of money before you went to Shoshanim, and we continued not to, even when you went to Shoshanim. *So maybe we had a few more dollars in the bank.* You know, and that was it. *But* money doesn't make for happiness, and that is one thing we've taught you, from the time you were a little kid, that you do not have to have a lot of money to be happy, and

Mother doth protest too much, and in the confusing doubletalk of "It pains me but it's nothing."

we're living proof of that. And, uh
... You shouldn't feel guilty, honey,
'cause we . . . .

David: I've always felt like this . . .
Oh, I don't know.

Mother: We have always, uh, you
know, we have a creative household;
we don't have very expensive posses-
sions around the house . . . .

David: Well the reason I feel like I
should . . .

Mother: We have fun things that I
can . . . .

David: The reason I feel . . . .

Mother: and I enjoy it.

David: Can you let me talk?

Mother: Yeah.

David: The reason I feel I should not
feel guilty is because you agreed to
this. You're the one who agreed to do
this; I didn't force you to do this; you
did this.

Mother: Yeah (not listening).

David: Well, let me finish (gasping
and thumping his chest uncontrollably)! You won't let anyone finish. . . .
And now I can't even think anymore
. . . I can't think. . . . You talk and
talk. It gets me angry. . . . Why can't
you stick with one point. I . . . my
chest . . . .

Mother: We are sticking with one
point . . . about your guilt feelings.

Mother's voice picks up the "don't
feel guilt" chorus.

Perhaps he has always felt like this.
Amnesia for all other feelings.

Symptom components, including
difficulty breathing, trouble thinking straight, and uncontrolled
anger, are in progress.

What happened to college
registration?

Finally, the last inductive segments mobilize and bring together
the many melody lines to synthesize preceding suggestive effects. They

culminate in a full-blown spontaneous manifestation of David's symptoms.

Step 5: Activating Unconscious Processes

David: Don't you see . . . you used to always hang it on me about goin' to Shoshanim and whenever you got upset, you threw it out my backside. Whenever you got upset. You always did that. Now don't tell me you didn't; I remember!

"Remember, you contributed to all this . . . how I feel now . . . I think . . . somehow . . . ."

Mother: For the simple reason, David, after the first year that you went, I told you it was gonna be very tight for us, that we could somehow manage, but it was going to be a really tight way to live, and dad went and got an application at Central. You remember? And you went into one of those tantrums . . . .

"Go on and nearly break us like you did before and without being grateful" is one of the indirect messages David might be getting.

David: The reason I . . . first of all . . .

Mother: As a result of it, I . . . decided to continue . . . for you to go to Shoshanim . . . so we can help. I mean, we can help him. You know, like half, or as much, whatever we can afford. But, he will have to supplement the rest. It's reached that point—a few years ago . . . we have $600 left in the bank. Uh, inflation, I don't have to tell you the way it is now. We live very modestly, actually, and yet, like most families today, it's hard to make ends meet. Now, we feel that we could help David, like maybe pay half of it, but David has to help.

Now, in the symptomatic trance, money is discussed concretely and benevolently in terms of "meaning."

For two reasons; not only because we need it financially, I think the college will have more meaning for him. If he's not going to do his work, I feel that . . . .

David: You're really putting a burden on me by doing that.

Mother: Well, we don't . . . we just don't have the money to put out, anymore. On the basis of one semester. Uh, we certainly, I think we could probably handle the whole thing, until David . . . .

Father: The thing that I put forth was not only in planning for help to help me, but also to help with David's negative manner, because he contributes, he takes a stand. So we shouldn't lose sight of the fact, David, that if you do, if you are able to get a part-time job, and you can choose toward your own education, you're really a hunk of man, and much more son than . . . .

Manhood, money, stressing father all converge, each full of suggestive meanings.

David: You have to be able to do that. Look, I'm having a tough time just living, I just don't think I can do that. Yeah, but you don't understand how I feel.

Mother: David is right, but also . . . .

Father: We're in a position . . . .

Mother: David is voicing something . . . .

Father: We're in a position to help for six months. After that, our money runs out.

Mother: Yeah, we can carry David for the first semester, totally, if need be. After that, we don't . . . the only money we could have would be from the income tax refund, which I was planning to fix that room with, I told them . . . .

The infantilizing of David is evoked by indicating that his parents can totally "carry him" financially.

David: (To therapist) Listen, I'm really . . . Could we have this thing over, I really want to talk to you.

Father: (To therapist) So, I'd like to say . . . I would do anything for this kid, and so would my wife, but it's only possible . . . because of my condition, changed, my physical condition has changed, and that makes a big difference. I don't have that pizzazz that I used to have (containing himself).

Back to the father's condition— "Now don't feel guilt!"

David: Maybe your new drug can bring it back; I hope so.

Mother: Well, I'm very optimistic. I mean, we had put that money away just for David's college, I mean, for nothing else. That $600 was for David's college. We had a little bit more, which you know, we had to spend since then, but that was for that purpose, that money, no other purpose, as far as I know. Wasn't it dear, that we had put that aside?

Father: Right.

Mother: That's all we have left.

"Go ahead, take all your parents have left."

Father: I think that David, things will be easier for David if he takes a stand, and he's every bit as tough as his old man is. The legendary toughness that I'm supposed to have is nothing compared to—David's every bit as t-t-tough as I am, or I was, or tougher. I have dreams . . . (bursts into tears).

Mother: It's okay . . . .

David: Are you okay, dad? (Gasping, twitching, gesturing ineffectually, thumping his chest, and uncontrollably gulping) Dad!

We might analyze the same induction in terms of activation of symptom component of mother or father in this case. However, we assume the symptom that has been offered to the therapist epitomizes a central conflict. Shifts in family structure and individual mind-set vis-a-vis the symptom bearer is therefore often our *best* entry into the whole symptom structure.

Despite conscious "insight" into his parents' induction of guilt, David is defenseless. Induced by the family structure, David cannot sustain a look outside himself to see major problems in the spouse subsystem, that is, between mother and father concerning, among other things, mother's fear and anger at father for being a poor provider. The bad trance is so powerful that David can find no way out and experiences as "autonomously occurring" both his physical symptoms and psychological confusion.

After the induction process, the inductive moment is erased. The conflict, the confusing messages, the emotional intensity, all evidence of external provocation, have gone in the amnesia-producing flow as the family moves on in the more routine style of family life. Mother says:

Mother: David is terrific, though. He's the only one who doesn't know it. David is a terrific person; we know it. We're not tough people. We believe in the gentle approach, to be loving and firm in a gentle way . . . and all that stuff.

Father: We just want David to . . . turn out better than I did.

Mother: Well, I think you're the greatest human being, so I'm sorry. I think . . .

David: Well, there's something wrong with my mind.

David is left with his own profound symptomatic state. Shortly after this inductive disappearance, David describes the interior aspects of the family inductive process. *Possible* exterior events that may be mirrored in David's internal experience are cited on the right side of the pages.

David: It's like my mind is off somewhere else. Like mostly mine. That's what I feel like. You know, I don't . . . this worries me . . . things are jumping out at you and things are just jumping around. It's like you still see the same thing, if you look at something carefully, you see different spaces, it's just little different spaces. That must be an anxiety. I wish it would go the hell away, you know. I can't . . . I wonder . . . I . . . I feel definitely crazy or something like that, you know. Or like I've lost my mind. All these sensitive feelings—there's something wrong with my head! There's something wrong! I don't know what it is, but there's something wrong. I don't know what it is! I mean, it seems to me my head's being pushed from different sides. It's like there's different people in me, one that hates me and one that likes me. Look, I have all kinds of pains and it feels like my body's curling up, and it's terrible! It could destroy a person. As long as I feel open to them, open

The wish to escape but nowhere safe or known to escape to.

Uncertainty about the changing relational spaces.

Feeling too open, too occupied with family life. David's psychic retreat has become property rental for his family. He is—even in reflecting—out of his mind.

Interiorization of conflicting hierarchies of family life, parental disagreements, disagreements from his own self-suggestions and mind-set and from the collective family suggestive processes.

feelings is the worst thing that I can
... That open feeling ... I don't
know if it's all psychological for this
being anxiety, but not for that reason, because I'm, you know, vulnerable, and that makes it open. Can this
be part of anxiety? ... I can't control
the thoughts that go through my
mind, or I can't get music out of my
head, and I just get things. ... That
might be guilt. ... I am totally
changing.

A prolonged experience of being
open to intrusion or collective
monitoring of inner experience. An
outgrowth of a contract in which
mother had served as David's
barometer of psychological and
physiological stress.

Chapter Seven, Case Study 2, "A Matter of Growing Pains," will
briefly describe the successful therapeutic counterinduction of David. For
now, we have seen a systematic family contribution to the spontaneous
manifestation of symptom components in a symptom bearer. Contextual,
sequential, and content issues converged, carrying a very negative and
immobilizing message to a young man about normal family life cycle
events.

We can see from these segments how dysfunctional families can
readily plug directly into members' ideas of self, through what they say,
and indirectly, both through the evocation of psychological and psychophysiological associations and revivifications of past events and through
the implicit framing of all events in an overriding symptom-maintaining
family structural context.

Summary

Under certain circumstances, whose nature is disputed in the field
of hypnosis, individuals can be given suggestions that activate reactions
typically conceptualized as occurring spontaneously and automatically,
without cognitive plan or intention. Whether or not the activation of a
trance state is an essential component to the production of such automatic
responses is uncertain. It is clear that the induction of trance is among the
forms of suggestion making that culminates in seemingly automatic
reactions.

We have proposed that the hypnotist is not the only person capable of making suggestions affecting reactions typically considered automatic. A vast literature on stress has documented that some external social factors are able to suggest changes in respiration, pulse, and heart rates and many other aspects of functioning considered automatic. We consider the hypnotic and therapeutic contexts as among many social-inductive contexts that potentially feed messages to families and individuals about how they are to behave. In keeping with this recognition, we have provided an open-systems model of hypnotic suggestion.

In this chapter, the family, itself the nexus of broader social suggestions, was described as a potential transmitter of messages about individual functioning. Special family inductive capacities and techniques were outlined, and a family induction of symptom components analyzed. Additionally, symptomatic behavior was introduced as containing *both* automatically occurring behavior—in that the subject and others experience it as happening to the symptom bearer against his will or without his intention—and intentional if not effective coping behavior. We considered the select circumstances under which family activation of the psychophysiological components of symptomatic behavior becomes analogous to the activation by hypnotists of classical concomitants of trance. Clinically, the symptomatic state is regarded partly as the result of a persistent contextual intrusion into an individual's private inner reality, which culminates in an abuse of that person's inner focus and of his state of readiness to respond to suggestion. Although we propose that, like hypnotists, families transmit suggestions to individuals, sometimes using various trance states and special inductive moments to do so, and although we recognize the potentially overriding powers of family suggestion, we also regard individuals as self-inductive entities, with some margin of individual freedom from contextual suggestions. It is in part this range of freedom that hypnotic family therapy capitalizes on.

Chapter Five ⚜ ⚜ ⚜

Case Study
of a Hemophiliac

⚜ This chapter, via excerpts from a case transcript, demonstrates how a therapist develops a dialectical two-person hypnotic intervention. A seven-year-old boy with hemophilia and his mother receive hypnotic therapy to help the boy reduce stress-related bleeds. In a life fraught with physiological interferences, mother and son have become wired together in a reciprocally worrisome rapport. Using two related but separate-track trance technologies, the therapist initiates a rewiring process that can create more room for competence. The case is referred to as "Getting Mind Control."

We detail the rationale and steps involved in developing a single dialectical intervention. Our final plan is tailored to the unique needs of the case. However, the general structural concerns that guide the decision-making process also apply to other families and problems. In this case, a single-parent mother is bringing her hemophiliac son to a child guidance clinic because she is interested in adjunctive hypnosis. She hopes that hypnosis can help decrease stress-related bleeds in her son's weakest joint and help him relax. Her *son's* problem is to be her gift, the aspect of her situation she asks the therapist to do something about.

Because the presenting complaint is a concern about excessive bleeding in a young hemophiliac, our starting point will be to gain some knowledge of the illness so as to consider what aspects of it may be psychosomatic and therefore responsive to a psychotherapeutic approach.

Hemophilia is a genetically transmitted clotting disorder. The daughters of a father with hemophilia will be carriers; any sons of the daughters have a 50 percent chance of having hemophilia. The hemophiliac lacks sufficient clotting factor needed to stop a bleed as quickly as usual. As a result, a hemorrhagic episode can result in bruising, bleeding into joints, painful swelling, and, if untreated by a synthetic factor, a threat to life. Physical traumas are not the only precipitants to bleeds; in fact, many incidents of bumping and bruising are not followed by bleeds, even in young men with a severe factor deficiency. On the other hand, anticipation of events, positive or negative, and interpersonal problems, including family conflicts, can activate serious bleeds even in males with mild hemophilia. The mechanisms through which certain mental-sets, family relational variables, and social stressors—including peer and economic pressures—translate into bleeds are still mysterious.

Historically, hemophilia has been regarded as a one-person problem, so medical and therapeutic treatments, including recent hypnotic work, have focused on the symptom bearer alone. If we consider the important role of external stressors in the course of the illness, however, this model of treatment is unnecessarily limited.

A young man with hemophilia, studying to be a therapist, stated some of the reasons he personally considers his illness a problem that extends beyond the boundaries of his own body:

> Normally there are three socializing agents: family, school, and peers. Hemophiliacs in my age bracket didn't experience that. You had a strong family influence, but not necessarily a healthy one, often a very overprotective mother and a father who was negative or just uninvolved.
>
> At school, when you were well enough to go, there was so much protectiveness that you couldn't go onto the playground for recess because you might bump yourself or get knocked down and aggravate your knees. And so you'd eat lunch in the classroom with a classmate to keep you company. But even then, the kids are not going to be strong playmates, because they don't want to stay indoors.

But you do have a strong socializing agent as far as the hospital. You get to know the doctors and nurses well, and you get to know your disease inside out. There you see all your friends, who are other hemophiliacs, and you fill up your whole vocabulary with an unusual life-style. You look ahead at your life. Pain is inevitable. Life is one bleed after another. You're used to needles. In fact, lots of hemophiliacs become drug addicts. The hospital is where your friends are, where you get acceptance. Therefore you stop doing anything on your own to fight bleeds, because when you have a bleed, you can be with your friends in the hospital.

Based on our approach, hemophilia has several components, each of which may contribute to the symptom and may be considered a potential point of therapeutic entry:

1. The first component is the symptom bearer's individual psychophysiology, including both his mind-set about his illness, as evidenced by a prevailing idea such as "I might as well be in the hospital so I can see my friends,"* and his idiosyncratic psychophysiological response sequences, as triggered by feelings of helplessness about fighting his own bleeds. Individual and group hypnotic approaches have documented that, using trance states, hemophiliacs can prevent bleeds (LeBaw, 1970, 1975) or reduce capillary bleeding, such as occurs in oral surgery (Lucas, 1959). With a mind-set and a psychophysiological response sequence such as the young man's, an individual's natural capabilities might not be spontaneously rallied on behalf of decreasing stress-related bleeds.
2. The second component is the family relational context, in which meanings and implications of hemophilia embody a highly personal psychomythology and take on lives of their own. Family interaction patterns around illness problems may become rigid and restrictive.

---

*The role of peers as bleed fighters is important, although not discussed in this chapter. Peers help buffer the child from family problems; peers outside the hospital setting could aid in normalization. Part of the efficacy of LeBaw's hypnotic work may lie in his peer-group format of induction (1970, 1975).

For example, a mother may feel guilty and become overprotective of her challenged child, and the father may withdraw from his frailer son, increasing the likelihood of intense mother-son involvement. Individual therapies alone, including hypnotic treatments, have found some relapse even in young men whose trance experience activated vasoconstriction or overall relaxation. From our knowledge of psychosomatic families and a large body of medical literature confirming the likelihood of family relational contributions to bleeds caused by stressors, we can consider family life a potential piece of the pattern which includes a young hemophiliac not in good control of his own natural resources. We can also consider the power of family structure to override individually based masteries over psychosomatic aspects of bleeds.

3. The third component is the broader social and economic systems, including hospital, school, and financial strains from medical expenses and work absences, which impinge on the family's routines and arrangements and the hemophiliac's psychosocial development. The hospital context can be refuge for mother and son from the social isolation that may accompany the illness. Bleeds that have had the negative power to take the family out of mainstream social contexts can accrue short-run positive powers of "open-sesame" into the accepting, familiar hospital context. Also, once mother and son are habituated to working in disease-related synchrony, the separation caused by, for example, the son going to school, and mutual worries about school mistreatment, can make them both uncomfortable. In fact, many hemophiliacs have school absences that the severity of their illness alone cannot account for. Thirty-five percent of hemophiliacs do not finish high school, and developmentally they are often immature, rebellious, and self-destructive.

Thus we have a three-level still picture of hemophilia. It is an illness that translates into many potential problems, ranging from society's lack of knowledge about it to chronic family pressures and anxieties to unhelpful individual patterns of responding to and thinking about the disease. To perceive the illness in motion, Figure 11 represents its three-level structure.

Start at the top center of Figure 11 and move counterclockwise. Aspects of family functioning (such as interdependence of mother and son

Figure 11. Holistic Structural Model of Hemophilia.

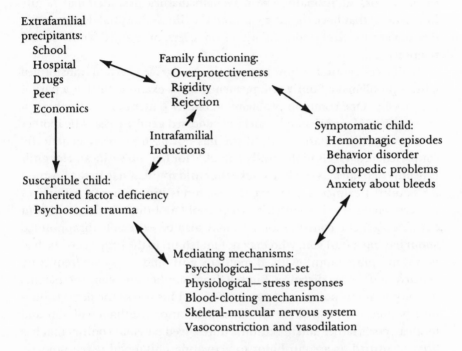

Note: The three levels of structure, including family and social context, are represented with the symptom bearer divided, for heuristic purposes, into three parts: the susceptible child, the mediating mechanisms of the child, and the symptomatic child.
Source: Revised from Minuchin, Rosman, and Baker, 1978, p. 21.

and withdrawal or exclusion of father) and such extrafamilial precipitants as hospital dependency, school overprotectiveness or inadequate peer relationships are represented as acting on the susceptible child through psychological and physiological mediating mechanisms (such as unconscious processes and the severity of the factor deficiency) to produce for the symptomatic child bleeding episodes, orthopedic problems, behavior disorders, school absences, or family relational difficulties. The psychological and physiological symptoms then feed back into the broad symptom-context system, activating family interactional and other problems. This model of the illness in motion gives us many potential points of therapeutic entry, depending on specific problems of any one hemophiliac and his family. A therapist may still act directly on the child's physiology, through drugs, surgical procedures, orthopedic treatments, and hypnosis, or, additionally, she may help disrupt dysfunctional family interactions that have rigidified around the illness, hospital dependencies that undermine the family, isolation from peers, or strained family-school relations.

To conceptualize how hemophilia can be recoded and transformed within problematic family arrangements, let us examine further a part of the process. One common problematic family pattern draws partly on a convergence of genetics and societally endorsed gender roles. The mother of a hemophiliac, particularly if she has not been properly genetically counseled, often feels biologically culpable for her son's illness. Her guilt is readily activated as she has to take the child night or day to the hospital for painful treatments or as the disease binds him to her in a flurry of protectiveness, starting with his two-year-old mobility. Father may resent his wife's genetic contribution and may also be extremely disappointed about having a frail son, who may not match up to the rugged boy he had hoped to "play rough" with. If mother's guilt and worry are frequently enacted and father distances himself from mother and son, the parents may argue about how to manage the boy and his needs; the perfect situation is then established for the cross-generational alliance of son and mother versus father and the chronic unresolved parental conflict that has been identified as a contributor to activating childhood psychosomatic patterns. In this case, the family structure becomes a second level of the illness problems.

When thinking of treating the boy's stress-related bleeds, we want to consider his psychophysiological responses as part of sequences of family interaction. We hypothesize that much as the hypnotist can help the hemophiliac affect the movement of blood through his body, to help ward off a building bleed, move the site of a bleed, or aid in vasoconstriction so as to slow down a bleed, his family, through secondary utilities of his symptoms, can affect the movement of blood through his body, if inadvertently.

Additionally, the family may also interiorize aspects of the broader social context of the illness. Especially before home care transfusions became possible, sons were frequently hospitalized, with teams of hospital experts taking charge of their lives. Because of strong hospital and societal indicators that it is mothers who are to bring their children to hospitals, mothers' bonds with their sons around illness problems are further intensified by hospitalizations, even if this intensification itself contributes to the family stress-related features of the problem. Also, if the hospital is a pleasant place for mother and son, a source of support, son and mother may derive secondary benefits from this kind of social life within the hospital setting. With marital conflicts at home, social isolation, and a supportive hospital environment, bleeds may help both mother and son temporarily "forget" other problems, offering them a more natural network, if in a nonnormative setting. In other words, the problems of the illness may have a secondary calming effect and become part of the routine in the ebbs and tides of family conflict.

Ultimately, parents face tremendous financial expenditures for good clotting factor and hospitalizations and losses of leisure time and social life. The child faces social isolation and school absences. The central management problem of the family then becomes their ability to handle the family communication aspects of the illness. Relational problems can translate inward into bleeds; bleeds can translate outward into family conflict or prevention of conflict resolution. Hemophilia becomes a symptom into which a therapist can afford to intervene at more than one point of entry. On one hand, the therapist is foremost called on to help the symptom bearer gain control of his psychophysiological processes. Other family changes cannot readily occur unless the child is stabilized. On the other hand, family structural problems may well have the power to override individual changes and ultimately destabilize the child once again. Hence, dialectical interventions may be desirable for so complex a symptom.

With these general ideas about the illness in mind, let us look at a single case as it recodes illness problems through family structure and individual mental-sets. Actual transcript is presented. This material, including dialogue and behavioral descriptions of mother, son, and therapist, are prefaced and followed by segments explaining the broader therapeutic interventions, particularly those pertaining to therapy steps outlined in Chapter Two. To the right, additional explanatory comments note the therapist's explicit considerations and movements. In this microanalysis of transcript segments, the use of language to facilitate the creation of an hypnotic atmosphere and tone and content in inducing trance are described in detail. A clinician might want to read the transcript and broad strokes first, returning afterward to evaluate nuances.

In this session, mother has been invited to be present during her son's hypnotic treatment. She has heard that hypnosis has effectively decreased the number of bleeds in young males with hemophilia, and she has some adult hemophiliac friends who have tried it. No formal therapeutic contract has been made. From the interviewer's vantage point, the first task is to determine the mother's and son's expectations for the interview and to determine what problem they are in actuality offering her to work with. Although mother has ostensibly come to help her son, the therapist regards mother and son together as her unit of focus. The interview, set up to help son relax, begins with a bang.

Stage 1: Preinduction—Reading Family Structure to Search for Rigid Mental-Sets

Mother: (Yelling) Bill, she put those chairs there for a purpose, now put that back! (Softening) Okay? I mean, she wants things for a purpose. You can take your jacket off and put it over there.

Therapist is arranging chairs for a videotaping of the interview.

Bill: (Surprised, then irritated) Uh uh.

Mother: Well, this is very hot in here. You're going to be here for a while, you know.

Bill: I thought you said we weren't going to be here very long.

Mother: No, it's not going to be that long, but it's not going to be any ten minutes either. You sit there, you know, I told you we're going to have a good time.

Ther.: (To mother) Okay. Great. What are you making (pointing to mother's sewing bag)?

Notes interactions. Mother-son argument is not seen as helpful first step toward trance. Therapist uses "needlepoint" to disrupt argument and indicate interest in mother.

Mother: It's not that I'm making anything. Needlepoint is very relaxing
to me; I mean, it requires minimal
concentration whatsoever, you can be
hyper and do needlepoint. And I'm a
hyper type person anyhow, you know,
and I, it drives me crazy to sit still.
You know what I mean, not only
does it drive me crazy, but the act of
sitting still causes me to get even
more hyper than I normally do. So I
just do it, you know. . . .

Ther.: Yeah.

Mother: And I like the relaxation,
even waiting outside emergency
rooms, you know, and you think
hours and hours and hours until I'm
done and you sit around. And I can't
get into reading, you know, when
you wait, because you do a lot of
waiting, you know that's most of
what you do, and you can't get into
reading, because the doctors are coming in and out and everything. This
is really neat, because you can pick
it up and put it down, pick it up and
put it down.

The therapist's tone is receptive,
inviting mother to go on. This is
an important interchange because
mother is indicating she is "bringing in" something other than her
son as her gift, and the therapist is
accepting it.

In this brief segment, several salient issues began to appear. In
terms of mother-son interaction, the intensity of the mother's reprimand
to the boy and her immediate, almost apologetic, softening are hints of
her ambivalence toward him and her anxieties about the strains of hospitals and appointments, including the present one. The arguing about
how long the appointment will last, placement of chairs, jackets, even
temperature suggest a kind of immersion in the minutiae of the son's
behavior. Mother's portrayals of time carry a sense of endless waiting and
frustration.

The therapist focuses on the needlepoint to disrupt the mother and son's bickering, which is not a useful beginning point for the hypnosis treatment. The needlepoint discussion suggests that part of the mother's gift to the therapist may be a sharing of her *own* nervousness about the illness and its management and of her wish for a means of relaxation and control.

The therapist wants to attain more information about why the family is here. She has spoken with mother, so she asks Bill what he thinks about why he is seeing her. Mother responds first.

Mother: Did you tell her what I told you. . .

Bill: Mind control. . .

Ther.: Mind control, that's a good expression. . .

This is the kind of language a therapist looks for as an opening into private realms of meaning.

Bill: For my hurts.

Ther.: Hmmm. Would you like to have some better mind control when it hurts?

The phrase is picked up and carried into the therapeutic plan, intensifying rapport.

Bill: Uh huh.

Mother: Is that an adequate explanation?

Ther.: So you like that idea, huh?

Bill: Uh huh. Once God helped me.

Ther.: Who did?

Bill: God. My elbow started to go up and he made it get better.

Ther.: How did he do that?

Bill: I don't, I don't know.

Mother: He said he would take care of things, didn't he?

Bill: Uh huh.

Therapist wants to continue connection with child, so she nods to mother but returns to child, as though not interrupted. "Our connection can continue despite interruption, brief separation." This is a micromessage of the therapy.

"God" has been doing good therapy. Therapist wants to know more about this God and how he works.

Ther.: God did. When was this that God said he would take care of things, in a dream, or. . . ?

Therapist probes, hoping to make this God an ally, not another powerful foe who induces reliance on outside forces.

Mother: (Whispering, as if to create a boundary around her and therapist) We don't go to church regularly and I'm trying to get the idea across that there are higher powers and what I'm telling him is that God doesn't actively do stuff, but, he sees us and he makes ways available to us, so that we can help ourselves, and I'm telling him if you get a bleed, if somebody bleeds, we know now that we can do something about it, if we take care of it right away, that's what that's all about. That's, you know, symbolically, what that's about.

Mother whispers, as if to create an adult boundary around therapist and herself. She and Bill live in such proximity that whispering is a way to suggest to son that "this is private."

Ther.: Ummhmm. (To child) So God's on your side, huh, if you know how to do it right?

Therapist ponders mother's explanation and uses it to return to son. God too is then able to be incorporated into the therapeutic plan.

Interestingly, in a family routinely subject to the higher authority of outside powers, like physicians and hospitals, mother had selected to explain the boy's getting "mind control over his hurts" in terms of another outside superior power, God. Mother has been using God to help her son hunt for the benevolent powers of the unconscious. She has explained the idea that a bleed in Bill's elbow stopped itself because "God makes ways available to us to help ourselves." The therapist wants to capitalize on mother's approach. To facilitate Bill's taking as active a role as possible in his own hypnosis treatment, the therapist slightly tailors mother's explanation as she exits from the adult boundary mother has thrown around the two women, saying to Bill: "God's on your side, if you know how to do it right." She suggests that Bill become a competent partner of God.

Mother frequently introjects herself into interactions between the therapist and Bill, offering to answer adult-type questions or otherwise rescuing the son from a question he cannot answer, or offering additional information, with that kind of neck-craning helpfulness of the mother of a smaller child, feeding vocabulary to nascent phrases, to help them grow into sentences. Likewise, the child invites his mother to nourish him with tidbits of information. The therapist does not actively resist this process at this point, regarding these verbal interventions as interactional features of the symptom offering (see Chapter Three). The therapist does, however, continue to address questions directly to the son, both to assess the level of contact allowed and to demonstrate to mother that she will not hurt her son or try to undermine her role. She wants to see how the boy contributes to the twosome.

The therapist continues, intentionally focusing on positives, probing for areas of competence in the son that will reflect the mother's competent role as a single parent. The goals are to continue to establish rapport while finding out more about family life and the son's and mother's mind-sets about the boy's symptom. The child is allowed to actively present his universe before going into trance.

Ther.: Tell me a little bit about you, Bill, okay, so I can. . .How old are you?	"Tell me a little" is a safe request, indicating "not more than mother would like" and "I won't ask more of son than he can handle." Therapist then narrows request down to age.
Bill: Seven.	
Ther.: Seven. And what grade are you in?	Introducing school for chitchat because Bill has missed so much school.
Bill: Umm. Second. And I didn't even have to go in on the other grade twice.	
Ther.: Oh yeah.	
Bill: And I've got every single grade so far.	
Ther.: Good for you.	Conveys how impressive an accomplishment of his and mother's this is by nodding. This is something Bill did for himself. Therapist seeks information about other abilities.
Mother: All two of them.	
Ther.: That is very good. Do you read this (picking up his King Kong book); do you read some of the stuff in there? Do you just look at the pictures or do you really read?	
Bill: I read some of them, parts of it.	
Ther.: Ummhmm.	

Bill: Sometimes I don't read very much of it. There's the old stories I didn't read yet.

Ther.: The old King Kong?

Bill: Yeah. I didn't even read the planet of the apes one either (a little disappointed).

Ther.: No? So you've got that left to look forward to.

Bill: Uh huh.

Bill sounds disappointed. Disappointment in Bill might convey to mother that therapist is too rough with her son. Such emotions *cue* mother to rescue Bill. Therapist introjects the idea that not having done something yet leaves something good for the future, an indirect suggestion to transform disappointment to hope.

Ther.: What kind of stuff do you do with your mom? There's just the two of you alone at home now, right?

Therapist wants some influence over mother's ins and outs. To take charge of mother's likely intrusion at this point, therapist introduces mom herself.

Mother: Except for the pets. Do you want to tell her about the pets?

Bill: Yeah, we have a kitty who died, a dog, except we had to give him away. His name was Sparky. He really barked when we left him alone in the house.

Ther.: So you had to give him away?

Metaphorical empathy for things lost in general. There is a tone of sharing loss and compensations for loss with an empathetic listener.

Mother: And he'd eat the furniture and the shoes and. . .even people. I mean he'd chew us.

Bill: And then we got this new dog called Whiskers, then we got a bird (turning to mother) or was it the fish?

Mother is activated as the boy's memory bank.

Mother: The fish.

Bill: The fish.

Ther.: Which one do you take care of most?

Therapist focuses on caretaking and competence. In this way, the boy is elevated from "one who is cared for" to "one who takes care of," in this case, animals.

Bill: Well, Whiskers needs a lot of attention.

Ther.: Yes.

Bill: I take care of him a lot. I have chores. I have to feed Whiskers, do my little professor.

It is as if son has answered "I take care most of the one who needs me most." Therapist's "yes" confirms the reality of special "needs for attention."

Ther.: What's the little professor?

Bill: It's this thing you work on math problems.

Mother: It's like a calculator.

Ther.: So you like to do that?

Bill: Uh huh, and, uh, then we got a bird named Tweetie. Then we got. . .

Therapist hints at the possible burdens of so much responsibility to create a little place of acceptance for them too.

Mother: Hermit crabs.

Bill: Yeah, hermit crabs.

Ther.: My goodness!

Mother: And you got the two monkeys. . .

Ther.: My goodness.

Bill: All the crabs died, but we still have two more named Flash Gordon and Buck Rogers. And do you know what Flash Gordon's real name is?

Ther.: What?

Bill: Buster Crabbe.

Ther.: How'd you find that out?

Bill: My mom told me.

Therapist has a good idea how but wishes to convey clearly to mother her recognition that "many of his successes are associated with you."

Ther.: Ohhhh. Some mom. . . .

Particularly valued are such contributions as mother's wit.

And you help take care of all the pets, but *especially* Whiskers?

Bill: Umhuh. And then we got these sea monkeys. They're pretty small and one of them died. Just one of them. And *then,* we got a guinea pig. It was a piglet.

Ther.: I can't believe this. . . !

Bill: Which we named Clarabelle. And then we got another one that was a little piglet, too.

Mother: Now you have to tell her, you know, that, if you don't have a family . . . (everyone is talking at once).

Bill: (Talking over mother) And the house is, the house is turning into, the house is turning into a zoo!

Focusing in on the boy's private feelings, to increase a climate of rapport.

Death reappears in the boy's tale of himself, but he diminishes it as if interiorizing a reassurance of his mother's: "Just one of them." Perhaps the quantity of pets is a protection for son and mother. Some can die and they will still have a full house. But in the meantime, they have chaos.

In the simple act of sharing "a little about himself," Bill has revealed a great deal about his life. He is a responsible child who has been given chores, and he follows through on them. He is proud of his school accomplishments, despite many illness-related absences. His life centers around his house, which is full of animals. His mind is full of concern for the animals and their care, and he recognizes death. Mother has also offered that her loss of social life and family has been compensated for by filling up the empty spaces (another kind of needlepoint) with many little creatures to care for. Kicking his legs wildly during the culmination of this duet about an accumulation of animals, the boy's voice swells over his mother's to describe their house as turning into a zoo.

The boy's statement is a good metaphor for the lack of structure and routine in the external family context and the rapidly changing and permeable boundaries between mother and son as they enact their roles in relation to each other and the illness. There is a sense that mother and Bill both lack private spaces to which they can escape from the other's "special needs for attention." Perhaps inspired by Bill's analogy of their house as a zoo, mother goes on to explain that the worst thing about their situation is that they do not have control over their own lives. She says, "We're denied the opportunity to find ways to solve our problems ourselves." She goes on:

Mother: (Agitated) We have a . . . Bill! Stop kicking your foot! (Regaining her composure) We have a very unstructured life, because of this. . . this situation. . .you know. And the things we do don't always fit into a normal pattern, if you know what I mean. This is, we have our life unstructured, because we don't have control over our time like a normal person would.

Mother again wants to tell therapist things that she does not want to say in front of Bill. She says "this situation" and "if you know what I mean," again inviting therapist into her private illness-related problems.

Ther.: Well, tell me about that, let me get a picture of what goes on in the house that is, that makes your schedule hard to control. . .

The therapist wants full details on what this mother is routinely up against.

Mother: Okay, because we can never predict his bleeding. 3:00 in the morning, 9:00 in the morning, 2:00 in the afternoon, we never. . .

Now for mother's view of the problem, framed in terms of the central therapeutic issues of "control" over their lives.

Ther.: Okay, how old was Bill when you first found out that he was a hemophiliac?

Mother is becoming upset; she seems to want to unburden herself of chronic suffering around the illness. Therapist invites her to unload the chronology of the problem.

Mother: When he was twenty-four hours old. Yeah, they circumcised him and he didn't stop bleeding and then they looked in my folder. . . . And my father was a hemophiliac and so I knew that hemophilia comes through the mother's side of the family and you know, all of that stuff. But they never bothered to tell me that all the daughters are carriers!

And so I knew, I knew that my father had hemophilia, that. . .

Ther.: Was it severe?

Mother: Yes. I didn't know it at the time. My father. . .had a drinking problem, all right? And never coped with what was going on. I knew he was a hemophiliac, but, I thought hemophilia was cutting yourself and you bleed to death kind of stuff. All his drink stuff, he said, was because of pain from arthritis and I never thought any more about it. The doctors who were involved with my father told us that hemophilia comes through mother's side of the family, you know, and all of that stuff which is true, but they never bothered to tell us that all the daughters of a male hemophiliac are carriers. They didn't bother to tell us that. I mean, I knew that my mother didn't have it. We thought we were terrific. My sister had three kids, all of which were girls, and I came up with the only boy.

The word "severe" refers not only to mom's father's condition but to the statement "I knew that my father had hemophilia." The mother responds to that latter message, saying, "My father had a drinking problem, all right?", as if to say, "There, I said it. My situation was rough, too, as a daughter of a hemophiliac."

This inadequate counseling of daughters of hemophiliacs is unfortunately common, even today.

"We thought we were terrific" implies that she found she was not. Why? Because *she* produced the abnormal child.

The therapist has begun to accumulate information suggestive of how mother experiences herself in the face of the illness problems. Even though the disease is *technically* lodged within the body of her young son, in *actuality* it is interiorized by mother as something terrifying that descends on her, disrupting her days and nights, unraveling the fabric of her existence. Blood, death, guilt, and pain become the imagery occupying her mind-set and preoccupying her daily activities. The lack of control over herself and her destiny translates outward or exteriorizes into her alternately overly critical disciplinary actions and overprotective helpful actions. It is as if society, hospital domination, and the illness all joined forces and are in control, hierarchically, over her. Then, under the shadow of these controlling forces, she is supposed to remain a calm and competent parent to her young suffering child. She is clearly experiencing these seemingly conflicting demands as overwhelming.

Throughout the preinduction phase of the interview, the therapist is induced by experiential influences of the mother-son interaction to allow mother the right to interject comments throughout the conversations between therapist and son. Although mother has shared with the therapist what needs relief, she has not yet *transferred power* over her problems to the therapist. As part of allowing mother to give the problem to the therapist, the therapist continues, with greater intimacy and rapport, to draw the problem-offering gift more closely to her, to examine it more fully. Mother and son have permitted her to "enter into their house" via a discussion of it. Will mother let the therapist examine her son's somatic complaint?

Ther.: Umm, I can ask you, Bill. You have, you bleed sometimes where? Where do you get a bleed?

Bill: My elbow.

Ther.: Which one?

Mother: (Sounding impatient) Take your coat off so she can see!

Bill: This one (rolling up his sleeve for therapist to inspect).

Ther.: Left one?

Bill: Uh huh. That's the only one that seems to go off.

Ther.: Just the left, huh?

Bill: Always that left side. It's always bent like that, always.

Mother: Bill had a broken arm when he was. . .

Ther.: Bill, is that true? Can I see (looking more closely)? Oh yes. Mine does that too, can you see? They go

Therapist enters gingerly, asking ("I can ask you, Bill") if she can indeed ask Bill about his actual physical complaint. Again, in this case, where fear and pain loom large, she asks in the diminutive "you bleed sometimes. . . ?" This movement inward is a step toward the work on internal processes that will culminate in the trance induction.

We are going to get very specific about the symptom. He shows his illness-related joint disfigurement.

Again the therapist uses the content of mother's interruption to bring her back to Bill, as if mother were

like that, kind of out like double-jointed.

Bill: Not mine! This one goes like this (straight) right arm. Just this one goes like that . . . (left is disjointed).

not disrupting but *bridging* (a distortion technique).

To intensify rapport and convey comfort with the joint disfigurement, therapist shows her double-jointed elbows. This suggests "We are alike."

Ther.: Yeah, some people have that.

Mother: Well, he's had this same arm broken three times.

Even people without hemophilia have that sometimes.

Ther.: Ummm.

Mother: And that was the start of his elbow. Now, he's got a weak elbow there.

Ther.: Ummm.

Although son wants reassurance of normalcy, mother wants recognition of the severity. Therefore therapist nonverbally conveys recognition of severity, so as not to have to support mother by addressing Bill's abnormalities more than is respectful to Bill.

Mother: And now he's started, is it your right ankle where you have those bleeds every once in a while?

Mother's tone softens, as if she appreciated the therapist's hesitation.

Bill: Sometimes I have it in the right (looking at his ankles). Sometimes I have it in my right ankle, sometimes I have it in my left.

Mother: This is the first year we've ever had legs. We've never had any leg involvement up until this day.

Bill: No, this is the one I have it in, my left ankle. . . When it hurts, it has this bump on it, always.

Mother: But it's mostly in his elbow. That's his big spot.

The central spot therapy will focus on is this real material spot, the boy's left elbow.

Ther.: How many times do you get it? Like where you feel like it's a bleed? How many times a week? Do you know these things? Or does mama know these things?

Bill: I don't remember.

Ther.: Okay, I'll ask mama, okay? Okay, how many times would you say that he. . .

Mother: Once a week.

Ther.: Okay, once a week and this requires a transfusion?

Mother: Yes.

Ther.: Bill, how do you let your mommy know when you think you're going to need a transfusion?

Bill: I just, uh, if she's asleep. I would just wake her up and tell her. If she wasn't, I would just go over to where she is and tell her.

Ther.: Okay, and how do you know that you're having one? What kind of feelings do you get that tell you you're getting one?

Bill: Well, sometimes I get a little bit of pain, you know. And if it's an elbow bleed, I can see it starting to go up, but when it first starts, there's not that much.

Therapist asks the boy's permission to ask his mom, as a way of conveying "This is your private realm, but until you're ready to take it over completely, we will check with mom. . .but only about what you don't know or can't do for yourself." The boy remains gatekeeper of information about himself.

Mother's tone is snippy, her pace fast. The subject is provoking anxiety.

Back to Bill as soon as possible for the information he is expert in.

Therapist is accumulating the idiosyncracies of how mother and son communicate the onset of a bleed, how son recognizes the internal cues that activate him to alert his mother to a bleed. These will be essential threads to weave into the induction process.

At this point in the interview, the rapport between mother and son and therapist is established, and the actual transfer of power over the symptom is about to occur. The therapist has a hunch concerning what in the family context *might* be a kind of coded statement about the psychosomatic component of Bill's hemophilia. The negative intensity in the bond between mother and son seems to be an exterior manifestation of the bleeding problem being out of control. Bill also misses much school, and it seems possible that the kind of connection between him and his mother might make separation something each seeks to prevent. She might not find the school's treatment of him adequate; he might not want to leave her alone in their zoo.

Figure 12 is a map of the way mother experiences herself vis-a-vis society. In the face of this negative environment, mother must take responsibility for her son with at least weekly "hurts." The mother-son connection, although characterized by love and caring, seems to be shaped by two problematic conflicting arrangements, which shift rapidly, unsettling both persons. In one arrangement, Bill is like a little husband to his mother, and in this capacity, they argue like husband and wife, carrying on a sort of bickering. In the second arrangement, mother acts as a mother, but as an overly critical or overly protective mother of a younger child, censuring his movements, or feeding him words, lines, and endless, creative ideas. Figure 13 shows these two troublesome arrangements. In both hierarchies, their interactions, when problematic, are characterized by a kind of developmental imbalance.

Figure 12. Mother's Interiorized Image of Herself in Society.

Society

⑁

Mother

The bond of dependency is great, and the social forces are overpowering; therefore the nature of the connection is negative.

Key: ⩵ Negative and intense bond

Figure 13. Two Troublesome Family Arrangements.

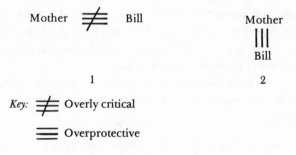

Mother ⩵ Bill

Mother

|||

Bill

1

2

Key: ⩵ Overly critical

⩵ Overprotective

Regarding the actual cuing of anxiety in Bill in the course of his relating to his mother, the techniques are evident throughout the interview. For example, after yelling at Bill as the session begins and "losing her cool" because of her own pressures, mother tells him in an irritated voice that the interview is not going to be that short and that it is going to be fun, thereby confusing Bill. Her talking over the boy, answering for him, and in a sense occupying too much of the space designated for helping him needles him and makes him swing his legs wildly, become impatient, and try to talk over her voice. While trying in every way to give Bill a normal life, because of doubts about her own normalcy in the face of his disease, mother expresses and invites anxiety about how abnormal, how unstructured their life together really is. Above all, while resorting even to God to reassure Bill that there is nothing to be afraid of, mother—especially as a single parent—confronted as she is with the real isolation, the serious economic pressures, the relentless and unpredictable problems of the illness, is afraid. The boy is told at once: "I am in charge of you, don't worry," and "I am out of control, help me."

Based on (1) observation of the dyad, (2) experience of the patterns of conflicting messages and confused roles that seem to activate reverberating stress cycles from mother to son, and (3) our crude map of the three levels at which the symptoms of hemophilia can be problematic, we can begin to formulate requisites of the hypnosis format. We want to take into consideration the following factors:

1. *The boy's inner realities,* including his mind-set about his illness, his psychophysiological processes and his sensations associated with bleeds, his connection to his mother regarding illness problems, and his atomic inner reflections of outer chaos.

2. *The mother's anxieties* about her management of her son's illness problems and her strong wish to help ease his pain. Because of mother's experience of herself in the world as the mother of a hemophiliac, she would benefit from an experience that elevates her and enhances her competence with her son.

3. *The relationship between mother and son* as a family unit, especially regarding the establishment of balanced hierarchies and clear boundaries.

In this case, because of the importance of mother feeling in control of her son's experience of relief, the induction process ideally will incorporate her. Also, because Bill is very much tied to his mother as a twenty-four-hour nurse and lifeline, it is also in his interest that she come along for this journey into mind control. The difficult decision the therapist must make at this point is how much involvement mother should have in the actual induction process. On the one hand, some form of shared trance phenomenon could be sculpted to actually *disrupt* the negative intensity of the mother-son relationship. Suggestions might be given and circumstances provided to partially defuse the diadic intensity through trance. The boy might learn to gain in control over his own psychophysiological processes *while* his mother learns to remain calm and self-assured, encouraging the boy to draw on his own healing resources. On the other hand, in some families, involvement of a parent in trance phenomena with a child could be abused or distorted into a means of increasing control over or engulfing the child. Also, some children so resent the involvement of their mothers in their lives that they refuse to report bleeds and suffer joint problems rather than admit dependence. Such a child would not appreciate connecting mother to his mind control.

There are no simple answers to the therapist's questions at this point. One reads the family members' motivations and wishes and decides how and where a thinner membrane, a thick wall, or an almost impenetrable barrier must be established.

In this case, the therapist is impressed with the mother's successes with her son and the depth of her longing to help him. She is also impressed with mother's fear of the illness. The plan the therapist begins to consider, then, includes:

1. Defining mother as remaining in charge of her son's hypnosis treatment.
2. However, in this first session, having mother learn about how to help him use trance by herself relaxing and observing.
3. Through this and repeated sessions, having mother gain skill in ultimately developing ways to help cue Bill to enter trance, to foster her son's independent management of the psychosomatic aspects of his illness, and ways to relax herself while helping son.
4. Ideally, beginning to defuse the negativism in the mother-son bond by this setting up of circumstances of relaxation for both *while* treating the son's illness-related problem.

5.   Focusing the induction itself on decreasing the flow of blood to Bill's weak left elbow joint and using whatever material Bill comes up with in trance to help loosen his rigid mind-set about his illness problems.

At this point, then, the therapist begins the process of receiving the problem for therapeutic purposes by formally starting the delicate negotiations around establishing the hypothesized treatment plan. In the following exchange, notice mother applying the brakes in her efforts to not do "a sloppy job." Bill, seemingly impatient, then expresses his reservations too, in the form of worries about not waking up from a trance to get transfused. Finally, the last postponement of the trance entails their bickering about Bill's fears.

Ther.: So I think that what I would do with Bill and with you would be I'd like to try to evolve a relaxation method that *you* would then do with him. Whatever I'm doing with him you could do with him.	It is therapist, "I", who will do something; they can relax passively. What therapist will do is "with Bill" and "with you"—the hypnosis will be directed at both, separately. But its purpose is to evolve a relaxation "that mom ('you') would do with him." Mother is reassured that son will be reconnected with her and that she can interiorize the son-therapist connection for the future.
Mother: That's what he was afraid of. He said that he was, he said that he might forget what you told him. . . He wanted to make sure that we. . .	Mother confirms that the thought of son getting mind control without being connected to her was frightening . . . to him.
Bill: When are we going to get the mind control?	
Mother: Well, we have to discuss these things first, Bill, that's why it's important for her to learn about us.	
Bill: Mom, you're being too long.	
Mother: Well, you don't want us to do a sloppy job, do you?	

Bill: Well, mom, then hurry it up, you're talking too long.

Mother: No, we have to get all this stuff talked about, so that we don't do a sloppy job, so that you can really learn it right. Okay?

Bill: I might forget it.

Child confirms that he needs mom as a memory source.

Mother: That's why I'm here, so then she's going to help me to help you.

Mother vindicates her presence for mind control by using therapist's explanation. A sign of good rapport and trust that this therapy will not rob her of power.

Ther.: And your mother will help you to remember it and you'll probably remember this better than you remember most things. Okay? But first, I'm going to talk with you a little bit and tell you what one boy, I don't know if you saw it on TV. . .

Mother: He didn't.

Therapist defuses this conflict by transforming it into a suggestion that reassures that mother will help and son will remember. Therapist then puts this suggestion out of reach by moving on to "But first . . . ," opening up a different issue about a show on TV in which the use of trance with a hemophiliac was presented. This elevates the illness.

Ther.: Oh, he didn't. But, umm, because going under, going under, whenever he feels the bleed, in your case, just tell your mommy that you feel a bleed, you can "go under," it's called, and get very relaxed. Just as if you were going to sleep. . . Okay? And I'm going to tell you how to. . .

The therapist is careful to tie strings back to mother when suggesting the boy *will*, like the boy on TV, enhance his self-control.

Bill: And if I do fall asleep and I have a bleed and I forget how to do it and my mom forgets how to do it and I fall asleep?

Ther.: First thing, you'll go to your mom and do what you need to do and then you go down under and relax.

Therapist wants the boy to express his fears so she can address them. this issue of reporting bleeds is an important one. Therapist does not want the child to stop experiencing

Bill: What if. . .What if. . .

Mother: Don't worry about what if, just pay attention to what's going on now, all right?

Ther.: Okay. Well, I think it's okay for him to give me his "what ifs" because otherwise, they'll crop up.

Mother: He's being silly.

Ther.: Are you being silly?

Bill: What if I'm too tired to tell her and I fall asleep?

Ther.: Well then, I don't know for sure what to tell you about that. I think it's better if you. . .I think it's better if you don't let that happen. And you just stay awake and tell mommy.

Mother: Ummhuh. Let me just point out he always tells me anyway. I think he's playing. I. . .

Ther.: All right. So, I'm going to, let me do a couple of things in a couple of steps (to son), and then I'll break down for you what I was doing and why I was doing it. (To mother) Would that be a good way to do it, you think?

Mother: Anything. Go with whatever you're comfortable with because I can pick up the steps. . .

Ther.: You'll get what I'm doing, because I'm not going to be doing anything fancy. Okay. So Bill, we'll talk more about it afterward, okay?

Bill: Okay.

cues of a bleed but to fight the bleed himself while awaiting a needed transfusion.

Again therapist draws a boundary, protecting son's fears from mother's intrusion.

The suggestion to continue to tell mother of bleeds and to not use trance to pretend bleeds away or to ignore or not report them is now made. Also, the boy is indirectly reassured that trance will not be misused to pull him abruptly away from his mother.

"All right" is said as if to say "I know how you feel, and it's all right; nevertheless, we can continue." Again, "I" removes their responsibility of having to actively do anything. Therapist simplifies, demystifies, again reassures nothing scarey will happen, and asks if this is acceptable to mother.

Mother demonstrates her confidence and competence.

Therapist reconnects to son in the present "conscious" domain as if to say, "I'll see you again after the journey, okay?" Implicit is the suggestion that there will be a special experience.

Mother has now *invited* therapist to take charge of the problem.

The following induction is based on a dialectical goal. On the interior side of the dialectic, the therapist seeks to heighten feelings of self-control by working with the atomic inner reflections of outer chaos. On the exterior side of the dialectic, the therapist works to secure clear relational functions and draw the kinds of boundaries between mother and son that, when interiorized, can provide security and enhance self-control.

In the interior work, the primary physiological goal for Bill will be to stabilize his illness problems. The therapist will help him learn to use the trance state to reduce stress-related bleeds, partly by increasing, through indirect suggestion and posthypnotic suggestion, his automatic use of vasoconstriction at the site of his most distressing bleed, his left elbow, and vasodilation in other parts of his body. The induction therefore will include the son putting an icy right hand to this left elbow to withdraw blood from that area while awaiting an imagined transfusion.

In the exterior work, the induction will be used to draw boundaries between mother and son and specify functions mother can serve to help son. Mother and son will be provided the structural-corrective experience of being physically side by side while remaining *separate* in their own special imaginings. The rationale for mother's joining son in trance is that it will enable her to learn by experience how to later carry out the induction of her son. By using the induction to clarify specific functions, mother can help her son relax, and the therapist clears the way for specifying later those functions mother might discontinue serving. Even while eliciting private imagery in the son, the therapist has to be careful to protect aspects of that domain from mother's intrusion. Likewise, within son and mother, their own unconscious material will be identified as a sacred territory meriting protection from conscious intrusion as well. Note that the issue of separation is built in from the start of the formal induction by the separate but related technologies for entering into trance. Through the trance, the therapist will work with the small inner processes that may be exteriorized as outer boundaries and the broad external boundaries that ultimately can be interiorized. The dialectical hypnosis, designed to affect related interior and exterior system-sustaining contexts, will be the therapist's fair repayment to the family for the initial interview offering.

Stage 2: The Therapeutic Induction

Ther.: (To Bill) But I want you to learn that what I'm going to teach about today is just how to use yourself. It's all to put you in control of yourself, so I'm going to tell you how to do that, but you are the only one who can do it. (Change of tone to include mother directly) And you can do it for yourself, with your mommy's help whenever you need to, and you might even want to try it every single day, once a day, just to practice, okay? (To both) So put your hands on your knees and that's nice to do, yeah, that's right, what I always do while I'm helping other people do it, and (to mom) if you do it while I say it. . .

Using "I" takes some of the responsibility off them and suggests they can be passive—the word "you" is used alternately for mom, Bill, and the diad so that all that follows will have a direct line to those three units.

Mother: Now wait a minute, till I get ready, now. . .

"What I always do when I'm helping people" is a suggestion to mother. If therapist can go into trance while inducing it in others, mother can too when she does it with son. This begins separating mother's and Bill's trance experiences.

Ther.: When you're ready, put your hands on your knees. You put your hands on your knees and you can feel the warmth of your legs and your hands all together. . .like. . .

To both of them. Trance is suggested as "neat." It just happens, and it's "neat" to notice it—no work at all. Both have hands on knees and are awaiting some wonderful experience.

Bill: My hands seem warmer than my pants.

Ther.: The warmth of your pants, okay, it's going to come from your legs right through your pants, too.

Therapist makes a safe prediction to continue "yes set."

Bill: I can feel it.

The boy responds, warming his hands with his legs.

Ther.: Can you feel it a little more? And that's happening all the time.

The boy will enter hypnosis attached to mother, but the rules are he cannot be attached with all his

We just don't notice it. Now you can't watch your mother all the time. Okay, I'm going to tell you what to do, so you don't watch your mother all the time. Okay. Close your eyes. I'll close my eyes, too. Okay. I'm going to peek sometimes though. I'm going to cheat, but if you keep your eyes closed, feel the warmth in your fingertips and really feel that warmth—and that is the blood circulating in a very good healthy way through your body. And it circulates like that and goes through your body. It's happening all the time. I'm just going to tell you some things you can do so you start to notice it. You start to notice the way that you feel like that and you can feel very relaxed and very comfortable.

Bill: I feel sleepy (he stretches).

Ther.: And you feel very sleepy and that's another way to feel relaxed and comfy. And while you're sitting there in a chair, put your hands on your legs and feel that tingly sensation as a normal, healthy sensation of the blood flowing through your body. And if you notice that you're breathing every now and then, you can even take a very deep breath at one point and breathing it out, relax more.

Mother: (Takes a deep breath and closes her eyes, relaxing)

Bill: (Takes a deep breath) Is it all right if I scratch my nose, under my nose?

senses, for example, his eyes. Therapist will play by this rule too but will have therapist's license to peek. A boundary is drawn between mother and son.

Therapist caters to playfulness of childhood and gives the boy license to carry on *his* trance even if *he* cheats too.
First image of blood flow is to be positive. Warmth and comfort are associated with blood and the wonders of the normal aspects of blood circulation.
Once you notice what you feel, *you will relax.*

Bill is experiencing the relaxation as similar to sleepiness.

The sleepiness is defined as a way to feel more relaxed. Further suggestions of focusing inward on psychophysiological cues include "sitting there in a chair" and "tingly sensation."

Of course they are "breathing every now and then," so a very self-cued suggestion of taking a deep breath and so on is made.

Bill indicates his wish to cooperate, his connectedness to therapist.

Ther.: By all means, scratch. That's okay. And you just feel the comfort and relaxation of your own body, okay? And now what I want you to do is turn on a TV screen in your head; make the TV screen and turn on the on button. Now *your mommy might want to watch something else on TV than you do,* and I might want to watch something else. You're going to watch what?

In the security of one another's presence, a clear boundary is drawn in the trance format as mother and Bill are offered *separate TV screens* and the opportunity *to watch different shows.* Because mother and therapist are connected as trance teacher and trance trainee, therapist models "I might want to watch something else."

Mother: (From this point to end enters into a medium trance, not moving or talking, occasionally smiling in response to internal stimuli).

Bill: Superflick.

Ther.: Okay, turn on Superflick. I want you to watch the show of Superflick, and in this show of Superflick today I want you to imagine that you're somewhere where it's very very cool, where there's cool air—comfortable, it feels good—but it's very very cool and when you've got that picture, tell me a little bit about what's going on on *your* TV screen with the cool, cool air. What's going on on *your* TV screen with the cool, cool air?

Bill tunes in to the canned imagery of the collective dreams of young children, based on Saturday morning TV. The job of the therapist is to capitalize on whatever Bill comes up with.

"Your" is used for both mother and Bill, repeated as if said once for each one, each with a *separate* trance technology.

Bill: So far the creatures of the Invisible Man attack me.

The exterior lack of boundaries is reflected in the interior feeling of being invaded.

Ther.: Right there in the cool air?

Bill: Uh huh. They all attack me.

The boy is entering stream of consciousness.

Ther.: And then what'd you do when they attacked you?

Bill: I don't know. Then I fell down.

Ther.: You fell down, huh? Then get yourself back up and really feel that cool air makes you strong. . .

Bill: Yes.

Ther.: I want you to fill up with that cool air, fill up with that cool air. As you fill up with that cool air, you get very, very strong.

Bill: Now I turn into Superboy.

Ther.: You're Superboy now in the picture? Okay, now, while you're Superboy, I want you to imagine that one of your hands is getting very, very cool, and this is your strong strong strong hand, getting very very very cool. Okay?

Bill: Uh huh.

Ther.: And this very very cool hand is going to be very powerful for you. I want you to feel the coolness even in your fingers of that hand. That's good.

Bill: Uh huh.

Ther.: That very very very cool hand is going to be very powerful for you. I want you to feel the coolness even in your fingers of that hand, that very cool hand. It's like ice. Okay, you got that?

Bill: Uh huh.

Ther.: Now I want you to take that very very very cold hand, and when Superboy takes that very very very cold hand he can touch it to any part

This is the kind of material therapist wants to use to symbolically enact Bill's picking himself up when he's down.

Cool air is to be used to fill him with strength, ultimately a weapon against bleeds. He inhales, filling his cheeks with air.

Bill shows he is able to use suggestions to guide his dangerous fantasy.

The suggestion is to rescue himself from danger by using his right hand, the one he can get so cold that he can use it to freeze the bleed in his left elbow (vasoconstriction) by touching it.

Therapist continues to help Bill use imagery to affect psychophysiological processes and go more deeply into trance.

The icy hand, with associated psychophysiological sensations, is linked metaphorically in Bill's imagery of being unsafe, to his power to regain control. Instructions are

of his body and cool that area of his body. He can touch another monster with it and cool that monster or he can touch it to a part of his own body and cool the body. And I want you to imagine that Superboy's hand, the very cool hand, gets very light now and starts to move over to his elbow and cool that elbow, freeze that elbow. That cold hand gets very very light and floats and I don't know which hand it is now, but you'll know which hand it is when it starts to get light, that cold cold hand and floaty, kind of all fluffed up and floaty.

Bill: My eyes are watching it.

Ther.: Your eyes are watching it happen? Is it happening now?

Bill: Yes.

Ther.: That light hand goes over and touches the elbow, and cold cold in that elbow. Cold hand. And that feels good, doesn't it?

Bill: Yes.

Ther.: It feels really good. It can feel a lot like getting a transfusion feels, there's that rush, kind of rush. That cold hand can give you that kind of rush.

Bill: (Neck shivers)

Ther.: Okay, now what's happening on the TV screen?

Bill: The creatures are capturing me.

Ther.: They're capturing you?

Bill: Uh huh. With the bad guys.

explicit at this point as therapist moves from fantasies of Superboy versus creatures to Superboy versus his own super elbow.

It will need to be the right hand, but he can decide that. Therapist need not intrude.

Bill hallucinates the upward movement of his strong cold hand. Bill gasps as the hallucinated arm touches his elbow.

Bill's head shakes with the hallucinated transfusion of factor, which sends a rush to the neck. Therapist returns to the TV screen to put these psychophysiological suggestions out of reach, *to draw a boundary around them*. Therapist returns to visualizations about being overpowered.

Ther.: Okay. Now, what are you going to do with your super strength? You know how to make your fingertips cold or you know how to make your fingertips hot, what can you do with that?

Bill: I don't know.

Ther.: Okay. Let's take your cold cold hand and use that hand to. . .

Therapist suggests Bill practice fighting back against attacking agents by directing his newfound skills *outward*. The freezing hand is compatible with the boy's Superflick format.

Bill: But there's a lot of them.

Bill expresses fear he cannot do it alone.

Ther.: Okay, then you need your mother there.

Therapist offers that this may be a time to call on mother.

Bill: I don't think . . . Superman doesn't have a wife.

Ther.: Oh, he doesn't have a wife, huh? Does he have a friend? He needs a friend. He needs somebody to help him.

Bill transforms "mother" to Superman's "wife." It is as if he gets to say "I don't need her" while at the same time bringing her along symbolically, then letting her go, in a situation of parity.

Bill: Then I call on Flash.

Ther.: Okay. Bring in Flash. And Flash has two icy hands to join with yours and together they're stronger than other hands.

Bill: Flash isn't strong. He's just the fastest man on earth. He can do anything faster than the speed of light.

Strength is not enough. Bill spontaneously adds the need for "speed"—quick responses as well. He is beginning to embellish his own trance controls.

Ther.: And you join up with him?

Bill: Uh huh.

Ther.: And you still have your cold cold hand, right?

Bill: Uh huh. And I knock out my arch enemy: Hex Luther.

Ther.: Okay.

Bill: And then Flash knocks out Captain Cold.

Ther.: Okay, and have you won over everybody? Have you beat them? I want you to beat them. I want you to beat them this time.

Notice, in the face of her son's trials, mother, who interrupted at every sign of discomfort before the induction, stays out, sitting still, hands on knees, immobile, smiling slightly, throughout. Therapist, however, does want Bill to find within himself an exit from helplessness.

Bill: They knock Flash out.

Ther.: Does he come back up again?

Bill: Uh uh, Captain Cold froze him. And he froze me. 'Cause I couldn't get out. So I called Superman.

Ther.: Then what happened?

Bill: Then he calls the rest of the Superfriends.

Ther.: Then what happens?

Bill: Then one of them gets trapped.

Ther.: Can you figure out some way to get out? Not every time, but just sometimes?

Therapist considers that Bill might need to produce endless horrors if he thinks he is being urged to never get attacked. She adds "Not every time, but just sometimes." Part of salvaging benevolent or useful symptom features.

Bill: My cold hand is free. I grow back and Flash turns into a tornado and breaks out.

Bill responds favorably, using the cold hand *spontaneously* as his own idea of "some way to get out."

Ther.: Okay. So when you need to, when you can remember very carefully the scene when you and Flash and Superman can break out. . .

Of the entire sequence of Bill's interior events, *this* is the memory to salvage and exteriorize.

Bill: And Green Lantern. . .

Ther.: And you can use your icy hand to freeze out someone else that tries to hurt you or to freeze out a part of you that hurts you.

Therapist embellishes this option the son has selected and suggests that this is the ending point of the show. He can remember it *when he needs it.*

And now turn the TV off and just leave it with the white fuzzy stuff blinking. And now I'm going to talk to you a little bit. And you can feel the blood returning to your finger-tips, not painfully, just comfortably. What I'm going to. . .

Bill: Now my hands are all sweaty!

Ther.: That's good. That shows how warm you can get your hand and that's very important 'cause if you can get your fingertips very very warm whenever you need to, when-ever you feel pain in your elbow or your ankle, if you can get your fin-gertips warm, it won't feel as badly. Now you might not want to do this every single time, but if you want to feel relaxed, and you want to feel comfortable when you get a bleed, you can just tell your mommy it's coming, sit down in a chair with your mommy next to you. She can remind you to put your hands on your knees, close your eyes.

Bill: That's what I'm doing.

Ther.: That's good. Feel that warmth of your own body and in control of yourself, the warmth of your hand on your lap. As the temperature gets greater in your fingertips, you can then feel all relaxed, comfy. We can imagine the TV screen goes on and you're feeling safe, even if the monsters and the bad guys come. You have a weapon against them. You are strong, and if you remember that

Therapist begins a slow awakening process by harkening back to the psychophysiological suggestions preceding the turning on of TV. This also begins to put the TV *in-formation* out of reach, to draw a boundary between conscious and unconscious material. TV show goes off.

Bill responds quickly with the phy-siological component of increasing blood flow to a particular body part following first induction sugges-tions of warming hands.

Bill is ready for the next round and indeed, while starting the awaken-ing process, therapist is embedding an abbreviated replication of the trance induction, taking a kind of detour back through the trance ex-perience, to make some suggestions and let the experiences of mother and son settle in. Also, by shifting across levels of trance material, boundaries can be drawn to sepa-rate them, facilitating amnesias. Therapist does not want them to obsess about their "unconscious" learnings: "You don't need to think about this process."

scene, you won't forget this experience. You won't forget what it feels
like, because it will be useful to you
and you have a better memory than
you think. You might be surprised to
find that out. Today is just a start,
and since you're going to practice
this soon, you'll be in much more
control over yourself in a short
amount of time. And I'm going to
count from one to ten, and at home,
after you've spent time relaxing very
quietly, if your mommy helps, she   Mother is again tied to Bill's relaxa-
should count from one to ten too,   tion. It is as if the last thing said
very slowly, and at the end of the ten, had been: "Tell Bill to relax, and
then you should open your eyes.   put his hand on his knees" and
Then you should open your eyes, but   "then count from one to ten to
not until then. And let that good feel- wake Bill up." The whole middle
ing stay there until the time is up.   of the trance becomes erased. This
                                         is useful for amnesia.
And when you wake up, you can feel
very refreshed, as if you went to sleep
and woke up with a good dream.
You don't need to think about what   The emphasis is on remembering
happened. You don't even need to   the *steps* of the trance induction
remember it in your awake state, for   and forgetting the *content* of the
it to happen again. Just whenever   trance material. Amnesia is a way
you need it, and you just give your   of drawing a boundary between
mommy the signal and she'll help   conscious and unconscious states.
you relax. So we count from one to   Therapist simultaneously suggests
ten. One, two, three, four, now   what mother will do to induce
slowly start to wake up as I get   trance while suggesting that at
toward ten. Five, six, seven, eight,   "ten" the boy will wake up.
very slowly now, nine, ten.

Stage 3: Postinduction—Pegging and Securing Changes

Now the induction is done. Mother and son each had a unique
experience of trance, and mother did not intervene between the therapist

and her son. Mother has received some ideas about cue words, such as counting, and routines she can suggest, such as putting hands on legs, to retrigger the associations with the trance states. Now the goal is to draw a boundary, to protect the trance state's privacy and maintain it in the waking state as at least a partial refuge from the intrusion of the other. The reciprocal pattern of intrusion begins to be activated immediately as each person starts to awaken. The therapist stops it by defining the trance experience to each person as something they need not document to the other.

Bill: I'm the first one up (eyes opening, body reorienting, stretching)!

Ther.: First one up, uh! I think I'm the last one.

"Last" is good with trance. Here slowness counts too. Also models "I was in my own world also, while working with you."

Bill: (Giggle)

Ther.: Okay.

Bill: My hands started to get cold a little bit again (the counting reinitiated the initial trance sequence).

It is likely that Bill's sweaty hand got cold again in response to the detour through an embedded review of the induction process. The actual therapy room was fairly warm.

Ther.: At the end? Or when we were doing it in the middle?

Bill: Uh huh. At the end.

Ther.: At the very end, huh?

Bill: A little bit at the end.

Ther.: That's right. That's fine that it started to do that again. . . .So I think that I don't need to review it with you today. I think you will remember.

Mother: I'm sure. . .you know, we're talking about the, uhm coolness. Now I. . .

Mother is still slowly arousing and cannot speak with her usual facility.

Ther.: You were not watching that same movie?

Therapist asks with mock surprise.

Mother: (Happily) No, I was in there, I was in the middle of a beautiful forest and the snow was just coming down and I was watching kids coming down, sledding down a hill and I was, you know. . .(staring off).

Mother confirms her own trance experience by volunteering an independent well-developed reverie. It is interesting that in selecting a comforting image, mother partakes of the experience of "normal" children sledding. The trance state spontaneously activates a different sense of herself, mesmerized by snowfall and natural beauty.

Bill: You should have been watching your soap operas.

Mother: You said cool, and you know, I think. . .

Bill: You should have been watching your soap operas.

Bill begins to intrude into his mother's unconscious processes. This is the kind of exterior situation therapist will want to help prevent. Therapist will help mother and Bill draw a protective skin around their visualizations.

Mother: Does it matter what scene you see, I mean, I got the impression that. . .

Ther.: Don't mention the scene. . .

Bill: Mom, you should have watched the soap operas!

Ther.: (Inaudible)

Therapist does not want mother to evoke her or Bill's trance events in the waking state. They might be tampered with by premature conscious intrusion.

Mother: Okay, because I was, I thought, hey, you know. . .

Ther.: She gets to watch whatever she wants.

Therapist draws a protective boundary first around mother's reverie.

Mother: He isn't paying attention at all to what. . .you know what I mean?

Ther.: No, no.

Mother: It doesn't matter?

Ther.: Umm. Let's see. Well. . .

Mother: Because I was afraid he was missing what was going on.

Ther.: No, no, no.

Mother: He was missing a lot.

Therapist then draws a line around son's reverie, which mother is not to trespass. Therapist is allowed

Ther.: No, no, no, not for a second. We should maybe talk about that separately.

Bill: Mom, weren't you watching. . .

these intrusions into the relationship because the rapport is good.

To further enhance boundaries, therapist will now see mother separately.

Each one fears the other did not do well. At this point, to draw a sacred line around the privacy of the trance experience, to elevate mother, and to free Bill from parent talk, the therapist suggests that if Bill is satisfied—and clearly he is—he can wait in the waiting room.

One goal at this point of the interview is to *encourage mother to express her objections,* to minimize the possibility of sabotage and prevent external facets of the symptom structure from engulfing mother's or son's newly ordered internal events. A second goal is to use mother's trance experience as a body of information and learnings that the therapist can introduce in abbreviated form into mother's self-anxiety inductions to help her disrupt her own illness-related rigidities (see discussion of trance insertion in Chapter Two).

As mother talks alone with therapist, after the induction, she starts to make statements that are anxiety producing, rushing into a speech about her worries and self-doubts. Because of the shared trance experience, the therapist simply interrupts the speech, as if mother had been talking about something else, and inserts into the anxiety talk the cue words of relaxation. Mother immediately relaxes, laughing. Shortly afterward, she expresses the same fear Bill had expressed immediately before the induction, when she accused him of just being silly. After the shared induction, she is in a state of receptivity to a gentle challenge. This challenge pertains to both overinvolvement in her son's inner life and the negative reactivity that charges the current of their relationship.

The therapist wants to highlight less intense or worrisome ways mother can function with son.

Mother: In a single-parent situation like this, there's such an incredible tendency on my part to be an overprotective mother, it isn't even funny. I mean, I think I go completely the other way because. . .

Ther.: (Talking over, inaudible)

Mother: And with Bill, so much of
the stuff he's got to do himself, you
know, with his hemophilia, and as
much as I'd like to take all the problems that he's going to have in life
away from him, I can't. He's got to
come, and all I want to do is to get
him all the things that he can get, so
that he can find a way that works for
him to cope with what. . .

Mother talks quickly of her worries.

Ther.: (Quietly) So when you do this
with him, then talk about that. Turn
on the TV screen and imagine whatever you would like for him. . .

Mother: That's a great thought, boy.
Oh, it's so hard. I should do it, talk
in that great voice, even if he laughs
at me, I'm going to be practicing
talking s-l-o-w-l-y, and nodding
out. . .

Therapist suggests that it is when
she feels upset, as she is starting to
now, that she can turn to her own
new inner resource, *her own TV.*
Therapist uses the trance voice,
language, and timing as if slowing
down time. The suggestion is "Imagine whatever you would like for
him" while "You watch *your* TV
screen when he has a problem you
can do something about." She is to
imagine *what she wants for herself*
and do it for his sake, *or* imagine
what she would like him to have.
Either is offered as an option.

Ther.: If you get into that trance
state while you're doing it with him,
you'll really know the right thing.
No, because. . .

Mother: I think I'll have to get myself half drunk (laughing) just to
slow. . .myself. . .down. . .enough. . .
to. . .talk like that (putting her hands
on her knees).

Mother jokingly reenacts the trance,
but manifests the perseverative nodding characteristic of light trance
and enjoys a brief but relieving stay
in that state.

Ther.: It's good if you can do it here,
you just have to feel your. . . .

Mother: Yeah, I'm going to have to
consciously do that (nodding slowly).

Ther.: And I find it very helpful. I
will just, if I need to, I'll close my
eyes and I will just do it while I'm

Therapist attempts to prolong her
self-induced trance, again using the
"You and I are alike as trance

talking to people and I have to occasionally open my eyes, because I have to make sure, you know, that the person didn't leave the room or something. Pretty much, though, you'll be in good touch; you can even stay in touch with him with your eyes closed, because you'll hear him move around and you can just look at him now and then to make sure. . .

teachers" to model safely for mother.

Mother: He's a worker, I mean, he thinks it's a game now, and I think he's going to get into it.

Mother has other issues she wants to get to.

Ther.: Oh, if he does, that would be very good. All reports seem to indicate that this can really make better. . .

Mother: You know that I have a friend who hypnotizes himself. . . He's into that—it scares me to death.

Ther.: Why?

Mother: Oh, I figure, you know, I've always. . .It sounds to me. . .I'd love to be able to hypnotize myself, but I kept thinking what if I couldn't get myself out of it, you know what I mean? And that upset me and then I was concerned, about Bill—I was concerned that he'd hypnotize himself to the point where he actually would have a severe problem and. . . that he wouldn't feel any pain—he wouldn't tell me, and. . .

Mother expresses fears about hypnosis, about not waking up, about Bill's not waking up. These things "scare her to death" and might, if not discussed, undermine the hypnotic work.

Ther.: See, that's what Bill was afraid of, that's what Bill was saying. That's what Bill was saying and you

"You and Bill have the same fear, and that's natural. It need not interfere."

were saying to him "You're joking, you're joking." Do you remember that?

Mother: Yes. . .yes. . .I do.

Ther.: That's what he was saying. That's what Bill was afraid of. Bill said "What if I go to sleep. . .?"

This exchange suggests to mother she let Bill worry, without interfering. A good mother may allow her child some discomforts.

Mother: (Laughing) Oh God, all my parent effectiveness training and I don't even hear what my kid's telling me.

The hypnosis gives mother a concrete task she can engage in to help herself and Bill relax and to increase their sense of control in their own lives. This goal was clearly synchronous with mother's goals:

Mother: My ultimate goal was for him to grow up not thinking of hemophilia as a handicap. He'll think, that he's a person and he's got all these options and he happens to have hemophilia. And to learn that the rest of the world isn't going to understand it and that they're wrong, you know, that he knows, because of his age, he knows better now if there's something he can do, whatever it is, you know, that's what I want for Bill. I don't want this hemophilia to be the central focusing. I don't want him to be Billy Rogers, hemophiliac, but to be Billy Rogers who is a young man with hemophilia, you know what I mean. . . .

It was important for this interview to close on a positive note, with mother back in control. The hypnosis must not meet with overriding family relational patterns. Mother agrees not to ask Bill about his trance events. And Mother does leave in a more confident, positive spirit than when she first came in, as if she had gotten back something for the trouble of sharing her problems. Thus, an essential goal of our model of cooperative exchange has been satisfied for this interview.

Ther.: I think that his relaxation should be linked with you. I think that you should do it with him, although he should be in control of his body. I think that you should do it with him, because I think he needs to still feel a reliance on you *first.*

Therapist reiterates that son will go into trance connected to mother *at first.* Therapist emphasizes that Bill should remain in control of his own body even when mother helps him. Future sessions may wish to emphasize further incremental steps of separation. Nuances of separating are hinted at.

Mother: I think so. He has, I think he's, we have a, I think he's very very solid in his relationship with me. Very solid indeed. He trusts me. I see, well, another thing, I would never lie to the kid. If he's going to go into the hospital and it's going to hurt. He knows it's going to hurt and, you know, I'll explain to him why we have to do this, that, you know, it's not that everybody's out to hurt him, but I don't say, oh, we'll get a butterfly and it's no big deal, I mean, you know. . .

Ther.: Do you think that maybe you're doing a good job?

Therapist suggests mother *is* doing a good job.

Mother: I hope so. I really hope to hell I am, because I've only got one kid, and I expect him to be president! (Laughing)

The therapy of mother and son continued in the same format with a different therapist, including practice inductions by mother in the sessions. Also to be dealt with over time would be related boundary issues, for example, mother's expanding her idea of a "good mother" to include some periods of inaccessibility to her son, separation, even moments of uninterrupted *inner reverie,* and Bill's finding other ways than stress bleeds to fill his place in his mother's life. The result of a seven-month data follow-up was Bill needed less factor with each transfusion (976.42 as opposed to 1473.57 units prior to treatment), which was evidence of a psychophysiological change, and missed much less school, despite school problems (two days, as opposed to twenty-seven in the seven months prior), suggesting better mother-son separating skills. The negativism of the mother-son interaction was successfully diffused, and plans were being made for mother to resume home care of Bill (see Ritterman, 1981).*

Summary

Regarding the generalities of this case and others similarly treated, this approach entailed hypnosis with three potential structural goals:

1. To affect the mind-set of the symptom bearer, including his physiological behavior
2. To affect any dysfunctional aspects of family structure
3. To establish more functional hierarchies and clearer boundaries.

Additionally, the hospital context can be used, or hospital personnel can be involved, to activate the hypnotic response during treatment as well as parental and patient competence in face of treatment. An example of such a family-hospital interface concerned Mike, a two-year-old with a severe factor VIII deficiency with inhibitors, who frequently needed weekly transfusions, often for mouth bleeds. It took four adults to pin Mike on his back and straighten his arm to give him his transfusions. Especially regarding mouth bleeds, his nonstop screaming made it extremely difficult to arrest the bleed and unsettled all the nursing staff involved. Usually, after the traumatic transfusion experience, Mike returned to his mother's lap and fell into a deep sleep. The therapeutic goals for this

---

*Although results are not attributed to the interventions in this single interview, the long-term follow-up is that four years later Bill is averaging four bleeds in sixteen months, has straight A's, is a computer whiz, and has home treatments. All this despite his mother's continuing single-parent pressures and loss of a long-term relationship with a man. These results suggest a decrease in the stress-reverberating patterns in the mother-son diad.

simple aspect of bleed management were to help the child "sleep" before and during each transfusion. A multiperson hypnotic approach was developed, in which both mother and father learned to hold the child in their lap and engage all his senses with repetitions of present caresses, good flavors, loving gazes, and favorite songs. Alternating turns, when the child needed hospital treatment, they would bring him in, sit in a special chair in the hospital, and establish the intense rapport. Then the nurse would come in dressed in street clothes and administer the needed transfusion. In this simple manner, the family induced its own hypnotic atmosphere, in which they remained relaxed and in control of their son's treatment, even in the hospital setting. A six-month follow-up confirmed that treatment was no longer associated with extreme anxiety for Mike, his parents, or the hospital staff.

A general paradigm of childhood psychophysiologically related dialectical therapy—including both the interiorization of new family interactional patterns and the exteriorization of newly developed trance skills—suggests that the therapist:

1. Assess the nature of the relationship between parent(s) and son regarding illness problems (family context).
2. Evaluate mental-sets of each member regarding illness (context of mind).
3. Evaluate related social factors (social context).
4. Using a diagram of illness in motion, map problem sequences in the related contexts and select pertinent points of entry (including work with peers, for example, to increase autonomy from excessive family dependencies).
5. Because of the complexities of such cases, select a dialectical intervention that will simultaneously work on the internal and external representations of illness problems.
6. Build a single-parent mother into the hypnotic treatment of her son's psychophysiological problems if she seems trustworthy to not abuse her trance skills.
7. In a two-parent family, engage father by inviting parents, if the family is suited for this process, to take turns doing the induction.
8. Negotiate boundaries, even in a family in which a parent(s) is thought ill-equipped for conjoint trance work or the child is unwilling. In one case, a young boy had seen his older brothers suffer

excessive dependency on mother and did not want to end up like them. He rebelled by not reporting bleeds and thus unnecessarily weakened his joints. To help him strengthen the boundary between himself and mother, the boy was given individual hypnosis. In trance, he learned to "blow the whistle" he wore around his neck on intruding monsters. It was suggested that this was a *manly* thing to do. Mother was then seen alone. After using a light trance in helping her get relief from her routine hospital migraine, the therapist cautioned her to resolve to stop nagging her son and was assured he would change. The boy "spontaneously" began to report his bleeds and to be promptly treated for them. Mother also kept her end of the deal (see Ritterman, 1981).

9. Gradually help parents foster the child's autonomy, teaching him to "hold onto their hand" even when they are *not* with him, thereby enhancing his self-control and relieving him of serving secondary communications functions for the family via his illness, encouraging his search for peer support.

10. Keep records of amounts of factor transfused before and after treatment, numbers and durations of bleeds, location of bleeds, and days of school missed, to document therapeutic efficacy and refine the approach accordingly.

Chapter Six 🙝🙟 🙝🙟 🙝🙟

Case Study
of a Suicidal Woman

🙝🙟 This chapter details the use of an indirect induction of a symptom bearer to facilitate needed trance work with an entire family. The sequences transcribed from a single interview also provide a model for the broader sequences of the entire therapy. The first part is background on special features of the interview, the case, and the epidemiology of suicide. The second part describes the steps for creating an hypnotic atmosphere. In this atmosphere, the clinician's capacity to "read" family inductive techniques is enhanced. In the third section, trance is used in the reading of the symptom bearer's self-inductive techniques and the creation of a family therapeutic hypnotic counterinduction. Separate but convergent trances are employed to (1) affect symptom-related rigid mind-sets of all family members and (2) activate *shared trance reveries* for specific purposes. The fourth section clarifies the steps involved in eliciting and working with postinduction resistances or objections. The therapist inserts "atoms" of the trance experience into family interactional events, to facilitate new family sequences, connections, boundaries, and suggestions.

Throughout, despite the shifting from inner to outer realities, the therapeutic focus is on the principal symptom offered to the interviewer: a woman who wants to kill herself. The case is referred to as "The Young Woman with the Bad Body."

The Consultation Format of the Interview

The family interview is a consultation on an ongoing case. The interviewer is from out of state and is seeing the family only once, in the capacity of consultant to the ongoing therapist and his cotherapist. The two ongoing therapists (OTs) are present during the interview, while a group of clinicians attending the consultant's workshop view from behind a one-way mirror. Because this context is slightly unusual, contributions of this special format are briefly discussed.

Prior to the family interview, the consultant held a presession with the entire workshop group. At this time, she was given a comprehensive background on both the history of the case and the six months of prior treatment that the OTs felt had dead-ended. This format makes several unique contributions to the therapy:

1. Although the consultant is new to the family, she is directly connected to it via the OTs.
2. She has much background on the case and the attempted approaches, which failed. By the time of the interview, she has had a chance to establish a good rapport with the primary therapists, who will carry the case, and she has some general ideas about issues that may be roadblocks for her as well.
3. The format heightens the interviewer's power. Bringing the interviewer in from out of town accords recognition to both the therapeutic and family systems and carries the unspoken message of appreciation of the power of the gift. Recall from Chapter Three that the gift is a feature of symptomatic expression that the family generally disapproves of but that has defensive or refuge functions for the symptom bearer. The therapist or consultant links into this part of the symptom with respect, gentleness, admiration, and interest, always with the consent or by invitation of the symptom bearer. In a situation like this, the interviewer must be particularly cautious to not let the circumstances of social pressure cloud her judgment about what aspect of this gift is acceptable to her. She must look for invitations family members extend to her about what problems she is to deal with and accept a problem she can begin to realistically do something about.

4. The consultation interview is a moment in the events of the broader therapeutic context. The goals of the interview are to introject a new thrust to the treatment setting, to sharpen the focus on a central conflict, and to help evolve a treatment model compatible with the observing clinicians' skills and understandings. In this case, the OTs have knowledge of both family and hypnotic approaches and are interested in their integration.

The Case

The parents of the family coming for therapy emigrated during the Nazi occupation from a small and poor area of Germany to the United States. Father had been a tailor in Germany but had to become a maintenance man once he came to this small mining town. Mother, originally a housekeeper, has run a grocery store for the last three years. The store, which was to stabilize a poor economic situation, was bankrupting the family. The parents have a twenty-four-year-old daughter; the index patient, who is twenty; and two sons, eighteen and ten. The oldest daughter left home approximately one year before the interview. She became pregnant, disgraced the family in the eyes of its fundamentalist church, but then married afterward, redeeming herself. She lives in another town, where she raises her child. The eighteen-year-old son had been attending a boarding school and returned home approximately a year before the interview to help his mother manage the store, as a bad economic situation turned into a terrible one.

The index patient had a history of obtaining therapy for various problems since she was five years old. In the course of her therapeutic tutelage, she had been seen and treated by most psychiatric specialists within a radius of 100 miles and had obtained a number of diagnoses, from hysteria to multiple personality. In the last year she was hospitalized twice for suicide threats. The OT had seen her individually for several months, using various paradoxical techniques, and had begun working with her parents to stabilize a situation in which the girl was to either go to work or to college by a certain date. The girl had chosen to go to another town, where she had been attending a college. She had trouble concentrating at college, and her grades were only average. She was socially immature, and she made the mistake of telling the teacher of her early childhood development course that she had been in a mental hospital; the teacher then told Gretchen that because of her history she should not work with children. Several months prior to the interview, she had been threatening to kill herself, and when she became actively suicidal, she had been hospitalized until she felt in control. At that point, feeling overwhelmed with the demands of the case, her therapist invited in a cotherapist. This therapist came from a similar background as the family's, so it was hoped that his presence might ease entry into the *private* domain of the family, those aspects of life ordinarily protected from strangers or nonkin.

In a previous session, the father had said that "This house isn't big enough for two women." Nevertheless, the night before the consultation session, the daughter had gone to the junior therapist and informed him that she has just dropped out of college and that it was impossible to go back this term. This was to be the fait accompli handed to the consultant. Also, the young woman is notorious for carting around a stuffed animal, which the consultant had been forewarned about. (Indeed, the young woman arrives for the session—having just quit college the day before—barefoot, her hair and clothes unkempt, carrying a small blue rhino.)

The therapists, conceptualizing the case as a classic leaving home situation, had tried reframing her "crazy" behavior at home, prescribing it at circumscribed times and bolstering the mother and father regarding their parenting. The OTs felt concerned (1) that the young woman had not expressed authentic seeming emotions, hence that their rapport with her had not been adequately established and her mind-set was unaffected; (2) that as they jostled the family system at one place, another, equally powerful spurt of water would burst through another hole in the dam and so it might be necessary to affect the family structure at several openings at once; and (3) that they were insufficiently informed of this family's edicts, such as the rules and roles they had based on socioeconomic, fundamentalist religion, and gender issues. These special concerns of the therapists would orient the consultant's therapy. Because the principal presenting complaint was that the index patient was suicidal, we look briefly at aspects of the epidemiology of suicide in the United States and Canada to help frame the young woman's specific problem in the broader context of adolescent suicide, which is a wildly proliferating social phenomenon.

Suicide Attempts as a Social Problem

Gretchen, the index patient, is only one twenty-year-old living in a unique family context, with a unique way of perceiving herself and the world. However, she is also a contributor to an alarming set of statistics. Likewise, these statistics comprise part of the social context of her symptoms. Death by suicide is an increasing problem for adolescents over the age of fourteen; recent international comparisons indicate that suicide rates for fifteen- to twenty-four-year-olds have risen more sharply in the United States and Canada than in most other countries ("Suicide—International Comparisons," 1972). In both countries, suicide has advanced directly as a cause of death in adolescents, as evidenced by increasing suicide death rates. It has advanced indirectly in association with the decline of deaths from other causes. As the tenth cause of death for *all* ages, suicide ranks as the third cause of death for fifteen- to twenty-four-year-olds, Gretchen's age group—only accidents and homicides resulted in more deaths than suicide in that age group.

Although there are more male suicides than females, the female rate has increased more rapidly than the male, with females, historically users of poisons, now joining males in the use of firearms. Girls who have tried suicide, or "gestured" before, run a greater risk than those who have not. Childless teenagers and married teenagers run the greatest risk. As many as 13.5 percent of female suicides of childbearing age and capacity have been found pregnant at the time of their death. Physical illness, particularly if it affects sex-role identification, or, in the case of females, if it deprives them of care and support from important others, increases the likelihood of suicide. A family history of suicidal behavior also appears prominent among youths attempting suicide. (See Petzel and Cline, 1978.)

Adolescent suicide attempts have been described as part of a process that includes long-standing problems, escalating problems during adolescence, increasing failure of adaptive techniques, progressive isolation, a relatively acute dissolution of residual relationships, a conceptual justification of suicide, and, finally, the attempt (Jacobs, 1971). Translating the process into the context of this book, we consider adolescent suicide a potentially three-level metaphor for persistent social situational conflicts, problematic family relations, and a rigid mind-set that provides the conceptual justification of suicide.

Step 1: Creating an Hypnotic Atmosphere and
Reading Family Inductions

The entire transcript of the consultation follows. This is the first interview with the entire family present, except for the older, married daughter. Note that: the first three statements of the interview are between the ongoing therapist (OT) and mother and father while the consultant is behind the mirror observing with the group. The consultant decides to enter after these initial statements, to prevent the family from jumping into the problem before she has a chance to connect with them. From behind the mirror, the arrangement is: Gretchen on the far left of an oblong half-circle. Her blond hair is disheveled; her glasses are filmy, almost concealing her blue eyes. She is wearing an outdated blouse, is barefoot, and is carrying her blue stuffed rhino. Next to her is the junior therapist. To his left is father, who is gentle, quiet, reserved, and conveys a formality. To his left is mother, who is a round-faced, rosy-cheeked, large, informal, friendly woman. The younger son, Chris, is neatly but casually dressed and has brought his own entertainment with him, a Rubik cube. The older brother, John, is dressed in a suit and tie. He looks formal and very stiff. To his left is the OT and the camera operator.

OT: Do you want to tell us how that visit was?

Father: Well, you know, she does want to come home.

Mother: Yeah, yeah. Gretchen decided she wants to come home. She spoke to Clide [father] last night and Clide told me that.

Consultant notes sequences described. Daughter calls father. Says she wants to come home from college. Father okays it, *then* tells mother. OT will look for replications of this pattern, in which father and Gretchen have power to make decisions independent of mother.

The consultant notes that Gretchen had told her father she had decided to come home from college the night before the session. Without discussing it with his wife, there apparently being no "rule" to do so, father had then simply told his wife of the fact. From this initial observation, the consultant decides to make a good connection with father, assuming that in at least one aspect of family life that affects Gretchen, he has the decision-making power. The consultant has also noted that

Gretchen looked very pleased with her power to come home, like a little girl enjoying getting away with mischief.

OT: This is Dr. Ritterman, Mr. Clide.

Cons.: Mr. Clide? I am pleased to meet you. (Consultant looks questioningly at father, indicating his family)

Father seems to want responsibility, so consultant treats him as head of family.

Father: Maybe we should introduce the rest of the family to you: Brenda, Gretchen, Christopher, and John.

Cons.: (Nods, meeting each one) Christopher?

The women—mother and daughter—are introduced first, contrary to actual order of seating arrangement, in which mother is to father's left and Gretchen is to father's right (with the junior therapist between them).

Chris: Chris.

Cons.: Your nickname—okay.

Father introduces young son with his formal name. Son corrects.

Although she has been introduced first, Gretchen is the last person the consultant contacts in this casual social capacity. The consultant wants to convey that *she* will determine when and how much she will interact with Gretchen; Gretchen is not going to run the show with her. The consultant assumes that Gretchen is not simply *subject to* certain family and social inductions but that she too is actively maintaining the symptom structure, however lamentable she might appear.

Note in the following section that the consultant uses her joining with Gretchen to both (1) begin a process of activating "unconscious" associations, a basic component in creating an hypnotic atmosphere, and (2) challenge Gretchen.

Cons.: (To Gretchen) Hi. I am glad to meet you. You know, I was just admiring your—what is this—rhinoceros.

Gretchen: Yeah (attentive, beaming like a child who thinks she can control a situation).

Consultant goes directly to an aspect of symptom. While ostensibly praising Gretchen and effectively joining her, she is connecting to the three-year-old child aspect of Gretchen's behavior.

Cons.: I wanted to show you what I just bought my children, because I had to leave my children to come out here to do some work with you; I got my daughter this raccoon.

Consultant shifts from "playmate" connection to "My children play with toys like yours. . .the children I love."

Gretchen: That's nice. . .

Cons.: And I got my son this beaver.

Gretchen: A beaver.

Cons.: Yes. Do you like those? How about if we put yours in here (box holding animals) with these—or would you just like them to sit next to you?

Consultant teases Gretchen: "If you won't give me your toy, I won't give you mine either." Consultant and Gretchen are at a standoff.

Gretchen: They can sit next to me.

Cons.: Let's keep them over with me; they remind me of my little children. (To Gretchen) You know, my children are three and a half and one and a half (turning to include parents).

Consultant changes her mind. She speaks to parents as well, but in an indirect way, a way they cannot respond to in this social setting. "I too am the parent of a three- to five-year-old child!"

Gretchen: Oh, wow.

Cons.: They really like animals (change of tone, erase past message). (To Gretchen) Would you bring your chair in? You're a little far away from the rest of the family there.

Asking Gretchen to bring chair in closer is done in a different tone. Here consultant has begun a process in which subjects will be opened and closed by a change in tone of voice. Gretchen has made a connection. She agrees to move in.

Gretchen: Okay (moving chair in).

In this initial encounter, still prior to any formal giving of the gift, consultant and Gretchen have engaged in play therapy. In this exchange about toys, the consultant is speaking in the symptom bearer's language about issues of fantasy life, and about what constitutes age-appropriate feelings for toys. She is talking to both Gretchen and her parents. She indicates her own separation from her children to accomplish important work, dropping that as a seed to the mother. She also attracts Gretchen with the toys and then suggests that when one becomes a mother, one may get stuffed animals. She then drops the bomb, looking at Gretchen and her parents, that her own children are one and three. The tone suggests that "I, too, am a parent of a very young child." Gretchen will not be regarded as "crazy" here but as capable of being immature.

In this simple exchange of praise for toys, the consultant has conveyed "I will play with the little girl in you, but it will be on my terms." This is part of a careful creating of an hypnotic atmosphere, in which metaphorical language, innuendo, and rapid shifting from levels of communication will be part of the therapeutic context. To put aside the unconscious issues about acting like a baby, the consultant changes her tone and, not unlike father responding to Gretchen's isolation, asks that Gretchen, who is seated on the periphery of the room, move closer to her family, suggesting nonverbally, "Now let's deal with you in your family" or "Let's see what happens in your family when you move in closer." Gretchen concedes.

The consultant proceeds to join with father. Note how she develops a style of communicating with him in which she responds to indirect messages rather than taking his statements at face value. She notes the ordering of his words and the tone of his voice and responds to them. However, she also drops this level of indirect communication as soon as father indicates discomfort with it. In this way, rapport is established carefully and respectfully and at a less superficial level than father might ordinarily entertain.

Cons.: So, I have heard a little bit about your family from the OTs and let's see, they didn't know too much about your sons, but maybe you could, you know, just tell me a little bit about yourselves—you know, what you do and. . .

Consultant is casual and open-ended toward father.

Father: Well, I am a maintenance man with the board of education. I have been employed with them for about, close to eighteen years now.

Cons.: Eighteen years?

Father: Yah.

Cons.: (Slowly) I have never worked anywhere eighteen years.

Consultant praises father and uses his on-the-job record, which is superior to hers, to elevate him.

Father: I do general maintenance work and I get to like it after so many years. . .

Cons.: It's hard work, isn't it?

Father: Sometimes it is hard work, but I don't mind that. . . . It's challenging.

Cons.: What kind of hours do you keep at work?

Father: I work from eight to four mostly.

Consultant notes great sadness in his voice and also his language about getting to like something (not liked) after so many years with it. Consultant begins a process of relating to the body and voice tone messages, not only the content of his speech. Father brings up difficulty and adds that he does not mind. Remember, in terms of *suggestive continuity* in families, such indirect messages as tone of voice may affect a symptom bearer more than words.

Cons.: And you have a store also?

Father: Yah. Yah.

Cons.: How do you do that?

Father: Well, just lately we work the store ourselves and split up the shift. John comes in after school from four to seven, then Brenda works from eight to twelve, and I take the last hours, from seven to eleven.

Cons.: So, you work all day and all night? My goodness, you are a hard-working man.

Father: Oh—it's only temporary, we hope.

Father introduces heavy economic problems. This big problem is converted to a praise of father: "You are a hard-working man."

Cons.: Okay.

Father: I am not that fussy about work (laughs).

Cons.: You don't mind. . .

Consultant establishes rapport, nodding at the indirectly conveyed sadness. "Okay" is said to the emotions associated with father's doubts about how temporary it will be.

Father: I don't enjoy it that much, but I don't mind it. It is just that it is necessary at this time.	Now father states it more fully as "not *that* enjoyable."
Cons.: For survival?	Consultant introduces *life or death* issues. Father assents "I work this much because I must, to survive." He is complimented again. Consultant turns to mother.
Father: Yes.	
Cons.: You're a survivor. Okay.	

We begin to get a picture of father and his life. He combines an underlying tone of sadness with a disapproval of complaining and "fussiness." He sounds like someone who swore to God that if he survived he would not bemoan his earthly situation again. His English is not very good and his accent is heavy, confirming the social isolation of a maintenance man working night shifts for eighteen years.

The consultant drops this discussion charged with the kinds of emotions father does not like to have, framing it as "He is a survivor." In this way life can be admitted to be hard for him, *without his being weak or a failure for perceiving it as such.* Indirectly, the consultant has suggested that she hopes to help ease father's burden. This is what she can "barter" with him about when she wants to give him something in exchange for his share in his daughter's symptoms. She has also as invisibly as possible begun to challenge his tone, which may not be helpful to his daughter.

The consultant now turns to mother. Her opening statement suggests "We were just talking about work hours," thereby drawing a protective boundary between the emotionally laden talk with father and the *overt* content of that exchange. Mother is not invited into that private talk with father.

Cons.: And, you work in the store then, Brenda?	
Mother: Yes, I work during the day in the store.	Mother's English is much better than father's, her speech direct.
Cons.: So, most of the time you work alone and then John *joins you,* or does he *relieve you?*	Consultant's language is used slowly and deliberately, suggesting that messages may have more than one meaning. Ambivalence and doubt about whether mother can

Mother: He joins me. He comes in and we cook supper at the store.

Cons.: Mmmmhmm.

Mother: Then, we are together and it's usually about quarter to seven before we go home and my husband will get cleaned up and come back at 7:30. So, that makes us together for supper. Otherwise, we don't ever get together as a family. That's our only time together.

Cons.: How long has it been the only time you get together as a family?

Mother: Well, I guess it got bad last fall—but before. I have had the store for almost four years and it was bad before, but it wasn't that bad that we had to work it all the time. We had staff and then we'd be home at night. But, things got really bad, so we have to work it in order to—so that we don't have to pay out so much so that we can at least pay our bills.

Cons.: And, this has been for *under* a year or *over* a year now? This particular. . .

Mother: Well—that we'd be all at the store? Well, last summer we didn't even have any holidays. Like, my husband had his holidays and we worked in the store most of the time. We didn't go away. So it's been getting close to a year now.

get relief from a man or only assistance is introduced. One wonders whether mother sees son and father as similar.

Mother introduces consultant to economic survival worries and lack of family unity time.

Consultant uses mother's language carefully, to talk on several levels of meanings at once while having some control over how directly an issue is discussed.

Mother answers *"It* got bad" a year ago. But it had not been good for a while. Hard times are called bad times. Is there a sense of self-failure here too?

Careful articulation, suggesting that we are narrowing in on a specific issue.

Cons.: No time away from the work or the kids?

Mother: Hardly. . . no, not really. I haven't been out, just my husband and I, since September (laughs) anywhere. Except in bed at night and then I am—once I get to bed, you're. . .

Consultant moves inward toward emotional issues, inviting mother to comment on herself and/or husband.

Mother lightly alludes to sex life, bringing their bedroom into the therapy.

Cons.: You are really tired after all that work. Well, you have my husband and I beat. We have two tiny kids and we have hardly gotten away either. So, it's not a good thing, is it? (laughs)

On behalf of father, consultant diminishes the scope of mother's statement, focusing not on bed interactions but on "tiredness" and then empathizing parent to parent. Intimacy is cued as "getting away" from kids, money pressures, and so on.

Mother: No. We're going out on the eighth of February—it is my husband's birthday. We are going—that weekend—we're going down to see our married daughter.

Cons.: Oh.

Mother: But we probably will stay in a motel. So that we will have some time alone. That way, I get to be alone with him and I get to see our granddaughter.

Father: (Folds his arms, and tenses)

Consultant notes that father folds arms and looks uncomfortable at his wife's anticipated proximity.

Only minutes into the session and already dire economic matters and an absent sex life have been raised, in a very understated, slow-moving, quiet-toned way. The consultant's job is to show recognition and appreciation of symptom-related aspects of the family troubles while being very selective about which aspects will be addressed directly and hence be part of the collective domain of family interaction and which will be addressed indirectly as part of a private discussion with a particular family member.

With father, the consultant has established cues about discussing carrying burdens and being emotionally withdrawn and depressed. With mother, she has established cues about mother-daughter analogies, between herself and her own children and Mrs. Clide and hers; about wife-husband analogies; and about the relationship between gaining space from one's grown children and proximity to one's spouse and grandchildren. These cues are part of the seeding for trance that occurs in the creating of the hypnotic atmosphere.

Father folded his arms protectively when his wife referred to having time alone in a motel with him. The consultant wants to convey her interest in being respectful of his body messages. She uses a shift in content to do so.

Cons.: Yes, oh. What is your granddaughter's name?

Consultant focuses on the granddaughter to comfort and reinvolve father. She keeps the emphasis on positives and the future, the gift of grandchildren when parents let go of a child moving to her next developmental stage.

Father: Jessica (relieved, he unfolds his arms).

Cons.: Is she the apple of your eye, as they say?

Father: Yah. We are all—every one of us here. Even Christopher, and *he is not so fond of girls.* I was surprised when she was up. He even changed her diaper and takes quite an effort— for a young boy to do.

Although many ten-year-old boys are "not so fond of girls," there seems to be a battle of the sexes in the air.

Cons.: You changed her diaper? Oh. Really.

Chris: Yes.

Mother: That is a good uncle. This kid over here (mother points with joking accusation at John) says, "Yuk, take your daughter. She is poo." And Chris says "Give her to me—I will change her."

Consultant notes that mother, unlike father, calls son by his nickname. The older boy—and anyone

John: (Looks hurt)

Cons.: Smart one over here (consultant assuages John) prefers to stay in the store, huh? You prefer store work to taking care of your niece?

John: No—I think I would prefer taking care of my niece (said with a chill).

Mother: Except when she's dirty!

John: Yeah. Sometimes I take a break.

else?—thinks the girl is "poo," not "covered with poo."

Consultant does not accept mother's definition of this son; she instead tries to tie his alleged preference to competence.

Touché to mother. "Even hating baby poo as I do, I'd prefer it to helping you in the store!" Mother reiterates her criticism. Consultant wonders: "Do older son and dad think females are dirty?" Mother and son are fighting out some family issue.

Although the tone is subdued and slightly playful, the consultant notes that older son takes some flack from mother. He is a great support to her in the store, yet she indicates that he does not like to deal with his niece when "she is poo." John is embarassed by the mention of "poo," and there is a hint of joking about "girls being poo" and awkwardness over male-female relations in the family. "Christopher will change her diaper although he is not so fond of girls." Father empathizes that it takes "quite an effort" for a young boy to care for a girl. Mother and son bicker mildly, revealing how overburdened mother feels and how "unrelieved" by son, while son too feels overworked and underappreciated. From a structural vantage point, the consultant automatically considers the *possibility* that the son-mother conflict *parallels* disagreement and disappointments between mother and father.

The consultant is careful not to accept mother's characterization of her son. She simply keeps in mind that mother finds son inadequate and critical of babies and bodily processes and that son feels overburdened by mother's expectations. She uses this entree of mother's to join up with the young man.

Cons.: So, okay. You moved back home recently?

John: Well, it was last November or October?

"Forget the 'pooey' introduction mother gave you, John; let's talk about how helpful you are."

Mother: November 11th.

John: Yeah, last November I came back home.

Cons.: That was when times got very hard for your parents, that you came back home—it was around the same time?

John: Yeah, well, it was long after, but yeah.

Cons.: So, it had been hard for a while. You had been in college?

John: No, it's called college, but it is a high school and college. It's separate.

Cons.: I thought that you looked awfully young for college.

John: Yeah (blushing).

Cons.: How old are you?

John: Seventeen.

Cons.: So, you—were you able to finish high school, then?

John: Yeah, I am finishing it up here.

Cons.: And do you have plans after that for yourself?

John: Yeah, well, I have plans, but I don't know if other people are going to agree with them, but what I want to do is join on as a police cadet at one of the places that sponsor it and so, I am just checking into that right now. By the end of the week I should have all the places that sponsor it. Then I can get into contact with

Mother remembers the exact day her son came home to help her.

Son suggests that emotionally, financially, or both, things had been hard before they got terrible.

Consultant wants to equalize John with his older sister. He acts and is treated as if he were much older.

He blushes deeply under a fine and smooth cheek, suggesting sexual embarrassment. Consultant notes this strong response, but as with father, talks directly about the son's accomplishments and strengths.

Son does not want further education. He wants a steady job as a policeman.

them and see what they say. That's what I want to do.

Cons.: By other people who might not agree—I wonder who you might mean.

John: Oh—it's not my parents. It's just the people who would hire me. I don't know if they have any need for me or anything. I am just hoping because that's what I have my heart set on.

John's clear plans are in stark contrast to Gretchen's state of uncertainty.

The consultant notes that John is a parentified child. He fills in dad's shoes when dad cannot be around, supporting and fighting with his mother. He likes to act much older than his sister and is encouraged to do so. While respecting his competences, the consultant wants to identify some area in which John could develop more, hoping that Gretchen may have strengths in this area that the consultant can draw on to equalize the balance of functional hierarchies in their relationship. It is hypothesized that this imbalance somehow reflects the marital imbalance as well, and the consultant will probe to confirm or rule out this structurally derived analogy.

The consultant, after a brief contact with the younger brother, now addresses Gretchen.

Cons.: Hmm. Now let's see—what's your name again? I've forgotten.

Gretchen: Gretchen.

Cons.: Okay, Gretchen. And where do you live?

Gretchen: I live in _____ , but I am moving to _____ today.

Cons.: So you live with your parents?

Gretchen: I am going to, yeah.

Cons.: You are *going* to live with your parents. Oh, but you *lived* in _____ .

Consultant intentionally suggests confusion and forgetfulness with Gretchen as if enacting Gretchen's internal state.

Gretchen: Right.

Father: Yah, yah. She is coming home with us this afternoon after this session is over.

Father is a little impatient with all this confusion and again jumps in to rescue both Gretchen and consultant.

Cons.: Okay. You haven't been living with your parents. *I am confused.* Where do you. . .

Through her confusion, the consultant sets a communication she will use with Gretchen to further trance—by suggesting confusion, a second step in trance induction, and by suggesting "See yourself reflected in me," which she will use later.

Gretchen: I *used to* live in _____ . Yeah.

Cons.: Did you get an apartment? Or. . .

Gretchen: I lived with an old lady in a house.

Cons.: And, then you are moving *back* with your parents today?

Gretchen: Right.

Cons.: Are you also moving back, like your brother, to help?

As soon as she is clear about housing for Gretchen, consultant asks why she is back and throws the motive "to help" into the question.

Gretchen: Oh, not really.

Cons.: Well then, to hinder. . .? Which one?

Gretchen must choose within this set of choices.

Gretchen: Umm, to help, yeah, I guess.

Gretchen selects a positive and active motive.

Cons.: To help. And, what happened to your shoes?

As soon as Gretchen chooses, consultant shifts again, focusing on Gretchen's bare feet.

Gretchen: Well, I left them in the office.

Cons.: Oh. I just don't want you to get cold feet.

Consultant offhandedly gives rationale that she is just concerned that Gretchen not get cold feet. The metaphor is obvious to observers but subliminal to Gretchen, who is very much thrown off balance by this interaction.

The consultant has wanted to rock Gretchen's cradle. Gretchen has been altogether too happy in a position that may lead to her death by suicide. If the consultant affects only the girl's family context, failing to recognize the girl's symptom as a hybrid of family- and self-induction, Gretchen may kill herself. Therefore, one of the consultant's goals is to shake Gretchen up enough to affect her rigid mind-set but to leave her with the idea that she will get help. The consultant conveys that she is a formidable opponent to Gretchen's symptoms. Framing it in maternal concern for Gretchen's getting cold, she presents a worry that Gretchen will get cold feet, thus leaving Gretchen pondering whether she is home to help or hurt and what might she chicken out about: going back home or staying away?

At this point, a number of seeds have been sown for the creation of an hypnotic atmosphere. While she has been exploring interactional features of family structure, the consultant has been identifying, on a one-to-one basis, unconscious or more private feelings, ideations, and bodily cues. Rapport with the parents and two adult children has been firmly established. Cue words and private themes have been set up with each family member. Certain family conflict patterns have begun to repeat themselves; they center around gender roles and the distribution of economic and emotional burdens.

Note that the creation of an hypnotic atmosphere and the seeding for trance are not necessarily done with minute-to-minute continuity. As long as the unconscious communications occur whenever certain themes or cue words or a special cuing tone of voice is established, indirect suggestions can be picked up and ultimately more fully developed over a discontinuous time period. It is as if each individual's associations, which bypass his or her ordinary frame of reference and public communications, were left in a to-be-continued status or awaiting further information. Meanwhile, conscious and interactional phenomena go on simultaneously or alternately.

Now the consultant wants to *observe family induction techniques.* She therefore sets up a family interaction. To initiate this process, she turns from Gretchen to her parents. She asks them, in a tone of disbelief and confusion, enacting the emotions she thinks the parents could manifest more, "How did this happen that Gretchen just suddenly moved back home?"

Mother: Well, she told us on the weekend that she wanted to come home.

Mother is ambivalent, but there seems to be a collusion in Gretchen's return home.

Father: We asked her how she was making out and she wasn't making out that well. I don't know what it was, but I think probably she had her mind made up that she wanted to go back to _____ .

Cons.: Hm!?

Mother: She wanted to come home. She had asked us at Christmas. We— like I really didn't think it was best for her *or* for us.

Cons.: You didn't?

Consultant *collects negatives* like these to use later.

Mother: I didn't. And, she is just— Sunday she was just—she *has* to come home. So.

Cons.: She just says that she *has* to come home?

Consultant acts innocently baffled at how powerful Gretchen is. One word of "please" and "have to" and the doors fly open! In this way she probes indirectly for the parents' deeper responses and emotional tone about Gretchen's homecoming.

Father: Umm—I am a little bit leery. I think Gretchen has a hard time functioning on her own (voice lowers and speech becomes slower while looking at Gretchen).

To explain how it was decided that Gretchen come home, father introduces his doubts about Gretchen. He also starts an induction of Gretchen, as he focuses inward into her functioning, using a sad tone.

Mother: She found it lonely here where we live.

Mother fills in this general focus with "loneliness."

Father: Yah. You see, for a while there she was staying with that elderly lady and for a while she was alone up here. We didn't know what

Father joins in the details of loneliness. (See Chapter Four on family inductive technique for discussion of father's inadvertent affect on his daughter.)

time the college started up here and
she came up a week earlier. And, she
was alone in the house and I don't
think it is best for her.

Cons.: So, you were worried for her.

Consultant defines what father has
said about Gretchen in terms of
himself and then vanishes that
focus.

Father: I didn't want her to come
back, but then she would be better off
at home.

Father expresses his ambivalence
and double message to Gretchen
about his expectations of her.

Father's statement "Umm—I am a little bit leery" is the beginning
of the family induction process. We do not yet know for sure what family
structures make this statement powerful, but somehow the family, wishing to support and rescue Gretchen, inadvertently finds a way into Gretchen's inner workings by focusing on how worried they are that she
cannot function. Mother furthers this inward focus by labeling it "lonely."
Father confirms that being alone is not best for Gretchen. He does not
want her home, but it is best for her to be home. Mother does not *want* her
home and does not think it is best for her, but she is worried about her
daughter feeling lonely. The consultant notes that this family experiences
Gretchen's need to come home as a great failure for them all, which
perhaps adds to Gretchen's "need" for a big problem in order to get back
home.

The consultant recognizes that the parents are reluctant to raise the
real reason that their daughter's loneliness has so much power over them.
She wants Gretchen herself to bring the issue to the therapy. The ball is in
Gretchen's court concerning this issue. Therefore, the consultant decides
to not have the parents talk with Gretchen yet but to bring out the hinted-
at dangers of loneliness by having the girl take charge of the issue. To do
so, the consultant uses the approach of distorting father's statement to
amplify his nonverbalized sentiment. The consultant wants to enhance
the inward focus the parents activated by ultimately diverting it into a
therapeutic counterinduction of the young woman. Note that the consultant replicates the young woman's statements, to "track her scent" very
closely, to be let into her symptomatic suicide attempts and ideations.
Here the consultant and Gretchen talk, not about the toys of childhood

but about loss and death. The continuation of suicide threats are an aspect of Gretchen and her family's gift that the consultant does not wish to receive. It is a response *and* a coping device that has become potentially lethal.

Cons.: So, your Dad has been worried about you. Worried that you are lonely?

Consultant uses tone and word "lonely" to pick up the thread of father's induction.

Gretchen: Yeah. I think he is. He is worried that I might hurt myself.

Cons.: That you'd hurt yourself?

Five minutes into this session and we have talked about money, sex, and death.

Gretchen: Uh-huh.

Cons.: Why would he be worried that you would hurt yourself?

Gretchen: Because I have done it before.

Cons.: You have hurt yourself before?

Gretchen: Yeah.

Cons.: How do you hurt yourself?

Gretchen: I cut my wrists.

Cons.: You cut your wrists? What wrist did you cut? (Consultant gets up concerned and curious and goes to Gretchen)

Gretchen: My left one.

Cons.: Where did you cut your wrist? This one? (Consultant, kneeling, holds her hand)

Gretchen: Yeah.

Cons.: When you cut, you tried to cut across this vein?

Intimately, they both focus intensely on this single spot across the vein of Gretchen's right hand.

Gretchen: Uh-hmm.

Cons.: It is a very difficult vein to cut. It is nearly impossible, I am told, to die by that. Did you do cigarette burns, or is this a birthmark?

Gretchen: No, it's a cigarette burn.

Cons.: A cigarette burn. Did you do that when you were in the hospital?

Gretchen: Yeah.

Cons.: So—even when they put you in the hospital, you still hurt yourself?

Gretchen: Uh-hmmm.

Cons.: So, your parents think that somehow keeping you home—what do you think they think they can do—if you really want to hurt yourself? What can they do about it?

Gretchen: They can't really do anything about it.

Cons.: So, if you are determined to hurt yourself, couldn't you do it in the house?

Gretchen: Yeah.

Consultant then dares to explore a bit further up the arm, touching two red circles. Are these inborn or self-caused? Self-caused.

Sets up again the model of "When I talk to Gretchen, I am also talking to the other family members." This model is used to ease indirect communication with family members as the session progresses.

This is a fact. It clarifies a boundary issue. The family can affect how she feels, but they cannot stop her from the act of suicide.

The consultant wants to defuse the power of the suicide threat so Gretchen cannot wave that single banner of authority over her relatives' heads. Of course, she will want to trade with Gretchen this currently used self-destructive strength for some other self-constructive strengths in the family.

She now redirects the parents to talk with Gretchen, but she serves as a facilitator, initially to shape the nature of the interaction. She wants to turn up the volume on the affect in the coming therapeutic event, so that she maximizes the likelihood that she will see a family induction at a point of real difficulty.

Cons.: (To Gretchen) It seems to me that I would talk to your parents about this and (to parents) I guess it might be one of your worries.

Consultant focuses on "worry" to turn up the affective intensity for clinical observation. New interactions arise in different family emotional states. Greater intensity may,

Mother: I worry about her, especially like—even when she is at home—when she cut her wrist, she *did it at home* and I am scared of what she would do if she will do it—maybe not like, I think suicides are usually accidents. They try to prove something (nervous laugh). They do a good job, and I am afraid—like, I cannot imagine going and finding her really hurt or dead, like that bothers me. She says she won't do it anymore.

in some cases, lead to a deeper level of intimacy and a sharper focus on problem connections.

Mother now offers the suicide issue as her own concern.

Mother uses tone of a little girl caught stealing a cookie, promising mommy she will be good.

Mother reveals that having Gretchen home is no panacea. She was at home for her last wrist slashing and she may try again. Mother uses "anymore" instead of ever describing Gretchen's attempt. The statements' tenor would be apropos for a little girl promising she will not be naughty again; it does not match with a young woman terminating her life. Must mother "baby" Gretchen to let her come home?

Mother evokes the image of "going and finding her really hurt or dead." This is the image that haunts mother, activating her ambivalence, stoking whatever *personal* interest mother has in letting Gretchen come home with the dry wood of real fear.

Cons.: And you too are worried and it is not just loneliness that worries you?

The truth, dad . . . .

Father: No—but I think that Gretchen has a hard time if she lives alone. I guess everybody gets lonely, but she has a harder time to function on her own, I guess.

OK. I get lonely, too. . . it is that she "can't function." Father still does not mention the forbidden word, "suicide."

Cons.: (To father) I find life to be a lonely thing much of the time.

Father: Uh huh (nods intensely, head bobbing).

Consultant uses this moment to continue her discussion of carrying the burden and isolation with father. Father's head nods perseveratively in agreement. Consultant ponders

> whether Gretchen is a solace to her
> lonely father.

Because of the nature of his relationship with Gretchen and the relationship of Gretchen to her parents' marriage (that is, because of family structure), father is able to resume his loneliness induction of Gretchen, even though this segment is temporally broken off from the earlier segment. It carries an *emotional continuity* because of underlying family relationships. (See Chapter Four.) For this simple reason, sequential analyses of family contributions to symptoms are not sufficient; they fail to capture the underlying continuity of family inductions, which are charged with meaning, innuendo, and the powers to converge and activate certain associations and memories based on the often elusive rules of family organization.

The consultant uses father's embedded statement "I guess everybody gets lonely" to deepen their rapport for hypnotic purposes. The consultant looks intensely into father's eyes at this moment, sealing out others, continuing their discussion about life's struggles, talking privately with him: "I find life to be a lonely thing much of the time." Father enters a light trance at this time, his head nodding up and down, and he says slowly "uh huh." In this manner the consultant has suggested a shift from father's activating Gretchen's memories of loneliness to father's focusing on his own loneliness. As this line of association is initiated for father, the consultant returns to conscious issues at hand, maintaining that touch-and-withdraw style of communicating with father. The consultant does not want to be experienced as nagging.

Now the consultant wants to push Gretchen to see whether she can talk with her parents outside the family-induced state about "whether you want to kill yourself right now, or soon, in their home," about "wanting to die." This is a *probe* to see whether Gretchen can talk from an *active position* about her state of mind rather than enact passively the loneliness inadvertently suggested by the family. The consultant is also helping her prepare for a new future. The interaction of the subsystem mother-father-Gretchen is initiated as Gretchen talks to her parents about wanting to die, that is, her "bad" feelings.

Cons.: But, the other problem is the wanting to hurt herself that I—if she	Consultant's proposal of talking "death" especially increases parents' anxiety.

is going to move back in with you, it
seems to me that you need to talk
about this problem if she is still—you
need to tell your parents whether you
want to kill yourself right now. Or
soon, in their home. I think you need
to talk to each other about this problem. It affects everyone. If you were to
come into the house and find her
there, you know, or Chris finds her,
or John. Maybe you ought to tell
your parents about wanting to die
(turn up affect).

Consultant is intentionally graphically activating a shared imagining
of what could lie ahead. Consultant
involves everyone with seeing Gretchen dead.

Gretchen: I just feel awful.

Cons.: (To OT) Could I ask you to
let her sit near her folks so they can
talk better?

Gretchen: I don't want to sit there.

Cons.: At least—because you need to
talk to your parents so that, uh—this
is a terrible problem, a serious problem. (Gretchen reluctantly moves
near her father) You were saying to
your mother that you feel terrible,
that you don't know that they were
going to be able to see you. . .

In this intense frame, consultant
helps Gretchen move closer to parents. Gretchen has come home to
get something from increased proximity to her parents. Physically
moving her to them will help us see
what goes wrong when they communicate. At this point, the goal is
not change but observation of family induction techniques.

Gretchen: I just feel awful. I don't
want to tell them.

John: Why?

Gretchen: Because.

John: Why do you feel awful—
because you are lonely, or what?

John intervenes, enacting his parentified position by speaking in father's place. Interestingly, he
reintroduces the explanation of
"loneliness."

Gretchen: I don't know. I just feel
angry.

"Angry" is a little stronger than the
"lonely" mother, father, and John
offered.

Cons.: (To John) How about if we
let your parents do this job?

Seating changes provide a metaphor for structural sequences. Structurally, Gretchen has moved from the shadow of the family closer to the family circle, to "near her parents." This proximity is set up to observe how the family may contribute to an induction of the young woman's symptoms.

Because family structure is redundant, although the consultant staged the interaction to occur between parents and Gretchen, John intervenes, taking father's voice and words. The consultant recognizes this action as another manifestation of a dysfunctional suggestion-bearing hierarchy (see Figure 14). In this hierarchy, John plays dad for mom and sister. This structure merits disruption for at least two reasons. (1) If John is above his older sister by "helping" her with her symptom, he maintains his rigid functional superiority over her, and she remains in her position of consistent inferiority and powerlessness in the sibling subsystem. (2) If John acts in his father's place, stepping in to help out, we know he may join mother, but he cannot ultimately relieve her—only father can relieve her. The maneuver is a typical family structural intervention, in which the "parental" child is given a vacation from chasing his sister's ghosts.

Figure 14. Dysfunctional Suggestion-Bearing Hierarchy.

Mother   John
— — — — — — — — —
            Gretchen

John: (Confused) What? Ask?

Cons.: Since you are already helping in the store.	Helping in the store is enough. Parenting need not be his purview.

John: Okay. Go ahead.

Cons.: I think, mom and dad, you need to find out—is she suicidal, how are you going to handle this with her moving back into the house and your life as difficult as it is?	Responsibility lines are again delineated. This is parent work.

Father: I think the story with me—I try to ignore the fact that she wants to take her life because I cannot understand it. Personally, I am an optimist and I cannot understand why anybody would want to take their lives. (Bites his lip) You know what I mean?

Father's first mention of the suicide attempts.

Again consultant is concerned that optimism plus denial leads to inaction or symptom maintenance by father.

Cons.: I know what you mean (intensifying rapport). But, I know I just saw a family with a similar problem who ignored the suicide threats and the girl could have died. Like your wife said, she didn't really want to, but a mistake could have happened. So, I would be doing a disservice to you not to have you take it seriously.

Consultant accepts father's statement but seasons it with the bitter salt of death.

Father contributes denial and not seeing what is really there to the family inductive repertoire. Ignoring threats can make someone who is threatening up the ante. Insofar as Father's optimism is defined in terms of ignoring *the fact* that Gretchen wants to take her life simply because suicide is against *his* belief system, the consultant regards it as contributing to father's rigid mind-set. He will not be able to stand up to the challenge of Gretchen's threats of dissolution unless he shifts some aspect of the rules by which he organizes his thinking. The consultant challenges father's habit of ignoring rather than his description of being optimistic.

Mother, in her attempt to rescue Gretchen, spontaneously continues and intensifies the induction by embellishing a vivid inner state for Gretchen while describing her own memory of herself at fourteen. Her rescue attempt is flawed and intensifies Gretchen's feelings of shame, fear, and anger. (We look at the steps of this aborted rescue attempt afterward.)

Mother: I know it's serious. I can understand, in a way. When I was fourteen, life at home was *unbearable.*

This is also part of mother's gift to the consultant: "Help me, too, my life has been unbearable."

Note that in other therapies focused on problem solving without emphasis on identifying family inductive patterns, the content of this interaction might not be accepted. Here it is assumed that this heart-to-heart mother-daughter interaction will inform the consultant of subtleties of family inductive patterns, which may then be used in elaborating and expanding the hypnotic atmosphere to produce a therapeutic counterinduction. Family inductions, like fish, are slippery; the therapist intentionally selects the bait to catch them. Therefore, in this case, instead of preventing mention of the past, the consultant is less interested in content and tries to get a chance to study the often elusive or private family induction procedures.

Cons.: Would you say this to her?

Consultant redirects mother to Gretchen.

Mother: (To Gretchen, leaning forward, gazing intensely into her eyes) And, I tried to—I took a whole bunch of aspirins. I took too many and so all I did was get sick. I just threw up. And, every time I take an aspirin now, my stomach goes yecch because I remember the taste of throwing up twenty-two aspirins. *And, life is so unbearable* and I can understand that feeling of anything is better than living, in me, but I cannot understand it in you because I am *good* (looks in Gretchen's eyes) to you and dad's good to you and we love you and we don't fight and I don't go out with men and I don't drink and dad doesn't beat me up. And that is why *life was unbearable* at home. Because my mother called me a whore and I was a virgin. Just because—I don't know why. And so, I don't understand it—like I don't understand—*I can understand life being unbearable,*

As mother leans forward, Gretchen gazes into her eyes. Mother leans forward and lowers her tone; mother and Gretchen are alone in an intense rapport.

Note the vivid recollection and re-vivification of the taste of aspirin. Mother's tense changes to the present: "life is so unbearable." (See Chapter Four regarding the interspersal effect in mother's induction.) Inadvertently, suggestions of feeling bad and lonely are seeded throughout. These messages then can take on a suggestive life of their own. Because they are embedded in a context of helping Gretchen, they may be harder for her to detect and defend against herself.

Positives for Gretchen are defined as the negations of mother's nega-

but I don't understand why it would be for you. Because the circumstances aren't the same. *And yet, if you believe that life is unbearable, why, why is life unbearable,* and *how can I help you to make it bearable?* That's why I said to you, if you come home, one of the conditions is that we have to continue to see the therapist until you're better, because *I cannot handle it* on my own. Because I don't know how. You are a Christian and we are Christians. And you know that *the only reason to live is to go to heaven afterwards,* and if you take your own life, there is no—it makes it hard for me to understand. Because, that is not right as a Christian to feel that way. If I was a Christian then, I wouldn't have done it when I was a kid.

tives. A dismal and gloomy mother-daughter Cassat portrait is painted.

Mother uses repetition well, with "unbearable" exerting an emotional undertow, despite her *intended* message.

Suicide attempts are more likely in a child whose parents tried.

In the hypnotic atmosphere established, mother automatically enters trance as she talks, glassy-eyed, with Gretchen, revivifying—complete with tastes, memories, and the use of the present tense—events of her own childhood. Gretchen gazes into her mother's eyes. Wanting to die is not a foreign issue to this family. Mother raises a critical concern of this family, however, that charges her personal message: she introduces her interpretation of the fundamentalist religion and Gretchen's being *born* a Christian. Mother's rescue effort is flawed by unintended suggestions, and as a result, it offers an excellent induction of sadness and guilt. Let us examine step by step mother's statements and their embedded or unintentional messages.

1. I can understand.

    Suicidal thoughts are something I, [unlike Mr. Clide], can understand. (We are alike.)

2. I tried to kill myself with aspirins.

    Not a good technique, just makes you sick.

3.	Life is so unbearable.	A potential suggestion as well as a description.
4.	My mother was a drunk and a whore. My father beat her. I was not a Christian.	Picture my misery, feel for it. (If Gretchen feels sad for mother, how can she feel good about herself? Especially if mother and Gretchen are alike.)
5.	Dad and I don't do. . . .	Paired with "and that was why *life was unbearable at home.*"
6.	But I can't understand your feelings for you.	If there is no contextual contribution in Gretchen's case, there must be something wrong with Gretchen herself.
7.	But if *you believe it is for you.*	Suggestion to believe it is is embedded.
8.	Then why is it?	(The case that it *is* unbearable. Life *is* unbearable again embedded.)
9.	How can I help make it bearable?	(I will help you and it *is* unbearable.)
10.	I can't do it alone.	(I really can't be counted on.)
11.	Anyway, Christians live to go to heaven.	(Anyway, life will always be miserable.)
12.	If you take your own life as a Christian.	Don't give up hope for heaven (after death).
13.	It's not right as a Christian to even feel bad.	You're unethical for feeling life is unbearable.
14.	If I were Christian as a girl.	(As you are now.)
15.	I would not have done. . . .	(What I did then, like you, was as a non-Christian.) Hence, you are really worse than I and for no good reason!

Perhaps from a caring parent depressed by her own bad social situation, some efforts to help the child may accidently contribute to the worry and guilt that make life seem overwhelming. Perhaps abortive rescue attempts like these may even partly contribute to the increased incidence of suicide attempts in families in which a parent made a previous suicide attempt.

The consultant recognizes in mother's induction how easily she had established a "join-then-kick" style with Gretchen. Mother is pulled in to Gretchen by maternal concern and then tries to separate from her with a kick.

Clearly, we are not considering that mother's intention is to bring her daughter to a miserable immobilized state. We are simply noting how she might be inadvertently contributing to the activation of that state. Mother's own sadness colors her best efforts to support her daughter. We are interested in getting a view of her techniques for establishing rapport and entering into Gretchen's mind-set because we will want to use these old familiar routes to help the family carry some new messages to Gretchen and to help Gretchen identify possible alternative forks in the road of family communications.

Father now highlights the ultimate rescue paradox. It is as if he unintentionally said: "In a context in which life *is* unbearable, one must not even carry the recognition that it is."

Father: Well. . .even to carry those thoughts in your mind is not right (shaken, biting lip).

Mother: And, I have to help you or else your being home would be too hard on me if I can't help you and you help me. And, I don't know why. Why do you feel so *angry?* Do you feel angry because you don't feel well (wiping tears from her own cheeks)?

Mother now fills in Gretchen's emotion.

Gretchen: Yeah.

Mother: Why don't you feel well? Like—physically, emotionally?

Gretchen: Emotionally, I guess.

Mother: You know that we are a lot alike, you and I. We have a lot of feelings the same and what makes me different from you—like, how did I cope and you don't.

This is the *bad-twins* induction the present therapy of boundary renegotiation will want to challenge. (See Chapter Four, the section on blurring of boundaries.) Gretchen and mother are intensely connected.

Father: Well, I can understand that a person gets depressed once in a while. (To consultant) This is understandable.

Cons.: Tell your daughter so, because this—she needs to talk to you very much.

Father: (To Gretchen) I do understand that you do get depressed sometimes, but why so depressed that you want to take your life? That's one thing I don't understand. So, things don't always go the way we want them to go and then we have a hard time dealing with problems here and there. It is no reason to think about taking your life, though. This is something I just cannot understand. (Bites lip, folds arms, holds back tears)

Let us open this moment in the interview and examine in synchrony father and mother's consolation efforts in a context of perceived failure and futility.

1. Even to carry those doubts is not right.

   Un-Christian like mother?

2. And you have to help me or it will be too hard on me.

   Life is already too hard on me.

3. Why are you so angry?

   Now the emotion suggested is anger. This is also an attack.

4. Are you angry because you don't feel well? Why don't you feel well?

   I wasn't attacking. You are really just "sick."

5. Physically or emotionally?

   Once Gretchen picks either, she agrees to being "unwell."

6. You know that we are a lot alike, you and I.

   The twins technique. We are negative twins, but you are worse than I.

7. Occasional depression is "understandable," but to think about taking your life. . . .

   There is no room for this idea. An attack, but sweetened with tears of self-failure.

8. Father cries.

   How can you do this to me! How have I failed you?

This family induction culminates with mother looking angry, with tears in her eyes, father holding back his sea of tears, and Gretchen having proceeded from monosyllabic conversation to staring vacantly during this interaction. She has become a passive receptacle of some very confusing prescriptions: "Suffer all you want. Life *is* unbearable. But *pretend* it is not because *knowing* it *or acting* on the fact that it *is* is against our religion. Perhaps you are a little un-Christian from your mother's side."

This is the moment at which the consultant has a first clear sense of the family induction style and the way Gretchen's interior or private self becomes a public domain, predominantly a pool reflecting the despairing images of family life. The danger is that she will become a mirror of blood. It begins to seem that Gretchen's symptoms may be related to both the exterior contexts she has been part of and her own solution to her dilemmas, a solution fraught with danger. Failing to measure up at school, and worried about herself as a member of a family under duress, Gretchen may have wanted to come home for refuge. Fearing that her failure might deepen that of her parents if she came home and disappoint her therapists as well, she may have needed to become very upset (suicidal) and very infantile (disguised as a three-year-old). What might ordinarily have been an atavistic regression or a return home that helped her healing and forward movement was distorted by a lens of family and personal belief into a cue for family despair. Gretchen's symptoms got her out of an impossible school situation and idealized parental and personal expectations for herself but gave her no respite, only a life-threatening, symptomatic limbo.

The consultant has seen a moment in which the family context has contributed to the activation of potentially self-destructive feelings in Gretchen. The consultant turned up the heat by addressing survival and life and death issues and then set up the circumstances under which parents and Gretchen are seated in such a way as to talk with each other about the young woman's misery. In this context, the family *spontaneously* produced the kinds of *suggestive forms* the consultant will use to formulate family hypnotic style and structure. Also, at this point the consultant has a first hypothetical map of the symptom structure she will use to consider possible points of therapeutic entry. A central problem is within the family's gender subsystem. The symptom-structure proposed in Figure 15 is hypothesized as adequate to account for a chronic family

Figure 15. Part 1 of Symptom Structure.

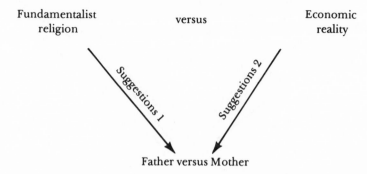

circulation of destructive suggestion *to* Gretchen. Let us first look at the symptom structure in parts and then as a whole. Part 1 is the broader social conflict that is affecting the parents' mind-sets about gender roles.

Mother and father are responding to conflicting messages in their own social situation. Raised to believe that a Christian woman's place is to reproduce and manage children and to tend to the kitchen and go to church, the parents find themselves confronted with an economic reality dictating that mother join and remain in the productive work force. Father then interprets suggestion 1 as: (1) a woman's place is in the home; (2) a working wife suggests the presence of either an inadequate father or an inadequately Christian wife. From mother's economic circumstances, she interprets suggestion 2 as: (1) although my place should be in the home, it cannot be; (2) men may join you, but in reality they cannot relieve you; (3) perhaps a woman would do better to work; (4) but in the meantime, life is unbearable and confused for a woman, and it is hard for a woman in trouble to rescue herself.

To sharpen the issue about which Mr. and Mrs. Clide disagree, Figure 16 shows a version of fundamentalism on Mr. Clide's side and a version of economic reality on Mrs. Clide's side. The figure reveals the messages their marital conflict transmits to Gretchen. Clearly, Gretchen *can* get and interpret her own messages directly from society's fundamentalist and economic subsystems. Certainly her own one-down position in college affected her self-esteem. Nevertheless, a principal conflict affecting her seems to be charged via her family structure and a resulting transmission of morose messages.

Father's suggestions (1) might seem to be to Gretchen: "Don't feel

Figure 16. Part 2 of Symptom Structure.

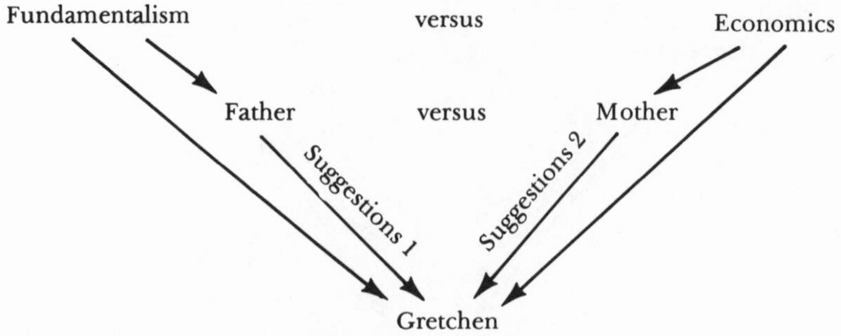

what you do feel because it's non-Christian and not right for a woman."
One senses also his disapproval of a girl's leaving home by going to
college. A girl is easily understood as not having the stamina for such
things. She should find another man to carry her on his shoulders; then
father could feel more at ease.

Mother's symptom-related messages, suggestions 2, are very different from her intended messages. She has the effect of conveying by her
own emotional tone "Either you can be like me and find life unbearable,
but do nothing about it, or you can be worse, acting like a non-Christian,
and kill yourself." While trying to help, she produces an undesired effect.
The parents' unintended suggestions converge at one point only, as
things stand. If Gretchen will find life unbearable but accept it, she can be
eternally mama's baby, thereby saving mother as a reproductively centered Christian in father's definition. Likewise, she can continue to be
carried by father, thereby confirming father's capacity to provide. These
suggestions may converge with Gretchen's own personal wish to come
home for respite. The family contribution to Gretchen's situation may be
an unconscious or unintentional suggestion that Gretchen's coming
home is disquieting evidence of family failure and conflict.

These suggestions then converge with Gretchen's own mind-set,
producing her symptoms, which are a hybrid of her mind-set, family
suggestions, and social problems. (See Figure 17.) At this point we have
yet to explore Gretchen's mind-set. We suspect, however, that Gretchen
has her own rigid ideas about her own development and gender identity,
partly because her symptoms include suicide attempts (mutilation or
destruction of her body) and carrying a baby toy. She also seems unable to
"transcend" the family logic of equating leaving college with failure or

Figure 17. Part 3—Whole Three-Level Symptom Structure.

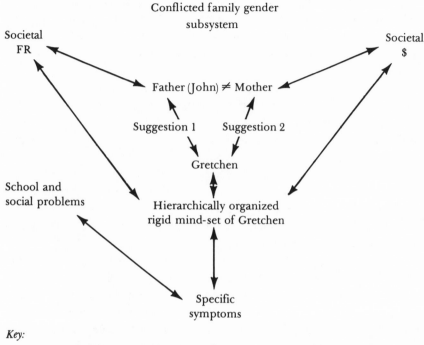

Key:

——— Significant suggestive channels

≠ Disagreement

(John) John can fill in for father in this gender subsystem

FR   An interpretation of rules and roles of fundamentalist
     religion

$ Economic reality

proof of helplessness and simply present a reasonable case for coming
home for a rest.

We will explore the creative aspects of Gretchen's turning of self
against self. The consultant does not perceive Gretchen as simply *the
subject of family induction*. Her suicide threats may be part of a perverted
manifestation of a wish for help, which is in itself quite healthy. Perhaps
in a family that perceives itself as failing and experiences the returns
home of the child as cause for despair, Gretchen's symptoms are a way of

coping with this system, a way of saying "I'm not ready for college, help me get it together again." Her symptom is both a response to and an action against the seemingly irresistible directives of those she loves! But suicide attempts are not the best way for her to exercise her margin of freedom from a family tradition of suggesting you are either a hero or a nothing.

The therapist assumes that Gretchen's state is not simply a consequence of enactments of sequences of family grief messages. Gretchen, and her interior realities, are also a starting point, an initiating moment in family interaction. The consultant wants to enter into such a moment, helping it become pregnant with inductive suggestions that can then be fed into the family system. This way, (1) Gretchen can learn to add her own new input to the family, including abilities to ignore their destructive suggestions, and simultaneously, (2) other family members will be instructed in the arts of inducing hope and experiences of competence and success in Gretchen and one another.

As we turn now to the therapeutic counterinduction processes, it is important to keep in mind that the therapist's goal is *not* to rescue Gretchen from her parents. This is a therapy designed (1) to block family members from being "homeostatic discouragers" of Gretchen's self-help attempts, (2) to invite family members to participate in catalyzing Gretchen's self-help attempts, and (3) to help Gretchen transcend the confusing cross-contextual logic she is confined by so she can *rescue herself* asymptomatically.

Step 2: Therapeutic Counterinduction

This section begins a series of moves that will culminate in a family therapeutic counterinduction. First the consultant eases into an exploration of the impact on Gretchen of the parents' efforts to help and considers ways of disrupting the power of family induction techniques. As is common in the present therapy, she will use a form of insight to awaken Gretchen from the family trance by calling her attention to the relationship between her inner state and outer contextual events. This way a microevent or moment in objective or clock time is opened up in subjective time. The therapist suggests "let us linger in this central moment of your situation." Thus, she begins to activate Gretchen's response against her father's tone by comparing Gretchen's ability to talk with her parents with John's ability to talk with them. The consultant will often pattern her style along the family style of making suggestions, to facilitate for them a useful way of incorporating what she offers.

Cons.: Did you stop listening to your dad? What happens to you when your parents are talking to you like this?

Insight is to disrupt the induction process, to see whether Gretchen can become more active in this discussion and stand up against father's tone. Thus begins an hypnotic immunization.

Gretchen: I get scared.

Mother: Why do you get scared?

Gretchen: I just do.

Consultant does not want mother to intervene here. Gretchen, supported by consultant, sounds a bit braver.

Mother: What do you mean—scared? Of something, or just scared?

Gretchen: I don't know.

Mother: Are you scared of us?

Gretchen: Yeah.

Mother: Do you think we would hurt you?

Gretchen: No—not that.

Mother intervenes again and Gretchen weakens into doubt. Consultant is concerned that the process she is starting *not* be taken over by mother. Ultimately, consultant wants to have a different affect on Gretchen than mother has had. She does not want to rescue Gretchen, only set in motion other needed parts of Gretchen's personality.

Mother: Then, why be scared of us if we wouldn't hurt you? Do you know that we love you?

Mother confuses love and discipline.

Gretchen: No (her head is nodding yes). . .yeah. . . .

Gretchen says "no," nods "yes," and looks confused.

Cons.: Let me talk for one moment, all right? Can you get scared—did it make you angry when they say "don't have doubts—it's against our religion?" Does that make you *ashamed* or angry?

Boundary line is drawn. Mother is silenced. Consultant enacts a harsh tone, pointing finger, showing a critical face, slightly exaggerating, and distorting father's message to Gretchen. Rewording is also used to create a sense of her versus them.

Gretchen: I kind of feel guilty, in a way.

Cons.: Guilty that you want to die sometimes, that you get so lonely and

you feel so helpless and so inadequate that you want to die, and then
you feel ashamed of that, that you
want to die? So—how are you going
to be able to talk to your parents so
that you can live in the house with
them until you are ready to leave?

Gretchen: I don't know.

Consultant summarizes an *interior*
cycle of Gretchen's teaching where
her mind-set is stuck. She then
frames it in terms of how will she
learn to act differently with parents
so she can move on. This hypnosis
will focus on *doing,* not on feeling.
Feelings are *used to mobilize a person to act in the world.*

Here the consultant has begun to take the gift of the symptom and
propose a therapeutic repayment plan. She has arrived at a definition of
the problem by amplifying and distorting certain family messages, such
as by focusing on shame and anger rather than fear and falsely quoting
the father in a stern tone as saying "Don't have doubts, it's against our
religion" when, in fact, father indicated predominantly sadness rather
than threat or demand.

The morass of incapacitating emotions is put in a basic frame of
leaving home. Gretchen's job will be to use trance to not only reorganize
feelings but to talk and act differently. Her problem is to learn to talk to
her parents in a way that does not leave her feeling unable either to leave
home or to use the family as a nontoxic retreat in her leaving home
process. The unconscious search for ways to talk differently with her
parents is activated and will continue after the first search yields uncertainty. The consultant knows Gretchen has no answer to this question. In
this way she also takes over some of Gretchen's self-doubt, to bring it into
her counterinductive work with Gretchen: "Let us *use* part of the doubt
your family life is rich with," but in a new way.

Although much else has been communicated, the family induction
of Gretchen is now framed as Gretchen being unable to talk with her
parents. Can John? To probe for parallels, Gretchen is left in her state of
doubt as the consultant turns to work on an interactive feature of the
symptom structure. The consultant probes to assess further gender rules,
family morality rules, useful analogies, or differences in the brother's
relationship with his parents. As is common in this therapy, the consultant moves easily from working with *family interaction* to challenging
Gretchen's rigid mind-set to affecting another symptom-related aspect of
family interaction.

Cons.: (To John) Can you talk to your parents?

Your sister cannot; can you?

John: Sure. Yeah, I can talk to them. But like, I think if I was ever in trouble, sure I could talk to them. But like—I can't, I would find it difficult if say I was, like how can I put it, there are some things that we never have talked about before, like my dad has never really sat down with me and like, explained things about life, what it's like to be a teenage guy, things to look out for, the type of *people to refrain from,* stuff like that and *things to refrain from.* But, like if I was in trouble, I could talk to them, you know. Like—say something happened and I got a girl pregnant or something, well, I have no intention of doing that, but if that ever happened, yeah, I think I would talk to them. I would find it hard, because I never have before. But, I think I could.

He can't talk with them either about certain things.

The son's refrain is about sexual developmental issues, hence his earlier blushing about looking so young.

Getting a girl pregnant is *again* raised as a way of shaking up this system. Pregnancy is something the parents *hear.*

Cons.: So, it's a *little hard* to bring problems to your parents because your parents are *very strong.* I get— your parents are very strong people and they have survived very, very difficult situations and something about it makes it hard to fail in their eyes, or. . .

Clear distortion of John's statement—selecting the soft underbelly of his possibly threatening remark.

John: It's not really that—it's just gee, I don't know how to put it. It's just that we have never really talked about that before and so it's, I know it is not wrong, but I don't know—it is

just something I have never done before. I feel funny because I have never
done it before. Maybe that's it—like if
dad talked to me about it before, and
he explained like, he explained
things to look out for and stuff, sure.
Well, I don't think I would find it
hard. Because, we are all human and
he's human, I'm human, you know. I
know that and I can grasp it with
him.

Cons.: But still, he seems like a god?   The defense is leading the witness.

John: Sure. Not exactly a god, but
yeah, I admire him. Yeah. *He is a*   This is good to tell dad to elevate
good man. He has treated my mom   dad. The consultant does not want
really good, she tells me that and I   son to put down his father. Father
feel proud. I kind of said gee, that's   will need power to help his family
nice. I would like to grow up and be   during Gretchen's visit.
like him in some ways.

Cons.: You can go ahead and tell   Father shakes head no.
him right now because you know he
is listening in and that's important,
what you said. (To father, who is
shaking his head and signaling with
his hand that it is not necessary) You
are not going to let him say it to you
now?

John: Okay—I would like to grow
up and be like you in some ways. I
would like to be a good husband like
you. I would like to be able to say
when I have been married for twenty-   Son also gives voice to father's sup-
two years, that *I have never ever*   pressed anger. As a substitute hus-
walked out on mom when I am mad,   band, he has probably felt like
and *I would like to say that I have*   hitting mother and he admires his
never hit her when I was angry, and I   father's restraint.
would like to say that, you know, I

have never fooled around on my wife.
I am sure I won't. I have decided that
right now, even though I have not
even thought about marriage much. I
would just like to be able to say a lot
of things that you have been able to
say.

Father: I am sorry son, if I have
failed you.

Father still self-effaces. Consultant
does not want to leave this part of
father in charge of his family!

John: Oh you haven't, Dad.

Father: In some ways, I have failed.
Sex is always one of those, you know,
things that I always have a little
problem with. I wouldn't ever go
into detail with any of my children.
Maybe I am not qualified for it in the
sense of it is something. . .

Sexual issues and things about
women are all areas father has "a
little problem with."

Cons.: Maybe it is something that
your son would like to talk with you
about even though you are not
qualified?

Consultant suggests perhaps even
as limited as father is, he and John
could still talk. She will then
quickly change the subject, preventing his responding to the suggestion.

The consultant used the father-son communication to suggest to
father that as unqualified as he is, nevertheless, maybe it is something his
son would like. For this interview, the consultant wants to *recognize*
father's having problems about sexuality and discussing bodily and reproductive functions. The consultant wants to challenge father, but only
indirectly, and only insofar as his problems are central to the life or death
issues concerning Gretchen. The father-son interaction further sharpens
the focus on gender and sex-role family problems that transform somehow into Gretchen's symptoms.

In this family, the consultant selects Gretchen's rigid mind-set as a
key point of entry into the symptom structure. The consultant wants to
explore how Gretchen perceives herself in this system and her self-, religious, economic, and reproductive goals.

Although what the consultant says to Gretchen will be used to carry on specific lines of suggestion with other family members as well, she will want to draw a protective boundary around Gretchen at this point of focus on issues of context of mind. In this case, she symbolically initiates the boundary making by asking Gretchen to move again. Thus far, Gretchen has moved from outside the family to inside the family, to close to her parents, to next to the consultant, who is seated within the sibling subsystem, between John and Gretchen.

The consultant represents a sort of island within the family that serves a transitional purpose. Gretchen is home, but she is not safe. She is stuck with her parents. Now the consultant will do something to help Gretchen and her parents move somewhere else. A step to facilitate this movement is to physically draw a boundary around Gretchen and the consultant.

Cons.: Would you like to come over here? How did you decide to move back into the house, it seems like a hard decision.

Consultant asks Gretchen to move across the room from her parents, next to consultant.

Gretchen: I am. I have decided. I just thought about it a lot and because I knew that I could not go to school anymore. Because, in not that many classes, I can't really concentrate. I can't do my work. And, I have a hard time really paying attention to what is going on. And, I knew that I couldn't do the work. And, *I can't take care of myself.*

Gretchen now volunteers the words suggesting conscious intent: "I have decided." The consultant listens to Gretchen's statements, as both descriptions of self and injunctions or directives to self derived from Gretchen's context of mind.

Cons.: You can't take care of yourself (repeating slowly with a tone of "So this is what you tell yourself").

Consultant speaks slowly, making eye contact as if she is a slightly modified reflection of Gretchen's inner voice or mental-set.

Gretchen: Right. And I need somebody to take care of me. That's how I made the decision.

Did she have to threaten blood or dress as a baby to get nurtured?

Cons.: So, *the part of you that's a tiny baby made the decision to come home.* The part that says, "I can't take care of myself, I can't concentrate. I don't even know how to think yet."

The whole family becomes silent and immobile at this parts-of-self induction. Consultant speaks slowly, continuing eye contact with Gretchen, emphasizing each phrase. Her lament makes Gretchen's decision making more tangible, more accessible.

The consultant is using a *parts-of-self induction procedure.* Gretchen's dominating symptom-related personality features are accepted, but they are reduced in size: the part of her self credited with decision making, the part that is a "tiny baby," the part that does not even know how to think yet. Gretchen now asserts she made a conscious deliberation to come home, but it was based on emotions out of control.

At this point, the entire family becomes silent and physical movement ceases. The parts-of-self induction also taps into the consultant's connection with each parent and John. Throughout the first part of the interview, the consultant has established a model for this indirect communication style. Thus, her talk of parts-of-self with Gretchen readily cues mother that the consultant will address parts of her concerned about reproductivity and *easing burdens* and father about *coping with loneliness.* John is cued that sexuality will be discussed, *that part of him that is psychosexually immature.*

In the following section, the consultant continues to close Gretchen off from the family and to indicate to the other family members "I will now address issues we've raised pertaining to each of you *indirectly.* I will do so by addressing Gretchen's private contributions to and interiorization of family and social conflict." The consultant does not arbitrarily select the content of the induction. Concretely, she picks up pieces of rapport drawn from the hypnotic atmosphere. She collects and uses cue words, body parts, voice tones suggestive of earlier inductive moments. At this point, just the slight turning away of her own gaze from parents and brother to Gretchen cues the family that private talk will now take place. Contributions will be accepted by invitation only.

Cons.: Whose hands are these hands?

Gretchen: Mine.

Cons.: Are you sure of that?

Consultant refers to "the hands" she has touched and explored earlier. This is a dissociation technique and suggests inward focus.

Gretchen: Yep. They are there.

> "Hand" focuses on body parts of a woman who has hurt her body, perhaps at times when she wanted to reach out for help.

Cons.: They are there. That's how you know they are yours?

> Activating doubt.

Gretchen: Yep. They are part of this body.

Cons.: They are part of this body you live in?

Gretchen: Yeah.

Cons.: So, you know they are there, because you can move them.

Gretchen: Yes.

Cons.: They are part of this body of yours, but you don't seem to own that body yet. You keep it all wrapped up as if it's something terrible—something to be ashamed of.

> Gretchen's answer reveals her disconnection from her body. She calls her own body "this body." Consultant redefines it as "this body you live in." This brings other family members in as well: The family body that each of them lives in, the sexual body, the body that has "poo," the body defined by an interpretation of fundamentalist religion. We will talk about *bodies* but at a safe level of communication.

> Consultant picks up the earlier induction that culminates in being "ashamed."

Gretchen: It's not a very good body . . . it doesn't work very well.

> This is a central revelation of Gretchen's mind-set, about her body, its badness, its ineffectiveness.

Cons.: What's the worst thing about it?

> Let's go for the very worst problem, *now.*

Gretchen: It's sick.

Cons.: What's sick about your body? Think about a really sick thing in your body.

> Consultant does not want to stop here with a "sick" body; she wants to go beyond medical metaphors.

Gretchen: It is sad all of the time.

> "It is sad" says Gretchen. Consultant accepts this state.

Cons.: So, your body is sad all of the time. Where do you feel the sadness most (lowering, looking up at her)?

> Consultant lowers herself to Gretchen by accepting "the body that is sad," asking to be let in further into Gretchen's experience of herself.

Gretchen: The sadness is in the heart.

> Gretchen uses "the heart," not "my heart."

Cons.: It's a sad body (redefine).

Consultant defines "it is a sad body." She accepts dissociation from "the body." Rapport is inten-sified.

Gretchen: Yeah, it feels sad.

Now Gretchen is letting herself sense what "the body" feels.

The consultant considers that the sad body also refers to the family body. She assumes each member is feeling some of that sadness and seek-ing help for it through Gretchen.

Cons.: When was the first time you remember feeling really, really sad?

Consultant builds on the culmina-tions of the mother-father-Gretchen induction, as she now suggests that Gretchen further recall her sad memories. To mother she invites memories of life being so unbeara-ble; to father she suggests periods of his life when he barely survived; to John she suggests his losses of in-nocence and sexual ignorance.

Gretchen: I don't remember not feel-ing sad. . . . It's in the body. . . . It is always there. . . . It was there when the body was born.

Gretchen poses a chronic innate problem! At this point she is in a moderate level of trance. Her eyes are fixed on the consultant's eyes, wholly absorbed. Her speech is slow and disjointed. She also refers to a tradition of sadness into which she was born.

Cons.: (Each is looking into the oth-er's eyes, detached from family con-text) Well, when a child comes into the world, gets a first smack on the butt and they scream and that's a cry of shock, but not of sadness. It seems like every baby starts out with some degree of shock and curiosity at just what hit you. And, early on in your life you do discover your hands. When you were a tiny baby in your crib. (Consultant wiggles her fingers playfully while talking seriously) That took a lot of learning, discover-ing those hands. (Gretchen starts to cry) And that was a joyful experience for you. You are going to have to find those tiny, happy times. Look back on those happy times. Your problem in concentrating isn't in terms of learning schoolwork—it is in terms of memorizing the joy, even if it only lasted thirty seconds. You need that joy for yourself and for your parents. (Gretchen is sobbing) And, even the saddest of bodies has a right to feel some joy. You have a right to feel sadness—*it's your own sadness. It's not mine.* To feel your mother's sadness or your father's sadness—it's *useless*, isn't it? And you know that your father and mother suffered a great deal.

As consultant introduces joy to her hands and acceptability *to her having been* a tiny baby, Gretchen begins to cry, showing the first spontaneous display of emotion ever in therapy. Gretchen has let the consultant into her interior reality.

Although messages are sent to parents about needing her joy and not letting her reverberate to their unexpressed grief, boundaries are also drawn among mother's, father's, and Gretchen's sadness, between the consultant (who is a mother analogue at this moment) and Gretchen. Gretchen is forced to acknowledge interpersonal boundaries. She sobs for the first time in any therapy. It is important to highlight that this automatic expression of emotion is Gretchen's own possession.

The parents' suffering is openly addressed in relation to the sadness in Gretchen's body. In this simple way the therapist assures that while she talks with Gretchen about *her* body and *her* sadness, the parents will think also of *their* bodies and *their* sadness. Ultimately, then, as the therapist guides Gretchen toward drawing on her own unconscious resources to find happy memories, the parents will also cue into this search for strengths. The consultant is "in" with Gretchen. However, she does not want to leave Gretchen activating only sad memories, even if they are her own and *not* her mother's or father's. She selects a likely positive domain.

Cons.: When was the first time you smelled a flower?

Gretchen: Uh huh (slowly wiping tears). I must have smelled flowers before. I must have been that small.

Gretchen speaks, omitting details as if talking to herself. Tears are streaming down her face.

Cons.: You were just a toddler.

Gretchen: Yeah (head keeps nodding).

Cons.: Do you remember the kind it was, or just the smell of them?

Gretchen: (Sniffing) Daisies.

Cons.: Daisies?

Gretchen: Daisies. Couple of daisies. I think so (sniffing).

Cons.: The smell of the daisies is special for you?

Gretchen: Yeah. They are pretty.

Cons.: They *do* smell good.

Gretchen: Yes. . . they do (wiping tears, rubbing under her chin).

Cons.: When you cried just now, you cried for yourself. And you cried for some of the things you've lost. You're only twenty years old and you've lost a great deal. And you know it.

Gretchen: Yes (very faintly).

Cons.: And you paid a heavy price, heavier than you knew at the time. And what other positive memories do you have besides smelling the daisies at three?

Gretchen: I remember riding on my dad's shoulders and we were delivering toothpaste and we were going down the hill (laugh). It was cold, it was freezing cold that day, and we were delivering toothpaste to people's houses (laughing). And I remember it

Consultant uses age progression to help Gretchen move to next stage from babyhood. Consultant assumed she was young when she first smelled a flower.

Gretchen sniffs before she answers.

The goal here is to work for something small and tangible that Gretchen can continue to hold onto now and in the future. (This approach was common in Erickson's hypnotherapy.)

Consultant acts as if she too is smelling the hallucinated daisies.

Consultant comments on crying after she has helped Gretchen use positive memories to collect herself. The consultant's tone is stern and supportive, not unlike the father's tone, but without the suggestion of guilt.

Again consultant teaches Gretchen to move from sadness and loss to positive memories. The mental-set of positive memories now opens to Gretchen much more readily than only minutes earlier.

Gretchen has had a change of mood. The next memory comes easily. Gretchen is laughing, and her head turns slowly, to allow her to gaze at her father as she speaks. She is staring at father and talking to consultant, describing in detail a vivid memory of a time when her father supported her happily.

was fun, it was fun riding on his
shoulders.

Cons.: It was freezing cold but you   So your exterior reality can be
and dad were comfortable.   harsh and you can still feel good.

Gretchen: Yeah. Then I got to ride
on the sleigh, too. He pulled me on
the sleigh. And I was small and I was
comfortable. And it felt good. There   Gretchen incorporates the consul-
was fresh air. It was wintertime.   tant's language into her revivifica-
                                               tion of this young girlhood
                                               memory: "I was comfortable." Con-
                                               sultant notes the literalness that is
                                               characteristic of trance.

In the ensuing section, the consultant uses a *shared family reverie*
technique. This basic hypnotic family therapy technique helps the family
affectively shift from morose to hopeful. Gretchen has been looking intensely and happily at her father, as if she were a little girl. In the memory
she is three. Following her lead, and given the ongoing family trance, the
therapist can easily invite the parents to participate in the shared recollection of a positive event. The critical therapeutic issue will be to activate
developmentally and clinically useful memories and draw a boundary
between Gretchen and her parents if the parents begin to induce her
associations away from feelings of comfort and pleasure. The consultant
now carefully invites father, who is in a light trance, to join in the remembered day.

Cons.: Do you remember that day?

Father: That's how it was (nodding).

Gretchen: I remember we were giving out toothpaste?

Father: I didn't remember that part
of it.

Mother: You must have mixed up   The consultant is concerned that
two things. Dad wasn't selling tooth-   mother's memory not intrude on
paste yet. I came home from the hos-   Gretchen's.
pital with baby John that day.

Gretchen: There was soap. . . .

Mother: Yeah, the soap was earlier. Yeah, you were working for Ivan, delivering soap and remember toothpaste? The toothpaste was the day I came home from the hospital after having John. And that was May.

Father: Seventeen years ago.

Cons.: Yeah. Seventeen years ago, that makes you really think about that memory. You were little, you could see it as if it's happening now.

Gretchen: I remember that. Yeah. I just remembered that about a year ago. I started thinking about that and I remembered it.

Cons.: About a year ago?

Gretchen: Yeah. It just popped into my mind for a day and I started thinking about that happening.

Cons.: And that was something very special, to be on dad's shoulders. And warm, even though it was cold.

Gretchen: Yeah. That was fun, yeah. I remember that.

Consultant lets mother elaborate and helps father participate in the memory. Here the family, each bringing personal experiences into play, build and share in a positive memory. For Gretchen, it was her last day as the family baby—John was born!

Consultant wants to stop the shared event at a positive moment and continue to build it into helping Gretchen take a more active and constructive stance in her planning.

The shared family reverie helped advance three therapeutic goals:

1. Mother and father in the *present* were introduced positively into Gretchen's *past* associations, to a time when she felt comfort and a joy of life throughout her *body*.
2. Mother and father participated in recalling and visualizing a time of joy. This event was key in activating a needed affective shift. Dad enjoyed Gretchen. Mom was happy to bring home her new baby.
3. Most importantly, the family was allowed to embellish and beautify the memory but not to take it away from Gretchen or keep the thera-

pist from going beyond the memory to difficulties that lie ahead for the three-year-old girl. Having accomplished these goals, the consultant renews her private rapport with Gretchen, to continue to work in a special state on each individual's and the entire family's symptom-related problems.

Cons.: So the little girl in the little body had some good times after all.

A shift has occurred in Gretchen's thinking.

Gretchen: I think she did, yeah.

Cons.: I had good times when I was little. Getting older I had to give up the toys of my childhood. It's a sad thing when we give them up. It's been a lonely thing to give up those toys of being a little girl. It's been a frightening thing to give up those toys of being a little girl. I felt safe on my daddy's shoulders and I knew he wouldn't let anything harm me.

Gretchen now confirms some happiness in an otherwise sad body. She refers to her younger self as "she." Consultant now wants to turn Gretchen away from family and back to rapport with only her.

Consultant uses the mother-daughter aspect of her rapport with Gretchen to fit in to the mother's "We are a lot alike, you and I" induction. Here the consultant as a young girl becomes Gretchen's twin. "I had good times when I was little." From that point of connection, the young version of the consultant is used as the engine to pull Gretchen from the joy of childhood, now confirmed, through the pains of growing up and "giving up those toys of being a little girl."

We all have to learn how to grow up, grow up or die. And death might not look attractive after all.

"We all have to learn to grow up" is also directed toward parents.

Gretchen: Why do people want to die?

Cons.: They'd rather die than give up the toys of their childhood.

Gretchen: Yeah (wispy).

Cons.: What do you think death is?

Gretchen asks this question with total curiosity and detachment. This is the kind of open trusting a therapist can be most helpful with. It often becomes accessible in trance.

Consultant sounds curious too.

Gretchen: Death is going away and never coming back ever again.

Cons.: Going away from what?

In part, death has been Gretchen's option to leaving home as a stoic hero. Perhaps "never" can be transformed to coming back on a p.r.n. basis.

Gretchen: From knowing you're
alive.

Cons.: From the life we know?   Consultant revises Gretchen's
                                             statement.

Gretchen: Yeah.   Gretchen concedes to the revision.

Gretchen and the therapist and the quiet, stationary, wholly immersed family have confirmed past joys, the need to choose to grow up rather than die, and the painfulness inherent in growing up. Suffering is built in as part of this process. It is not shameful or immoral but innate and normal. However, the bleak view of reality dominating Gretchen's and her family's mind-set must be "put in its place." The therapist challenges Gretchen's knowledge base. Issues of responsibility are clarified through the suggestive process. Gretchen demonstrates a significant shift in her mental-set.

Cons.: How do you know what life   Consultant hopes Gretchen will
is?   realize that her feelings derive in
                                         part from narrow and context-
Gretchen: Because you remember it   bound life experiences.
in your mind.

Cons.: You remember what you've   Consultant is speaking slowly, au-
already seen or where you've already   thoritatively, and sternly, indicat-
been. You have absolutely no idea of   ing "this idea is the bottom line for
the future. Let me give you an exam-   choosing life over death." Consul-
ple. When you were six years old, did   tant introduces a sexual aspect of
you ever know you'd have full breasts   development as proof that we know
and a plump behind?   the past but not the future, so the
                                         future may be brighter. (Erickson
                                         commonly used this technique.)
                                         Consultant publicly credits Gret-
                                         chen with "full breasts" and
                                         "plump behind."

Gretchen: No. . . yes. I thought I   "Like a woman" as opposed to a
would be like a woman.   *real* woman?

Cons.: You thought you'd be *like* a   Consultant and Gretchen, on behalf
woman?   of the whole family, are now pub-
                                         licly discussing the issues of sexual
Gretchen: Yeah.   development father has never felt
                                         adequate to discuss. He *is* part of
Cons.: Did you know how full your   the discussion now.
breasts would actually be when the
time came?

Gretchen: No.

Cons.: Why didn't you know that? I always wanted to have children starting from the time I was your age. I never had any idea what it would be like to actually get pregnant, be pregnant, until it happened. Now I know. And you don't know.

Consultant's tone is warmly challenging and ends up with the child-like tease of "I know something you don't know" of young girls playing together.

Gretchen: Is it fun?

Cons.: It's a lot of fun and it's a lot of hard work like everything else. But I never knew I could be as happy then as I am now. And I don't know how you can know, that you can predict the future. Even if you are intelligent.

Gretchen is becoming curious about future developmental unknowns.

It is not ignorance we are talking about, suggests consultant; it is a matter of emotional stance for survival.

Gretchen: The only chance is through. . .

Cons.: When you were little, did you look forward to being a big girl?

Gretchen: Yeah. You want to be as big as everybody else.

Cons.: As big as your mom?

Gretchen: Yeah.

Cons.: And pretty *like your mom?*

Gretchen: Yeah.

These statements including mom are to give hope and support to mom too that she has been worthy of emulation in a number of ways. Also, they contribute to a good twins option to mom's bad twins fears.

Cons.: And why don't you have the right to be that big, pretty girl now? Not right away. But in the future. Like your mom.

Why can't you carry your good memories into the present, not immediately, but over time? Last sentence also said *to mom.*

Gretchen: Maybe.

Cons.: Maybe. In the meantime, you're going to feel lonely and sad

Consultant accepts "maybe" by repeating the word but *suggests* "def-

sometimes. And I can't keep that away from you. And your dad can't and your mom can't. Until you're ready to let your body be your guide, because it's trying to teach you something and you've been saying to it "not good enough."

initely" by talking about "in the meantime" and inferring that "in the meantime" will not be very pleasant. Again consultant is suggesting to parents that they cannot save Gretchen from the inevitable suffering *until* she decides "to be a big girl." Further, Gretchen's body—not the consultant's, mother's, or father's—is to be her guide. Gretchen's *body is now hierarchically elevated in her mind-set as a superior authority*. Gretchen is censured for her disregard of *this* higher authority.

Gretchen now spontaneously offers a self-healing proposal. She manifests hope for change. This is a turning point in the interview.

Gretchen: But *maybe* it could get *better and then I could listen to it.*

Gretchen concedes. This is central, demonstrating a first self-motivated reorganization of beliefs and a permission to be flexible and self-helping and to heal.

Cons.: And how *are you going to let that happen, instead of always meddling and interfering with it?*

Gretchen: How do *I interfere with it?*

Consultant tests Gretchen further, puzzling how Gretchen will do this. How will she stop being so nasty to her guide? "Without meddling and interfering" is a suggestion to mother as well.

Cons.: By constant criticism and by your arrogance that you think you know where it's going.

Gretchen: Hmmm.

Consultant emphasizes that Gretchen's body can best guide her if she has room in her mind-set to consider that the future can be different from the past—instead of room only for the "arrogance" and "constant criticism" she has interiorized.

Cons.: Everyone knows you have to discover from your body what you want to do.

Gretchen: Oh.

"Everyone knows" is a suggestion to everyone listening. It also has a tone of girls at play being a bit competitive.

Cons.: You have to listen to your dreams, feel your emotions.

Gretchen: Oh.

The consultant *counters,* for both mother and daughter, *mother's bad twins induction:* "We are a lot alike, you and I." The consultant suggests "You are different from your mother, attractive like her, but in your own way." This kind of intervention is important in using multiperson trance inductions, to facilitate the creation of new relational boundaries.

Cons.: And look in the mirror at yourself and see if maybe you've started to become attractive as your mother is attractive in her way.

Gretchen: Ehmm.

Cons.: And you never know what a man finds good looking. You'd be surprised at some of the things out there catching their eye. And as a young woman, you can't possibly know what a man would like.

Gretchen: Mmm.

Cons.: Take a look next time you're sitting around somewhere, maybe go and have some coffee somewhere and sit and watch the people go by. And study how they act with each other. And look at what the men will go for.

Gretchen: Hmmm.

Cons.: You can't believe it. I always wondered if there'd be a man foolish

Consultant wants to differentiate, to detwin mother and daughter, so Gretchen will not feel destined to repeat mother's "un-Christian" ways and mother need not feel guilty for passing on "non-Christian" ways. Also, for father to see mother and daughter differently, especially to view mother as attractive.

This is an Erickson-derived example, a variation on beauty being in the eyes of the inscrutable observer.

This example also appeals to "the other side" of Gretchen's feelings for her mother as not as good to dad as *she* is. Her narcissism is appealed to by requesting that she allow herself to be appalled by "what some men" find attractive.

Here consultant uses the "we are twins, you and I" modality estab-

enough to fall in love with me. For-
tunately, a poor guy came along and
stuck it out thirteen years now. And I
never dreamed of that when I was
nineteen. If I'd given up then, I
would never have known that I could
be totally accepted by some male,
even though I'm far from the most
beautiful and interesting person.

Gretchen: Hmm. So that kind of
makes you special.

Cons.: And special to him in his
eyes.

Gretchen: Yeah.

Cons.: And I'm special to myself.
You see, *even your mother isn't perfect,* or haven't you found that out
yet?

Gretchen: Oh yeah.

Cons.: And even dad, *strong as he is,
knows* he has his weak points. And
you don't know yet *how to enjoy
being a big girl or a young woman*
and that's why you hold onto that little toy, because you think if you let
that toy go, you'll have nothing to
look forward to. And you think the
only joy is looking backward over
your shoulder.

Gretchen: Hmm. I see (nodding).

Cons.: Do you remember that daisy?

Gretchen: Uhmmm.

Cons.: That flower is just for you. It

lished between mother and Gretchen, suggesting "You at twenty
and I at nineteen *were* alike," so
Gretchen may think of acceptance
by a man as a possibility in her
near future.

This is also a suggestion to father
about making his wife feel "special
to him in his eyes."

Consultant humbles self and then
includes mother, inviting Gretchen
to look critically at mother, to disengage from her without insulting
her. Mother is simply "not perfect."
Also, to refer again to father's accepting his wife as she is.

It is suggested that father too could
stand to tolerate some of his "weak
points," "strong as he is." Now
consultant talks metaphorically to
the whole family, still *through*
Gretchen, about losing toys of earlier stage as they move on to the
next life stage. Each family member
is holding onto a little toy, including Chris and his Rubik cube.

Gretchen has been criticized (for
being overly self-critical) and reminded of her sadness habit. This is
the time to teach her to reactivate
the "daisy memories" to comfort

should be *your special flower to re-mind you of the talk we had and of your hope for the possibility that you can go beyond where your mother's gone*. And you might be *something really special*.

Gretchen: Uhmmm. I think so.

Cons.: Do you think she'd forgive you if you even did her one better?

Gretchen: Yes. I think she would.

Cons.: And would your dad? How well would he put up with it? A more grown-up you.

Gretchen: I think he would. Yeah, I think so.

herself. This is a basic technique of introjecting trance events into new sequences of thought and action.

Transcending mother is suggested as a credit to mother. Joining mother in grief is undesirable.

Again, spontaneous hope and self esteem.

Consultant also asks mother "Can you forgive Gretchen if she breaks away from being your sad twin?"

Consultant suggests to father "You have an investment in her being a baby. Think about how you will let her grow up and away from you." Parents are asked to consider the negatives of giving up Gretchen and her rhino as *their* "toys."

Because the family is in a receptive and unthreatened state, the consultant can help remake the "crazy" contract between mother and daughter (that daughter cannot outdo her) and between father and daughter (a developmentally excessive adoration). At this depth of trance, this procedure of forging a new contract can be used. Gretchen starts to examine her father's face at this point. The consultant does not want Gretchen to let her father influence this decision, so she prevents Gretchen from looking away by intensifying the privacy of what she and Gretchen have been talking about. Gretchen's job is not to focus on her parents' approval but to go on and "grow up," "choose life," and let her parents grapple with the consequences, let her parents give up their "toys" of raising a young girl.

Now the consultant wants to draw a line across which she suggests parents and brothers not trespass. In fact, they have only been in on their own experience. Gretchen's feelings are inside her, not visible to them.

Cons.: And these things we've been talking about today? I think they should stay between you and me, even though your mom and dad have

All the family is immobile, attentive, breathing deeply, their bodies in positions of openness and receptivity.

heard them and your brothers. No
one knows what you've been thinking. No one knows what you've been
feeling, just you and me.

Gretchen: Uh huh.

Consultant includes herself so
Gretchen will interiorize consultant
as her ally in future conversing
with her body as her guide.

Cons.: And what's inside of you is
what's most important. And what's
in your body is most important. Your
body has always wanted to be alive
and has continued developing in
spite of you. And if it had really
wanted to stop growing, it could
have. You could have not developed
breasts. You could have never had
your period. You could have not
grown. All those things happen
when a person's body doesn't want to
be alive and growing. I think your
body has been telling you lots you
ought to know.

Consultant reviews and summarizes
before awakening Gretchen. "You"
embraces the family body.

Sexual development is a sign of
health and will to live. Emphasized
again is the hierarchical elevation
of Gretchen's natural psychophysiological cues as constructive
mental-set guides.

In this summarization before she awakens the family, the consultant uses an approach that can be helpful for amnesia: *She refers back to
various aspects of trance material out of their previous sequencing.* This
has an effect similar to that of shuffling a deck of cards—some of the cards
last seen will be recalled, but the inexperienced person will be hard-
pressed to remember the previous order of the deck. In this way, nuances,
lines of association, and recall of suggestion can be jostled.

Cons.: I wonder if you'll go sometime dressed nicely and sit in a coffee
shop or somewhere in the suburb or
near home or school and watch the
people walk by, just to look, what
some men will find interesting.

Referring back to this suggestion
helps give amnesia for interim
suggestions.

Gretchen: All different things. All
different.

Rapport is intense.

Cons.: And you know less about
yourself than you would like to think
you know. And you have a whole
world to learn about yourself. How
are you going to find out about
yourself? It's a big problem. It's a
serious problem.

It is also a problem assigned to
other family members.

Gretchen is now given a new big and serious problem: To learn
about herself. To teach her how, the consultant returns to Gretchen's
hand, the body part Gretchen has hurt before. *Now her own hand will
teach her.* Returning to the hand also jostles the order of suggestive
events.

Cons.: How'd you find out that that
hand was yours?

Gretchen: 'Cause I felt it.

In the preconsultation, it was
agreed that Gretchen needed a very
serious problem. Consultant wants
to be sure she does not take away the
symptom and leave an empty hole.

Cons.: You felt it. And if your hand
fell asleep and you couldn't feel it. . .

Gretchen: I can see that it's a part of
me.

Consultant returns to "the hand,"
to use it now not as a means of taking Gretchen's life but as a vehicle
for learning about herself, an embodiment of her new "big
problem."

Cons.: And if you had to close your
eyes and your hand fell asleep, how
would you know it was yours?

Gretchen: I wouldn't.

Cons.: You wouldn't know.

Gretchen: I remember having arms
before.

Cons.: You remember having them,
but you don't even think to answer
that you could, that you could move
the arm, that's the way you find out
where it is. That it's still there, that
it's yours.

Consultant picks up her hand and
holds it. Gretchen's hand remains
in the air.

Gretchen: Even though it's asleep?

Gretchen offers that her hand *is*
asleep.

Cons.: Even though it's asleep.

Gretchen: It will still move?

Cons.: It still moves when you want it to move. That's your hand. That's how we learn. How do you think you learn where your ear is?

This is a direct suggestion, tied to her own timing of "wanting it to move." Gretchen looks at her hand curiously. Consultant puts her pinky playfully in her own ear, suggesting a moving hand can explore one's body.

Gretchen: Yeah. I can feel it and move it. Yeah. (Staring at hand)

Gretchen slowly discovers that she can move her fingers. She moves them as if for the first time.

Cons.: Well, why do you think it's going to be any different learning what you want to do for your life's work, where you want to live. . . ?

Gretchen: You've got to try it out.

Consultant uses Gretchen's discovery as a model for Gretchen's upcoming "movements" in finding work, home, and so on. Consultant assumes she will make those moves by saying "Why do you think *it is going to be any different. . .?*" The emphasis is not on feeling different but on making new movements.

Cons.: What about the kind of girl-friends you want to make? What about whether you like nail polish or not? I bet you don't even know if you like it or what color you like best? . . . My daughter likes shocking pink and I think it's *absolutely awful,* but *she* does look good in it. I prefer pale. You don't know about what you'd like to put on your fingers.

Nail polish is selected because it provides a concrete and easily accomplished task of caring for one's body.

Gretchen: Hmmmmmmmm.

Cons.: What colors do you look good in? Mom looks beautiful in maroon. It brings out her rosy cheeks. What color do you look good in?

Gretchen: Red.

Cons.: Red.

Gretchen: I like red. And blue.

Cons.: Blue. Deep blue or. . . ?

Color is used to separate consultant from her daughter. "My daughter and I don't have to like the same things." Consultant finds her daughter's color preference "awful". . .for herself. These suggestions are for both mother and daughter. Both can be attractive. Each can be different.

Gretchen: Dark blue.

Cons.: And do you have anything red
or blue you wear?

Gretchen: No. I don't have any red
things, but I do have some blue
things. I've got my blue pants.

Cons.: And you will look a lot more
attractive wearing something blue
than carrying a blue friend who will
wait for you at home like all our
stuffed animals wait for us at home.
But that color does look good on you.

Consultant wants to appeal
to Gretchen's narcissism about her
hidden good looks to mobilize her
to wear something blue other than
her stuffed rhino. She starts and
ends the suggestion on color pre-
ferences, hiding the suggestion
between layers of blue.

The transformation is being made. The stuffed blue rhino is
"saved," but it has been matured. It is first transformed into a *color*
Gretchen is wearing. It is then suggested that this blue-colored "garment"
is less attractive than some other blue thing Gretchen might wear. Furth-
ermore, "we all" have stuffed animals who can wait for us at home. But,
the color of the animal does "look good" on Gretchen. The color can
come out in *public,* and the cuddly baby toy can remain for *private* comfort. This salvaging of benevolent aspects of the rhino is a logical outgrowth of the present approach in which a nonadversarial attitude toward
benign features of symptoms is basic.

Gretchen: Hmm.

Cons.: And maybe you can get yourself something blue when you have
enough money, something special.

Gretchen: Yeah.

Cons.: And how about your hair?
What way do you look best?

Gretchen: I like it best when it's
clean and curls properly.

Cons.: Is it clean and properly curled
now?

Gretchen: Not today.

Cons.: When you knew you were going to meet someone who's a specialist, who came all the way across the United States, and you didn't fix your hair for me?

Gretchen: No, I tried to, but it didn't work for me.

Cons.: It didn't work for you?

Gretchen: No.

Cons.: So you really don't know how to fix your hair yet.

What an insult!

Gretchen: It was because I didn't wash it before I curled it, that's why.

Gretchen put some effort into looking disheveled.

Cons.: You mean you didn't wash your hair for me.

I insulted you because I was personally offended.

Gretchen: No, I didn't, but my brother did. He got all dressed up.

Gretchen too is part of the family praising of brother juxtaposed against criticism of herself. She maintains the inductive system.

Cons.: He looks quite handsome, doesn't he?

Gretchen: Yes, he does.

Cons.: He's a handsome young man. And I don't see why you don't have the right to be a lovely young woman. Not right away, but in the next year.

Consultant agrees he is handsome and suggests that they can *both* be attractive, not caught in a mutual contradiction based on rigid family structures or characterizations.

Gretchen: In the next year? (Makes it sound like forever)

Cons.: Well, I might rather it be in the next year, and you might rather wait two months over that. Your dad might want you to wait a year and a month. Your mother might wish you'd hurry up. She likes to get on with things. You'll have to make

An Erickson technique for providing a class of suggestion to allow a subject to pick her own date, but to not argue the *fact* of picking a date to "be a lovely young woman."

your own decision and the ongoing
therapists might think nine months
is rather enough.

Gretchen: Maybe the therapist and
dad are right.

Gretchen's statement points to her
choosing dad's side over mom's
rather than transcending their argument and making her own
decision.

Cons.: You're going to have to find
your own time. And not have any of
ours. And your body will tell you,
because you will get longings.

Listen to your inner longings.

Gretchen: Hmm. I see. . .I tried nail
polish before.

Cons.: But you don't know what
color looks best on you.

Gretchen: No, I didn't try very much.

Cons.: And I wonder who even gets
to take a look at you and make their
own decision. You have a big problem on your hands. I think it's bigger
than you ever dreamed of and more
serious than you ever thought. It's
the worst problem you'll ever face in
your life. In some ways, although
there will always be hard ones.

Now she has the *worst* problem
ever. The hole the symptom filled
can be filled even better! It was decided in the preconsultation session
that Gretchen needed some sort of
awesome problem. Consultant has
looked to prescribe an appropriate
challenge.

Gretchen: Yes.

Cons.: You have to get to know
yourself. What you want to make of
yourself. But you ought to keep some
daisies on hand, because you're going
to need them.

Again, hard problems are followed
by a now-established cue word for
activating a sense of well-being:
"daisies."

Gretchen: Yeah. It's a good idea.

Cons.: And think about those daisies
when you need them, when times get
hard and *they do smell good.* You
can think about them now while I
talk to your family.

Now consultant draws a boundary
around other family members, after
resuggesting Gretchen return to the
early positive memory she
unearthed.

Earlier in the session the consultant prepared for this phase of turning back to the family. The entire family is in trance. The consultant will now ask them to shift gears. She knows they have no plan for homecoming. She uses the next communication to break any intrusion into Gretchen's inner state and to place the entire trance experience out of reach. The final phase of an hypnotic family interview will reactivate aspects of the trance, but only selectively, and in a manner fostering desirable amnesias of other trance events.

Step 3: Working to Draw Boundaries and Address Postinductive Objections

The consultant is now looking to observe parents' and brothers' reactions and objections to suggestions. In fact, she wants to elicit as many of the doubts as possible, to increase the effectiveness of suggestions made and better tailor them to each family member. The consultant also wants to be on guard to block inadvertent family reinductions of Gretchen. She will use a variety of techniques to do so, *especially drawing on learnings from and reactivating components of the trance experience.*

Cons.: And the things we've talked about today are not important to talk about again. And you can understand that. Now I suppose you have a *plan* for the homecoming of your daughter.

Parents are totally immobile. Their speech is very slow, and their responses are delayed. They are still in trance.

Mother: It just doesn't seem that that's what she's going to do.

Father: It doesn't seem to work, no.

Mother: So I've done what I could.

Cons.: That's right.

This is an interesting sentence structure. It is mother's summary of what has happened in the trance. Mother volunteers an insight from all she has heard: "I have (already) done what I could."

Mother: Whenever, when she's come home, like when she's coming home with us today, well, we have to go

Mother has trouble speaking, enacting her beginning of emotional upset. The consultant wants mother's upsets and "resistances"

over, her landlady doesn't even know that she's leaving, so we have to go and tell her and bring her stuff home.

brought out *and* to help her and her husband deal with them in the rest of the session.

Cons.: Now, I wouldn't say that because certain things *haven't* worked out that they *can't* work out. In fact, I think there's a lot of *hope* that they *can* work out, but maybe it is going to take a little bit of *time.* So hopefulness on your part is useful *now.*

Consultant responds to only the parents' *affective state,* not to the *subject* mother responds with.

Father: Ummhmmm. I never give up hope.

Mother: He's always the optimist.

Father's tone conveys some worry. His responsibility is about to begin, and he feels its weight. Consultant responds only to his tone.

Cons.: There must have been a time when your first daughter left home, when things looked pretty bleak.

Mother: (Laughing nervously).

Cons.: Leaving home is never easy.

Mother: Why can't they do it nicely?

Cons.: Even in the worst of situations, it doesn't, uh, even in the best of situations, either one, it's always hard.

Mother: Yeah, I guess so.

Cons.: Hard on the parents. Hard on the kids. There's nothing more intense than the family relationship.

Mother: It's when they're growing up that you say, oh joy, they're growing up and then when they grow up, you say, oh help! (Laughs) Where's my baby?

Here mother expresses the kind of internal ambivalence that contributes to Gretchen's acting like a baby. Mother misses the "toy" of her reproductive years.

Cons.: That's hard.

Mother: And then you look forward to grandchildren.

Cons.: That's right.

Father: (Folds arms)

Mother volunteers this idea suggested in trance as moving onto the next life stage.

Since the start of the therapeutic counterinduction, this is the *first movement* by father. Therefore, it suggests to consultant that this subject is challenging to father.

Mother: But I'm really looking forward to the time when we're alone, and yet I know when I look at the kids when they're growing up that it's going to be sad, too, in a way, to see that the last, especially the last one leaves home, because that's the end of having babies.

Cons.: But you wouldn't want her to be there with you until your old age?

Father: Well, it wouldn't be normal for her to, you know, be living at home, and I would like to see her go out and function on her own. And that was one of the reasons why when she came up here we thought, we were hoping, it would work out then, but she's not ready yet.

Mother: She had a real nice little apartment at first. On Elm Street. Yeah. It was a nice apartment, but she just couldn't stand being alone. All alone.

Cons.: It's hard to be alone there.

Mother: Yet I think, joy, to be alone . . . (laugh) but if I were alone, I probably wouldn't like it.

Cons.: I often have those thoughts. . .

This is the kind of material consultant hopes to have offered to her so she can affect mother's mind-set as well. Gretchen's leaving home is tied to facing up to the end of mother's reproductive years. She was not programmed beyond those years. Mother describes the "toys" she must part ways with; these are not stuffed toys.

Father starts what could be a renewal of his induction. Is he suggesting her coming home now must be "abnormal?" This could "suggest" to Gretchen that she must hand a ticket marked "crazy" to pass through dad's door. Perhaps dad too is not ready yet for Gretchen to leave. Perhaps this is no cause for despair, just a *normal* refueling.

And mother continues what could be a renewed loneliness induction of Gretchen.

Consultant prevents this induction by containing the loneliness issue in her exchanges with mother.

Using the twins induction "We as mothers."

Mother: You know, when you're at the store and the customers are there and then your kids come home and your husband's there and you never have two minutes and you think "Oh, she sure is stupid. I wish I could be home."

As consultant blocks the way for father and mother to induce Gretchen, mother expounds spontaneously on her unhappy situation and jealousy of Gretchen's freedom.

Cons.: It's too bad sometimes you couldn't just switch. . .

Mother: Yeah. Just for a day or two.

Mother and consultant engage in a moment of fantasy about being kids again.

Cons.: That's why it's so important to somehow find the way to feel that this moment of my life is the best moment. I'm going to live it to the fullest. 'Cause otherwise ten years up the road, you look back and say, "I was healthier then; I was younger; I wasn't sick and my back didn't ache as much and why didn't I just enjoy it."

The fantasy is then used to endorse the beauty of the present as an opportunity they will not want to look back on as having been wasted!

Father: Well, we look back sometimes and we didn't have no problems when the children were small. And then they become teenagers and all the problems seem to come along and I guess they want to live their own lives and, you know, they rebel against the authorities and you think, boy, was it ever nicer when they were small!

Father too concedes a contribution to the undertow in the family that inadvertently pulls for Gretchen's immaturity. Now both parents have conveyed the aspect of their feelings consultant suggested in trance. In "losing" their children, they give up that younger period of their own lives when they were the parents of babies.

Cons.: So she has tried to accommodate in a sense by becoming the baby again. And she really can't do that—for you or for herself.

Gretchen's problem is defined as being helpful by acting like a baby.

Father: Yah.

Cons.: But the grandchildren, you
have the chance to have quite a few.
If she's as good at it as you were. . . .
It would be interesting to find out
(looking at Gretchen).

Gretchen: Yeah.

Cons.: But first things first. . . .

We just saw both parents, affected by the family trance material,
enjoying the memories of the time when the children were little, when
they were "no problems at all." They convey *their own fear of loneliness
and of their grown-up children not doing well;* they have yet to develop
dreams for their shared future. These spontaneous expressions of concern
in the consultant's frame of developing plans for Gretchen are what the
consultant *hoped* for. She can work with these concerns now that they
have spontaneously emerged.

Note how the conversation has flowed from the trance suggestions,
especially (1) the joyous memories of childhood to (2) the need to give up
the "toys" of childhood to (3) to go on to the next life stage. The discussion has remained *focused* on the symptom bearer. Nevertheless, mother
and father have each voiced a personal sense of loss, spontaneously.

The consultant hopes to ultimately help move Gretchen from her
position of triangulation in socially related marital problems to her sibling subsystem. Toward that end, she now activates brother, looking to
set up some possible brother-sister dialogue.

Cons.: Little brother, anything you
want to say today?

"Little brother" vis-a-vis Gretchen.
She is empowered indirectly as head
of her sibling subsystem. It is up to
her to learn to take this position.

John: Okay. I'll say anything I want
to say. Okay, I was just thinking
while you and she were going on and
on. . .well, I'll talk to her. Like you
heard when we were talking and you
were talking about you're always you
and stuff like that, well, you know,
Gary [both Gretchen and John's

John takes what is for him an unusual liberty. The "on and on"
carries a sense of the trance event's
lulling monotony for him. Bore-
dom is a prime trance inducer.

friend] and I get together and talk
sometimes, he said that at times you
were a really beautiful person and
there are times when you shine so
much more and you are a beautiful
person.

Cons.: Could you. . . ? (Indicating he
talk directly to Gretchen)

Consultant points to Gretchen,
suggesting John talk to Gretchen
directly. Brother, after trance experience, spontaneously offers positive response to his sister.

John: Sure. Okay. (Gretchen takes
consultant's seat)

Cons.: She needs to hear this from
you, something positive. (Consultant
moves across room to next to father)

Consultant points to Gretchen
again and moves away from between John and Gretchen. Gretchen
is now physically within the sibling
subsystem. The consultant is now
seated beside father and mother.

John: Like there are times that you
are a very beautiful person, like Gary
mentioned when you helped him
move into his apartment on Clarence
Street.

Gretchen: (Laugh) Yeah.

John: He said that you were very
helpful and that, well he said, that
you really shined. And aside from
that, Bernice (Gary's sister and John's
friend) said—and I don't know if
Gary would appreciate me saying
this—but Bernice was saying that
Gary is sometimes really intolerable
around the house. But she was saying
"I like it when Gretchen comes over
'cause. . . ." Well, that time, I guess
you went to see a movie or something, last time you were home?
(With great curiosity)

John is, for his age, appropriately
curious about whether Gretchen
went on a date with this friend!

Gretchen: With Gary? Oh, we went
for a walk. (Coyly, with innuendo)

Gretchen enjoys her special knowledge of "dating." In this context, in
which psychosexual development

John: Okay, you went for a walk. Bernice said he was tolerable for a few days after he was with you. I don't know, you must make him feel good or something. But, yes, there are times that you are really a beautiful person. And then on the other extreme there are times that, maybe it's the fact that you're my sister, but I'd just rather not have you around.

has been discussed more than ever in family history, Gretchen's potential knowledge of boy-girl relations is electric!

The consultant has awaited this likely "other extreme."

Gretchen: (Nervously laughing) Yeah.

Gretchen laughs, but she is defenseless.

Cons.: Don't you ever feel like that back to him? That sometimes you wish he wouldn't be around?

Gretchen: Sometimes, yeah, I do.

Consultant suggests Gretchen carry the same message back to John rather than taking his feelings as an indication of her badness. Brothers and sisters often wish each other were not around.

The consultant's goals in this brother-sister interaction were to:

1. Help Gretchen move to the sibling subsystem and strengthen especially the teenage rapport
2. Foster a positive age-appropriate exchange
3. Prevent brother from acting as Gretchen's superior
4. Help Gretchen assert herself with her brother

The consultant wants to have Gretchen end on an equal footing with John. Having one such experience is not an end point, simply a guide to the family and the OTs for an event that needs repeating.

In the last minutes of the interview, the consultant wants to use everything family members raise to delineate areas for future work, to secure appropriate boundaries between people and clarify issues of responsibility.

Father raises the issue of Gretchen's beauty. It is a loaded issue in a house that was described as "not big enough to hold two women." The consultant will work with this issue to help dad move from Gretchen to his wife and to help mother not feel undermined by daughter's mature strengths. The discussion is still about the parents' fear of Gretchen leaving home.

Father: If we ever look at some family pictures, I think Gretchen is the prettiest, and no offense to the boys, but I think she's a pretty girl.

Cons.: (To John) It's the women who have to find you attractive. . .

John: Ummhmm.

Cons.: And she certainly has a good-looking mother. I was struck by how attractive you were when you first came in there. I had to mention it.

Father: You should have seen a picture of her when she was Gretchen's age.

Cons.: Younger, huh.

Father: And she didn't have all that weight on her, too.

Mother: (Laughing) When I was. . .

Cons.: Gretchen may be able to do a little better. We always hope our daughter can do. . .

Mother: Yep.

Cons.: Better than us.

Mother: You want something better for them, a little better.

Cons.: That's what you work so hard for.

Mother: It's a surprise growing up and having a family when I think

Father has gone off into his own inner reverie of Gretchen's beauty, perhaps taking off on John's description of Gretchen as a beautiful person. Note that he apologizes to his sons when his wife may be more envious!

Consultant wants to help direct father's attentions from his beautiful baby girl *back to his wife.*

Father accepts, conditionally. Mother *was* beautiful; she *is* overweight.

The trance suggestion of a mother's success being tied to her daughter going beyond her is reiterated. This way mother can see Gretchen's beauty as a credit to her rather than as a threat, as was seemingly posed by father's adoration of Gretchen.

Mother accepts this suggestion. Her attitude at this moment is quite different from her "You're worse than me" approach only minutes earlier.

Consultant endorses this statement to bolster mother's tolerance of Gretchen actually doing better than she is. She suggests that Gretchen's success is related to mother's hard work.

Mother commends herself for doing "just right!"

ours is just right! Two and two, two
girls, two boys.

Cons.: Oh, I think you're lucky. I
have one of each and I have to . . .
Well, I just want to thank you so
much for letting me into your family,
and I'm honored that you made me
so welcome to it and, uh (to father), I
think you have a really beautiful
family.

Consultant indicates she is about to
leave. Father is credited with a
"beautiful family."

Father: Yeah, I'm (nodding, looking
dreamy) I wouldn't wish for—
sometimes I think I'm a lucky man to
have nice healthy children, then, anyway, like everyone is normal and my
mother always used to say that the
main thing is that they're normal and
they're whole. When you have little
ones and some of my older brothers,
they're a little disgusted with me in
Germany. They know it's rather hard
to have four children and they think,
well, it's too many children and I
didn't think so.

The "optimist" now says *"sometimes* I think I'm a lucky man."
And he volunteers some negative
information about his older brothers, who have condemned his being
too much of a family man and
hence poor economically.

His brothers contributed—in their
worries for *his* well-being—to father's feelings of failure, inadequacy, and so on.

Cons.: You knew it made you rich.

Father: Yah, Yah. I feel sorry for
some people who don't have a family.
It must be awful too just being by
yourself. I, we, get along very well,
but still just to look and stare at each
other and. . .

Consultant defines what father's
brothers suggested made him poor
as actually what "made him rich."

Father now volunteers his fear of
living without this wealth. Living
alone with one's wife is projected as
"looking and staring at each
other."

The consultant wants to respond to family members' concerns
while preventing them from culminating in problematic suggestions to
one another. For example, she wants to respond to father's expressions of
doubt that perhaps his brothers in Germany were right and he could not
handle the economic strain of four children. Anyway, now what will he

and his wife do with no children around? Just "look and stare at each other and. . . ." To prevent his doubts from leading to weakness or despair, the consultant therefore reintroduces some of the earlier trance material, reminding father of his real choices: ultimately, a blue rhino or a marriage-eligible, potentially grandchild-producing daughter. As usual, she then quickly takes the heat off father and turns to mother, to join mother to father in this issue of parents losing their babies.

Cons.: I think the hard thing ahead will be, you know, dealing with them going off, and that's always hard for the parents, and letting her rhinoceros turn into a beautiful blue sweater or shirt and so on, it'll make you cry. You know mothers cry at weddings.

Consultant uses this to emphasize their planning to let go of Gretchen, "letting her" transform Werner the rhino into clothes. *This,* rather than suicide threats, will make them cry.

Mother: They don't know what to do?

Cons.: That's right, because that little brat isn't going to depend on them anymore. So I think that'll be the next real rough spot.

Mother: When I think about that now, I think, well, that would be really fantastic. And when I was a little girl, I always wanted to have babies. I think that's all I ever wanted was babies and I couldn't wait. I know I was sixteen when I got married, and at seventeen I had Sophia (the older daughter) and then Gretchen and then John and Chris you know. Like that was my goal in life. Was to have babies, so I was lucky I had four, like some people can't have children.

Mother volunteers that her goal has been having babies. Now what is she to do? Mother keeps sliding back. She cannot help push Gretchen forward from this position.

Cons.: Hopefully, you'll get to be an active grandmother.

Mother: Yeah. I think that would be fantastic to see her married. I see wedding dresses sometimes and I think, oh my Gretchen. . . .

Cons.: First she's got to learn what color nail polish she likes. . . .

Mother: (Laughing)

Cons.: What kind of girlfriends? What color is the best?

Consultant wants to prevent mother from taking over Gretchen's fantasies for her own future building.

Consultant slows down the imagining process to prevent mother from inducing feelings of inadequacy in Gretchen or fears she must live up to mother's expectations of her.

Consultant talks as she did in trance, only to Gretchen, to redraw that boundary separating mother and Gretchen, *now.*

The family now yields to another Gretchen—a kind of family secret whose identity is hidden away in Gretchen's purse! Her "other" personality, who threatens mother by attracting dad and threatens dad by attracting young men! The family body spontaneously exposes a different self- and body image.

Mother: You haven't seen Gretchen here, you haven't seen Gretchen dressed up.

Father: She used to dress real sharp.

Mother: We have pictures.

Cons.: I bet that these therapists would hardly recognize you, even though they're extremely perceptive, when you'd come in the door dressed up.

Gretchen: I've got a picture on me.

Mother: Blue dress?

Gretchen: Yeah. Umhm.

Mother: Where is it, in your purse?

Gretchen: Yeah.

Mother: Well, why don't you show the lady?

Mother now offers that consultant has not seen the real Gretchen. This less frequently activated aspect of Gretchen and less often induced Gretchen is now elicited. Father too remembers this Gretchen, spontaneously.

Gretchen herself, entering barefoot, carrying a blue rhino, has left hidden in her bag in another room a purse, with a treasured picture of herself. She had left her purse, the photo, and her shoes in the other room so that she would be dressed a certain way for the interview.

Cons.: Want to bring it in?

Gretchen: It's in my purse right here.

Mother: That's it, that's the lady Gretchen. Sometime we'll shock the OT and we'll walk up here and you won't know her.

OT: I'm easy to shock.

Mother: Yeah.

Gretchen: Right in here. That was me, when I was how old? And pounds lighter!

Cons.: My goodness, absolutely beautiful.

Mother: That's that blue dress, I don't even know. I guess Sophia has that dress. That was a few years ago.

Cons.: You never saw this?

Mother: Yeah, we took that in. . .

Gretchen: The date is on the back of it.

Father: Maybe in '77.

Gretchen: That's three years. . .

Mother: That's three years ago, four years ago. . .

Father: Yeah.

Cons.: So you were sixteen?

Gretchen: Yeah. Sixteen.

Consultant again does not want mother to push Gretchen to show this self, but to invite her to. She softens mother's push.

Mother follows consultant's lead about therapists not recognizing her.

Handing picture to father; mother looks on over his shoulder.

Father takes out his glasses and takes the picture.

Before things (especially economically related) got "really terrible."

Father, engrossed in the picture, is holding it, beaming.

Note that the family has now spontaneously and collectively evoked a shared image and shared enjoyment of Gretchen, who can succeed, who can, thanks to her parents' suffering, suffer less and look better. Just as the family in shared trance had viewed happy little Gretchen together, they all now mark their own personal seasons against Gretchen's growing up.

The therapist wants to use this final stage of the therapy session to also model the final stages of the therapy for the observing clinicians and to continue to more fully develop the indirect trance suggestions made to the parents. Most importantly, she wants to (1) direct father's overflow of adoration of daughter over to his wife, so that he will (2) help her find places other than in Gretchen to put all her intense maternal feelings. The content is of less significance than the family structural issues under consideration. Sequentially, father focuses on Gretchen in the picture and the consultant tries to redirect his attention to his wife. Wife focuses on babying Gretchen and consultant offers that father step in at moments like this to hold his wife back, instead of allowing her to foster Gretchen's dependency.

Cons.: (To father) And there's no face as beautiful—did you want to see the picture, Chris? There's no face as beautiful as the one you've traveled with for several decades. And you can see the whole journey in the face.	Consultant redirects father's attention to—if not his wife's beauty—her familiarity. "The journey of their shared life is in her face" (borrowed from Alex Haley's *Roots*). "She whom one loves best is loveliest. . . ." (from Sappho).
Mother: Isn't that true.	
Cons.: She's going to need a lot from you, eh? You've got good shoulders? The whole family attests to your shoulders.	Consultant does not wait for father's response. She turns to mother, changing the subject while focusing on related family structural issues.

It is suggested that father can continue to carry large burdens but that wife will take children's place. This transmits the message about separating marital problems from parenting ones.

Cons.: Now where are you going to put all that mothering, mama?	Once father blocks your pouring it into Gretchen. . . .
Mother: Well, when sometimes I would just like to, when Gretchen is like this, then the mother instinct is in me, like Sunday morning when I got up to get ready for church and I stopped by her, she called me and I	Mother brings up her "mothering" instinct and the collusion of that part of herself with sustaining Gretchen's babyish behavior.

stopped by her bedroom and she
cried, she said "mama, please, please,
let me go home" and well, you're a
mother, eh, and I say I want what's
best for her. And she said "[The OT]
thinks, he says I should come home
and I'll be good and I'll do all these
things," you know, and I don't want
her to be *good*—I mean, it's not that.
I don't want her to hurt herself. I
want the best for her and I'm scared,
too, with her coming home—how it's
going to be.

Cons.: (To father) I think it is *where
you need to step in* because it's not
the time for mama to baby her anymore. And I think somehow you're
going to be the only one to be able to
help mama deal with her natural
mothering instinct and say to her,
"Not now, you know, let's wait for
the grandchildren." Because she, it's
not good to encourage her not to
suffer through her difficult time now,
just as you had to, you suffered
through yours. (To mother) Your
husband suffered through his. And it
made you strong.

> Again this is designated father's
> burden. He will need help from the
> OT to carry it. Although very
> straightforward, this structural in-
> tervention is counterinductive to
> both mother and father. Gretchen
> needs support. She does not need to
> be infantilized.

> Suffering is associated repeatedly
> with strength to enable parents to
> tolerate growing pains in Gretchen.

Mother: But when I had mine, I was
married, eh, it was different.

> Mother resists this idea. A girl can
> only suffer if married.

Cons.: Then she'll have to have a different one.

Mother: She'll have a different kind,
eh, because most girls are not married
at sixteen.

> Mother accepts that the times have
> changed.

Cons.: Not any more.

Mother: Not any more, but for me, for me, it was the best thing. I had my babies, to fill that need, like when I got pregnant, especially the last time was because I needed that baby, like I really needed it. Like some women say they go through it when they're in their forties. I hope I don't have it again, 'cause I'm not going to have any more children. You know, that, I really needed a baby. And so when you get that way. . .

Cons.: Right. I think in some ways that your daughter has wanted to fill that need and she's paid, I think she knows today she's paid a price and (to father) I hope you'll hold her (wife's) hand and pray together a lot, so that she can feel that loving and nurturing transfer back over to you. You're a good handholder.

Drawing on the family trance, consultant refers back to "the price paid by Gretchen." The single sentence is spoken to everyone, starting with looking at mother, to Gretchen, to father. This *family structural sentence* is made easily because of the family hypnosis. For Gretchen, it returns her to trance suggestions advising against being a baby for her mom.

Mother: (Laughing) He doesn't sit still long enough. He's a doer. I'm a talker and he's a doer.

Cons.: Handholding is doing. (To father) You could have a busy handholding.

Consultant teases father about his impatience with affection. She does not want him to fold his arms.

Mother: (Laughing)

Cons.: Some on top, some on bottom (wiggling the index finger). If you need to be restless, you can tap your feet, dance while you do it?

Mother: Well, how do I handle . . . what do I do?

Mother asks her help with Gretchen.

Cons.: I think you really will need

Gretchen is not mother's problem

your husband. I don't think you can do that alone.

Mother: But Gretchen. . .

Cons.: What she has to do she has to do alone, because it's the nature of her age. You do have your husband and I think that when you feel that urge to baby your daughter and she wants to come in to that soft bosom, that you, you have to say, no dear, and let your husband. . .(To father) You have to pull her away, really.

Mother: So, I should be hard. . .and make her do the things that are good for her.

Cons.: Well, you can't make her.

Mother: No, but I mean, not let her do. . .

Cons.: Not that she can't, she can't be babied by you anymore.

Mother: So even the tears on Sunday that made me let her come home, *I should have said no. . .*

Cons.: Maybe so.

Father: We just want what's best for Gretchen, *but we don't always know what's best for her, that's the trouble.* I don't know. I guess to come home at this time probably would be the best for her. (To OT) Is that what you've been suggesting?

Cons.: Perhaps you want to go on and just talk to each other for a bit now. And talk about your plans together and. . . . Well, again, the best of luck (extending her hand).

alone. She needs father's collaboration.

Father nods perseveratively, reentering an inner reverie.

Again, structure is betrayed by sequence. Father wanted her home; mother was not so sure. A turning-point decision is now spontaneously reviewed.

Father indicates he is ready to get help from the OT to carry out the general suggestions of this consultation.

Father: Thanks very much (shaking hands).

Cons.: Yeah. Oh, warm hands (prolonging the handshake).

Mother: (Laugh).

Cons.: You're a better handholder than you know.

Father: Thank you.

(Mother and consultant shake hands).

Cons.: (To Chris) A pleasure to meet you. Goodbye. I didn't get to talk to you much, but I hope you figured out how to do the cube. (To John) Good luck with the cadet job. I hope you get it.

John: I do, too.

Gretchen: 'Bye.

Cons.: Goodbye. (Extending her hand) Can you give me a squeeze there? All right. Take good care now. (Consultant and Gretchen hug) I'm going to be writing to find out about you and the latest thing you learned about yourself, okay?

Gretchen: Okay.

Cons.: So be sure to keep me in touch.

Gretchen: Okay.

Cons.: Okay. You know I don't want to separate from these. I don't want anybody walking out with my children's presents.

Mother: Your special stuffed animals to take home.

In shaking hands with father, consultant again teasingly reiterates her "suggestion" that father's less-than-Don-Juan sexual prowess is more than he gives it credit for. As always with father, the consultant uses a "mention it and drop it" approach, rather than pushing as mother does.

Consultant ends as she began, by referring to the toy animals. She jokingly expresses worry that family members might want to keep these baby things that are for her own children. Referring back to the pretrance start of the session further helps place the trance experience out of reach.

OT: Thank you. I really appreciate
you. You were of invaluable
assistance.

Carrying her stuffed animals, the consultant now leaves the family
and joins the observing therapists behind the one-way mirror. The original discussion between father and OT ensues with little reference to the
interview. The consultant takes this as a positive indicator, regarding
amnesia and other forms of distancing-from-trance phenomena as allowing suggestions received to settle in with a minimum of conscious or
interpersonal intrusion.

Although the family is very eager to get help, the tone has changed
from despair to celebration. This authentic sense of hopefulness was successfully inserted through the steps of the therapeutic counterinduction.
The return home can now be seen as a normal moment in a sequence of
events culminating in leaving home—an "atavistic family regression."
"Celebration" is premature. However, the therapeutically enacted sequences *leading* to celebration provide the *kind of format* that, if followed
over the next year, are likely to lead to something to celebrate about!

Father: We kind of made up our
mind that it's probably best for Gretchen to come home. And I did make
the suggestion that we all come to
therapy.

There is a tone of hope and choice.

OT: I think that the next time
Gretchen leaves home, that she can
leave much better than she has in the
past. And lead a much healthier life,
so that is good news for everybody.

OT resumes as before the consul-
tations. By defining the return
home as positive toward the goal
of Gretchen's leaving home in a
better way, the OT employs the
goal of therapy used by the
consultant.

Mother: Will you continue to see us?

OT: I would like to, if you all. . .

Mother: Because I, like that's what I
said to her, Gretchen, you have to
continue to go to the OT, because *I
need help, we need help, and she
needs help.* And if you would, be-

Mother has begun to include father:
"*We* need help." She also clarifies
three subunits of the family: herself,
the marriage, and the daughter.

cause, I mean, we're traveling up anyway, so whether we're traveling up
with Gretchen or coming and meeting her here, it's the same thing.

OT: I think we would really like to
continue with all of you. And sometimes we'll see just Gretchen and
sometimes all of you. We can work it
out as we go along. But I think you
have to, I assume that you have to
agree with that, too, Gretchen.

The OT offers Gretchen some power.

Gretchen: Oh, yeah. I'd like to make
a suggestion though.

OT: Good.

Gretchen: I would like to, instead of
us coming up every second week, I'd
like us to come up every week and
one time I meet with you alone and
then my mom and dad can meet with
you alone and the next week we
could have our family therapy, all
together.

OT: (Sounding irritated) I think it is
a really good suggestion, but I think
that the way we meet should depend
on what we want to accomplish and
we could decide that as we go along.

Gretchen: (Getting defensive) 'Cause
I'm not, I'm not going to be able to
make it like if it's just every once,
every two weeks.

The OT's tone suggests *irritation* with Gretchen. The consultant
wants to ensure that OT does not return to a former pattern of relating to
Gretchen. He will want to convey a fresh start as well. From behind the
mirror, suggestion is made to *praise* Gretchen for wanting to initiate a

plan to care for herself, emphasizing that the parents need to agree. While OT is receiving input to help him convey a clear structural issue, the family talks playfully about how hungry the youngest child is.

Chris: I'm starving!

John: Oh, you can see him, he's shriveling now.

Gretchen: He's shriveling.

Father: He's an inch shorter since he came in. Oh, my god.

There is a tone of festivity and celebration.

John: His pants are falling off.

Mother: They're better off.

Father: We need to rush him to the hospital for some food. Starving a kid on his birthday.

Mother: Does he have a snack to sustain him? Uh oh, oh I messed up on that. There we go.

Father: If you want to go to Paisan's, we'll have to go all the way back to ⸺ .

Mother: Oh. I guess we can settle with Ponderosa's, I guess. I'll take Chris to Paisan's later. I don't know if Gretchen wants to come, too.

Gretchen: We can eat supper at Ponderosa's and then when we get home, go to Paisan's and have some garlic bread.

Father: We can leave Betsy to work in the store. That way we can save the money it's going to cost us to eat the garlic bread (laughing).

(All of them talking at once) Oh yummy, yummy, yummy garlic bread. (OT returns)

OT: And we thought that it was really a good idea, that, uh, we kind of follow your plan, Gretchen, but I think it's okay if you make plans for what you would really like to accomplish, but we have to talk to your parents about whether they want to do that, too.

OT returns with his modified position vis-a-vis Gretchen's input.

Gretchen: Okay.

OT: I would find it really helpful when we got together if you would have come up with some kind of plan of really what you would like to get done in that time, too.

Gretchen concedes, grateful that OT recognized her wish to take part actively like a grown woman.

OT further enhances Gretchen's new position.

Gretchen: Oh. For our family therapy. . .

OT: And for. . .

Gretchen: And for us alone.

Gretchen is delighted.

OT: (To parents) And, uh, what you—do you agree that that would be helpful to you? Gretchen I think is making a good suggestion.

Mother: Yeah. That would be fine. I know that we have to come, like that. I do know, because I can't help her without, we can't help her without somebody helping us.

Mother spontaneously corrects herself, introducing her need for her husband and herself to work together. It is both their problem.

Father: As long as we could come in the evenings, then I could really take off some work.

OT: I understand that. Did you agree that you could manage evenings?

OT looks for parental agreement.

Gretchen: Every week?

Mother: I think from what we've talked about that anything that's going to make Gretchen better.

OT: Ummhmm. And you know that
the whole family has to create a plan.
So you've already begun it. . .

Mother: And maybe if only Gretchen
had to come for certain sessions,
maybe John could drive her out.

Mother connects John and
Gretchen, following consultant's
approach.

John: Yeah, I could go see Justine.

John could see a girlfriend, too.

Mother: He could go see his friend
here.

OT: He would really like that.

John: Yes. I would like that very
much.

OT: Something somehow that we
should mention—I think it's really
generous of Chris to come today, because today is Chris' birthday. So it's
really nice of you to be with us on
your birthday, as part of your birthday. Sorry there's no Paisan's pizza
here for you—hope you settle for the
cherries or something like that (all
laughing). Happy birthday.

Chris: Thanks.

OT: And we can stop now and we
can make arrangements to get together again, okay?

Everyone: Okay.

The session is over. Now there must be careful planning with the
OTs. The movements made in this session will be reflected in coming
sessions across the entire therapeutic sequence.

Follow-Up

The way was now cleared for family therapy to take place. A difficult year of therapy followed, in which therapists helped parents identify

and set limits and realistic expectations for their daughter and helped daughter negotiate maturely with them. Gretchen and John grew closer. During this time, Gretchen corresponded with the consultant. In the first letter, written on daisy-yellow stationery, she wrote that upon receiving her parents' renewed edict of work or school, she returned to a local college. After describing the wish to "be dead without killing herself because she would not want to upset her parents," she wrote: "You know something beautiful I never noticed before, my quilt has beautiful yellow daisies on it. It's so beautiful, and soothing. My curtains are yellow to match." In this way, Gretchen demonstrated her spontaneous interiorization of the idea of inserting trance events to activate hopefulness into an otherwise unhappy chain of ideations.

She indicated that she did not like her local college. "I find it so hard to concentrate on my work because I have so many feelings inside of me which control me." She reported that she bought three colors of nail polish to see *which color* looks best on her and went skiing with her girlfriend and her brother John.

Several months later she wrote her second letter, after she had quit college and gone to work at her parents' store, but not like John had— Gretchen requested pay. In this letter, also on yellow stationery, she said she missed the hypnosis and found her family sessions embarrassing. Her mother was supposed to have gotten a dog to take care of, but instead she was making visits to her granddaughter. Gretchen stayed at home alone during these visits. For her best friend's wedding, she bought a long light blue dress (the color of a stuffed rhino) and had started jogging. She also wrote: "Two weeks ago my mother went for an interview at the college. She applied for the nursing program starting in September. I really hope she is accepted. She has always wanted to be a nurse, but never took it up. So that means I may be running the store for my mom."

There had been a shift in her parents' agreement about mother's rights to work and develop herself in nondomestic capacities. It seemed that father—perhaps not wishing to inherit an increased emotional burden—may have okayed his wife getting her need to be needed met elsewhere. Several months later, while her family was at her sister's, Gretchen wrote her third letter, on an envelope with a yellow daisy drawn all over it. In that letter from the store she wrote: "I wish so much you were here to help me. Sometimes I find it hard to remember the daisies. I have a jar full of daisies on the counter here at the store. They are so beautiful, and everyone who comes in can see the daisies and *know* their beauty. Also, my therapist gave me a pendant, it is a yellow daisy. I always wear it wherever I go." Gretchen has her stuffed rhino with her.

Gretchen wrote that the last three months had been hard. She had caught her girlfriend's bouquet at her wedding. She had left home and worked as a nanny, for a woman dying of cancer, and was doing well until she was unexpectedly fired by the husband when the wife was hospitalized. She stayed in that town looking for work but could not find another job after looking for three weeks. At this point, she felt she was a failure and that the therapists and her parents felt she was too. Hurt, she clung to her rhino. She was going to burn down the therapist's office if he would not see her. The therapist called her father, and her father caught her at a bus stop and, as therapy had charged him to, he physically fought with her to keep her from getting on the bus. He punched a man who told him not to hit her. The police helped her father take her home.

The letter continued: "I feel like Werner [the rhino] and I are in a huge balloon, and inside the balloon are all my feelings but they are not inside my body. And nobody can get inside nor can I get out because my feelings are blocking the entrance. Only once someone has come inside, that's you! For just a short while. You came in, but I was scared and I cried. . . . I want someone to come in so desperately to help me. I don't think anybody will be able to help me. I wish so badly I could come see you. I miss you a lot. The letter ends that she took from 8:45 to 2:32 to write the letter and that she met a man in the park who gave her a tract from his church.

Several months later, Gretchen wrote that her mother had decided to go into nursing and her parents planned to sell their store and use that money to pay their bills and cover their mortgage. Father continued working for the school board. Brother was becoming a police cadet. Gretchen herself was teaching Sunday school and feeling conflicted about fundamentalist religion and the role of women. She was looking for a job and felt that hypnosis had helped her.

Exactly *nine months* after our session (recall our discussion of how long improvement might take), she wrote, using a stamp with a yellow flower on it, that she had met a slightly older man, Roger, had moved in with him, and was (as her older sister had been) disfellowshipped from the church. Her parents, brothers, and sisters like Roger very much, but none of them is allowed to associate with her anymore. "Also, I enjoy the hardships we are facing together. These hardships make me feel stronger inside. I feel strong, much stronger than I have ever felt before. I was like a little girl inside and sometimes I still am. I never believed I could be so strong as to be able to stop seeing my therapist. . . I love my parents very much, I never knew how much before, but now I know that they are an important part of my life. There is a human thriving within me that has been fulfilled. I am a total woman, and I don't ever want to go back to being a little girl again."

Gretchen also writes a parallel of her mother to her: "My mom is having a hard time in the RNA program. She finds it difficult to concentrate when she has so much sorrow. But she believes in the church and feels she must stay there." This had been one of Gretchen's original problems at college. Gretchen's parents saw the OT alone when she moved in with Roger, to see if the OT thought this was okay. He identified it as Gretchen behaving as a self-willed normal young woman. He pointed out that she had *none of her presenting symptoms,* had selected a *nice man,* and was *quite happy.* She was simply acting differently than they expected. Reassured, they discontinued therapy.

And *the day after she met Roger her parents sold their store!!* Gretchen and Roger relate a lot to Roger's parents, who are quite old, sometimes ill, but cheerful. When, because of religious problems, Gretchen's parents did not have her over, she wrote: "Life is so short—too short for petty disagreements over religion! I was rather disappointed and angry when my parents told us we couldn't go over—not even on Christmas. Oh, bother! Silliness—that's what I think it is! But I was expecting that reaction, so I wasn't the least bit surprised. But Roger and I are getting along fine."

Clearly the battle is not over for Gretchen. Her parents are now, as they had been with her older sister, unified with the church in an outward rejection of Gretchen's position. Privately, they are relieved she has a good man to care for and who cares for her. Mother and father have worked through some of their gender conflicts. Mother has stayed a good Christian, while father has let her go on and get the nursing education she wanted, without feeling that her efforts are a sign of his failure as a provider.

Gretchen is still epidemiologically at risk. She is somewhat socially isolated. However, as of a one-and-a-half year follow-up, she now has problems *outside,* and *inside* she is clearing a way for a *private reality*

278 Using Hypnosis in Family Therapy

separate from her parents' conflicts over economics and religion. She is more self-possessed and more open-minded. Perhaps Gretchen will get pregnant and Roger will marry her. In terms of her original complaints, Gretchen is asymptomatic. With the therapists' approval, she has discontinued therapy. The consultant is looking forward to a visit from Gretchen and Roger.

Had Gretchen's mind-set been different, her family structure different, or their family's economic and religious situation different, Gretchen might not have been suicidal or infantilized. The consultation and *nine* months of subsequent therapy did not produce miracles, simply a young woman, alive, and parents facing harsh realities with more satisfaction.

Summary

This chapter described aspects of the treatment of a suicidal twenty-year-old woman and her family. As is common in people who attempt suicide, the young woman's self-destructive symptoms included social and adaptational problems, difficulties in her intimate relationships, and a conceptual justification of suicide in her belief system. She had experienced difficulties at college and was fraught with societally based conflicts concerning the role of women in the eyes of the fundamentalist church versus the economic realities of a single woman. Regarding her intimate relationships, she was a member of a white, German immigrant, working-class family, which drew on the fundamentalist religion to determine their rules and roles. Economic hardship necessitated that mother work and intensified gender-related conflicts between mother and father, which exacerbated the parents' difficulties in helping their two older children, both girls, leave home. In the case of this younger daughter, the dismal family mood colored her need to come home for refuge. The girl herself brought to the multilevel difficulties of her situation a belief that she had a "bad body" that was sad and did not work well. In her private logic, a bad body was a justification for eliminating that body. As an expression of her own, family, and societally based conflicts about reproductivity, sexual maturation, and social immaturity, the young woman manifested the symptom of carrying a toy in public.

The actual case consultation was conducted in three phases:

1. Creating an hypnotic atmosphere to establish rapport with each family member and to join with the whole family as a system. This was also done to help the consultant get a good reading of private family induction techniques.

2. Reading the symptom bearer's self-inductive techniques, during trance work, and carefully building *separate-track trances* for family members, which converged at points, producing *specific shared reveries*. In this building of a family hypnotic counterinduction, family members were instructed in how to turn off unhelpful directives from self and others and improve their attempts to be good hypnotists for each other. Suggestions were made to each member, which, when enacted synchronously, would help activate *new family structural arrangements*, including better parenting cooperation between parents, a deparentification of son, heightened rapport between the two older children at home, and more mature daughter–parents negotiations.

3. Postinduction work, in which family objections to trance suggestions were elicited and responded to. Atomized trance events were introjected on an as-needed basis into this phase of treatment to help family members *introduce components of the trance learnings into their routine family life.* In this way, new family suggestive sequences and new rules of relating were inserted and rehearsed.

Overall, the clinical priorities in such a therapy are to offer first aid by:

1. Resurrecting hope via helping family members (*a*) draw on and develop resources of refuge *within* themselves (such as the daisies) and (*b*) improve their attempts to be useful resources to each other.

2. Intervening at conscious and unconscious levels of symptomatic functioning while simultaneously intervening into related interactional levels. During the trance events, *private* and *deep-seated* issues can be worked with, such as giving a *young woman's body hierarchical ascendance within her family context* as a unique and separate source of positive directives that can guide her self-healing. For parents, each can feel his or her equipment for spousing and parenting is good enough and can then be invited to move out of a self-doubting

mood, to take the actions that will help their daughter separate slowly and successfully.

3. Ultimately, ending the therapy with a *new affective tone,* activating a sense of hopeful reunion while blocking family members from imposing new unrealistic expectations on one another.

Thus one clears the way for a therapy of enabling.

Chapter Seven

Adapting
Intervention Strategies
to Particular Problems

Thus far we have studied the choreography of specific interviews *within* ongoing family hypnotic therapies. Here we back our lens
up a bit, to get an overview of *cross-session* considerations. We also look
at instances in which parts of the therapy paradigm must expand or steps
be omitted. Each case study selected exemplifies common clinical challenges and includes a concept or technique that has been developed to
address them. Although the interventions discussed are *tailored to the
idiosyncracies* of a case, they are also described in terms of their general
clinical applicability. In all cases, the interventions were designed to affect dialectically related inner and outer symptomatic realities. Each case
ends with a brief formulation.

It is important to note that hypnosis is not always needed to affect
an individual's context of mind or mental-set. Sometimes certain qualities
of a situation and a willingness to receive guidance places a person in an
adequately receptive state, without the need to clinically search for it. One
case highlights this point. Similarly, families do not always change in the
way we might hope. There are times in some families in which the only

way the symptom bearer can transform his exterior reality is to rehearse for increased psychological distance by putting maximal physical space between self and kin. Another case highlights this point.

What emerges at the end of this chapter is a sense of the kinds of variables the clinician must weigh when selecting and coordinating balanced therapeutic entries into a multilevel symptom structure. The hypnotic family therapist recognizes the importance of enhancing, renovating, reconstructing, supplanting, and activating boundaries between and within people. A common therapeutic goal is helping people attain a balance across the subcontexts they inhabit. Coordinated interventions directed toward inner and outer boundaries may lead spontaneously to such balance.

Case 1. A Study of Family Hydraulics: Enuresis and Alcoholism

Session 1. Latona, a seven-year-old black girl, was brought by her mother to a therapy session at a child guidance clinic; her father waited in the car. He refused to come in to the session so long as Latona was in the room because he feared mother would blame him for Latona's problems.

The therapist agreed to see the family in shifts, starting with the diad the family offered first: mother and daughter. In that segment of the interview, the therapist established rapport with mother and daughter and kept the focus on identifying the presenting complaint and minimizing talk about father. Mother and Latona displayed a strong bond to one another. When mother cried out about her daughter's problems, Latona cried harder. Latona said she was worried she peed so much and "worried about her daddy." Mother sobbed at one point and said that they lived in the poorest ghetto area of Philadelphia and survival was getting to be a question too. *It seemed likely that social and family turmoil could override attempts to hypnotically immunize the girl against family contributions to her symptoms.* For the time being, the therapist tried to seal some issues raised, to help the family save face and not feel that they had given too much for a first get-together. The girl was thanked and told that she was to look forward to her mother and father cooling things down for her, although neither she nor the therapist would know how until her daddy came in. Calm, and for the moment dry, Latona waited in the waiting room.

Father was then invited in. His breath stank of alcohol. He and mother immediately fought so badly that the therapist could not stop them. Father confirmed mother's ineptness and, by screaming at his wife, told the therapist that she had been twice hospitalized for suicide in the last five and a half years, since April 6, 1977. Mother, by screaming at her husband, told the therapist that her husband "had not had a dry day" since April 6, 1977, when she had left their three children, all older than Latona, to telephone her husband, who was in the service. While she was gone, all the children burned to death in a gas explosion. The stories themselves were excruciating. *Their format of presentation suggested to the therapist that perhaps Latona received some "symptomatic information" in much the same spill-over way the therapist had received her clinical information.* The therapist also noted a strong love between the couple and that each had suffered a serious loss of self-respect. The *structural challenge* presented was a sort of precarious balance of two hierarchies. In one, father behaved as older, more competent than his considerably younger wife. In this hierarchy, mother was helpless and could at anytime become actively suicidal. In the other hierarchy, mother described father as a derelict and a madman, setting a bad example for Latona by urinating into old wine bottles in the house. In this hierarchy father might comfortably remain an alcoholic. Figure 18 shows the primary family structure in which mother and Latona banded together in the face of a disturbed man in the house. An available substructure in which father—older, clearly better educated, having had broader social recognition—regarded mother and Latona as children is shown in Figure 19. In any case, lacking was a sense of coordinated parenting or mutually elevating balance of domestic functions.

Figure 18. Primary Hierarchy.

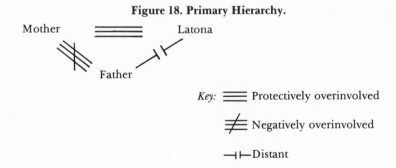

Figure 19. Secondary Hierarchy.

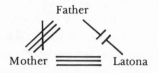

Note that this case demonstrates an instance in which the therapist was unable to catch a family inductive sequence because of difficulties in seeing the whole family at once. Therefore she drew on her own experience of ways the family conveyed information to make an hypothesis about the family's *effect* on the symptomatic child. The therapist formulated that Latona's enuresis was maintained within a rigid and destructively balanced family system in which her parents struggled to regulate guilt and grief by monitoring anger. The therapist noted that somehow Latona responded to parents' chronic emotional outpouring and blaming as a cue to lose self-control. Her loss of control over her output of fluids through crying and urinating seemed to give mother a chance to both fuss over her child, behaving as a demonstrative, if less than effective, mother, and prove her superior virtue to father in their ongoing battle.

In evolving a therapeutic counterinduction, the therapist considered that:

1. Although family structural intervention seemed a priority, work with the whole family together would be inordinately difficult.
2. Father's alcohol problem alone might override any individual self-suggestion with Latona.
3. Working with mother and Latona alone might reinforce the notion of father's uselessness.
4. Working with father and Latona alone might enhance mother's ineptness.

To attempt to affect the complex existential situation in which the enuresis occurred, the therapist decided to help father elevate himself by emphasizing his ability *to heal his daughter*. To prevent mother from feeling robbed of a chance to prove *her* adequacy, mother's role as *the only one who could save her husband*—who was indeed life-threatened by physical deterioration secondary to alcoholism—would be emphasized. *It seemed possible that if father stopped drinking and mother dried her tears, the family faucet would be something Latona might more readily get a handle on,* even in the face of other adversities.

The treatment planned remained predominantly focused on the presenting complaint, which was Latona's enuresis. In this context, mother was seen alone and told directly:

1. "You know your daughter is affected by your husband's drinking. You love them both very much. If you want your husband to set a better example, there is only one thing you can do as I see it. One time and one time only, when you are ready, calmly set him a deadline by which either he will have gone into detox, or you will leave him."

Additionally, a technique of "preparing for opposites" was employed. Thinking dialectically, the therapist postulates that if the father is elevated, there may be a tendency for hierarchy 2 to be activated. Therapy will then have simply awakened a secondary but dysfunctional aspect of the same problematic family structure. Therefore, the therapist builds in a protection against this opposite side coming to the fore.

2. "You must promise me *now* that no matter how lonely you get or helpless you feel while he's gone, that—for Latona's good—you will not try to get him to leave his program prematurely." The therapist promised the woman she would be her faithful ally through *all* this.

The key rationale was that mother needed a concrete, absorbing, and morally uplifting task as well as a chance to stand up on her own two feet *while* father regained his equilibrium. The therapist would be a temporary leaning post.

Afterward, mother joined Latona in the waiting room, and father returned from the car. The therapist established an intense rapport with him, joining the *parts of himself* that had been weathered by life's storms. She learned from him that the fire had destroyed the family's sense of joy, almost their will to live. Before that time, he had been an officer in the Navy, had always been a top nursing assistant student, and had worked well for fifteen years as a nursing assistant in a naval hospital. He indicated that racial tensions had held him back in a series of humiliating circumstances throughout his work career. Although he had been one of the few blacks occupying a semiprofessional position, ultimately, family tragedy and discriminatory work experiences converged in lowering his self-esteem and his will power.

The discussion with father enhanced the clinician's sense that *father was highly motivated and was the most open avenue of indirect clinical entry into the family system.* The following light trance induction was therefore used with father alone: "Now I think the problem you mention of your daughter's enuresis is a very important problem. And I think you are the only one in your family who can do anything about that problem. I think you know something about that problem no one else knows. Now when you were younger you somehow learned about controlling your own bodily fluids. And your daughter has not yet learned how to control her bodily fluids. It is imperative to know about the intake and discharge of fluids. When we are standing on a street corner, and it becomes uncomfortable, nowhere to go, we must learn to regulate our discharge of fluids. And you know how to regulate your fluids."

Half an hour of discussion of fluids (a metaphor for drinking) ensued while he gazed without blinking into the therapist's eyes, catching each word in order to go home and tell his daughter. At the end of this metaphorical discussion, he offered the therapist an additional personal facet of his problems. He mentioned a friend of his who "if he had known earlier that he was a dying man might have controlled his symptoms and lived." The therapist then graphed on a blackboard the man at twenty, at the patient's age, and at sixty. The father's full attention was on the graph. He was totally focused on the board, and it was reiterated that had the man known at this point or at that point, he might have lived. Even at this point, had he really known, he might have controlled himself and lived. The therapist repeated that he and only he was in control of himself and that he might have chosen to do what he needed to do to live. At the end of this discussion, the therapist changed her voice and returned to the social voice with which she had introduced herself at the start of the session. "You know your situation well. And I don't want you to act on any of your own problems until you are ready. You have to work with your daughter. You must not and should not do anything right now about your problems. Do not discuss any aspect of what we've discussed with your wife. It might only upset her."

The subject was then quickly changed and the father promptly dismissed, in a state of confusion, but eager to go home and talk to Latona about her problems. That night he called the therapist at home to say that he was determined to go through detox. The therapist doubted. He insisted. The therapist found a hospital bed for him within the next five days. Meanwhile, father talked with Latona.

The therapist joined mother and father as father was brought into the program and involved in all aspects of the program, making sure to mention casually to staff that the man had himself been a nursing assistant. During this time, mother weakened and wanted to tell her husband of her terror of being alone in the house with Latona. She called the therapist instead. The therapist called the father to reassure him that she was in touch with his wife. A niece moved in with the wife. In sessions 2 to 4, mother was worked with individually during the husband's involvement in the detox program, and the therapist visited father in the hospital.

However, in the face of the undertow of the past and no hopeful pull toward the future, when father came out, he started to miss his follow-up meetings and began to drink within a month. This was the moment that session 1 had prepared mother for. After she notified the therapist by phone, mother calmly reminded him of his deadline, this time more confident that she *could* survive alone if need be. The deadline came, and she and Latona and her niece moved to a relative's for a week. Father requested help to reenter a new detox program, with a more comprehensive follow-up therapy, ideally culminating in a job. Mother moved back in during this time.

In sessions 5 and 6, mother worked with the therapist on losing some weight and practicing swinging her handbag ever so slightly when she walked, modeling a carefree attitude in preparation for her husband's homecoming. Father came home dry and stayed dry. At the time of session 7, the therapist saw the couple and helped them plan *a mourning ritual over their children's deaths,* to pay homage to them, and cry together— although all the tears in the world could not put that fire out—over their shared and sobering loss. Finally, at a home visit, session 8, with the whole family, father said Latona was over her problem because of some "heart-to-heart talks they had had over the last six months." Mother had started a small ceramics business to bring in extra money. Dad had returned to a night school course to better his chances of getting a job. He was being treated for physical problems at the VA.

Two years later, mother phoned the therapist to find a heart specialist. Father's physical problems had caught up with him. Their VA physician recommended open heart surgery. They wanted a second opinion. Mother confirmed less crying, no enuresis, and no drinking! Family life was no longer a problem. Finances still were. Father survived the operation. And Latona remained a good student, in the roughest of school systems.

Formulation. "A Study of Family Hydraulics" exemplifies the kinds of therapeutic situations that weight the clinical scales toward the desirability of (1) insulating trance events from family interaction and (2) focusing hypnotic work on a family member *other than* the symptom bearer. The eight-session treatment entailed a dialectical therapy in which *individual systems-related hypnosis* with a family member *other than* the enuretic symptom bearer was coordinated with dialectically related *non-hypnotic* family intervention. The therapy permitted all family members less constricted exploration of their existential realities.

Case 2. A Matter of Growing Pains: Psychosomatics

Chapter Four described an induction by the Marad family that seemed to intensify components of David's symptoms. David had been brought to family therapy after a fight with his mother about whether he could live at a cousin's house part of each week. At the end of the fight, he threw a piece of garage sale furniture at mother, and the family sought therapy.

The therapist had been struck by several features of the case, which seemed to classically reflect interrelated socioeconomic and family life cycle problems.

1. Mother, out of the work force and largely socially isolated as she reared David, had never been paid for her work, had been 90 percent mother and 10 percent wife, and was now asked to abruptly turn this ratio on its head. This was especially painful and economically uncertain at a time when her husband—in this case seriously ill—had poorer odds than she for longevity, and she herself was not a "marketable product" in the work force. In her own fear of the future, she

found herself caught in the middle of husband and son, feeling that "A wife and a mother, you know, is love in both directions, love torn from two sides."

2. Father, who had been concerned with breadwinning, was now supposed to *spend more than ever* financially for college for *his child's future while he himself* was dreading the loss of his own health, fearing the inadequacy of his retirement and social welfare benefits, and uneasy about inheriting from his son an *increased emotional burden of his wife.*

3. The index patient, the child, was both financially and emotionally dependent on his parents. Until this time he had been the charge of his mother as both a source of responsibility and a source of joy. Now confronted with expanding financial and other worldly concerns and issues of manliness and gender security, he was increasingly drawn to a dependency on his estranged father.

Ultimately, as in David's case, the symptom metaphor of being "unable to think from one idea to the next" or the fear of "losing everything" may also reflect broader socioeconomic uncertainties that beleaguer an entire family. It is hard to move from A to B when B "looks like" the loss of everything one has known. The sessions prior to this family induction session were characterized by father's quietness in the face of screaming arguments about the past, which mother and her only child frequently engaged in. The therapist had been unable to create an hypnotic atmosphere and was still in the process of building rapport at this fifth session. She had put her energy into urging father and son to speak with each other while helping mother sit back and later critique their efforts. She also attempted to draw a boundary around mother by talking alone with her about her interest in growing things other than David, such as flowers in her backyard garden. Regarding content, the therapist had centered treatment around dollars-and-*sense* issues about what parents could afford to pay for David's college registration, without David having to inherit a debt of guilt. Meanwhile, David's own presenting complaints of chest pain and trouble breathing persisted, although they slightly diminished. The interventions thus far had not been powerful or well-coordinated *enough*.

Session 5. Recall that David alternated between playing an infantilized role in his family and being an heroic rescuer of mother. It was hypothesized that these roles were partly efforts to respond to and help out with marital burdens. After the therapist "awoke" from family induction, she suggested that David's parents talk as long as they needed to, to offer David an amount of money they could *reasonably* afford. The therapist would then help David decide how he would manage. While the parents talked and argued, the therapist turned to David, slowly and repeatedly suggesting that *at a time like this,* David could take a deep breath, close his eyes, and let the back of his mind anticipate some of the upcoming challenges he faced regarding the registration and related tasks. Basically an *on-the-spot immunization* to one aspect of family emotional undertow was thereby *given to all family members.* The parents were "free" to disagree uninterrupted by David and therefore to ultimately resolve their disagreement. At the same time, David was free to not feel responsible for helping his parents settle their accounts. In fact, their arguing was to cue him to enter into a self-constructive state. The technique employed demonstrates one form of *symptom cuing, in which some component of the symptom structure is introduced, often in an abbreviated form, into a therapeutic counterinductive sequence.* The economically reduced cue may derive from an external family or social component, as in this instance, or from an internal component (as we will see shortly). It is an aspect of the heretofore symptom-activating structure that is now used to activate a counter- or nonsymptomatic sequence of events. Symptom cuing can be employed with one or more family members, either in or out of trance. It is an opportunity to salvage an aspect of a symptom, which once in the background is benign. In this post-family-induction session, the *family contextual symptom cuing* focused on David, for the benefit of all family members. It was suggested that the very parental conflict that contextually contributed to the activation of his symptoms would now begin to *cue him to focus inward,* not on his feelings but on his plans for *doing.*

The previous therapy had laid the groundwork for the parents to sustain their interaction around finances and actually propose specific numbers of months and dollars. After the symptom cuing technique, Father told David the amount. He could realistically cover his son's first semester without being unduly taxed. No discussion was permitted at this point. Parents and David were praised, and a further boundary was drawn between the family's parent-spouse and young adult units.

The therapist then bolstered David, neither infantilizing nor aggrandizing his position. Whenever David said that he was worried that he had unused ability, the therapist adopted some of the tone of anger in the family but paired the feeling with suggestions for action by inserting: "It should get you angry! You're very bright, and it is not being used." He was invited to be as anxious as he could possibly tolerate while registering. In fact, it was offered that:

Ther.: You will feel unbelievably anxious when you do this. All I'm telling you is when you are functioning . . . like a robot, where you go in and you do all this stuff, and you fill out these horrible forms, and you talk to these people that bore you to death, and you ask, you know, all that crap about the first semester. When you're doing that all right, you will have more confidence in yourself. Then we can deal with these things that freak you out! The things that scare you too much to talk about now. That we don't have to go into now.

His anguish was described as representative of the margin of freedom he had from family conflicts, as his *own*, albeit incipient, outcry against an impossible situation.

Ther.: All this anguish that you're feeling is a sign of the freedom that you have.

David: How?

Ther.: It's a sign to me of the health that you have. Because if you weren't in pain, in your difficult situation, you might not be able to change. You might just stay at home and never go to school. I'm telling you, all the pain and confusion is the extent to which you're at a crossroads in your life.

David: I don't feel that, though. Why don't I? Because my anxiety stops me from perceiving the way it is? College must bother me more than I think it does, I just can't tell. I probably really can't tell. It upsets me. It really upsets me! If I felt, if I felt good. Look, I'd still be anxious. I have to be honest if I'm feeling normal, I'd still feel anxious about it. But now it's like I feel little butterflies in my stomach area. See it's a different type anxiety, it's the type you feel before a test. It may be stronger butterflies.

The young man left session 5 with strong butterflies in his stomach area to bring with his registration fee. At least he was stretching his wings.

Session 6. Mother did not feel well and did not attend. She was sent herbal seeds, soothing for arthritis, to bathe in. Father and David (who had registered) discussed remaining pragmatic concerns. Suggestions to David about how to remain out of parental discussions and work through decisions alone with father were highlighted. The tone was melancholy, but David was less symptomatic. He still gulped periodically. After this session, father and mother took their first vacation in fifteen years. David thrived alone in the apartment. Father's new medicine had an effect on his Parkinson's symptoms. Basically, there was a convergence of therapeutic intervention and good luck. David then went away overnight, and at the therapist's advice, *mother helped pack his bags.* This was David's first overnight away.

Session 7. David, a college student for a month now, had begun to grow a beard. He had shopped for his own clothes and looked handsome. Again, only father attended with David. There was still a mood of melancholy. Therefore the therapist proposed that their next session, the last one, would entail a *celebration of the family's accomplishments.*

From David's talk about girls and dating, from his stubble and demeanor, *and* from father's continuing air of melancholy and sense of being unmanly, the therapist used indirect suggestion, *focusing on David while father watched.* The therapist was going to *prove to both father and son how ignorant this intellectual son was about his own body.* (Father also watched as a young woman talked about physical concerns with his child.) Building on a version of an Erickson technique, the therapist turned toward David:

Ther.: I wonder if you know what eyed you are? Right or left? And do you even know how to find out? (Had David look at her through a circle of his fingers, closing one eye.) What legged? What eared are you? How can you tell? I'm sure you don't know what sided hugger you are? What sided kisser? What side of a person do you like to walk on? How good are you at nostril flapping? Cheek rotating? Backward? Ear wiggling? And you call yourself college material? And you don't know yet, do you, that if you take it slower, you get there faster, and it feels better?

Both father and son, convinced of son's ignorance, left in good spirits for the first time in nine months. Note that mother, who had had an infantilizing and intensive concern with David's body, would not have been included in this procedure; it was safeguarded as man-to-man talk.

Session 8. The last father and son session entailed eating cake (brought by the therapist) and drinking soda (brought by father and son). Father then left as son stayed on alone. Trance was then used privately to enhance the boy's own body image on a deeper level. David's own presenting complaints had not been that he had an angry outrage but that he suffered psychological and especially physical pain. To work on this deeper level, a trance was induced, and another form of symptom cuing was employed. David was told to look inward to find an image of how his unconscious mind perceived his body. Once a positive image was sustained, posthypnotic suggestion was given *to cue into this image after a brief period of anxiety in the presence of new male or female acquaintances.* In this form of self-symptom cuing, David was instructed in making a place for a reduced version of a likely anxiety in the self-curing process. In this way, when the anxiety occurs, it is not experienced as a roadblock but as a step on the way to new experience.

A one-year follow-up confirmed that David was continuing in college. He had become a Ping-Pong champion and held a part-time job. Mother and father regrouped as a couple. Mother became more closely involved with a previously estranged older brother. Mother's and father's physical problems continued.

Formulation. No formal induction was carried out with the entire family. Trance and indirect suggestion were *cautiously and selectively employed both in and out of the family therapy* context to immunize family members against the powerful charge of family inductive processes. Symptom cuing, a therapeutic counterinductive technique, was presented in several forms. Whole family meetings focused on pragmatic financial issues and were used to draw needed interpersonal boundaries in an intrusive family context. *Because of reciprocal invasiveness in the mother-son diad, self-revealing trance work with the index patient was not employed in her presence.* The boy was, however, cued that his parents' negotiations of finances was to give him a time to "worry about his own plans for the future" (family structural cuing). Sustained indirect suggestion about physical concerns was used with the boy in his father's presence only, *after* the major practical goal of registration had been accomplished. It was used as a chance for both men to improve their body images and sense of manhood. Finally, after father and son celebrated the fruits of their successful labor, a moderate level of trance with son alone helped in cuing him into a strong positive image of self and body that would be activated by an initial brief period of anxiety (self-symptom cuing) when making a new acquaintance. By shifting from dialectically related exterior (interpersonal) and interior (conscious and unconscious) phenomena, the therapy remained consistently symptom focused.

Case 3. Over My Dead Body: Suicide or Self-Ectomy

In Chapter Two, we referred to a twenty-three-year-old woman named Ellen, who had been depressed for two years and had made two nearly successful suicide attempts. We noted a prevailing self-belief that she was unworthy and should die. She lived alone and came to the therapist requesting individual therapy.

Session 1. At the initial interview Ellen was overweight, unkempt, did not make eye contact, was humorless, affectless, and offered nothing but an uncomfortable shrug unless prodded. The therapist had difficulty establishing rapport with her. The therapist learned that Ellen had lost a boyfriend to someone new and that she had parents who lived nearby and had no interest in helping her, not even when she attempted suicide. Since she had left home, Ellen's parents had traveled the world together. When asked if the therapist might interview her in her family context to see what she had been up against at home, Ellen conceded. She warned that finding a time when her parents were not at a concert, playing golf, or taking art classes would be difficult. She said she was afraid the therapist would be deceived by their charm.

Although the therapist expressed to the parents that she needed their help to explain what they thought Ellen's problem was, they were practically too busy to come. At the first family interview with Ellen, the parents, and the younger brother, Stu, the therapist was not able to establish an atmosphere of rapport. This wealthy Protestant family had developed a wall of courtesy and formality that effectively shut out emotional concerns. Mother did report that Ellen had been a model child until the last two years, when she had "strayed from the fold." Father had never been involved with Ellen, Stu, or the older sister. Stu was clearly closely allied to mother. He would indicate "worry" about Ellen's mental status and then protect mother from any of Ellen's statements about feeling rejected. The family conceded to attend four sessions if it might help prevent Ellen from killing herself.

Session 2. By the second family session it was evident that mother and Ellen, once mother's public formality was put aside, could not be in a room together without erupting into name-calling and accusations to which each was vulnerable. Stu would alternate back and forth, rescuing them from each other. Father would sit on the sidelines detached, smoking, as if watching a tennis championship match, with no real investment in either side winning. Rapport with the family was still poor. However, father agreed to talk with Ellen about what she would need from him financially to return to finish her last semester of college. He and mother would talk. *He* would present Ellen with the decision. Stu was to worry about his new girlfriend (who had similar problems with her own mother as Ellen did).

Session 3. Father came in with a sprained back and had to be placed on pillows on the floor. He had not talked with Ellen or his wife. At this point, everyone agreed that Ellen was stressing the family by upsetting everyone. Ellen said she was feeling suicidal. The family was asked whether they would work with the therapist in a coordinated effort to contain her and care for her in the home, and they unanimously agreed that they wanted her to go to an inpatient program.

*Session 4.*When Ellen came out of the program, having made no suicidal gesture, she said that she had learned that *some of the things she hated herself for were actually family limitations.* She had thought her mother was the problem, but at least her mother would send her money. She had confided in Stu, but it was always Stu who had reported her secrets to mother! She had thought her father was a "nice guy," but, although he was independently wealthy, it was when he had refused to supplement her college tuition two years ago that she made her first suicide attempt. *It seemed that the therapist's confirmation that Ellen's family was in fact toxic to her at this point in her life freed Ellen to work on her own self-suggestion and behavior.*

The therapist then developed the following plan based on what family members seemed willing to offer Ellen. She called father and said, "If you will cover Ellen's college costs, you need never come to therapy again unless there is a problem with finances. Ellen and I will work out a plan to cover her therapy costs." Father agreed.

At this point, the family work had served the purpose of helping Ellen recognize that her depression had some familial roots. She now *requested* hypnosis to get her body image together and improve her self-esteem by improving her looks. She conceded that weight had been a reflection of her troubled state; two and a half years ago she had been anorectic. Her mother was skinny and obsessed with food, both hers and Ellen's. In her rebellion against mother, in which to leave her she had to be regarded as "bad Ellen," Ellen revolted by becoming fat. She was now *obese* and *bulimic*. She wanted to gain control over her eating habits.

The therapist was now invited into the young woman's mind-set, to work on her interiorized family relational landscape and to help empower her to follow self-instruction even against the powerful tides of family suggestion. It seemed that family problems had crystallized within Ellen, and the family wanted to cast off these troubles by severing association with her. The family pattern was like the old English custom of casting out one's sins at year's end in a boat (see Frazer, 1922). The hypnotherapy of Ellen would simply help her learn to identify her own needs, ask for *only* financial aid from father, learn to express gratitude for what she *did* get, and *to separate by voluntary self-ectomy* from her family. She needed an opportunity to leave her family rather than feel self-pity that her growing up meant her family was abandoning her. Previously, to have power of self-removal, she had been attracted to death. The therapy offered her new options.

Ellen was seen seven times over the next year. In each session hypnosis was used for weight control, using the model of having her recall a happy memory of a time when she felt control of herself, approaching food in that state, enjoying, relishing what she did eat, feeling her meal and her pleasure were *as good as anyone else's*. Simultaneously, the therapist worked with Ellen on dialectically related exterior events. These included a session on:

1. Ellen's fight with a tall, thin, dormmate over food in the kitchen, which replicated Ellen's relationship with her mother.
2. Ellen's stealing food from other girls she thought more fortunate than herself.
3. Ellen's replacing food she had taken and explaining that she would not do that again.

4. Ellen's recognizing unhappiness in students other than herself in the dorm and taking pride in memorizing the characters of a new language.

5. Meeting with father to ask for money to move to an international dorm on campus, where social life was better. Father very reluctantly complied only when Ellen vowed to never ask him for any more money. Ellen did not criticize him for this. As planned, she was gracious in receiving *what he did give.*

6. Analyzing father's behavior and discussing Ellen's mother, who had been simultaneously pressuring her to attend family functions and having aunts and uncles call her to be "more involved in the family." Ellen was trained and helped in trance to go to only those events she wished to, to eat what she wanted, and to talk with whom she desired. She was trained to use humor to disengage.

7. Ellen's losing weight. She had already lost some pounds and so joined Overeaters Anonymous to speed that process and get group support. She made many new friends in the dorm and they gave her a surprise birthday party. Her brother called and was *incredulous* that people would do that for her. Her father expressed indifference. Her mother wrote her "Why don't you love me? I don't blame you if you hate me!" Ellen did not get depressed.

When Ellen graduated with all A's, no one called or sent her a card. Ellen decided to move away without leaving a forwarding address. Before she did so, the therapist wrote Ellen's parents a note that Ellen approved, commending them on providing the finances Ellen needed and commending their nonintrusion. Ellen was the first child in their extended family to graduate from college. Ellen wrote them a thank you note and told them how well she was doing and said she did not know exactly what she was going to do, but she would be in touch when the time was right for her. She then left town, remaining in touch with the therapist via correspondence.

During that time, Ellen wrote of many varied life experiences, rich with a full range of emotions. One day she felt a "knot in her stomach" and realized it represented her family and the things she had been through in leaving home. Instead of isolating herself at the place she was lodging, and bingeing, she sought female companionship. She wrote that "Many women there described being in my situation! A wall that's been there all my life fell away, and I saw the world, not as full of enemies and hostility, but full of people who are scared, lonely, and caring, like me. . . . I realized, if I don't enjoy today, what's the point of all this striving to set up my postgraduate life!"

Ellen had a very good year and a half. She then mailed a letter to the therapist that she did not want to keep because it had started to make her angry and she did not want to be irritated into contact with her family. The therapist showed it to a friend and together they laughed for an hour over so classic a guilt letter.

Dear Ellen:

We respect your decision to find your own way free of family interference. We hope that someday we can reestablish our relationship and share in each other's lives again. Mom and I both want you to feel comfortable with us *before you do this.*

However, there are two members of the family who I think you might consider contacting as soon as possible. One is Grandpa, who isn't getting any younger and may not be around too much longer. He desperately wants to hear from you and inquires constantly about you. The other is your brother. We will not *bother you, but Stu plans to use his entire Christmas vacation searching for you until he finds you!*

All my love,
Dad

Ellen got a job, an apartment, friends. She lost more weight and met and dated an interesting young man. Basically, the therapist formulated that there are situations in which, for various individual and family-contextual reasons, the choice comes down to suicide or person-ectomy. In reality there are families who, at least for a certain period in their shared developmental history, have earned the right to be held at bay, if not disowned. Ellen is hopeful that someday her parents and brother will share in her gladness. In the meantime (two years later), she writes:

The hardest thing is keeping up with the feelings—
how do people do it? Keep acknowledging them, dealing

with them and tracing them to the source. I feel raw and inexperienced in all this.

But life is so rich and more beautiful than I ever imagined, and I know I'm still only getting glimpses of reality—but it's enough to keep me working towards it!

Formulation. In this case, the therapist was confronted with resistances to both *hypnotic* and *family* treatment. Ultimately, these *resistances were employed* in developing an *individual systems-related hypnotherapy* of a twenty-three-year-old suicidal woman *after* an aborted family treatment. In this way, the woman was helped to remove herself from a family that had, in a developmental abberration, left her holding the bag of family troubles as she became a young adult.

Case 4. The Turtle with the Cracked Shell: Intractable Back Pain

In Chapter Two we discussed Patsy, a thirty-year-old who had lower back pain and was crying much of the time. At the initial session, Patsy looked like a poor southern black girl, disheveled and beaten down. The meeting ultimately entailed her sobbing and telling a story of profound racial discrimination on the job.

Session 1. Patsy was so ashamed and unconfident that she could hardly tell her story. One year ago, after raising four children with her husband, they needed more money to buy a new house. Although her husband felt he had failed as a provider, she had to go to work. She held the lowest level in her hospital job: filing clerk. She worked diligently. When a position at the next level opened up, she asked her boss if she could apply. From that moment on, her white boss changed from patronizing to hostile, and Patsy, historically shy and frightened by authorities, became increasingly compliant, to prove her worthiness to the boss. The boss gave her a trial of the new job. During her trial, the boss gave Patsy work that was more menial and required less knowledge than any labor Patsy had ever done. The boss knew Patsy was a religious Muslim, but she forced her to come in on Sundays during her church time and work night shift, although she had five children. She embarrassed her in front of her coworkers and harassed her to prevent other coworkers from speaking out. She had her spend most of her days, despite an inborn back problem (scoliosis), carrying files from the basement, up four flights of stairs.

When Patsy reminded her boss that she was required to give her on-the-job training toward her competing for the new job, the boss would agree and then not show up. Harassed and overworked, Patsy had to be hospitalized for her back problem. Once released, she returned to try for months to get support from her coworkers to appeal to their union. She herself finally appealed to the union following complex procedures, but the union was corrupt and unwilling to really defend its members.

The therapist formulated that there was a conflict between the budding sense of competence that Patsy had developed on her job and this exterior work-related denial of her self-worth. At the end of this first session, it was agreed, as if in a business deal, that Patsy and the therapist would figure out a way for her to regain her dignity on the job. To add to her understanding of the social and mind-set components of Patsy's problems, the therapist requested that the husband attend the next session. At this point Patsy was again overcome by a new sea of tears. She explained through sobs that if she complained to Harmon, he would leave her. The therapist held up the opposite face of the problem to the overwhelmed young woman. If he could not comfort her, what kind of relationship did they have? In relation to both husband and boss, the therapist *suggested directly that Patsy's pain be transformed into her cue for building greater determination to fight for her rights* (symptom cuing). It was planned that she take off from work for two weeks, using up accrued sick leave, until she could stop crying. She was not to shed one tear at work but to bring her saltwater home with dignity to her husband.

Session 2. In session 2, Patsy brought her tears to her husband. As she told him, for the first time, about her work situation, he did have trouble comforting her. Her anxieties aroused in him the painful associations of his own situation of racial bias on his job. He worked as an engineer in a fiberglass factory, where he had suffered long exposure to fiberglass. His skill had been recognized and his boss, a nonracist white man, slated him for a higher-level job. But then the boss fell ill and was replaced by a new man. As Harmon continued to compete with two other white men for the job, two masked men waited for him outside work, beat him up, and told him "Stay in your place, nigger." He was scared and gave up the fight. It seemed as if Patsy had protected her husband from remembering his own traumatic experience with racism by concealing hers from him. After this session, as he had done twice before in a stormy but loving ten-year marriage, he left her.

Patsy used the next three sessions to work through her problems of getting the new house, regaining control over her children, and developing a very careful plan and proper Muslim mental attitude toward her boss. Formal hypnosis was never used. Patsy was already in a state of unimpeded willingness to work. Very simply, she needed suggestions about how to feel confident and not be bent by the ill winds of anti-black sentiment or her husband's fears. The therapist proposed that if she could transcend her situation, both psychologically and behaviorally, ultimately her husband might rise to the occasion as well.

At work, Patsy calmly went over her boss' head. She became the most tranquil person in a chaotic and politically corrupt hospital hierarchy. She knew that "Quality work was the number one goal for the administrator and that was her interest as well." She was guided in many battle plans at work. She returned to work at the job for which she had always been the best candidate, at an appropriately increased salary.

When her husband appeared at church to see how she and the children were doing, she was neatly dressed and did not cry because she was not sad. If he wanted to come back, he would have to come home to her standing tall. She hoped he would. She would not bend in the meantime.

By her last session, her husband had not come back. Patsy was fine, however, and believed that he would. She had bought herself a new muslim white dress with gold beads and had a queenly air. She looked exceptionally beautiful. She brought the therapist a small ceramic turtle with a rose in its mouth and a chipped back. She said, "I wondered when I bought it, why I wanted it. Now I *know* why I want *you* to keep it."

Two months later, for Christmas, she wrote the therapist: "My job is going well for me! (Smile.) For Elizabeth [her boss], it's a joke to have to see her act so hard to be nice. It comes naturally for me. She won't even sneeze around my desk. Harmon has come back. He's acting a little bit different too Thank you for a strengthening therapy."

Formulation. The more general effects of racism on the social contextual level of symptoms in minority family systems may, as in this case:

1. Intensify other conflicts, such as gender conflicts. For example, the ways black men and black women are discriminated against, under-utilized, or pitted against one another in the white economy may contribute to domestic gender struggles.

2.   Intensify the family's sense of powerlessness to stand up as a unit in the face of chronic and no-end-in-sight social inequities.
3.   Tend to cause one or more family members to interiorize social categories based on ideas of racial inferiority, even in the less than 10 percent of the black population that is materially successful. Such racism may be powerful, but it is not necessarily an insurmountable antitherapeutic factor.

In this case, no *hypnosis* was needed to intervene in a woman's mind-set, family, and work contexts. Unconsciously, Patsy thought very highly of herself. She simply needed to learn to put up and then fortify a boundary against the bad messages from others. For Patsy, in a racist and sexist context, it was best to help her hold up her own mirror so she could get a clear self-reflection! We might say that some *narcissism was directly prescribed* as a means of intervening into related family and work aspects of a symptom.

Case 5. Too Close for Comfort: Claustrophobia

Session 1. In California, a young, stiff, engineering student who was about to become a father for the second time came with his remarkably nondescript wife to therapy. Three previous visits to an emergency room for "heart attack" had ended in his being diagnosed as suffering extreme anxiety. The man never had had symptoms before the summer, which was the first time in his three years of marriage that he was not very busy studying. He was also at a crossroads in deciding whether to stay in urban California after graduation in one year or to return to the midwestern countryside where he was born. Both he and his wife agreed clearly on one thing: The husband was the only problem; the wife need not be present for therapy.

Hypothesizing that the man's symptoms might well represent multilevel problems, the therapist requested that his wife stay *"to observe and aid in the relaxation therapy* of her overstressed husband." When asked what was the *deepest* complaint he would like to focus on in his hypnosis, he said that he would like help for what he believed was *claustrophobia*.

In the first part of the first interview, the therapist fostered brief interactions between husband and wife and noted from them that the husband seemed to be *compelled by the slightest movement the wife made.* If she changed position, coughed, patted her stomach (she was three months pregnant), or sighed, he looked to her *to remedy the situation.* At this point, the therapist hypothesized to herself that claustrophobia for the man might be a relational metaphor for his feelings about his wife, especially without the boundary mechanism of his studies. Also, it seemed that claustrophobia was a catchword for their where-to-settle conflict, in which she wanted to try to stay in an urban area (near her mother) and he wanted to live in the wide open spaces. Finally, he alluded to job and economic pressures being less stressful in the midwestern town.

In the second half of the session, the therapist carried out an induction of the husband. The induction goals were to:

1. Accept the wife's wishes to *not* receive treatment while hoping that the *effect* on husband would make her *envious* of enjoying a *complementary* version of such therapy, creating in her a state of trance readiness.
2. Help the husband relieve his claustrophobia by creating an hypnotic task that, as he enacted it outside therapy, could affect all three levels of his symptom metaphor, including: "I am closed in by the crowds and competitive pressures of city life"; "I am closed in by my responsibilities to my wife and child"; "I am privately afraid of close spaces."

Arm levitation was used in the formal induction procedure. When the man was in a moderate-level trance, the procedure ran as follows:

Ther.: You know, you've suffered a great deal in recent months. You've experienced a level of confinement that has been painful for you. You know a lot about this closing in, more than your wife and I can possibly know or understand. But what you don't know and what you have been *so cruel and unresponsive about* is your association with your own psychophysiology. Man is an animal not designed for confinement to closed-in spaces. He is a creature of movement in the fresh air. Anyone knows that this ancient being responds to its own ebbs and tides of breath, heartbeat, and blood flow. The human being is an animal that fears being caged. In all these months, you have ignored your own animal physiology. It has cried out to you, pounding in your chest, pounding in your head, but you have been *cruel and unresponsive* to it.

The hour-long induction continued with the therapist prescribing that the man find a time to go out for a walk at night under the starry sky, find a place that he could call his own and go out to after their first child was in bed, *for the good of his animal physiology*. His job was to think of nothing, just let his body breathe deeply, absorbing the stillness in the evening air and allowing his respiratory system to take over.

He was then awakened, and the therapist addressed more directly the *relational* aspects of this prescribed brief period of separation from family responsibilities to commune with human nature. The man was advised to do something both he and his wife would find strange. He was to either say "no" to a single small request his wife made or to ignore an unspoken request for assistance from her, such as a sigh or a mildly pained facial expression. He would be cued to an opportunity to follow this suggestion by a flitting sensation of claustrophobia (symptom cuing), felt in his wife's presence. The couple looked at one another and laughed. Therapy was not what they had expected. The next appointment was to be in three weeks.

Session 2. The man had begun to run at nights after he put his son to bed. He found a nearby wooded place and had even spotted some deer. He said "that part about the animal physiology was so true" and that he would "like that repeated." He had had no prolonged attacks of claustrophobia.

His wife was then asked to report on part 2 of their plan. She said she noticed how much he irritated her by jumping out of his seat in the living room if she sighed while she opened the refrigerator door. He once raced in to take a salad from her hands, as if she had screamed for help! The therapist pointed out to her, in a slightly mischievous tone, that this was very disrespectful of her capacities to handle things. After all, she had been an independent working woman her entire adult life before marriage. The therapist assumed that the wife was probably a contributor to the husband's feeling he needed to hover near her at all times. However, she did not point this out; rather, she set up the circumstances of separating husband from wife—and happily so—that might allow the wife to think of her own needs.

At this point the wife said that she was finding, now that her husband was better, that while he was out, she felt lost and lonely. She was feeling like a "nothing." After his hypnosis today, might she too be helped in trance with this problem?

After the husband received his booster hypnotic treatment, the therapist initiated a light trance with the wife, culminating in automatic hand warming to ratify the woman's special state. She then used a *parts-of-self induction technique* to complement the wife's end of her husband's claustrophobia treatment. Throughout each day she was to collect moments when she longed to be alone. Because her husband had all the responsibility of putting their son to bed, before his run, she was to go to her room, treasuring this opportunity to be unintruded on, to some personal project. She had no idea what this project might be. However, *part of herself* had begun *as a child* to long for certain things that would be attainable by herself *only as an adult*. She was to find herself dreaming of and reviewing these events and making plans for ways she could get some time to accomplish these goals.

Session 3. Three weeks later the husband was still running. The wife had taken up sewing. She reported it was great to have an hour to herself after a long day. The husband felt healthy and looked less rigid. At a four-month follow-up, they still disagreed about where to live, but the wife felt she could survive away from her mother, and the husband felt that he could find open spaces even in the city. The husband was still slightly overprotective, but the wife said they were "no longer too close for comfort."

Formulation. "Too Close For Comfort" is a complement to the man reading the poem "I Sing the Body Electric" in Chapter Two. Both cases exemplify the clinical situation in which a *person contributing to the system of the symptom "refuses" treatment*. However, in this instance, hypnotic treatment of a husband in his wife's presence was used to entice the wife into needed complementary hypnotic work. The hypnotically induced shift in husband's behavior *triggered* the wife's desire to make a complementary shift, but in the example in Chapter Two, trance experiences increased both spouses' recognition of a desire to revise the basic marital contract. Here, the elevation of the man's psychophysiological experience to a guiding principle toward health, rather than a problematic cue toward incapacitation, cleared the way for the wife's elevation to competence. The wife could then recognize her right to be the architect of her own aloneness, without having to experience it as evidence of neglect. The marriage—the broadest relational construct—was never threatened. In this case, the contract was dynamic enough, for the time being, to permit internal modifications; it had some room for breathing space.

Case 6. Divorcing the Dead: Alcoholism

Monks, in their world of contemplation, confinement, and self-abnegation, use discipline as a key orienting principle. By "discipline" they mean "instruction by the self to the self,"* hopefully charged with divinity. Such is the case of a woman who lives a *private* life of self-denial, confinement, and reflection, but all turned against herself. Although she has paid her legal debt to society of trial by jury and serving a prison sentence, she has served a life sentence of self-effacement. She has become her own worst hypnotist.

This case entails a seven-session treatment of a woman who has been an alcoholic for thirteen years, since the death of her husband. Her husband died an accidental death; she wielded the knife that killed him. After hearing the circumstances of their marriage and the events of the night he died, the court ruled manslaughter with a brief prison sentence. From that night on, after fulfilling her responsibilities to others, she drank herself to sleep. When depression penetrated her daylight hours, she sought therapy. Therapists searched for an underlying problem in her personality, associated with hypothesized early traumatic experiences. The woman continued to fulfill her responsibilities by day and by night drink herself to sleep.

Session 1. The therapist was working at a Philadelphia clinic that refused treatment to drug addicts. The intake worker informed the potential client of that fact. The woman sounded irritated and stated that alcoholism was not her *deepest* problem. The intake worker argued with her and in frustration requested that the therapist talk to the woman. The therapist told the woman she would see her herself, but they would have to work together to deal with the institutional problems that might hinder their efforts. In this way, the therapist strongly joined with the woman in response to her statement that she had a deeper underlying problem.

At the initial interview, Julia, a woman in her early forties, came in, dressed attractively in a business suit, her hair in a closely cropped

*I am indebted to Braulio Montalvo for bringing this understanding of "discipline" to my attention (personal communication, 1982).

afro, looking pretty and tired. She reported that every night at home, after work, and after she had cared for her seventeen-year-old son, William, she went to bed and drank herself into a stupor. She woke up on time to feed William and get to work as the manager of a large store. She had been doing this for the thirteen years "since my husband died." Her last sexual contact had been with her husband, whom she had killed accidentally. Before that time she had only had an occasional social drink, never drank alone, and had never gotten drunk. Now she *only* drank alone. She had raised four children successfully, William being the last. William was about to live his senior year among his father's side of the family in Missouri. Julia felt she had served her function as mother, and now it was time to get herself together and stop being an alcoholic.

Sensing the depth of the woman's motivation, the therapist used the clinic's policy of not treating drug problems to her clinical advantage. She told the woman that she could not treat her alcoholism at the clinic. However, if the woman would *stop drinking completely* as of their next session, she would *do everything in her power* to help her get a *just and honorable divorce from her husband*. The therapist said hypnosis could be used to provide "surgery with anesthesia." The woman looked the therapist over, considered the offer, and agreed.

The therapist had conceptualized the case from the broad structural perspective proposed in this book. It seemed central to consider that if conventional divorce proceedings do not *end* a relationship but only *change* it, murder certainly does not. Of the estimated 17 to 30 percent (Federal Bureau of Investigation, 1979) of North American family members who will kill parent, spouse, or child in any one year, some may be legally pardoned. Psychologically, however, the act of murder—even if deemed an accident, a pardonable *consequence* of prolonged brutality, or the just cause for a prison sentence of some duration—may effectively seal the actor off from the public world and thereby prevent healing.

The therapist's formulation was that the woman was satisfied the therapist had recognized the "deeper" problem she offered, what we have referred to as part of the client's gift. The therapist's offer to give back to the woman a very personal investment toward her own self-respect was well received. Julia's other therapies, through searching for disturbed childhood relationships, had left her attached to her guilt. For this therapy, the plan was to use hypnosis to create a new experiential event and suggest new actions. Because of the sensitive issues involved, all trance work would be done in private. The therapist and Julia agreed that it would be helpful if before the hypnotic, inner work there was one session in which her two children living in town were present. In this session, Julia would tell them that she had stopped drinking. She would also use the therapist to help her discuss with them any residual feelings they had about her accidental murder of their father. Her job was *to activate their resentments,* to bring them to the fore so that they might not come out *inadvertently* in a manner potentially harder for Julia to protect herself from. It was also hoped that Julia would be so eager to get on with the hypnotic divorce that she would tolerate any family animosities incurred to get there.

Session 2. By this second interview, two weeks later, Julia had stopped drinking. Her daughter Dawn and son William joined her in the session. Within an hypnotic atmosphere, first the alcoholism was discussed, that is, the symptomatic complaint that had brought the family via the mother into therapy. Dawn, an attractive college graduate, conveyed that she had always admired her mother and never understood her secret drinking. It had pained her while growing up to see her mother do that to herself. She said she was so relieved to see her in the last few weeks. It was a great inspiration to her. William, a very handsome and well-dressed young man, said that he was glad she had stopped drinking. Talking in a tone of pseudomaturity, he indicated that he had always thought it would be better for her to stop, but she just would not listen to reason. He said he had warned her that her drinking would drive him to drink. Sometimes when she drank she would be in a bad mood. Also, sometimes it made him worry about her. But now, there was nothing to worry about. Dawn teased him for trying to sound so big and wise, explaining to the therapist that sometimes William carried on like he was the father instead of the baby brother. William said the one thing that bothered him was that now he had to do some hard thinking about how much dope he smoked.

The therapist stayed focused on the mother's presenting complaint in this session, assuming that the number 1 hierarchical priority was to help the mother set an example for her children, not only by what she did for them but now *by showing how she cared for herself.* The therapist indicated that perhaps modeling her own self-care was to be her service to her adult children.

In discussing the murder of their father, both Dawn and William expressed love for their father. Because he was sexually molesting Dawn and her older sister and had raped her aunt, however, Dawn said she felt her mother had been understandably outraged. She felt that as a result she did better than her mom, picking men who were *loyal* to her as a top priority. William said that, in a sense, he did not have a childhood, because when he was six, and his father died, emotionally he had to be sixteen. In terms of the murder, he said "How can I ever know exactly what happened between them? Mom could have done it in shock or it could have been totally an accident or it could have just been meant to be, so I'm not the judge over that, but, if there'd been another way around and I wouldn't have lost my father . . . whatever was between *them*, because they both had so much love for me: that would have been what I wanted."

The family talked. Tears were shed. The therapist proposed that whereas, as William put it, a divorce would have been better, somehow there had not been support for it then. It seemed William too needed to somehow reconcile himself to the death of his dad. Perhaps he would do so by seeking a connection to his father's brothers in the Midwest. The therapist did not know how he would do it. To help William let off any steam of resentment toward his mother, it was suggested that he find himself periodically irritated with little things she did and telling her about it, until he left on his pilgrimage. He liked that idea. William requested one individual session before he left town. Never were two children more enthusiastic about a divorce!

Session 3. This session was planned for the therapist to get better acquainted with Julia, to help Julia experience her parameters in a trance state, and to take account of Julia's own unique ways of responding to trance and suggestion. The therapist knew nothing about the circumstances of the murder. She knew little about Julia's past. However, hypnosis was used not as much to look for evidence of prior trauma as *to share the parts of Julia's life that were significant to her and that occurred prior to and surrounding the murder.* This way, insofar as she was introduced to Julia's experiential life and self-instructional system, by the time of the divorce session the therapist would be a familiar part of the hypnotic landscape and could help Julia lay the past to rest.

Following a simple induction procedure, Julia fell into a deep trance, which she later described as similar to being under sodium pentathol. She was invited to relive and share memories of her life before the age of five. She described life for herself and seven adults in a shack in the South as one of psychological, if not economic, slavery. As her grandmother's beloved one, however, she was often happy. In trance she demonstrated a special ability to *revivify events in detail* and as *if seeing them for the first time, with all the shock, curiosity, sadness, or joy of real-life immediacy.* In this way she recalled figuring out her family had just returned from an uncle's funeral, by pondering why a relative was wearing his fancy shoes coming down a certain path, and reexperienced the joy of being taken out of her crib and bounced in her daddy's arms.

The therapist formulated that somehow these abilities to *be* in the past and *recall in detail* should be built into the trance divorce. The therapist wanted one more session, to continue to introduce her own voice as a kind of "invisible friend" into the woman's recollections.

The therapist saw William alone after this interview. He basically wanted reassurance that he could be normal under his circumstances. The therapist gave him data on violence in North American homes. She talked about social violence and the violence of poverty. She quoted King and Gandhi. She told him that he need never forgive his mother for killing his father, whatever the emotional and intentional circumstances, but that somehow he might find a way to feel that *he need not repeat the problems of either parent.* In this way the therapist suggested a means of extricating William from his parents' unresolved marital conflict. The therapist gave him a farewell book, *The Autobiography of Malcolm X,* and William agreed to return in one year for a checkup after his trip. The therapist wanted to close psychic doors, not open them, for William. He was quite well-adjusted and had many practical matters to deal with, including getting a job in a new part of the country. Also, the therapist reassured him she would watch over his mother in his absence.

Session 4. Julia was seen again one week after the previous session. She had continued to not drink. She opened the appointment by saying: "I feel like I'm making progress. I've been doing a little analyzing, too, and I think that I have somewhat of a low self-esteem. And I think it's that I don't feel as close to my mother as I think I should. So I punish myself." The therapist considered that the murder and guilt about it may have intensified and prevented the resolution of insecurities in Julia's other relationships.

In the context of divorce therapy, this issue was discussed both in and out of trance. Out of trance, Julia calmly described her hurt caused by mother's jealousies over her dad's love of her. In trance, in a quest for "memories to save and memories to discard," she began to describe a pattern, after the age of five, in which she reflected or interiorized the emotions of significant others around her. In recounting a day she caught a sunfish and ran all the way home with it for her mother, she burst into tears as she recalled that mama discounted it. She cried, "She hurt me! She hurt me!" as she relived running out the back door to the comfort of an old apple tree, hiding even the victory of tears from her mother. Later she cried with joy, explaining that she did so "maybe because everybody else is crying, too. Because their hearts are full, my heart is full."

Most importantly, the therapist noted that she was permitted to ask Julia questions *and to insert components of new emotional states into recalled sequences of painful events* and that she was thereby allowed to lead Julia, in a deep trance, to a reinterpretation of those events.

Finally, Julia came up through time and memory to her own adolescence and leaving home. She had to get work to help with expenses for her younger siblings. Father began to push her out of the house. She had always been poor, but now she was frightened about survival. She married the first man she met. Their marriage was never good. The military immediately stationed him in Vietnam. On one of his return visits, Julia was six months pregnant with their oldest daughter Linda, and she and her husband had to go to court for a paternity suit brought against him. He lied, denying that the other woman's child was his. During his next visit he raped her sister in their home. In the following ten years, incidents increased, including incest and beating the two older girl children and eventually beating Julia as well. *The reports were telegraphic in an hypnotic contract designed to scan major events of importance with detachment, "as if they were happening to someone else."*

At this point the therapeutic rapport was excellent. There was no fear that the effects of alcohol would dull the hypnotic work. The therapist was confident that she could insert a new voice into old versions of the woman's difficult experiential life. She and Julia agreed that they were ready together to conduct the hypnotic divorce next time. Note that it was never defined what that process would be like. As much as possible, the therapist perceived her job as one of *allowing the woman to heal herself, using the therapist, but not being too heavily intruded on by her.* The divorce session was to offer an induction to counter Julia's habitual self-instructions.

Session 5. The divorce session opened with Julia saying that the world situation, from the racial violence to the president's cutting school lunch programs, was enveloping her with a feeling of hopelessness. She could hardly bear to read about black history because of the suffering. She bemoaned the murders of the black leaders of the sixties, who held out hope and dignity and assuaged fear. She said that since she was uncertain how to affect social injustice, she wanted to start by helping herself. She indicated that lately she had been thinking of some way to help young black people but that she suffered some sense of inadequacy.

Julia: I feel inadequate, and I'm sure I'm not.

Ther.: That sounds like a good thing to discard. (Both women laugh) Isn't that our work today, a divorce from inadequacy?

This trance had two goals. One was to introduce the therapist as a kind of invisible friend into the emotional aspects surrounding the murder, which, to date, had remained private. Ideally, this would initiate a deep healing process, a change in Julia's communications to herself about herself. The second goal was to have whatever divorce event the client evolved culminate in some *action taken by Julia in the light of day.* It was hoped that this would help *break the spell* of Julia's hidden guilt.

The only therapeutic guideline was the suggestion to return to the day when she was "very much married to . . . painful associations . . . the day she realized her marriage was destroying her. . . ." In this deep trance, Julia cried, writhed, screamed, and had great difficulty breathing throughout most of the hour. She recounted an event, the day her husband told her about the other baby he had conceived, in full psychological and psychophysiological detail.

The therapist did not intervene into the content, only the sequencing and organization, of associations. Using a parts-of-self technique, she helped Julia *insert a new observing self,* who would watch everything to learn and understand what was happening to Julia then, in a way she was not ready to do when they had happened before.

Julia: I can't stand it. Oh . . . I . . . can't breathe . . . I'm . . . dying . . .

Ther.: (Waiting for a pause) When you finish crying . . . I want you to think about something . . . because with all your hurting you're learning something . . . *Part of you* sees what it is. *Part of you* is calm while the rest of you is suffering. . . .

This process was repeated throughout, with the therapist cothinking with Julia.

Julia: He's been messin' around since he been in the service . . . oh what am I gonna do? I don't think women mean a thing to him. He doesn't know how to love. . . . He doesn't know (crying) . . . got a baby . . . with another woman. . . .

Ther.: Gonna need to think. *Part of you's hurting. Part of you's thinking.*

Julia: (More deliberately, whispering) My child needs a father. He's gonna be a good father. I can put up with the other. We'll make it up. I'm supposed to stay married (shaking, shivering, scared). When you get married, you stay married. . . .

Ther.: Are you really ready to forget it? You don't know how to forget it, *yet*, do you?

The years roll on; a girlfriend of her husband's wrecks her car. Her family and his seem to know that he is causing her grief, but *no one believes in divorce,* so there is no suggested out. The husband's brother tries to slit his wrists rather than get out of a bad marriage by divorce. Her husband rapes her sister and starts molesting the children. Julia has four children in five years. Isolated, in the face of family consent-by-silence, carrying in herself many of the secrets of his deeds, after ten years of marriage she interiorizes her husband's disregard. She begins to think she is at fault. Perhaps she needs to be hated. The therapist inserts a wave of compassion into her ocean of self-blame.

Julia: (In a low enraged voice) I was dumb dumb dumb. What's wrong with me? You dumb stupid lady. You stupid stupid lady!

Ther.: You put your trust in the wrong man, Julia. You weren't really ready to be married.

Julia: I left one father and ran to another! Well, at least I can talk back to this one, can't I? But you are not supposed to get divorced. You are married forever. And he would never give me support money, what about my kids? I will take this other stuff, you go ahead—so long as you provide for me and the kids and you provide for us, I'll put up with it till the kids are old enough to leave home. But don't you ever ever hit me. (Screaming) I cannot, I will not take that.

Again the therapist inserted her voice:

Ther.: Can you go through that he's going to hit you?

Julia recounted several times when he started hitting her. The stories became increasingly brutal. Julia became hysterical, sobbing, caught between pity for him and terror of him. One night, drunk, home from a party, he twisted her arm behind her back. She almost lost consciousness. Julia decided to scare him because she could no longer tolerate this. The therapist inserted:

Ther.: Before you do, I want you to know how unhappy you are, that you want this all to end in a divorce from this man who is playing rough with you.

Julia then "realized" her feelings for him were over. She would leave him. She did not have to take this anymore. Her husband acted like nothing had happened and undressed for bed. Julia went down the hall. She wanted to scare the hell out of him. She did not pick up the knife on the counter but took one from the drawer, loudly slammed the drawer, stalked to the bedroom, and stabbed the knife into her side of the bed. In her husband's stupor, he had fallen asleep at an angle and was stabbed to death. Screaming, "Get up, fool," Julia went utterly out of control.

As Julia enacted the stabbing, in the next few minutes the therapist took the hand with "the knife" in her own hand, squeezing it, suggesting that Julia can understand now that it was getting to be a lethal situation, him or the kids, him or her. After Julia regained composure:

Ther.: I want you to understand something. Say "Never again will anyone treat me like that." To open the door to love again, you're going to have to say "Never again will anyone treat me like that."

Julia: (Whispering) Never. No more sorry for other people, hating myself.

Ther.: You need a divorce from this man.

Julia: (Later, spontaneously beginning to come out of trance, no longer needing to work at so deep a level): I realized something, I shouldn't have married him in the first place. But I *love* those kids. I felt sorry for him. But I didn't love him. I never did.

Ther.: How are you going to help yourself divorce *this dead man* who betrayed you?

Julia: I don't know how. I've got to stop feeling guilty. I've got to stop condemning myself for staying with him. I wasn't sick the way I thought. I had reasons. And they weren't that I wanted to be hurt. I thought for a long time I was sick, the reason I stayed with him, was that there had to be something wrong with me. There wasn't. Self-preservation, survival. *Those are real things you could put your hand on.*

Ther.: That's right.

Julia: Oh, in all those years I thought there was something wrong with me!

Ther.: Going to need to go to the graveyard to tell this man goodbye, to tell him really what you never could because of how dangerous it was, how alone you were.

Julia: Yeah, I was tired. I was tired. But I've got to be. I've got to be able to really care for a person. Based on feelings, things to do together. Respect. I never respected him. Never. . . .

Ther.: You need to respect yourself, because you protected your children all alone and you did survive.

Session 5 ended with plans for Julia to go to her husband's gravestone at least once alone and once with William before he left town. The therapist's formulation was that a pocket of Julia's psychic life had been locked away inside of her. By introducing herself into Julia's mind-set at the moment in which Julia's despair was at a peak, the therapist hoped to bring the pain out into the light of day. The *action* of going to the grave for a talk with husband and for his consent of divorce was to bring the murder to an intrapsychic stopping point. This is based on appreciation of the fact that trance is only as good as the actions and interactions it leads to! In this case, Julia needed to bury the dead.

Session 6. Session 6 was scheduled two weeks from the divorce therapy, to allow time for the process to settle in. The therapist wanted both a conscious and a trance report on Julia's thoughts about herself and actions. Throughout, there had been a marked discrepancy between the two. Her waking remarks would be mild and fairly calm, while her trance experiences tended to be very emotional and lead through a series of events in a driven fashion.

Julia reported that she felt kind of strange but pretty good. It was like she had to keep reading herself over and over again, as if she did not know definitely how she felt about things.

In trance she described a single event, poetic, allegorical, spontaneous, and healing.

Julia: It's like there's a light shining in from the outside but I can't see what. Kind of flashing. I don't know. I seem to be inside of something black but can't see me . . . I'm not scared . . . I'm just trying to figure out where I am. I don't feel bad . . . I can see the light. . . . It's like I'm in this cave, and I'm going toward the light. . . . It's like there's nothing, there's nobody but me coming out of this darkness . . . I don't know what's going on. But I'm not afraid (incredulous)! . . . Mountains, trees, sky, it's like it's a new world, like I've never seen it before. It's like a beginning. I've never seen it before.

At this point, the therapist lifts the hand that last week had enacted the stabbing slightly, leaving it cataleptic. She does so to give a posthypnotic suggestion to increase the likelihood that when it is carried out it will automatically bring forth with it the state of experiencing the new beginning that Julia has spontaneously arrived at and is so utterly absorbed in.

Ther.: It might be nice to feel your hand is detached from your body, only later I'd like you to find you can't pick it up, even if you want to.

Julia: (Arm cataleptic) I see me as two people, one big and one little. Inside is the small one (suddenly sobs). Can't understand the way I'm feeling (sniffing). I see me as those two people. But I'm not one of those two people.

Julia seems to be describing a vulnerable baby self in her old self as a grown-up, or perhaps her mother and her eldest daughter, with whom she has enacted some of her deeper guilt.

Ther.: Do you want to feel like they're you again? (Therapist treads cautiously)

Julia: No. No, 'cause it made me cry 'cause I don't understand it. I don't understand those two people together like that. Makes me sad. . . . They're still there. . . . Just outside the cave doin' nothing'. . . . Now they're kind of two people again . . . and they're walkin' . . . away . . . it's like a mother and daughter! . . . Now they're separating. . . . Now I'm standing there . . . (gasps) I don't know which one to go with . . . (sobbing) I'm not (with determination) I'm not . . . going . . . with either one of them. I've got to go my own way. I'm not going with them. I'll make it . . . I just found out I don't need them. I can be by myself. . . . When they left each other—when they first separated I was really upset. Because I'd always had them. But now that they're going, I didn't really need 'em. I was trying to hold onto them. But I didn't really need them. Because I'm me. I'm a person. I'm somebody. And I'm not afraid to go by myself. I'm gonna go straight ahead.

Ther.: And you can remember this moment a long, long time. Remember how you feel. Something you worked hard to get.

Julia: My head is cleared up (sighs). Heart still feels kind of full. Head is clear. Day is clear. Sun shining. I'm walkin'. Step stepping high. I feel good. I'm going. I'm coming out of the woods.

In freeing from her husband, Julia spontaneously decreased her own guilt and dependencies on her mother and older (and most maritally triangulated) daughter. Julia made steady progress emotionally from this point on. She had one session one month later. William and she corresponded regularly. He was good. She felt good. Eventually she visited William in Missouri, *where he helped her arrange a mass for his father. His father's whole family came. Together now, Julia and her son could bury their dead, in public.* One and a half years later they each came in for a checkup. Julia reported she had had drinks twice socially at parties, but that one night, just after William came home, she drank in bed and ended up vomiting on herself. At that time, however, she renewed her resolve to never drink alone. She had dated one man. They had stopped short of intercourse. She had graduated from a computer training program and was getting a top-level job. She was feeling better about her mother, even though no one celebrated her graduation. Although William had returned home during a time of heavy unemployment, he promptly landed two summer jobs. He was still grappling with his Don Juan tendencies toward "too many girlfriends." Mother was told that his "acting out" was an effort to help her recognize it was time to start noticing other men. She said that for his good she was considering it. She felt that was definitely her next project. She reported a recurring dream in which she was surrounded by a dome. The dome was not hard like glass. "It's like somebody could get through if they pushed hard enough and I wanted them to get through. If I wasn't sure, you know, and if they really tried, they could get through and it would probably be OK."

Formulation. The therapy in this case was designed to help a woman separate from her husband. Because the husband was dead and because of other special features, the separation was facilitated predominantly through individual hypnosis and processes of exteriorization of new trance events. Family work was done to bulwark the woman's new position and to establish complementary therapeutic goals for one of her children. The woman was helped to develop a new foundation for better self-discipline.

"Divorcing the Dead" is a model for dialectical intervention when significant family members cannot (or will not) be present. The case focuses on the role of *self-instruction* in symptoms and the utilities of deep trance work in both *countering "bad self-hypnosis"* and *truly burying the hatchet* of old, privately reenacting relational conflicts. The case demonstrates the *parts-of-self* counterinduction technique as well. The therapy was designed to use the woman's special capacities in trance, to create an *action-oriented* and *shared cathartic event* aimed at affecting an *interiorized relational system*, which until this time had been hidden away from the light of day, emanating unseen but toxic rays.

Summary

The process of selecting optimal inner and outer points of therapeutic entry can be complex. In some cases, the transition from establishing family interactional events to inducing family hypnotic events can be smooth and occur within the same session. There are cases, however, when this balanced form of unconscious and interpersonal work, even if theoretically desirable, is not possible. For example, if there is a central symptom-related conflict between a woman's mental-set and her relationship with her husband and the husband is unavailable for treatment, as in

"Divorcing the Dead," the therapy may of necessity be *more intra-actional* than *interactional*. There are also cases, such as "Over My Dead Body" and "A Matter of Growing Pains," in which hypnotic work is best cloistered from family interactional work and thereby used to help build less permeable suggestive barriers. In such cases, although the clinician might prefer the situation to be otherwise, there is reason to be concerned that the family might *override individual changes or abuse the trance state* as an opportunity to trespass already tenuous symptomatic boundaries. The therapy may then be more *interactional* than *inwardly focused* during family sessions, or trance may be induced in the symptom bearer while he is safeguarded from family interactions in a version of "You dream while they struggle toward unity."

Depending on each case's special needs and resistances, one side or the other of the symptom dialectic may offer a more readily accessible point of entry. Symptom cuing, shared hypnotic events, and parts-of-self inductions may all be employed in various forms during this process.

As mentioned in Chapter Three regarding the gift, sometimes a family or individual sets conditions on treatment that render the problem clinically impenetrable. Short of such an unacceptable offering, the therapist may wish to accept a family member's limited active participation or objections to formal hypnotic treatment, considering these restrictions and rites of entry as part of the gift from the client(s). The goal of dialectical interventions is to help clients coordinate changes in related inner and outer realities. The nature of the interventions must be suggested by the case.

Chapter Eight ❧ ❧ ❧

Hypnotic Family Therapy

Summary and Comparative Assessment of Related Approaches

❧ This chapter highlights essential features of hypnotic family therapy. To help the reader place the approach in its historical context, a table compares the therapy with Ericksonian hypnotherapy and key components of structural/strategic family therapies.

The Interiorization-Exteriorization Dialectic

In describing therapy, we have been especially interested in connections between interior and exterior symptom realities. We looked at clinical applications of a three-level experiential model of symptoms. The interior level is the individual's context of mind; the two exterior levels are the family and the social situation. Each level of the symptom structure is related but partially autonomous. Therefore, a change in one level or order of symptom phenomena is not necessarily sufficient cause for a change in the arrangement of another level. In other words, each phenomenal level of the symptom has some margin of freedom from the others. We therefore proposed that symptoms are sufficiently complex phenomena that it is often best to intervene simultaneously into related inner and outer symptom contexts. This type of related two-front therapeutic intervention is called "dialectical."

A therapy emphasizing the interior side of the dialectic, or the individual's margin of personal freedom, focuses on the directives of the self to the self. Hypnotherapy, especially Ericksonian style, specializes in using special self-directive capacities, often most readily accessible in trance—to help a person rearrange his view of his life situation in a way that permits new actions on his exterior reality. Ideally, Erickson himself often selected as his point of therapeutic entry a feature of the individual's mind-set that reflected a related conflict in his exterior reality. Changes triggered in the individual then tend to make a bang in the person's social context as well. Grounded in a belief in the powers of the individual, Ericksonian hypnotherapy is designed to create "a new phenomenal world in which patients can explore their potentials, freed to some extent from their learned limitations . . . . a period during which patients are able to break out of their limited frameworks and belief systems so they can experience other patterns of functioning within themselves" (Erickson and Rossi, 1979, p. 2).

In fact, we have proposed that trance is possible because of the human capacity to put external contexts, and even customary self-organizing arrangements, into the attentional background, bringing to the foreground select elements of one's interior landscape. Trance is one of the vehicles the interior-focused therapist uses to help clients transport themselves to a broadening conceptual framework. Also, trance gives the therapist a special connection to the individual. From the client's vantage point, it is akin to having the therapist interiorized as a gentle but strong guide, taken into his dream, or to having aspects of his bodily processes "spoken to," as his intestines gurgle, blood rushes to his cheek, or his arm hangs strangely in the air. The mysteries of how a hypnotist speaks to the respiratory system, affecting breathing rate, or to the hematopoietic system, affecting the supply of blood to a wart on the face, or how a hypnotist activates the vomiting reflex or affects menstrual cycles, breast development, or the hemophiliac's bloodflow away from a weakened joint, can be appreciated in part by recognizing the immediacy of the kind of coded communication between hypnotist and both the individual's own biological rhythms and the psychophysiological ordering of his feelings, sensations, and ideas.

On the other hand, a therapy concerned with the determining powers of the collective over the individual or based on a belief that there is no I without a thou will tend to focus on directives about how the individual is to behave, which derive from participation in various interpersonal arrangements. The family structural and strategic therapies propose that shifts in power and responsibility in situational rearrangements will activate and reinforce individual psychological, psychophysiological, and related special-state changes. The structural and strategic therapies therefore tend to promote alternative interactional sequences, to facilitate new contextual arrangements, which are then said to lead to interior changes as the individual functions and experiences new parameters of self and others in a new context. A study designed to explore family structure at the level of blood chemistry concluded that families do have the power to affect levels of free fatty acids (a stress marker) in the bloodstream of individual members. This finding is used to emphasize that individuals—besides being resources in their own right—are also subject to the rules of broader social structures (Minuchin, Rosman, and Baker, 1978). In the structural and strategic approaches, the emphasis tends to be on the exterior side of the symptom dialectic.

The dialectical approach brings to the clinical foreground both the "connective tissues" and the "membranes" between the self and the collective, between somewhat distinct but intertwined interior and interpersonal processes. Although we (like Family Therapists) recognize the often materially based hierarchical powers of the collective over the individual, we also (like most hypnotists) appreciate that the individual has a roving self, which scans and selects from multiple contexts he is part of: therefore in hypnotic family therapy, we search for ways to synchronize and amplify related interior-exterior changes and to complement interactional work (from the outside in) with trance and other individual work (from the inside out). The study of family interactions characteristic of structural and strategic approaches is seen as one means of learning about symptom-suggestive context.

In this book, we studied in depth families' suggestive power and the relationship of that power to the activation symptoms. In fact, the study of the family in symptom induction has a number of utilities in therapy. In the dialectical approach, the idea of creating an hypnotic atmosphere is designed to partly facilitate the study of family contributions to symptoms. Once a family is hierarchically organized, regardless of positioning, any family member may contribute to the contextual cuing of symptom components in a symptom bearer. Additionally, in our study of families' suggestive powers, we examined multiperson sequential directives and also explored the power of unintentional and difficult-to-detect contextually transmitted messages. *In this therapy, what we call the family suggestive tone and other unconsciously transmitted suggestive forms—associated with, but independent from family hierarchical arrangements—are also appreciated as part of the symptom-suggestive context.* They are both starting and end points of interactional sequences. Messages from several different family members may interweave with one another, orchestrating a single metamessage to a symptom bearer. Unconscious messages may be *in effect* interspersed throughout the suggestions a significant family member makes to a symptom bearer, carrying both the weight of a structural cue and a personal feeling tone of hope or despair. If a family is stuck in a problematic structure, the feeling tone may be one of hopelessness. This hopelessness may suggest to family members a reason to not take responsible action but to remain impotent in the mutually demoting processes of family functioning. Carefully, progressively, and individually activating hope in multiple family members can be an important part of enabling changes in family interactional and other suggestive events.

Basically, we recognized that part of the power of family suggestion derives from (1) economic and life-stage developmental dependencies, (2) responsibility structures of the family, and (3) the rapport that permits the transmission of unconscious messages from one family member to the unconscious mind of another family member. Because messages are often transmitted in a private family code, it is hard to catch this process. But catching this slippery event under certain carefully monitored circumstances is considered something worth writing home about. If the therapist handles the therapeutic situation optimally, she may get a multilevel action-demonstration of the relationship between the symptom bearer's problematic self-instruction and unhelpful family suggestive techniques.

Part of our study of symptom-induction processes includes an examination (through therapeutic activations of them) of the sequences of thought and other aspects of behavior—verbal and nonverbal and psychophysiological—that belie the habitual way an individual structures or organizes his thinking. Using trance when necessary or desirable, and possible, and employing other observational methods when trance is not chosen, the therapist explores the individual's inner phenomenal reality and assesses ways the symptom bearer immobilizes himself, drawing needlessly from only a narrow part of his potential behavioral range.

We also added a third fundamental level to the exterior referents of the symptom, the social situation. As therapists, we often see our domain as restricted to life cycle and developmental concerns. But the person we wish to help is not restricted to these issues. He is also subject to the laws of society and to epidemiological likelihoods of experiencing a traumatic event or becoming a symptom bearer of some sort. We mentioned that society too can play a role in the suggestion, even of psychophysiological changes in individuals, and that the hierarchies of context regarding race, gender, class, religion, and age may all exert real and symbolic threats of status changes to people as individuals and as family members. If domestic shifts in relative "altitude" pull on the strings of heart and psyche, certainly economic ebbs and tides have some association with rises in alcoholism, suicide, depression, murder, rape, child abuse, and other symptomatic outcries. Although social situation has played a minor role in this book, it is a symptom level worth further examination in its own right. We saw roles of religious, economic, and gender conflicts in the subsystems of family life and of social isolation and hospital-based dependencies in psychosomatic aspects of a chronic illness as they have been interiorized into the hierarchies of family and individual life. Basically, we proposed that it is worthwhile to search for possible problematic shifting hierarchies in a person's social context when confronted with his complaint of dis-ease.

The Symptom as a Gift

In dialectical therapy, the symptom is regarded as a gift for a number of reasons. First, within itself the symptom embodies the central contradictions in a person's life and hence becomes the central "object" of attention in the therapeutic exchange. Often the symptom may represent part of a person's best emotional, behavioral, or physiological product as he functions within nullifying sets of contextual expectations for his behavior. Symptoms may include, in their seemingly bizarre manifestations, automatic or eruptive psychophysiological components—as we saw in cases of lower back pain, stress-related bleeds (in a hemophiliac), trouble breathing, and persistent crying. Other components of symptomatic behaviors, even in the same individual, may include creative coping devices or forms of active outcry against the powers of seemingly insatiable intra- or intercontextual messages. We saw examples of these phenomena in a young woman trying to return home for refuge and refueling and in a young man expressing anger and indignation. We described symptoms as *hybrids* of the faithful living out of directives from the automatic pilot aspects of self, family, and society and active efforts to cope, create, and transform. Nevertheless, in the face of the symptom, whatever its multiple purposes, the individual's margin of freedom is compromised. Because the symptom is a totalization or epitomization of conflicts in a symptom bearer's inner and outer realities, however, we as therapists want to appreciate it so we may be offered the opportunity to observe as many facets of it as necessary for us to help its owner alter those life circumstances that have elevated it to the level of a law.

One facet we hope to be offered is an action demonstration of the relationship between self- and family-suggestive systems. Certainly, catching contextual inductions is not possible or essential in every case; sometimes family troubles *do not* pertain to a person's problems. Work and economic troubles might be central. When it does seem that a family is involved, however, and when the family is accessible, the therapeutic creation of a space for a family inductive moment is used to both bring together in proximity the molecules of the family and permit immersion in the most private of family suggestive contexts. In this specially charged atmosphere, the therapist may glimpse structure and suggestive tone and can begin to select benevolent interior and exterior aspects of symptom sequences to salvage throughout the therapeutic process and help the family shed undesirable symptom layers. In this way, as in the case of the young man with hemophilia, the family brings in both a concern about a bleed and a feeling tone of anxiety about the mother's hierarchical powers over the management of the bleed. In teaching mother to become the boy's hypnotist, the therapist helps her *transform the anxiety* into a benevolent energy source the mother can channel into the mastering of self- and son-soothing hypnotic techniques. She likewise *uses the bleed* to help elevate the mother, hierarchically, in the face of her son's illness problems and medical dependencies.

Regarding the symptom as a gift also has implications for the structuring and exchanging of power in this therapy. Therapy begins only after the client has transferred (if temporarily) power over the symptom offering to the therapist. The steps by which the client gives over certain powers and the therapist receives selectively from those powers may be critical for the outcome of the entire therapy. These are the moments when trust, cooperation, and the kind of rapport that facilitates multilevel communications are first designed. Throughout the transactions around the symptom, including the therapist repaying in kind, in which the approach is carefully tailored to match the symptom's inner and outer measurements, the idea of the symptom as a gift is used to classify the therapeutic process as one of cooperative exchange. This approach does not imply that therapy occurs in all cases without suffering or struggle; it implies that the therapeutic relationship, embodying whatever healing events are needed, is not adversarial and is ultimately shaped to functionally elevate all parties concerned.

Creating an hypnotic atmosphere is in fact the careful building of a therapeutic context that can foster the kind of quick connection, rapprochement, intimacy, and reciprocally responsive bonds to the therapist that permit the client, in a respectful process of exchange, to transfer selective powers over his problem to the therapist. This transferring of power over the symptom, in conjunction with the special suggestive capacities of the therapeutic context itself, enables the therapist to get the best possible reading of self- and family-instructional capacities and techniques.

In this receptive atmosphere of fair, if not always gentle, give-and-take, in which direct and indirect, interactional, verbal, nonverbal, and body language communications take place, the therapist may note, for example, that part of what a client is offering her is a glimpse at a kind of psychological outlet. Observing and appreciating the gift's interactional inductive facets, the therapist may note that, for example, mother, intending to support her daughter, accidentally plugs into the young woman's guilt outlet. In so doing, she sends a charge to her suicidal young daughter not altogether pleasing. Similarly, a mother may have an outlet in her mental-set for helplessness that her young hemophiliac son may inadvertantly plug into when he has a bleed. The diad may then become psychophysiologically wired to one another in a relation bond that transmits unhelpful directives to each member. The wish to support is salvaged, therapeutically in this approach, and family members are offered more effective healing techniques. Meanwhile, the therapist helps family members rewire the outlets for guilt and helplessness to develop-mentally *progressive* tasks, to seal them off from the family suggestive current or to otherwise convert them. Basically, the therapist who appre-ciates what is benevolent in what she is offered will be offered more. By rejecting those lethal aspects of the symptom gift she may lose some clients, but she will most often offer a person a chance to recognize *his right to reject those aspects as well.*

Coordinating Inner and Outer Interventions

We suggested that there seems to be a kind of convergence of prob-lematic situations across the sectors of a symptom bearer's life, a certain connection between rigidly hierarchically organized aspects of a person's context of mind and inflexible features of a family and social context. *One problematic level appears to sustain and promote the others, so that a movement in one does not automatically lead to a change in another but may meet with opposition from the other.* Sometimes, therefore, if the therapist intervenes in one sector, the symptom may be pegged in place by related rigidities in another. As Montalvo wrote: "A situation becomes transformable when a change brought about in one sector can be applied in another sector, or when changes happen almost concurrently in differ-ent sectors" (1973, p. 108). Hence, we mapped out an orientation in which the therapist intervenes at once into multiple levels of a symptom struc-ture. Because this project entails working both from the *inner* phenom-enal world of client and family members, to mobilize special capacities to help individual members make new exterior actions, *and* from *outer* interactional realms, to help individual members interiorize new expe-riences of self during the enactment of new relative functional capacities, we call this type of intervention dialectical. Basically, if the symptom captures the mysteries of multiple purposes, the therapy must know the mysteries of these multiple purposes as well.

In the dialetical approach, having created an hypnotic atmosphere, the therapist begins to intervene within a context energized by the closeness of intense rapport and carefully monitored unconscious communications. She then further simplifies this setting by progressively suggesting directly and indirectly, for all individuals present, an intense and inward focus on only select symptom-relevant phenomena. This phase of therapy, the therapeutic counterinduction, is more highly charged than the pre- and postinductive stages. In this stage, new interior and exterior boundaries can begin to be negotiated as the therapist uses methods resembling family inductive techniques to intervene into multiple family member mental-sets, clearing the way for new attitudes and interactional connections. In this inductive moment, multiperson hypnosis can provide the therapeutic technology for creating either selective convergent trance events or separate-track trances. The goal is to invite new complementary parts of self to join in new valences with one another. *In this way, coordinated interior and exterior trance-catalyzed events may be choreographed.* Self-instruction and transformed family directives may converge, producing the possibility of the enactment of new asymptomatic interconnections. Although the therapist does all she can to facilitate change, she is not the one who produces a new arrangement of the symptom bearer's existential furniture; it is up to family members and symptom bearer to reorganize their own relational and intraassociative pathways. The therapist simply creates an intense and highly charged problem-focused event, carefully delineating a new exterior relational path here and a new interior sequence of memories and associations that might be more inspiring over there. It is in their synchronous enactment that changes may occur. Ideally, the therapist, interfering as little as necessary, *helps* the symptom bearer and family become more *helpful* and *hopeful* hypnotists.

In the post-inductive stage of an interview, the therapist arouses the clients from the hypnotic event and encourages the expression of objections to the counterinductive proposal. Often these objections are actually questions posed to the therapist about how to use the suggestions made. For example, on awakening, the mother of a young hemophiliac is invited to express her worries about her son's use of trance. As the mother talks about her worries, she becomes anxious again, thereby expressing her doubts about her abilities to manage the boy's illness-related problems. It is at this point that the therapist *reintroduces specific components of the mother's own trance experience,* to convey to her "Now, at a moment like this one, now, go into trance and draw on those memories you just had of the young and healthy children sledding down a mountain, and draw courage from those associations to deal with your challenges." In this phase, the hypnotic family therapist may also modify her inductive suggestion or more directly explain aspects of her input. Objections that seem to threaten the dislocation of new connections before they have had time to stabilize may be defused. At this time the therapist does not wish to open up the entire sequence of inductive events. She wants to keep the deck of trance events well-shuffled, so she encourages the use of amnesias and other psychological capacities whereby family members may, for the time being, put all that has just occurred into the background.

Table 3 distinguishes the present therapy from related models. Essential differences are highlighted. The categories of differences include (1) the central symptom-related structural concern; (2) the primary model of the symptom; (3) the relationship between structure and spontaneous or automatic change; (4) the foreground therapeutic interest; and (5) capacities and structures most frequently mobilized in therapy. The language is that of the dialectical approach.

Further Considerations

Somehow it seems that our powers of proximity and distance enacted in life's exterior structures have their psychic representation within the margin of phenomenal freedom we associate with hypnotic experience. We have considered the possibility that an individual may be robbed of his psychic retreat, which might otherwise serve in a self-healing process, because even there, ineffective good intentions or the wastes of family and social troubles have piled up. Often, when the symptom bearer's rights and opportunities to diversely attach to (put in the foreground) and detach from (put in the background) aspects of his exterior contexts are inordinately or unusually curtailed, his interior associations and range of behaviors may become so narrow as to be mistaken for a diagnosable reality. That is, he may become so fixed in his proximity to and distance from certain dialectically evoked *inner* associative substructures—recalling again and again only certain chains of ideas, memories, and psychophysiological cues, even in diverse exterior contexts—that concerned observers might feel they can capture the essence of his psycho-

Table 3. Comparison of Hypnotherapy, Family Therapy, and Hypnotic Family Therapy.

	Ericksonian hypnotherapy	Structural strategic family therapy	Hypnotic family therapy
Central symptom-related structural concern	Individual mind-set	Family structure (including hierarchical substructures)	Structured connections between individual's contexts of mind, of family, and of society (the hierarchically organized existential tripartate)
Primary model of the symptom	Multifaceted coded statement about a person's situation as it is represented in and representative of his or her mind-set	Metaphor for conflicted or confused lines of power and responsibility in family arrangements, which are enacted in sequential patterns structurally analogous to one another	Metaphor for dis-ease in the relationships among interior (individual) and exterior (family and societal) contexts that in actuality or perception constitute a person's existential circumstances
Relationship between structure and spontaneous change	Transformed utilization of certain associative re-arrangements may activate new behaviors, start new interactional sequences automatically	Certain transformed interpersonal hierarchical arrangements may activate unprecedented relational patterns, individual psychophysiological changes, special states	New balance of power across the contexts of an individual's life may activate unprecedented internal associative and relational valences
Foreground therapeutic interest	Interior changes that lead automatically to other changes via exteriorization	Exterior changes that lead automatically to other changes via interiorization	Coordinated interior and exterior changes, thus, on both ends of the dialectic, interiorization and exteriorization are synchronized
Capacities and structures most frequently mobilized in therapy	Special individual states and individuals' unique responsive patterns	Family organizational capacities and unique interactional patterns	Special individual states and family structural inductive capacities

logical state in a single word. In this way, the individual's complaint, which may most significantly be evidence of a lack of exercise that one gains only by running more freely through the vast landscape of one's psychophysiological environment *while* establishing dynamic developmental relational valences, can be misrepresented in a manner that may prevent the person from arousing from his bad trance.

In this book we have explored special states as both derivatives of structured social circumstance and as proscriptive forces in their own right, as starting and end points of poignant and somehow symptom-associated relational sequences. We surveyed the symptom bearer's behavior—including aspects of special-state functioning—with a special interest in finding disputable boundaries between the individual as a self-instructional resource and as a member of contextual suggestive arrangements. We pondered the importance of there being balance across the contexts of which an individual is a part; of perceiving oneself, in routine functioning, as being in synch, existentially; and of experiencing some degree of self-possession in the face of collective claims to the self. *We considered symptoms as often creative efforts to meet exotic requisites of disjointed inner and outer realities.*

We proposed that people are capable of being either predominantly "in" or "out" of their minds at any point and that to go inward and shut out significant aspects of exterior reality is the hallmark of trance. To immerse oneself in outer reality so intensively as to forget oneself is the hallmark of love or other forms of interactional rapport. Somehow it seems that it is in the relationship between the mind's ins and outs that symptoms are situated. For some person, being "in" his mind may mean reliving over and over being locked in a closet as a boy by his mother or orchestrating debates among secret selves, meaningfully disembodied from outer realities, so that in this cluttered and troubled space the person "forgets" to look outward to make needed changes in his connectedness to others who might rightfully participate in his exorcism. Instead, as the person looks here or there, the air fills with hallucinations, voices no one else hears. It might seem that madness is not so much a product of being out of one's mind as a signal of misused, untapped, or obstructed powers over the ins and outs of one's existential arrangement.

❧ ❧ ❧ *Glossary*

Context of Mind. The interior system of an individual that regulates his accumulation and exclusion of information and experience and the arranging, putting into priorities, and sequencing of behavior. Although at any one moment the individual is subject to this system of rules, he is also capable, under certain circumstances, of transforming it. Insofar as the hierarchy of rules exists at any time below the threshold of the individual's perception of it, the context of mind may take on its own suggestive life. This interior and structured system is one of the three existential levels an individual inhabits.

Convergent Trances. Multiperson hypnotic events including shared reveries used therapeutically to affect family suggestive tone and to facilitate the development of new relational and self-directional boundaries.

Cooperative Exchange. One of the two fundamental social institutions connecting kin to nonkin (the other is warfare). Applied to therapy, this is a model of a nonadversarial, reciprocally elevating, transactional process.

Dialectic. (1) Method of exposition whereby contradictory facts or ideas are weighed with a view toward resolving their real or perceived contradictions. (2) Theory of change based on the concept that in the struggle between two opposing forces, a third force, more complex or more highly developed and that preserves essential features of the opposite forces, can be produced. (3) Model of relationship between interior and exterior symptom-suggestive contexts in which oppositionality is implied.

Dialectical Intervention. Therapeutic technique whereby the therapist attempts to coordinate the depotentiating of those related inner and outer manifestations of symptom-sustaining patterns that are not significantly benevolent for the symptom bearer.

Economic Subsystem. That functional family structure based on spoken and unspoken rules pertaining to the earning, spending, and distribution of money, material goods, and symbolic indicators of wealth, as well as to family service functions that could be given a monetary value if converted into jobs (such as housecleaning).

Exteriorization. One aspect of the psychological dialectic whereby an individual's internally activated events and associated experiences of interior phenomenal reality are organized and ranked in a manner that culminates in interactional and other forms of outer-directed behavior that are either intentional or automatic. Significant internal events may be activated by self, family, society, or therapy. This psychological capacity is basic to the effectiveness of hypnotic techniques that help individuals draw on internal resources to develop new models for action.

Family Induction. Moment within the enactment of rules of relatedness among the symptom bearer and other family members in which multilevel messages converge to activate the symptom bearer's automatic and intentional symptom components. This moment is used therapeutically to observe in action relationships among the symptom bearer's context of mind and his family as they pertain to the symptom. This event has neither nosological value nor the power to predict limitations on a family's capacity to communicate asymptomatically.

Gender Subsystem. Family life substructure of rules based on sex-role notions about what constitutes an acceptable range of behaviors, relationally, and particularly, in terms of relative domestic and social status and positions of responsibility among family members.

Holistic Structuralism. Biological model of developing organisms, which postulates that within any living entity, change occurs by transformations in the function-structure relationship, not by antecedent-consequent causality. Broader structures affect but do not determine the nature of substructures in that substructures are subject to many but not all the laws of the broader structures at any one time. The basic unit of any scientific study is the spontaneously and centrally active biological whole. In dialectical therapy, this model is applied to the symptom bearer's entire existential arrangement, including himself as part of his family structure, his social situation, and his own psychological structures, including his context of mind.

Hypnotic Atmosphere. Therapeutic climate established progressively, beginning with initial transactions around the symptom, principally by abrogating the usual social categories of time and space and instead, employing subjective definitions, separating conscious from unconscious communications and private from family interactional communications. Cue words are established in relation to both individual family members and specific diadic and triadic units. In this specially charged climate, therapeutic focus can readily shift interactional, conscious, metaphorical, or trance-related events to the background or foreground. This climate increases both the likelihood of therapist observation of family inductions and family receptivity to therapeutic counterinductions.

Interiorization. One aspect of the psychological dialectic whereby an individual, either automatically or intentionally, introduces externally activated events and associated experiences of self in relation to others into his internal representational and experiential system. These events and experiences are significantly utilized to rank any or all levels of behavior, from the psychophysiological to the emotional, and can be activated by self, family, society, or therapy. This psychological capacity is the source of the effectiveness of using family and other situational rearrangements to produce interior changes in a symptom bearer.

Public Versus Private Dichotomy. Essential contradiction in family suggestive powers between what ideas, relational connections, memories, and events are the possession of the family collective and what are part of the public domain. It is the analogue in family life to the interior-exterior dialectic within individual functioning. This contradiction is consequential for a therapist (as an outsider) seeking intimate knowledge of a family's workings.

Separate-Track Trances. Multiperson hypnotic techniques using individuated but related trance technologies simultaneously or in a coordinated manner to help family members reshape the contours of their relational and self-instructional boundaries.

Shared Reverie. One form of convergent trance, in which family members in trance participate in a mutually positive, collectively reexperienced event that is then used therapeutically to activate a readiness in the members to renegotiate aspects of suggestive tone and boundaries that delimit interrelational connectedness.

Structural Directive. That suggestion about how to behave that an individual derives either automatically or consciously from participation in a context. The suggestion may be a hybrid of direct and indirect messages from multiple persons in multiple substructures of the broader context of which an individual is a part. These contextual cues often have an irresistible power because they are difficult to detect and thus difficult to defend against. Broader social structures derive their power over smaller social units and individuals partly from the force of these contextual cues.

Symptom. Multipurpose phenomenon that may signal a dis-eased connection between two instructional sources an individual responds to. These sources are within an individual, as in a conflict between conscious and unconscious wishes or plans, and exterior, as in a conflict between the self and the exterior contexts the self (or certain aspects of it) is part of. The symptom is potentially a metaphor for antagonism within or between any of the existential contexts an individual inhabits. It is generally represented as a hybrid of active coping and automatic response behaviors. If it includes automatic responses, it is analogous to an abuse of the trance state. If benevolent features are included, they are therapeutically safeguarded rather than arbitrarily treated as adversarial.

Symptom Cuing. Therapeutic procedure in which abbreviated components of benevolent aspects of symptoms are transformed into signals used to help an individual turn on a newly suggested sequence of countersymptomatic behaviors. The technique has multiple forms, including family- and self-symptom cuing, depending on what context is used to provide the turn-on signal.

Therapeutic Counter-induction. That unity of interventions the therapist uses within an hypnotic atmosphere to depotentiate specific destructive symptom-sustaining suggestive processes among family members and within individuals' self-instructional systems. The common goal of these techniques is to destabilize related internal associative and external relational structures, so as to create the circumstances under which the symptom will no longer operate as a primary organizing principle in a client's inner or outer situations. However, benevolent aspects of symptoms are salvaged, in abbreviated or otherwise modified form, as secondary features of new self-instructional and family contextual arrangements. As the middle stage of a therapeutic interview, this process is characterized by intensity, simplicity, and sharpening of focus on related facets of what is perceived as the central contradiction within a client's problem situation. The efficacy of this event is appraised by how it affects the symptom bearer's personal and interpersonal adjustments within his existential situation, not by symptom removal per se.

Trance. State of intense focus inward into one's own interior phenomenal reality. It is predicated on the individual's capacity to detach from or disattend to significant aspects of his exterior context. This state can be activated by any person or event, internal or external, that successfully creates the subject's desire to detach from his exterior immediacies. Potential trance activators include self, family members, social situations, therapy, trauma, and listening to music. This state of absorbed inner focus can be used or abused by self or others to affect aspects of an individual's behavior. In it, inner realities may be experienced as actual external events and so be charged with personal meaning and accompanied by psychophysiological responses appropriate to corresponding external realities.

⬥⬥⬥ References

Aardema, V. *Why Mosquitoes Buzz in People's Ears.* New York: Dial Press, 1975.

Barabasz, A. F., and McGeorge, M. "Biofeedback, Mediated Biofeedback, and Hypnosis in Peripheral Vasodilation Training." *American Journal of Clinical Hypnosis,* 1978, *21,* 28–38.

Barber, T. X. "Physiological Effects of 'Hypnosis.'" *Psychological Bulletin,* 1961, *58* (5), 390–419.

Barnett, E. R., and others. *Family Violence: Intervention Strategies.* Washington, D.C.: U.S. Department of Health and Human Services, 1980.

Bateson, G. *Steps to an Ecology of Mind.* New York: Ballantine Books, 1972.

Benson, H. *The Relaxation Response.* New York: Avon Books, 1976.

Binswanger, L. "The Case of Ellen West." In R. May, E. Angel, and H. F. Ellenberger (Eds.), *Existence.* New York: Basic Books, 1958.

Cannon, W. B. "Voodoo Death." *Psychosomatic Medicine, 19* (3), 1957, 182–190.

Crasilneck, H. B., and Hall, J. A. "Physiological Changes Associated with Hypnosis: A Review of the Literature Since 1948." *International Journal of Clinical and Experimental Hypnosis,* 1959, *7,* 9–50.

Dugan, M., and Sheridan, C. "Effects of Instructed Imagery on Temperature of Hands." *Perceptual and Motor Skills,* 1976, *42,* 14.

Erickson, M. H. "The Burden of Responsibility in Effective Psychotherapy." *American Journal of Clinical Hypnosis,* 1964, *6* (3), 269–271.

Erickson, M. H. "The Use of Symptoms as an Integral Part of Hypnotherapy." *American Journal of Clinical Hypnosis*, 1965, *3* (1), 57–65.

Erickson, M. H. "The Interspersal Hypnotic Technique for Symptom Correction and Pain Control." *American Journal of Clinical Hypnosis*, 1966, *3*, 198–209.

Erickson, M. H. *The Collected Papers of Milton H. Erickson*. (E. L. Rossi, Ed.). New York: Irvington, 1980.

Erickson, M. H., and Rossi, E. L. "Two-Level Communication and the Microdynamics of Trance." *American Journal of Clinical Hypnosis*, 1976, *18*, 153–171.

Erickson, M. H., and Rossi, E. L. *Hypnotherapy: An Exploratory Casebook*. New York: Irvington, 1979.

Erickson, M. H., Rossi, E. L., and Rossi, S. I. *Hypnotic Realities*. New York: Irvington, 1976.

Erikson, E. *Young Man Luther*. New York: Norton, 1958.

Eyer, J., and Sterling, P. "Hypertension as a Disease of Modern Society." *International Journal of Health Services*, 1975, *5* (4), 539–558.

Fanon, F. *A Dying Colonialism*. New York: Grove Press, 1967.

Fanon, F. *Toward the African Revolution*. New York: Grove Press, 1969.

Federal Bureau of Investigation. *Report from the United States Department of Justice*. Washington, D.C.: U.S. Government Printing Office, 1979.

Foucault, M. *Mental Illness and Psychology*. New York: Harper & Row, 1976.

Frazer, J. G. *The Golden Bough: A Study in Magic and Religion*. New York: Macmillan, 1922.

Haley, A. *The Autobiography of Malcolm X*. New York: Grove Press, 1966.

Haley, J. *Strategies of Psychotherapy*. New York: Grune & Stratton, 1963.

Haley, J. *Uncommon Therapy: The Psychiatric Techniques of Milton H. Erickson*. New York: Norton, 1973.

Haley, J. *Problem-Solving Therapy: New Strategies for Effective Family Therapy*. San Francisco: Jossey-Bass, 1976.

Haley, J. *Leaving Home*. New York: McGraw-Hill, 1980.

Harburg, E., and others. "Sociological Stressor Areas and Black–White Blood Pressure: Detroit." *Journal of Chronic Diseases*, 1973, *26*, 595–611.

Herman, J. *Father-Daughter Incest*. Cambridge, Mass.: Harvard University Press, 1981.

Jacobs, J. *Adolescent Suicide.* New York: Wiley-Interscience, 1971.

Johnson, R.F.Q., and Barber, T. X. "Hypnosis, Suggestions and Warts: An Experimental Investigation Implicating the Importance of 'Believed-in-Efficacy.' " *American Journal of Clinical Hypnosis,* 1978, *20*, 165–174.

Laing, R. D. *The Politics of the Family.* New York: Random House, 1972.

Laing, R. D., and Cooper, A. G. *Reason and Violence.* New York: Vintage Books, 1971.

LeBaw, W. L. "Regular Use of Suggestibility by Pediatric Bleeders." *Haematologia,* 1970, *4*, 419–425.

LeBaw, W. L. "Auto-Hypnosis in Hemophilia." *Haematologia,* 1975, *9*, 103–110.

Levi-Strauss, C. *The Elementary Structures of Kinship.* Boston: Beacon Press, 1969.

Lucas, O. N. "The Use of Hypnosis in Hemophilia Dental Care." *Annals of the New York Academy of Science,* 1959, *240*, 263–266.

Madanes, C. *Strategic Family Therapy.* San Francisco: Jossey-Bass, 1981.

Maslach, C., Marshall, G., and Zimbardo, P. "Hypnotic Control of Peripheral Skin Temperature." *Psychophysiology,* 1972, *9*, 600–605.

Mauss, M. *The Gift: Forms and Functions of Exchange in Archaic Societies.* New York: Norton, 1967.

Minuchin, S. *Families and Family Therapy.* Cambridge, Mass.: Harvard University Press, 1974.

Minuchin, S., Rosman, B., and Baker, L. *Psychosomatic Families.* Cambridge, Mass.: Harvard University Press, 1978.

Minuchin, S., and others. *Families of the Slums: An Exploration of Their Structure and Treatment.* New York: Basic Books, 1967.

Montalvo, B. "Home–School Conflict and the Puerto Rican Child." *Social Casework,* February 1973, pp. 100–110.

Montalvo, B. "Observations on Two Natural Amnesias." *Family Process,* 1976, *15*, 333–342.

Naditch, M. P. "Relative Locus of Control, Relative Discontent and Hypertension." *Social Psychiatry,* 1974, *9*, 111–117.

Orne, M. T. "The Nature of Hypnosis—Artifact and Essence." *Journal of Abnormal Psychology,* 1959, *58*, 277–299.

Orne, M. T. "The Construct of Hypnosis: Implications of the Definition for Research and Practice." *Annals of the New York Academy of Science,* 1977, *296*, 14–33.

Overton, W. F. "General Systems, Structure, and Development." In K. Riegel (Ed.), *Issues in Development and Historical Structuralism.* New York: Wiley, 1974.

Petzel, S., and Cline, D. W. "Adolescent Suicide Epidemiological and Biological Aspects." In S. C. Feinstein and P. L. Giovicchini (Eds.), *Adolescent Psychiatry.* Vol. 6: *Developmental and Clinical Studies.* Chicago: University of Chicago Press, 1978.

Ritterman, M. K. "The Loyal Deviants." *Adolescence,* 1970, *4* (18), 223–230.

Ritterman, M. K. "Paradigmatic Classification of Family Therapy Theories." *Family Process,* 1977, *16* (1), 29–48. (Also published in *Terapia Familiare,* December 1977.)

Ritterman, M. K. *"Family Therapy vs. Ritalin vs. Placebo Treatments of Hyperactivity: An Open Systems Approach."* Unpublished doctoral dissertation, Temple University, 1978.

Ritterman, M. K. "Hypnostructural Family Therapy." In L. Wolberg and M. Aronson (Eds.), *Group and Family Therapy: an Overview.* New York: Brunner/Mazel, 1980.

Ritterman, M. K. "Hemophilia in Context: Adjunctive Hypnosis for Families with a Hemophiliac Member." *Family Process,* 1981, *21,* 469–476.

Rossi, E. L. "Hypnosis and Ultradian Cycles: A New State(s) Theory of Hypnosis?" *American Journal of Clinical Hypnosis,* 1982, *25* (1), 21–32.

Sartre, J. P. *Critique of Dialectical Reason.* Paris, France: Gallimard, 1960.

Sartre, J. P. *Search for a Method.* New York: Vintage Books, 1963.

Sonkin, D. J., and Durphy, M. *Learning to Live Without Violence.* San Francisco, Volcano Press, 1982.

"Suicide—International Comparisons." *Metropolitan Life Insurance Company Statistical Bulletin,* 1972, *23,* 2–5.

Sullivan, H. S. *The Psychiatric Interview.* New York: Norton, 1970.

Taub, E. "Self-Regulation of Human Tissue Temperature." In G. E. Schwartz and J. Beatty (Eds.), *Biofeedback: Theory and Research.* New York: Academic Press, 1977.

Weitzenhoffer, A. M. "Hypnotism and Altered States of Consciousness." In A. Sugerman and R. E. Tarter (Eds.), *Expanding Dimensions of Consciousness.* New York: Springer, 1978.

ᑌᑎᑌ ᑌᑎᑌ ᑌᑎᑌ *Index*

A

Aardema, V., 339

Age, in social context, 21, 22

Age progression, for suicidal woman, 237

Alcoholism: case study of, 23, 60, 62, 113, 306-318; and enuresis case, 51, 60, 61, 62, 74, 282-288

Amnesia: creating, 63; in dialectical intervention, 329; in family induction, 135, 139; in hemophiliac case, 177, 178; and sequence stopping, 94; in suicidal woman case, 247, 270

Anorectic girl, case of, 12, 74, 75, 91-93, 94

Anxiety, as freedom, 291

Aponte, H., xvii

Arm levitation, in claustrophobia case, 303

Associative pairing: in family induction, 127, 128, 129; and unconscious search initiation, 112-114

Asthmatic child, and shared reveries, 97-98

Attention focused inward: case of, 122-126; and denying aspects of family context, 90-95; in dialectical intervention, 328; and emotional and suggestive continuity, 98-100; in family interactions, 90-100; and

shared history, 95-97; and shared reveries, 97-98; in suicidal woman case, 233-234

Automatic behaviors: and cue words, 111; in family induction, 130; and hypnosis, 34, 36-37; by suicidal woman, 236; and symptoms, 7, 10

B

Back pain, intractable, case study of, 13-14, 18, 24, 52, 53-55, 60, 82, 299-302

Bad body. *See* Suicidal woman case

Bad twin. *See* Twins induction

Baker, L., 4n, 36, 40n, 118, 147n, 322, 341

Barabasz, A. F., 34, 339

Barber, T. X., 34, 35, 339, 341

Barnett, E. R., 17, 339

Barnette, L., 62n

Bartering. *See* Family bartering

Bateson, G., 43, 339

Benson, H., 34, 339

Binswanger, L., 26n, 339

Blame, of symptom bearer, 22

Boundary: in back pain case, 302; and confusion techniques, 104-105; and counterinduction, 59; in dialectical intervention, 328; and family and

343

Boundary (continued)
   social contexts, 27; in hemophiliac
   case, 153, 157, 168, 169, 172, 174, 177,
   178, 179, 180, 181; and new domains
   of privacy, 56-57; power and symptoms related to, 26-28; and psychosomatic case, 289; in suicidal woman
   case, 199-201, 211, 227, 232, 236, 238,
   244-246, 252, 253-274
Bridging, in hemophiliac case, 161

                          C

Callus, intractable, case of, 55, 80
Cannon, W. B., 23-24, 339
Carter, B., xviii
Claustrophobia, case study of, 61,
   302-306
Cline, D. W., 193, 342
Complementary separate-track hypnosis, technique of, 61
Confusion techniques: and boundary
   blurring, 104-105; and depotentiating problems, 100; of descriptive directions, 105-110; in family induction, 126-127; in family interactions,
   100-110; of nullifying hierarchical
   messages, 102-103; of parts-of-self
   inductions, 104; of structure versus
   content, 100-102, 132
Content-structure confusion: in family
   induction, 132; technique of, 100-
   102
Context of mind: concept of, 8n, 333; of
   symptom bearer, 8-15
Convergent trances, concept of, 333.
   See also Shared reveries
Cooper, A. G., 68, 73, 341
Cooperation, and gift exchange, 83
Cooperative exchange: concept of, 333;
   in therapeutic context, 43-45
Counterinduction. See Therapeutic
   counterinduction
Crasilneck, H. B., 35, 339
Cue words: in family induction, 131,
   132; for suicidal woman, 252; in ther-
   apeutic interview, 47, 57-58; in un-
   conscious search initiation, 110-112

                          D

Darwin, C., 5
Daughter-in-law, and family interactions, 102-103, 110-111
Denial: of aspects of family context, 90-
   95; in suicidal woman case, 216
Depotentiating problems: and confusion techniques, 100; and symptom
   cuing, 58
Depressed man, case of, 77-79, 98, 113
Diabetic child, case of, 36, 118
Dialectic: concept of, 321, 333-334; of
   interaction and special states, 25-30;
   interiorization-exteriorization, 320-
   324; public-private, 88
Dialectical intervention: concept of,
   334; coordinating, 327-329; in counterinduction stage, 53, 55, 56, 58; for
   hemophiliac case, 149, 169, 187-188.
   See also Interventions
Directives: descriptive, 105-110; in
   hypnosis, 32-33; hypnotic and waking, 57; indirect, 32; sequential, 32;
   sequential, multipurpose, 323; simple, 32; structural, 32-33, 336
Discipline, concept of, 306
Dissociation, in suicidal woman case,
   233
Distortion introduction: in suicidal
   woman case, 227, 229; technique of,
   62
Divorcing the dead, case study of, 23,
   60, 62, 113, 306-318
Doubt, activating, for suicidal woman,
   234
Dugan, M., 34, 339
Durphy, M., 342

                          E

Economic subsystem: concept of, 334;
   in family context, 18-20, 121
Einstein, A., 5
El Salvadoran woman, case of, 2-3
Embedded messages: in hemophiliac
   case, 177; in suicidal woman case,
   213, 217, 218-219, 250; and unconscious processes, 115. See also Messages

Entry points: considerations about, 55; family context as, 53, 56; individual mind-set as, 14-15, 53, 56; social context as, 53

Enuresis and alcoholism, case study of, 51, 60, 61, 62, 74, 282-288

Erickson, M. H., ix, xi, xviii, 19, 29, 30-31, 32, 33, 34, 39, 59, 61n, 73, 76, 78, 86-87, 106, 113, 114, 115, 118, 121, 237, 241, 244, 251, 292, 320, 321, 330, 339-340

Erickson, E., 5, 72, 340

Exterior context, and symptom structure, 26

Exteriorization: concept of, 334; in divorcing the dead case, 318; in hemophiliac case, 159, 176, 187; and interiorization dialectic, 320-324; and social context, 24-25

Eyer, J., 36, 340

F

Family: consensus or we-ness, and rapport, 89-90; in developmental cycle, 288-289, 298; primary and secondary hierarchies in, 120-121, 283-284

Family bartering: and repaying gift, 73, 80-81; in suicidal woman case, 199, 211; technique of, 62

Family context: and attention focused inward, 90-95; basic principles of, 15-20; boundaries in, 27; concept of, 15; developmental cycle of, 15-16; economic subsystem in, 18-20, 121; as entry point, 53, 56; gender subsystem of, 16-17; of hemophiliac, 145-146, 150-169; indirect clinical entry into, 286; inductive capacities of, 19; in interiorization-exteriorization dialectic, 322-324; interiorized hierarchies of, 11; and mind-set, 5, 17, 27-28; sequential denial of, 93-94; in suicidal woman case, 213, 222; as symptom level, 2, 6, 26; as toxic, 295

Family contextual cuing, technique of, 62

Family hydraulics, case study of, 51, 60, 61, 62, 74, 282-288

Family induction: capacities for, 118-119; case study of, 119-141; concept of, 334; continuity of, 213; observation of, 207-209, 214, 222; reading, and suicidal woman, 194-226; renewal of, 255; and symptoms, 36-41; and trance insertions, 63. *See also* Inductions

Family interactions: analysis of, 85-142; attention focused inward in, 90-100, 122-126; confusion techniques of, 100-110, 126-127; physiological and psychological phenomena manifested in, 117-119; rapport establishment in, 86-90, 122-126; summary on, 141-142; and symptom structure of suicidal woman, 228-231; symptom-suggestive, 322-323; unconscious processes activated in, 114-117, 136-141; unconscious search initiation in, 110-114, 128-136

Family members, engagement with, 46

Family therapy: as follow-up for suicidal woman case, 274-278; hypnotherapy and hypnotic family therapy compared with, 330

Fanon, F., 6, 23, 340

Fantasy, in suicidal woman case, 256

Federal Bureau of Investigation, 307, 340

Florist, interspersal technique for, 32, 115

Forgetfulness, as lying, and descriptive directions, 109

Foucault, M., 27, 340

Frazer, J. G., 66, 75, 296, 340

Freud, S., 5

G

Gandhi, M., 5, 39, 310

Gender subsystem: concept of, 334; in family context, 16-17; and genetics, in hemophilia, 148; in social context, 21; for suicidal woman, 223-224

Gift exchanges: analysis of, 66-84; background on, 66-68; in divorcing the dead case, 307; and intervention strategies, 319; model of, 44-45; pit-

Gift exchanges (continued)
  falls in, 84; rules of, 70-73; in suicidal woman case, 190, 210, 216, 228; summary on, 82-84; and symptom as gift, xii, xv, 68, 324-327; therapy steps in, 64-65
Giving: clinical cases of, 73-75; and gift not given over, 74-75; rules of, 70-71; too much, 73-74; of unsolvable problem, 74
Growing pains. See Psychosomatics
Guilt, in family induction, 123-124, 126, 132, 133, 134, 135, 138, 289

H

Haley, A., 5, 265, 340
Haley, J., x, xi, xiii, xvii, 3, 6, 15, 20, 73, 340
Hall, J. A., 35, 339
Harburg, E., 24, 340
Heard, D., xviii
Hemophilia: components of, 144-146; family-hospital interface for, 186-187; holistic structural model of, 147-148
Hemophiliac case: background on, 143-150; benevolent features of symptoms for, 176; boundaries in, 153, 157, 168, 169, 172, 174, 177, 178, 179, 180, 181; case study of, 74-75, 118, 143-188, 325-326, 328-329; dialectical interventions for, 149, 169, 187-188; exteriorization in, 159, 176, 187; family context in, 145-146, 150-169; giving in, 151, 152, 160; goals for, 169, 181, 186; interiorization in, 148-149, 157, 159, 163, 187; postinduction stage for, 178-186; preinduction stage for, 150-169; rapport in, 152, 154, 157, 161, 162, 167, 181; repaying in, 169; summary on, 186-188; therapeutic induction for, 170-178; therapeutic plan for, 165-166
Herman, J., 17, 88, 340
Hierarchical configurations, and levels of symptom, 6, 8
Hierarchical messages, nullifying, 102-103

Hierarchical positions, shifting between, 103
Hierarchies: balance of, in suicidal woman case, 205; body as superior in, 243, 247; and concealed opposites technique, 62; developmental imbalance in, 163; dual, 71; dysfunctional suggestion-bearing, 215; incongruent, of symptom bearer, 13-14, 17, 24-25, 29; issues in problems of, 54; modeling self-care as priority in, 308; primary and secondary, 120-121, 283-284; in social context, 20
History. See Shared history
Hitler, A., 5, 27, 39
Holistic structuralism: concept of, 334-335; and hemophilia model, 147-148; and levels of symptom, 3-8; and model of problem, 53-54
Hyperactive child, and family interactions, 105
Hypertension, and family induction, 36
Hypnosis: basic principles of, 30-36; complementary, in claustrophobia case, 305; in context, 7; goals of, 56-57; multiperson, 328
Hypnotherapy, family therapy and hypnotic family therapy compared with, 330
Hypnotic atmosphere: concept of, 335; and counterinduction, 59; creating, 46-49; creating, for suicidal woman, 194-226; in divorcing the dead case, 308; family contribution to, 323; seeding for, 196, 202, 207, 217; and symptom as gift, 326
Hypnotic family therapy: assumptions in, 43; basic principles of, 1-41; features of, xiii-xiv; further considerations on, 329, 331; hypnotherapy and family therapy compared with, 330; interior and exterior concerns in, xiv-xv; interview stages in, 42-65; maximal receptivity in, 67-68; goals of, 282, 319, 321; steps in, 64-65; structuring in, 43-45; summary and assessment of, 320-331; techniques in, 64

Hypnotic immunization, for suicidal woman, 227
Hypnotic private suggestions, and public versus private dichotomy, 89
Hypnotist, relationship of, with subject, 29, 86-87

I

Incongruent hierarchies, of symptom bearer, 13-14, 17, 24-25, 29
Inductions: contextual, reading, 46-52; family context capacities for, 19; goals of, in claustrophobia case, 303; for hemophiliac case, 170-178; issues of, x; learning structure of, 49-52; light, in family hydraulics case, 286; model of, 39-40; multiperson, for new relational boundaries, 244-246; paradigm of, 32; potential activators of, 38-39. *See also* Family induction
Inductive moment, erased, 139
Inner reverie: in hemophiliac case, 186; in suicidal woman case, 268
Insight, for suicidal woman, 227
Interaction, dialectics of, 25-30. *See also* Family interactions
Interior context, and symptom structure, 26
Interiorization: concept of, 11*n*, 335; in divorcing the dead case, 311, 313; and exteriorization dialectic, 320-324; in family induction, 140; in hemophiliac case, 148-149, 157, 159, 163, 187; in self-ectomy case, 296; of social context, 12-13, 22; in suicidal woman case, 228, 233, 247, 275-276; by symptom bearer, 11-14
Interspersal technique: in family induction, 124-125; and sequential directives, 32; in suicidal woman case, 217; in unconscious processes activation, 114-117
Interventions: adapting, 281-319; categories of, 56; formulations of, 288, 293-294, 299, 301-302, 305-306, 318; summary on, 318-319. *See also* Dialectical intervention
Interviews: analysis of stages of, 42-65; background on, 42-43; counterin-

duction stage of, 52-62; postinduction stage of, 62-63; preinduction stage of, 46-52; stages of, 45-63; summary on, 63-65
Intrapsychic stopping point, in divorcing the dead case, 315
Italian immigrant family, public versus private dichotomy in, 88, 89

J

Jacobs, J., 193, 341
Jewish immigrant family, and cue words, 112
Johnson, R.F.Q., 34, 341
Just noticeable difference (JND): and family context, 39, 41; and family cues, 85, 94

K

King, M. L., 310

L

Laing, R. D., x-xi, 68, 73, 92, 341
LeBaw, W. L., 34, 145, 341
Levi-Strauss, C., 44, 67, 341
Liebman, R., xviii
Linan, L., xviii
Lucas, O. N., 34, 145, 341
Luther, M., 5

M

McGeorge, M., 34, 339
Madanes, C., xiii, 6, 13, 44, 341
Malcolm X, 5
Mapping, of mind-sets, 9-10
Marad, D. *See* Psychosomatics
Marshall, G., 34, 341
Maslach, C., 34, 341
Mauss, M., 44, 67, 84, 341
Messages: in family interactions, 98, 101, 323; reconciling multiple and incongruous, 117, 130; in therapeutic context, 44. *See also* Embedded messages
Metacues and metamessages, in family interactions, 85, 110, 117

Metaphor: in claustrophobia case, 303; in family hydraulics case, 286; in hypnotic family therapy, 14-15, 25, 32-33; in suicidal woman case, 206, 215, 245; symptom as three-level, 68, 82; in therapeutic interview, 56, 59

Micromessage, in hemophiliac case, 152

Mind control. *See* Hemophiliac case

Mind-set, individual: concept of, 9; and family context, 5, 17, 27-28; of hemophiliac, 145; and inductions, 51; in interiorization-exteriorization dialectic, 321-322; mapping of, 9-10; in self-ectomy case, 296; and social context, 4-5; of suicidal woman, 224-225, 231-232, 234; as symptom level, 2, 5-6, 26; as therapeutic entry point, 14-15, 53, 56

Minuchin, S., xi, xiii, xvii, 4n, 9, 15, 36, 40n, 46, 75, 109, 118, 147n, 322, 341

Montalvo, B., xi, xiii, xviii, 8, 38, 46, 48-49, 94, 306n, 327, 341

Motivation, and descriptive directions, 107

Mourning ritual, in family hydraulics case, 287

Mutism, and family interactions, 105-110, 111, 118

N

Naditch, M. P., 24, 341

Negative hallucinations, and family consensus, 89

Negatives, collecting, in suicidal woman case, 208

O

Objections: concept of, 62-63; in dialectical interventions, 328-329; in hemophiliac case, 181; and repaying the gift, 77-79; in self-ectomy case, 299; in suicidal woman case, 253-274; and symptom handling, 69-70; using, and repaying gift, 73

Opposites, preparing for: in family hydraulics case, 285; technique of, 62

Orne, M. T., 29, 341 °

Overton, W. F., 3, 341-342

P

Parts-of-self induction: in claustrophobia case, 305; and confusion techniques, 104; and cue words, 111; in divorcing the dead case, 312-313; in suicidal woman case, 233; techniques of, 61-62

Peers, for hemophiliacs, 145n

Persistence, in therapeutic context, 43-45

Petzel, S., 193, 342

Play therapy, with suicidal woman, 196-197

Poem reading, case of, 51, 61, 79, 305

Positive memories, for suicidal woman, 237

Posthypnotic suggestion, in divorcing the dead case, 316-317

Postinduction stage: in dialectical intervention, 328-329; for hemophiliac case, 178-186; objections in, 62-63, 253-274

Power: boundaries related to, 26-28; exchanges of, 66-84, 326; role of, in symptomatology, 26

Preinduction interview stage: creating hypnotic atmosphere in, 46-49; for hemophiliac case, 150-169; learning structure of inductions in, 49-52; reading contextual inductions in, 46-52

Privacy, boundaries and new domains of, 56-57

Probe, in suicidal woman case, 213-215

Problem, holistic model of, 53-54

Progressive descriptions, as directives, 107

Psychophysiology: and family induction, 36, 132; and moderate trance, 60; paradigm of therapy in, 187-188; and trance, 321-322

Psychosomatics: case study of, 15, 16, 18, 50, 51, 56, 58, 60, 62, 141, 319; and family induction, 119-141; and family interactions, 29, 94, 95, 96-97,

103, 111, 113, 114; intervention for, 288-294

Public versus private dichotomy: concept of, 335; and cue words, 111; and rapport, 87-89

R

Racial subsystem: and back pain case, 299-302; in social context, 21, 22-23

Rapport: in dialectical interventions, 328; in divorcing the dead case, 311; establishing intense, and family interactions, 86-90, 122-126; and family consensus, 89-90; in family hydraulics case, 285; in hemophiliac case, 152, 154, 157, 161, 162, 167, 181; and interdependencies, 87; and psychosomatic case, 289; and public versus private dichotomy, 87-89; and rule establishment, 87; and self-ectomy case, 294, 295; in suicidal woman case, 197, 198, 213, 216, 217, 233, 235, 240, 247

Receiving the gift: in clinical cases, 75-77; and hierarchical power over symptom, 76; and rejection of unworthy gift, 72, 75-76; rules of, 71-72

Reciprocal empowering, and gift exchange, 83

Regression: in associative pairing, 112-113; in family induction, 133, 138

Religion, in social context, 21

Repaying the gift: in clinical cases, 77-82; and expanding on gift, 80; and family bartering, 73, 80-81; and resistance, 77-79; rules of, 72-73; in suicidal woman case, 228; and termination, 81-82; in therapy, 326

Repetition, role of, 7

Resistance. *See* Objections

Reverie. *See* Inner reverie; Shared reveries

Revivification: in associative pairing, 112; in divorcing the dead case, 310; in family induction, 128, 133; in suicidal woman case, 217, 218, 238

Rilke, R. M., xviii

Ritterman, A., xviii

Ritterman, J., xviii

Ritterman, M., xviii

Ritterman, M. K., ix, xi-xii, 3, 5, 6, 29, 105, 186, 188, 342

Rosman, B., 4n, 36, 40n, 118, 147n, 322, 341

Rossi, E. L., 31, 32, 33, 39, 59, 86, 118, 121, 321, 340, 342

Rossi, S. I., 340

Rule enactment, and symptom handling, 69

S

Sappho, 265

Sartre, J. P., 68, 73, 342

Scapegoat, and denying family context aspects, 91-93

School phobia, case of, 55, 81

Self-ectomy: case study of, 11-12, 14-15, 19, 61, 294-299; and family interactions, 90, 319

Self-symptom cuing: in psychosomatic case, 293; technique of, 62

Self-voice induction: for depressed man, 78-79; technique of, 61

Separate-track trances: concept of, 335; for hemophiliac case, 169, 170-178; technique of, 61

Separation, issues of, and gift exchange, 72

Sequence stopping, and family context denial, 94-95

Sequences, effects of, as proofs, 95

Shared history: and attention focused inward, 95-97; in family induction, 133

Shared hypnotic events, technique of, 61

Shared memories, and counterinduction, 57, 60

Shared reverie: and attention focused inward, 97-98; concept of, 335-336; in light trance, 60; in suicidal woman case, 238-240, 264; technique of, 61; therapeutic goals of, 239-240

Shared trance relaxation, and counterinduction, 57

Sheridan, C., 34, 339

Social context: basic principles of, 20-
25; boundaries in, 27; concept of, 21;
as entry point, 53; of hemophiliac,
146; and inductions, 51-52; in interiorization-exteriorization dialectic, 324; interiorized, 12-13, 22; and
mind-set, 4-5; new learnings in, 48;
suicidal woman, 223-224; as symptom level, 2, 6, 26
Sonkin, D. J., 342
Special states: dialectics of, 25-30;
further considerations of, 331; in
suicidal woman case, 240-241; and
ultradian cycles, 31
Sterling, P., 36, 340
Stress, and repaying gift, 72
Structural challenge, in family hydraulics case, 283
Structural intervention, as counterinductive, 266
Structuralism. See Holistic structuralism
Structure-content confusion: in family
induction, 132; technique of, 100-
102
Subsystems or substructures: in family
context, 15-20; in gift exchange, 70-
73; of social context, 25, 26
Suggestion: direct, in suicidal woman
case, 249; family, power of, 323-324;
graduated series of, 106; hidden, 250;
indirect trance, 265; posthypnotic,
316-317; self- and family- systems of,
325; unintended, for suicidal woman, 224
Suggestion-readiness, in hypnosis, 35
Suggestive continuity: and attention
focused inward, 98-100; in family
induction, 125; in suicidal woman
case, 198
Suggestive forms, in suicidal woman
case, 222
Suicidal woman case: background on,
191-192; boundaries in, 199-201, 211,
227, 232, 236, 238, 244-246, 252, 253-
274; case study of, 15, 46-47, 50, 51,
56, 61, 74, 189-280; clinical priorities
for, 279-280; consultation format of
interview with, 190-191; family con-

text in, 213, 222; and family interactions, 98-99, 100-101, 104-105, 112,
114, 115-117, 118; follow-up of, 274-
278; hypnotic atmosphere for, 194-
226; and postinductive objections,
253-274; rapport in, 197, 198, 213,
216, 217, 233, 235, 240, 247; self-
healing proposal of, 243-244; in sibling subsystem, 257-259; summary
on, 278-280; therapeutic counterinduction for, 226-253
Suicide, epidemiology of, 193. See also
Self-ectomy
Sullivan, H. S., 59, 342
Symptom: appreciating, 71; benevolent
features of, 47, 58, 69, 77, 176, 250;
boundaries related to, 26-28; as code
for conflicts, 4; concept of, 336; family interactions role in inducing, 85-
142; as gift, xii, xv, 68, 324-327;
handling, and resistance, 69-70; interactionally coded information
about, 50; level of, 2-8, 26, 320-324;
as living conflict, 68-70, 80; as multipurposed, 37, 68, 327; in social
context, 23; structure of, in suicidal
woman case, 222-225; summary on,
41; as totalization, 68-69, 82
Symptom bearer: blame of, 22; context
of mind of, 8-15; dual role of, 6; in
hierarchical organizations, 8; infantilizing and aggrandizing, 289-291;
rights and opportunities of, 329,
331; voluntarism of, 109
Symptom cuing: in back pain case, 300;
in claustrophobia case, 304; concept
of, 336; and depotentiating dysfunctional sequences, 58; in psychosomatic case, 293; and repaying gift,
72-73; technique of, 62
Symptomatic information, in family
hydraulics case, 283
Symptomatic trance, in family induction, 136

T

Taub, E., 34, 342
Termination, and repaying the gift,
81-82

Therapeutic counterinduction: concept of, 336-337; considerations in, 284-285; creating, 52-62; dialectical, 58, 60-62; in dialectical intervention, 328; and family inductions, 38; points of entry and strategy selection in, 52-57; for suicidal woman, 226-253; techniques for, 57-62

Therapeutic invincibility, and receiving symptom, 72

Therapeutic process, categories of, 44-45

Therapeutic relationship, gift exchanges in, 66-84

Therapist, and kin-nonkin connection, 67, 83

Therapy, struggle in, 67

Thinking straight. See Psychosomatics

Time, therapeutic magic of, 48-49

Tinnitus, case of, 9-10

Trance: for body image, 293, 296; concept of, 337; goals of, in divorcing the dead case, 312; indicators of, 33-34; levels of, 60; parameter experiencing in, 309-310; report on, and conscious report, 316-318; role of, 321-322

Trance induction. See Induction

Trance insertion: in hemophiliac case, 181; in suicidal woman case, 246, 262, 275-276; technique of, 63

Trance ratification, basic principles of, 33-36

Trance state: name in, 113; in suicidal woman case, 235, 238

Transpersonal system of collusion, and family interactions, 92

Twins induction: and blurring of boundaries,104-105; and counterinduction, 59; in suicidal woman case, 220, 221, 240, 242, 244-245, 255

U

Ultradian cycles, and special states, 31

Unconscious principles, of symptom bearer, 10

Unconscious process activation: in family induction, 136-141; in family interactions, 114-117; interspersal technique in, 114-117; and multiple messages, 117; and suicidal woman, 195-196

Unconscious search initiation: and associative pairing, 112-114; cue words in, 110-112; in family induction, 128-136; in family interactions, 110-114

V

Variable reinforcement schedule, and family inductions, 38

Voodoo death, and social context, 23-24

W

Warts, case of, 76-77

Waterman, B., xviii

Wealth, in social context, 21

Weitzenhoffer, A. M., 34, 342

Wendy, and family consensus, 89-90

Whitman, W., 79

Z

Zeig, J. K., ix-xii

Zimbardo, P., 34, 341